Republic and Empire

Republic and Empire

Crisis, Revolution, and America's Early Independence

Trevor Burnard
and
Andrew Jackson O'Shaughnessy

Yale
UNIVERSITY PRESS
New Haven and London

Published with assistance from the Annie Burr Lewis Fund and
with assistance from the foundation established in memory of
Philip Hamilton McMillan of the Class of 1894, Yale College.

Copyright © 2025 by Trevor Burnard and Andrew Jackson O'Shaughnessy.
All rights reserved.
This book may not be reproduced, in whole or in part, including illustrations,
in any form (beyond that copying permitted by Sections 107 and 108 of the U.S.
Copyright Law and except by reviewers for the public press), without written
permission from the publishers.

Yale University Press books may be purchased in quantity for educational, business,
or promotional use. For information, please e-mail sales.press@yale.edu (U.S. office)
or sales@yaleup.co.uk (U.K. office).

Set in Bulmer type by Integrated Publishing Solutions.
Printed in the United States of America.

Library of Congress Control Number: 2024951400
ISBN 978-0-300-28018-0 (hardcover)

A catalogue record for this book is available from the British Library.

Authorized Representative in the EU: Easy Access System Europe,
Mustamäe tee 50, 10621 Tallinn, Estonia, gpsr.requests@easproject.com

10 9 8 7 6 5 4 3 2 1

Contents

INTRODUCTION
The American Revolution as an Imperial Event   1

PART ONE
CAUSES OF THE AMERICAN REVOLUTION   33

ONE
The Seven Years' War and the New Empire   43

TWO
British Imperial Policy   68

THREE
Empire of Coercion   97

FOUR
Settlers and Indigenous Peoples   120

PART TWO
THE WAR AND ITS EFFECTS   149

FIVE
The Loyal Colonies   159

SIX
The War of Empires   185

SEVEN
Imperial Futures   217

Notes   247
Acknowledgments   293
Index   295

Republic and Empire

INTRODUCTION

The American Revolution as an Imperial Event

> The American Spirit, assisted by the ropes and chains of consolidation, is about to convert this country into a powerful and mighty empire. If you make the citizens of this country agree to become the subjects of one great consolidated empire of America, your government will not have sufficient energy to keep them together. Such a Government is incompatible with the genius of republicanism.
>
> —Patrick Henry, Speech to the Ratifying
> Convention of the Constitution, June 1788

JULY 4, 1776. IT IS AN IMPORTANT date in American and in world history. Delegates to a congress of thirteen British colonies in North America followed up their July 2 declaration—that the colonies would seek independence from the British Empire—by sending a document largely written by the Virginia planter and legislator Thomas Jefferson to the government printer for distribution to the American public and the world. It was the founding document of what would be the United States of America.[1]

We tend to think of Jefferson's Declaration of Independence as looking to the future—a new nation establishing founding principles of equality and unalienable rights to life, liberty, and the pursuit of happiness. But the authors of the Declaration of Independence also looked to the past, as seen in the less famous first paragraph.[2] In it, the revolutionaries listed the grievances that American Patriots had concerning their imperial condition. What followed was a list of the "repeated injuries and usurpations" that they had suffered from "the present King of Great Britain," who aspired to "an absolute Tyranny over these States."[3] The British Empire, in which the signers of the Declaration had grown up, had failed them to such an extent that they felt obliged to leave it.[4]

Why did some—but not all—of Britain's subjects feel so aggrieved that they wanted to establish a new system of government, one outside the British Empire? What about the subjects of the Crown who did *not* rebel? The American Revolution was an imperial event as much as it was an event in American history—an imperial-revolutionary conflict, in short.[5] To understand why it happened in the way it did and what resulted from it, both in the United States and in Britain and its empire, requires understanding the demands of managing a far-flung set of imperial possessions in a period of imperial reform. This was the undercurrent that shaped American Patriots' responses, leading to republicanism and to a rejection of monarchy. Breaking away from one form of empire, however, did not mean ending imperialism, which continued in the United States up to and including the removal of Natives from their ancestral homelands in the calamitous 1830s.[6] Empire is a central feature of American history, just as it is in British history.

Thinking Imperially

Connecting revolution with empire is part of the zeitgeist of thinking historically in the 2020s. Empire is "a thing," as any perusal of newspapers or a casual visit to a bookshop or museum shows.[7] We follow many scholars in seeing the eighteenth century, even in the realm of ideas, as less the Age of Reason, a vital moment in human history, when ideals such as freedom, natural rights, and constitutional government prevailed, than an Age of Empire, a less edifying part of Enlightenment culture, where states and individuals pursued wealth and empire by means of war rather than toleration, the progress of commerce, and the establishment and maintenance of liberty in free polities. Many of the great thinkers of the British Enlightenment, such as David Hume, Adam Smith, Edward Gibbon, Catharine Macaulay, Edmund Burke, and even Thomas Paine, did not share Jefferson's optimism that a new and just world was possible outside of participation in empire. They were coming to see that what Enlightenment thinkers were striving for in the first half of the eighteenth century—the replacement of superstition with reason—had not happened. Instead, the beneficial parts of "progress" that had seemed theoretically possible had been supplanted in real life by war, corruption, commercial excess, and the continual growth of violent colonialism.[8]

Empire is a highly diverse concept in the early modern world. Indeed, it is a problematic word that can mean many things. The pioneering imperial historians John Gallagher and Ronald Robinson stated in 1953 that "the imperial historian, in fact, is very much at the mercy of his own concept of empire."[9] Empire was "a chaotic pluralism" devised by many "agents in empire" which propelled the "irregular thrust of imperial jurisdiction into extra-European space."[10] Its chaotic nature led Adam Smith famously to talk about empire as inherently phantom, as being the "project of an empire."[11] Nevertheless, the "chaos" of empire was an ordered chaos. While the British Empire may have been uncoordinated, it did not grow in an unintentional way, with the major actors only sometimes being the state and often being private individuals and corporations. There were many colonial "projects" that came to cohere together around various themes that comprised colonialism. In short, empire was fluid, often inchoate, but far from meaningless. It resembled another protean concept—capitalism—that in the early modern world also took multiple and complicated forms. Commerce and colonialism had so much in common that the great imperial historian of the American colonies Charles McLean Andrews argued that they were "unthinkable each without the other."[12]

Empire was viewed in the early modern period in three broad ways. It was understood as a polity formed by a European metropolis and its colonies. It was also about the relationship between European states and their commercial and military arms and their overseas territories. Finally, empire refers to how power is exercised through the management of differences, especially legal, between territories and peoples placed under a similar sovereignty.[13] We look at all three approaches, with a particular emphasis on the last way, of thinking "imperially."[14] What is especially important is not thinking about empire as a monolith, as being as grand in its conception as it is in the word which describes it. When we think of empires we tend to think of imposing facades and remote, unapproachable, and unchanging structures—like the Roman Empire, which lasted for centuries. But, instead, empires were complex, varied, and ever-changing. The British Empire was "not made by faceless committees making grand calculations, nor by the 'irresistible' pressures of economics or ideology. It was made by men (and women) whose actions were shaped by motives and morals no less confused and demanding than those that govern us now." It was an unfinished empire, in the sense of always being an empire-in-the-making, made up of "hybrid components, conflicting traditions, and unsettled boundaries between races and peoples, a source of constant unease as well as extraordinary energy."[15]

Empires are composite, layered, and structured around hierarchies and communities with a dominant power. They have multiple structures of power and contain heterogeneous, usually polyethnic, populations. Stephen Howe's succinct introduction to imperial studies states that "a kind of basic, consensus definition would be that an empire is a large political body which rules over territory outside its original borders. It has a central power or core territory—whose inhabitants usually continue to form the dominant ethnic or natural group in the entire system—and an extensive periphery of dominated areas."[16] Empires are "a distinctive type of social formation" in which people inside them are either absorbed "to the point that they become fellow-members of the central society" or disengaged "from them to the point that they become confederates rather than subjects."[17] Empires also have a powerful cultural impact. The sovereigns gained support for their rule through cultural displays showing imperial grandeur, with dominance over poor, enslaved people, or people from ethnicities deemed inferior, being a symbol of how the cultural project of empire could be expressed.

An imperial approach has several advantages for understanding historical change in revolutionary contexts. These advantages have been highlighted in the last twenty years, when international affairs have had an imperialist tinge and when issues of globalization have been of intense interest. An imperial perspective helps answer questions about the past that bear upon the present, such as questions of identity and difference. Empires are long-standing polities, more so than nation-states, the latter appearing as "a blip on the historical horizon, a state form that emerged recently from under imperial skies and whose hold on the world's political imagination may well prove partial or transitory."[18]

In surprising ways, empire is presently seen by some in a positive light. Kathleen DuVal, in her study of the American Revolution on the American Gulf Coast, for example, argues that the end of empire in the region was a tragic event in which a world of cosmopolitan diversity and free exchange was overturned in 1776 by a modern democratic nation-state determined to achieve territorial control and cultural uniformity.[19] Krishan Kumar explains that "empires, for all their faults, show us another way, a way of managing diversity and differences that are now the inescapable fate of practically all nation states" through which "the pressing problems of the contemporary world and even the birth pangs of a new world order" can be traced. He concludes that "as scholars turn their attention away from . . . analyzing empire as a set of practices, they have discovered complexity, plurality, contradiction, and even fragility at the heart of imperial projects."[20]

British America in July 1776

Jefferson's text was just one of many texts, deeds, or conversations occurring in the months of July and August 1776. We describe here three of them, less because they are as momentous as the Declaration of Independence of July 4 (they are not) than because they exemplify one of the basic but important assumptions about empire that we want readers to be conscious of: there were many things happening simultaneously in a large, diverse, and complicated British Empire that had a bearing on what led to the American Revolution. If we were to take a longer perspective and look at events that happened after the passing of the Coercive Acts that both helped precipitate the American Revolution and can be explained only in an imperial context, we might add to these three events the Quebec Act of 1774, which suggested to Americans inclined to conspiracy that Britain was preparing to undermine its commitment to Protestantism, and the proclamation by Lord Dunmore, governor of Virginia, in 1775, that enslaved people and indentured servants owned by Patriots would be freed if they escaped their servitude to join British forces.[21]

One of these three events took place on August 8. The political economist Adam Smith, who in March 1776 had written a work of enduring importance in the economics of empire, *The Wealth of Nations,* visited his great friend, the philosopher David Hume, in Edinburgh two weeks before Hume's death at age sixty-five. Hume was pessimistic not just about his future, but about the future of the Enlightenment in Europe which he had previously celebrated as a turning point in human civilization. He worried about the consequences of ministers and merchants promoting a mercantile empire, fueled by spiraling national debt. That debt funded war. He was also concerned about how the selfishness accompanying the pursuit of material gain had corrupted national manners.[22]

Both Smith and Hume saw that Britain's commercial empire centered around the Atlantic slave trade, and more recently around the exploitation of India, and they believed this was inimical to the nation's virtue. Smith considered government by merchants, who made their own interests sovereign at the expense of Indigenous peoples and the interests of nation-states, "the worst of all governments for any country whatsoever."[23] The result, Smith and Hume argued, was ceaseless war by "larger states for commercial domination both by arms and by political and economic strategies of control."[24] Smith argued in *The Wealth of Nations* that the British Empire would collapse because it had turned into a mercantile system addicted to war and empire-building. Empire was a policy of madness, for "under the present system of management [Britain] derives nothing but loss from the dominion which she assumes over her colonies."[25]

Hume agreed. Looking at what was happening in America, the West Indies, and especially India, he saw that liberty was failing in an era of global wars fought for trade or empire, with both settlers and Indigenous peoples embroiled in disastrous conflict, while the cost of war would create such high levels of debt that it would bankrupt the state.[26] For Hume, this dreadful prospect of global war, the jealousy of trade, and the unstable cultures of commercial society could be blamed on William Pitt the Elder's reckless warmongering, designed to win the Seven Years' War. That war plunged Britain into huge debt and into false imperial jingoism. He anticipated that Pitt's evocations of nationalistic patriotism and xenophobia would lead to the breakup of the British Empire. He explained in 1768: "O! how I long to see America and the East Indies revolted totally and, finally, the Revenue reduc'd to half, public Credit fully discredited by Bankruptcy, the third of London in Ruins, and the rascally Mob subdu'd."[27] Jefferson was not the only thinker in 1776 wanting imperial disaster.

A month earlier, an event happened in Jamaica which confirmed all the negative views of empire that were held by Smith and Hume. It was a massive and planned slave revolt involving enslaved people from estates on which as many as 9,000 enslaved people were held in bondage. Whites found out about the plot on July 15, 1776, when an enslaved boy was discovered to be removing the balls from his overseer's pistols and filling them with cotton and oil. What was remarkable about the plot—possibly intended to take place on July 22—was that the conspiracy was not betrayed, as so often happened in plantation America, but was discovered either by a young conspirator's carelessness or by chance.[28] The full extent of the conspiracy started to emerge on July 20, when Colonel John Grizell wrote that enslaved people in Hanover Parish, in a newly settled sugar-planting area of northwest Jamaica, where the ratio of whites to Blacks was as low as one to twenty-five, "are deeply Concerned in the Intended Insurrection, the Number of the Troops is small and the Duty severe." He warned that "Our apprehensions are great upon the occasion as we know not where it will all end."[29] White soldiers were already making sure that the plot did not, as in the great slave rebellion of 1760, turn into reality, having detained "forty-Eight Ring leaders." Eventually, 135 enslaved people were put on trial for treason, seventeen were executed (some by being burned alive, others by gibbeting), forty-five were transported to Central America, and eleven endured "severe corporal punishment."[30] On July 23, the wealthy planter Sir Simon Clarke reported that "at least 20 or 30 more principal Negroes are impeached, the number before being about 100; in short there appears no end to this horrible affair."[31] On July 28, Pontack from Blue Hole Estate, a center of the plot, claimed under examination that the rebels were going to be supported by Maroons (an autonomous group of warriors with an African background who had agreed with the British government, as part of a peace agreement from 1739, that in return for independence they would support Britain in the case of any enslaved insurrection) and that the aim was to "take the Country to themselves, and drive the white people entirely out of it."[32]

The Jamaican governor responded quickly and forcefully as Jamaica, it was claimed, had "never been in such imminent Danger since the English Conquest" of 1655.[33] He declared martial law and put an embargo on shipping while bringing numerous enslaved people to trial. The intended insurrection kept Jamaica in a high state of anxiety until late August 1776. The plot stirred the worst fears of white Jamaicans, as it showed that enslaved people were able to overcome ethnic divisions, which whites had fondly imagined prevented them from conspiring together. Moreover, it involved native-born or Creole enslaved men, previously thought mostly loyal to slaveowners, and was led by the most elite enslaved men on plantations. The island was placed on a high alert. Simon Taylor was obliged, for example, to return under martial law to his home parish of St. Thomas-in-the-East, noting at the end of August 1776 that "we still keep guard and must continue it . . . for we are not at the bottom of the plot yet," discerning in Blacks "evil intentions" and "a spirit of insolence." The plot led him as an assembly member late in 1776 to petition Britain for Jamaica to have greater military protection. Through elite Jamaicans like Taylor, what Britain itself realized was that if the plot had turned into reality, as in 1760, the British Empire would have faced a nightmare scenario similar to that in Haiti and Grenada in the 1790s. Cataclysmic Caribbean wars against rebel enslaved people would have required large forces to combat them at the same time as more conventional wars against European enemies were being fought.[34]

If whites were anxious, Blacks were terrified. Facing cruel punishments and relentless interrogations, some of the enslaved people on trial tried to save themselves by incriminating others. Of course, as with all such events, even those as well chronicled as the Hanover plot, archival silence is abundant, with no mention, for example, of religious motivations or any female involvement. In addition, it is never quite clear what the intentions of the rebels were had the slave conspiracy succeeded.[35] It seems that the plan was "to set fire" to estates and "then to Rise in General Rebellion and Attack the several Estates and put to death all the White People they could."[36] The leaders of the plot had meticulously planned what would happen once the plot had succeeded. Creoles, Ibos, and Coromantees would each have separate kingdoms, each with specific headmen or ethnic kings.[37]

Seen from the perspective of the enslaved, this plot is evidence of a Black Jamaican and African-Atlantic politics of resistance, one that was the product of "a radical pedagogy of the enslaved."[38] The conspirators had learned several lessons from the great Jamaican slave rebellion of 1760. They took care to manage ethnic diversity and ethnic divisions, and decentralizing the rebellion ensured that the plot when implemented would proceed in stages, moving from estate to estate, with the rebels firing a gun "as a Signal to the *next,* and *so,* till their Plan of Carnage was complete."[39] Enslaved people, of course, did not need much reason to rebel against white rule. Adam related that Coromantee Sam of Baulk Estate had told him "That he had been ill-used by the Overseer and that the Hardships on Negroes were too great and that if all the rest of the Negroes' Hearts were like his, the Matter would have been finished long ago."[40]

The tumults in North America leading to the Declaration of Independence also played a part in creating ideal conditions for a slave revolt. Pontack claimed that the loss of food imports from America, alongside a severe drought, causing a subsistence crisis in Jamaica, made enslaved people angry, as they believed that whites "had taken from them their bread."[41] More concretely, the rebels planned the rising to coincide with both the removal of British troops from Jamaica to North America and the withdrawal of naval ships escorting the merchant convoy to Britain against the new menace of American privateers. John Purrier, a Kingston merchant, claimed that "the taking away the few soldiers we had left, at a time when there was a great scarcity of provisions . . . was the chief cause of the late conspiracy among the Negroes in Hanover."[42]

The Hanover slave plot points to another kind of ever-present conflict in British America that coexisted with political and constitutional strife: the perpetual war between Black and white in oppressive slave societies. It provides a different narrative than the standard account of the American Revolution. What would the British government have done if it had to confront simultaneously a settler revolt and a slave revolt? Would the American Revolution have started to resemble the much bloodier and transformative Haitian Revolution of 1791 to 1804? The near miss that white Jamaicans had in Hanover Parish in 1776 reminds us of the biting sarcasm of the English critic Thomas Day, who commented that "if there be an object truly ridiculous in nature, it is an American patriot, signing resolutions of independency with the one hand, and with the other brandishing a whip over his affrighted slaves."[43]

It might seem from these examples from Scotland and Jamaica in July–August 1776 that the British Empire was under severe strain. There is some truth to this assumption. Within five years, Britain had lost thirteen of its twenty-six Atlantic colonies.[44] The events of the American Revolution showed the Anglo-Irish politician and adherent of Hume William Petty-Fitzmaurice, Earl of Shelburne (later Marquess of Lansdowne) (1737–1805) that the empire was corrupt, unstable, and too expensive to be maintained. Unlike Hume, however, Shelburne, as prime minister and statesman, was determined to reform the empire, by promoting free commerce with North America, stifling Britain's addiction to commercial and military domination, and restoring virtue and morality to government.[45]

July 1776 also saw the beginnings of a new British Empire in the little-explored Pacific Ocean, one based not on commerce but on science.⁴⁶ One week after the Declaration of Independence was printed, on July 12, 1776, the ship *Resolution,* commanded by the foremost explorer of the age, the working-class Yorkshireman Captain James Cook, and its companion ship, *Discovery,* weighed anchor and slipped from the Thames into the English Channel, bound for the northwest coast of North America. Their aim was to discover the fabled (and illusory) Northwest Passage that might link together the two great oceans of the Pacific and the Atlantic. The voyage intended to add to the "Increase of Geographical Knowledge to the Benefit of Mankind in general," as Benjamin Franklin declared in 1779, ordering all American ships to grant Cook safe passage in what Franklin believed was an enterprise "truly laudable in itself."⁴⁷ This voyage was Cook's third and last trip to the Pacific. He carried with him the famed Tahitian Omai, who had gone to London with Cook in October 1774 and who returned to the small island of Huahine in the Society Islands in August 1777.⁴⁸ After Cook traveled to New Zealand and returned Omai to Tahiti, he became the first European to visit Hawaii before exploring California and Nootka Sound on Vancouver Island, and mapping the coast all the way to the Bering Strait, thus determining the northern limits of the Pacific. With his ship blocked by sea ice so that a northwest passage could not be sought, Cook returned to Hawaii. The warm welcome Cook had received on his first visit to Hawaii had vanished and fracas ensued, leading to Cook's death on February 14, 1779.⁴⁹

Cook's voyages presaged a new empire in Australia and New Zealand. They also established what would become by the twentieth century the westernmost state of the United States of America. The immediate impact of Cook's arrival in Hawaii, however, was profoundly negative. European diseases ravaged the Indigenous population so that within fifty years the archipelago's population had plummeted by half from a precontact population of 275,000. One hundred years after Cook's arrival, Hawaiians had been reduced in number to just 54,000.⁵⁰

The American Revolution

These three imperial events in July and August 1776 show that the American Revolution was an imperial civil war as much as a nationalist rebellion.⁵¹ The imperial context matters. That is a central theme of this book. We do not deal very much with the traditional story of the American Revolution as a struggle for independence and a series of overlapping conflicts between and within groups of North Americans. Some of the major interpretative battles over the Revolution, such as whether it is best explained as a contest between rich and poor North Americans about who was to rule once the British had been defeated, or how much the Revolution was indeed "revolutionary" in its political and social contexts, are not issues we explore.[52] Nor do we engage extensively with the debate about the ideological dimensions of the American Revolution and whether North Americans were guided in their actions by a belief in a radical form of republicanism derived from oppositional Whig thought in Britain, predisposing American Patriots to see British actions as tyrannical and corrupt acts intended to take away the liberty of virtuous Americans.[53] Readers wanting a general account of the American Revolution as the founding event in American history can find what they want in many excellent narrative histories of the American Revolution.[54]

A summary of how the American Revolution occurred is useful so as to place our imperial perspective on the American Revolution and our emphasis on Britain's "other" colonies into context.[55] Its immediate origins lay in the Seven Years' War and Britain's conviction that Americans and West Indians needed to contribute more than they were doing to the increasing expenses of empire, not least in maintaining order in a troublesome western frontier.[56] Britain looked into its huge and diverse global empire in 1763 and tried to bring North America into line in an increasingly rationalized system where local differences were eliminated and empire-wide decisions implemented. The aim was to make the empire more harmonious and safer through policies that brought all parts of the empire into common submission to a beneficent but authoritarian metropolitan rule. That plan badly backfired. As one historian notes, "Britain succumbed to the predictable hubris of modernizing states, so confident in their technologies for order but which almost inevitably fracture when faced with unforeseen contingencies, especially when people resist schemes that they believe aim at their subjugation."[57]

The events that made up the American Revolution are easily told. Reforms to empire from the early 1760s, such as a Royal Proclamation in 1763 that sought to preserve the interior west of the Appalachians for Indigenous peoples; plans to incorporate Catholics in Quebec into a Protestant empire; and various acts such as the Sugar Act of 1764 and a Mutiny

Act in 1765, all provoked opposition from white North American colonists. The problems of reform were especially apparent in the Great Lakes and Ohio Valley region in the interior, where there was a rebellion—Pontiac's War—in the spring and summer of 1763. It helped harden racial animosities and encouraged settler vigilante groups, such as the Paxton Boys in Pennsylvania. The Paxton Boys massacred peaceful Natives in Conestoga in western Pennsylvania before marching on Philadelphia in February 1764 to demand more violence be taken against Natives in the western interior so that settlers could acquire Indigenous land.

The real furor came in 1765 when Britain tried to make Americans pay a greater share of imperial costs by imposing a tax well known in Britain, a Stamp Act that taxed legal documents. It was designed less to reduce Britain's enormous war debt than to pay for British soldiers in western America. Everywhere in British North America, though not in the West Indies, attempts to collect taxes through the Stamp Act were met with fierce, sometimes violent, resistance. The Stamp Act was repealed in 1766, but further attempts by the British to tax North American colonists in ways that Americans found acceptable failed. Moreover, the dispute increasingly turned upon differing institutional interpretations, with settlers in North America refusing to accept Parliament's insistence that it alone had the authority to make laws in the empire.

Americans tested British authority repeatedly, especially in the northern port town of Boston, which formed a center of opposition to British imperial rule, with unrest leading to violence—the Boston "massacre" of 1770—and flagrant disobedience in 1773 when colonists refused to allow tea to be landed.[58] Britain responded to this colonial opposition with draconian legislation—the Coercive Acts of 1774—which, when combined with the Quebec Act of the same year that offended anti-Catholic Protestants in the northern colonies, increased tensions further. The impasse between Boston and Britain quickly escalated into war by 1775.

New England was central to the American Revolution, and not just because resistance to empire emerged quickly and strongly in the mid-1760s as imperial reforms hit the region especially hard. The end of the Seven Years' War had cut off military spending that had been useful to New England's economy, while plans for taxation and greater enforcement of current tax rules hurt an economy that was in the middle of a post-war recession. New Englanders also found British actions objectionable because they felt especially betrayed by Britain's perceived lack of concern toward a region that, as its name implied, had conspicuously embraced the British imperial ideology of an empire that was Protestant, commercial, maritime, and free. They also felt betrayed by Britain because it had been the region of British America that had contributed easily the most troops and money to Britain's military endeavors, as befitted the most martially inclined colonies in British America.[59] Their hostile reaction to British actions also stemmed from their historical imperial experience dating back to the 1640s and their memory of standing up to Stuart tyranny in 1689. The Coercive Acts of 1774 were the last straw: "by closing the port of Boston, remodeling Massachusetts' government along authoritarian lines, undermining its judicial autonomy, and strengthening the military's law enforcement powers, Parliament pushed the region into a second armed rebellion against imperial authority."[60]

The other region that was critical to the progress toward declaring independence was Britain's oldest and wealthiest continental colony: Virginia. Like New England, its background was culturally English, though as a slave society it was more relatively hierarchical and aristocratic than the poor and egalitarian New England colonies. Britain did not punish Virginia in the ways it did Boston, but its actions toward Boston accentuated Virginia's discomfort over British restrictions on westward expansion and disquiet about the 1772 *Somerset* case, decided by Lord Mansfield, which signaled a metropolitan willingness to limit planters' "freedom" to control enslaved people as they saw fit. Many Virginia planters became fervent revolutionaries, endorsing the cause of Boston as the "cause of all America," and providing, with New England, most of the soldiers to the Continental Army, led by Virginian George Washington. Virginia's support of Massachusetts turned a localized rebellion into a continental revolution. It led to a divided empire, where the West Indies stayed loyal to Britain, while most mainland colonies formed a Continental Congress that in 1776 declared that it wanted to break with the British Empire.[61]

Britain felt it had to take action against recalcitrant colonies because if it did not its standing as a great power in the eyes of other European states would be fatally compromised, showing that Britain could not impose its will on its own colonies.[62] Britain was convinced that it could run the risk of forcing the colonies to back down because it thought France was momentarily weak and pacifically inclined and would not take advan-

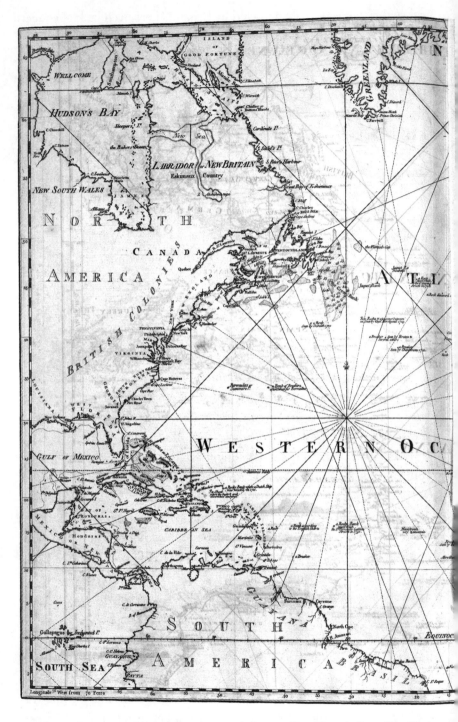

Thomas Jefferys, *The West-India Atlas, or, A Compendious Description of the West-Indies.* London: printed for Robert Sayer and John Bennett, 1775. (Library of Congress, Geography and Map Division)

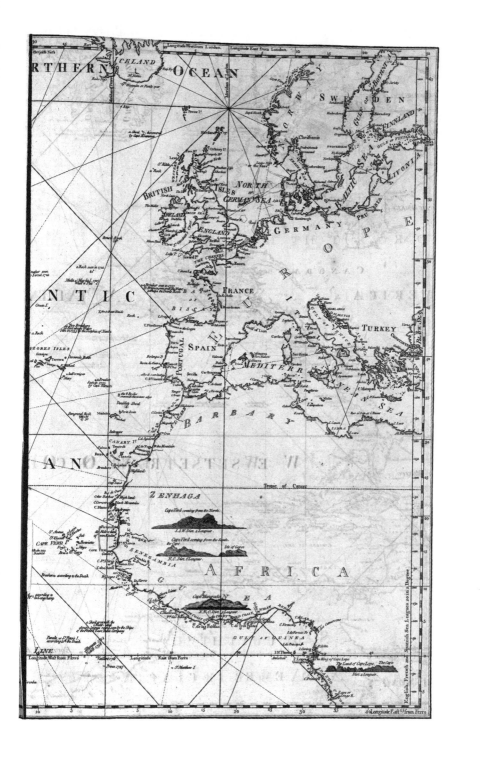

tage of any conflict in the Americas. That was true until 1778, but after American troops under the inspirational leadership of Washington managed to hold off British attacks and won a crucial victory at Saratoga, New York, in October 1777, France entered the war. The War of American Independence thus became a global war, as we discuss at length in chapter 6 of this book. It led in 1781 to the decisive victory at Yorktown, where Washington defeated an understrength British army, weakened from the British navy stopping a blockade of the American coast to chase French and Spanish fleets planning to capture British West Indian islands. American victory at Yorktown ensured British defeat. The two sides settled for peace in 1783 in Paris. When Britain lost at Yorktown, its army musicians played a tune called "The World Turned Upside Down." It was a fitting tune that noted a remarkable turnaround in imperial futures from the triumphs of the early 1760s.[63]

The Themes of this Book

The American Revolution was an imperial crisis, one of the most severe in the history of the British Empire. It was part of a larger imperial history of Britain and its actions in the eighteenth-century Atlantic world. Our book contends with the causes, course, and consequences of the American Revolution if we take an imperial perspective on events. We show that the American Revolution can be thought of as Britain's imperial problem as much as the birth of the American republic. The greatest crisis of the eighteenth-century British Empire did not result in the end of British imperialism, or even in as many changes in that imperialism as such a crisis might be expected to generate. Indeed, the height of British imperialism was not reached until well into the nineteenth and even the twentieth centuries.[64] Moreover, the new United States of America might have been a nation-state founded on republican principles, but it maintained many of the features of imperialism.

Empire is very much part of the modern zeitgeist, as it has been for all of this century.[65] The Thirteen Colonies formed part of a larger whole—a British Empire that had more than double the number of Atlantic colonies in it than those colonies that rebelled from Britain. This book is about the whole of that empire in the Atlantic world from around the start of the Seven Years' War in 1756 to the establishment of the United States of America in 1787–88, including treatment of British imperial possessions in Asia and Africa as well as how Ireland and Scotland fit into an expanded eighteenth-century British realm that also included England and Wales. A central fact about the American Revolution is that it happened in an empire that was larger than just the Thirteen Colonies that became the United States of America. What readers will find distinctive and unusual about our empire-centric rather than American-centric account is that we spend a lot of time on British policies toward those colonies that did *not* rebel, such as the West Indies, Canada, and Ireland, with side glances to India, Africa, and even Australia.[66]

Such an approach illuminates wider themes in the history of the American Revolution and British imperialism. Britain in the 1760s pursued several parallel initiatives in an increasingly diverse empire, the aim of which was to increase central control of imperial policy and provide mechanisms whereby a powerful and central government mediated between colonial elites and metropolitan stakeholders.

In this book, we concentrate less on the colonies that rebelled than on those that did not in assessing responses to this centralizing trend in imperial policy. We do so in the belief that we can learn a lot from the experiences of other colonies besides the thirteen which rebelled. These colonies had problems that at least equaled and often surpassed in seriousness the problems faced by the Thirteen Colonies. Ireland, for example, confronted rural agrarian protest in the 1760s from the Whiteboys, an insurgent and violent protest group, while its ruling elite argued with an authoritarian lord lieutenant who wanted to change the comfortable rules by which the Protestant Ascendancy had long lived. In Quebec, the great majority of the population in the decade before the American Revolution were unassimilated French Catholics, who faced severe economic hardship as British merchants moved aggressively into French Canadian space. Many ordinary French Catholics refused to accept Anglicization and threatened to join with Indigenous peoples during Pontiac's War of 1763–65 to taunt British rulers. In the eastern Caribbean, French Catholics who were brought into the empire after 1763 contended with issues similar to those their former compatriots in Quebec faced. In addition, they were confronted by rebellious Indigenous peoples just at the time that massive investment into islands like Grenada was enlarging the highly profitable plantation sector. The plantation sector also boomed in the fifteen years before 1776 in older Caribbean colonies such as Jamaica, but enslavers were haunted by the near success of the great slave rebellion of 1760, an attempted armed coup to transform Jamaica into an African society. They also engaged in protracted and contentious battles with their governor in 1764, confirming their well-deserved reputation for disputatiousness earned from being the only colony that before 1765 had been formally reprimanded for their insubordination by the British government.

In short, colonies everywhere at the time of the Royal Proclamation of 1763 and the Stamp Act of 1765 had issues that caused concern to imperial officials. Yet these loyal colonies did not revolt in 1776. The irritants of the 1760s were not harbingers of an inevitable revolution. They were the normal tensions that arose as part of running a large empire. The British Empire was powerful and resilient and its leaders were used to solving imperial crises—as they mainly did everywhere outside the Thirteen Colonies from the 1760s through the 1780s. A major contention of this book is that an imperial perspective helps us not only to understand when imperial policies failed, as they did so conspicuously in the Thirteen Colonies before 1776, but also to appreciate when Britain was able to solve imperial problems, as was frequent in Ireland, Canada, and the Caribbean. Indeed, one conclusion emerging from our survey of parallel initiatives made in the 1760s to try and solve imperial problems in the colonies that did not revolt is that it is easier to see why the empire stayed intact than why it fell apart. Explaining why revolutions occur is extremely difficult, which is why historians are wary of inventing typologies that suggest that a revolution will occur when certain things happen.[67]

The standard explanation of why America rebelled in 1776 is a version of the pressure cooker model of popular resistance, with small acts of irritation building to substantial colonial unhappiness and then rebellion. It is sometimes accompanied by an interpretation of imperial officials as out of their depth, unable to understand, let alone control, the new forces of the 1760s arising from Britain's rapid acquisition of a worldwide empire. Barbara Tuchman memorably described British actions in the 1760s as "an act of folly," similar to how "the best and brightest" American officials and military men got events in Vietnam all wrong.[68] This dual interpretation, however, elides one of the main issues in the coming of the American Revolution—when did the Revolution become revolutionary, and indeed was it ever revolutionary, and if so in what ways?[69] Our imperial perspective does not address that question, though we hope it provides a wider context for people seeking answers on that point. We show that different parts of the empire resolved imperial problems successfully enough that many British colonies remained committed to empire before and after the Revolution.

Looking at how imperial policies operated in multiple places and were solved, to various degrees of satisfaction, through non-armed negotiations, however, makes it hard to accept the pressure cooker version of how the American Revolution occurred. It is just as hard to place it within the interpretative schema of modern revolutions, such as 1848, 1989, or the Arab Spring of 2010–11, when revolt seemed to spring simultaneously from seeming voices in the air, following a single event that galvanized communities into resistance. The empire, we will demonstrate in the first half of this book, was in good shape in 1763 with the Peace of Paris, at least if you were a white male Protestant of British heritage or if you were a British statesman. We will show how slavery nurtured and sustained the empire and how wealth from slavery and the prosperity of a growing settler population made empire especially important in the aftermath of the Seven Years' War. The future of the British Empire, in the Atlantic but also in new areas for British imperialism such as India and Africa, looked assured with the conclusion of the Peace of Paris. William Pitt the Elder, the British politician most responsible for British victory in the Seven Years' War after becoming Britain's chief minister in 1757, may have disliked the settlement agreed to in Paris in 1763. He warned of problems to come from not destroying French power in the Atlantic entirely. Nevertheless, the result of the Seven Years' War was terrible for France, Britain's eternal enemy, leaving it permanently embittered. France's foreign policy for the next thirty years was based on avenging its losses in the Seven Years' War by reducing Britain in Europe and in the Atlantic.[70]

Britain was left with problems in dealing with its new empire but ones far less grave than those faced by the European countries that had lost the Seven Years' War, notably France and Austria.[71] Revolution and war fifteen years later seemed unlikely in the early 1760s. But war and revolution did occur. We explain how colonists outside the Thirteen Colonies responded to what most of them thought was a highly unfortunate set of events and how their response to a global and imperial war reflected their imperial experiences and perspectives, altering the ways in which imperialism developed in both the United States and the British Empire once the fighting had finished.

An Imperial and Civil War

Ours is not a new interpretation. There is a venerable imperial school of American historiography from the first half of the twentieth century, led by Charles McLean Andrews and Lawrence Henry Gipson—but they focused on the colonial period at best up to 1776.[72] Andrews insisted that "if we are to understand the colonies . . . we must study the policy and administration at home and follow continuously the efforts which were made, on the side of Great Britain to hold the colonies in a state of dependence and on the side of the colonies to obtain a more or less complete control of their own affairs."[73] That approach is now back in fashion, though not just with a broad geographic scope but with an appreciation for less heralded people and different kinds of events, some of which involved enslaved people. An imperial approach is one that shows an entangled, embedded world, informed by a larger Atlantic context. It helps us understand better the perspective that London had on the American Revolution. But it also encourages us to look at places like Kingston, Dublin, Montreal, and Madras as being as involved with the American Revolution as were traditional centers of rebellion such as Boston and the plantation houses of Virginia.

If we take an imperial perspective on the American Revolution, seeing "the empire whole" rather than as a series of discrete parts that did not interact with each other, we can demonstrate that British policy toward America in the 1760s and 1770s was neither exceptional nor malicious but came out of a parallel set of initiatives throughout the British Empire, notably in Ireland and the West Indies.[74] The causes and aims of these policies are more comprehensible when understood in the broader imperial context which illuminates the origins of the American Revolution.

The Revolutionary War was a global war—a world war as much as a struggle for America's future. That was especially obvious from 1778, when France and Spain entered the war on the American side, but was evident from the start of conflict in the Americas. What we most need to know more about is the European aspect of the conflict. As British ministers well knew, "for the European enemies of the British, as well as for the

British themselves, the war became a great deal more than a struggle for and in America."[75] The French wanted to get revenge for their humiliation in the Seven Years' War. They also thought they could regain lost French territory and advance their geopolitical influences in the West Indies, West Africa, and Asia. Spain and the Netherlands also had global ambitions and entered the War of American Independence to advance those ambitions. Americans were very aware of the international dimensions of rebellion. The Declaration of Independence was not just an announcement for domestic consumption of America breaking free of the British Empire and an iteration of fundamental political philosophy. It was primarily written to persuade European powers that American rebellion was serious and irrevocable; that America intended to be an independent republic; and that they were not going to return to the status quo ante 1776 as a dependent part of the British Empire.[76]

Moreover, as well as being a global conflict and a civil war between various groups of colonists in the Americas, the American Revolution was a civil war between Britons and Americans—people who had seen themselves as brethren, not as different people. It was also a civil war, or counterrevolution, between various parts of the empire, for when the empire is looked at in its entirety, Loyalism was more pronounced than rebellion. Only thirteen colonies broke away into rebellion. The Canadian colonies, the British West Indies, Scotland, Ireland, and West Africa did not evince more than minimal revolutionary tendencies. And finally, the conflict split Britain itself. A sizable part of the British political nation sympathized with American rebels, at least until France and Spain entered the war in 1778. The onset of the war occasioned the largest anti-war petition movement in the history of the nation, joined by towns that had never previously petitioned Parliament, in 1775. Why they opposed the American war often had less to do with their support for the American position than with their hatred of the government in power and even more so their worries over what the American Revolution implied for British constitutionalism and for the future of the British Empire.[77]

And all these civil wars had their roots, in one way or another, in the Seven Years' War. The American Revolution started well before the usual start of the conflict. Surveys of the Age of Revolutions rarely begin with the Seven Years' War, instead locating the origins of the American Revolution in the 1760s. An imperial perspective makes us aware that the roots of the American Revolution go back at least to the 1740s, if not to the 1720s and even to the Glorious Revolution of 1688, for "the underlying reason for the colonies' rejection of British authority was not their changing nature but their clinging to old ways, particularly their continuing adherence to seventeenth-century English political culture."[78] The Seven Years' War, which was even more a global war than the American Revolution, was a great imperial triumph that produced a series of imperial headaches which an inexperienced British government under a brand-new monarch handled badly, at least in respect to British North America.

That is an unremarkable and much-repeated conclusion, but it makes clear just how useful the imperial perspective is in evaluating the causes of the American Revolution. By keeping Quebec rather than Guadeloupe in the exchange of colonies that happened in the Peace of Paris in 1763, due in part to pressures from West Indians eager to keep their tariff privileges in plantation produce, the British Empire accentuated the likelihood of colonial assertiveness by removing a common enemy that prevented settlement in western lands.[79] More important, the nature of the empire changed radically after 1763. Before then, the empire was an empire of white people, mostly of British heritage and overwhelmingly Protestant, as well as African slaves, viewed as chattels more than people, and subordinated Catholic Irish. From 1763, the empire was full of people of non-British background and from a variety of religious traditions, including Catholics in the West Indies and especially in French Quebec—the latter group being especially disliked in firmly anti-Catholic New England.[80] Moreover, the new imperialism of the United States after 1800 was driven by similar factors as in the old empire, influenced "less by nation-building impulses than by land hunger, profit seeking, and eagerness to exploit new resources."[81]

Did the Revolution Matter?

These multiple dates of importance for the American Revolution within a diverse British Empire, where even under a strong fiscal-military state it was generally impossible to compel one part of the empire to act like another part of the empire, make one wonder whether the Revolution was as momentous an event as it is customarily thought to be.[82] We might ask, first, whether the American Revolution mattered and, second, whether it was just a reconfiguration of imperial imperatives.

Whether the American Revolution "mattered," however, seems a silly question to ask, given how much ink has been spilled in the last 250 years on establishing its causes, course of conflict, and consequences. We know that the result of the American Revolution was the creation of a new nation that has become the richest and most powerful nation in the world and its only superpower. The American Revolution was thought to be significant at the time because "men and women, Black and white, moved by the incendiary rhetoric of the Americans, made common cause across continents, spanning the vast differences arising from divergent places with unique traditions."[83] The American Revolution helped inspire revolutions elsewhere—Geneva in 1782, the Dutch against the stadtholder in 1787, and most famously France in 1789, before spreading to Saint-Domingue in 1791, Sierra Leone in 1792, and to much of Spanish America from the second decade of the nineteenth century.[84] The universalistic call of the American revolutionaries for a global push to liberty had a particular effect on people of African descent, especially as the Haitian Revolution expanded the possibilities open to a highly oppressed people. In Sierra Leone, John Clarkson tried to insist that it was the ideals of the American Revolution that inspired Black Loyalists to settle there. The settlement of Sierra Leone had been, Clarkson wrote to the Marquis de Lafayette in 1792, "established on the true principles of Freedom and intended to promote the general Happiness of Mankind."[85]

Many Americans and Britons, however, recoiled from the radical directions taken in France and the Caribbean and endeavored to distinguish the American Revolution as exceptional and the founding of the United States as singular. This view has had a long influence on American revolutionary scholarship, separating what happened in North America from what it meant globally. But the example of revolutionary America as the living site of Enlightenment and civility, despite white Americans' commitment to chattel slavery and their much-criticized tendency toward excessive worship of wealth over status or birth, was very important as inspiration for overturning old regimes. Its example was summed up by Thérèse Philippine d'Yve in Brussels. She rejoiced in 1788, a year before the fall of the Bastille, that revolts were erupting everywhere that "sovereigns submit their subjects to the yoke of despotism."[86]

Yet not every scholar has thought that the American Revolution was all that important. Hannah Arendt notoriously argued that the American Revolution was globally insignificant, with only local rather than worldwide implications. According to Arendt, little changed in America because of revolution in terms of regime change and in its intellectual effects: "the sad truth of the matter is that the French Revolution, which ended in disaster, has made world history, while the American Revolution, so triumphantly successful, has remained an event of little more than local importance."[87]

Certainly, recent scholarship on how the American Revolution should be viewed within larger global and imperial networks has tended to support Arendt's position. Continuity is stressed over change, with the American Revolution depicted as neither an end nor a beginning but an event that happened in the middle of an age of imperialism that was part of a longer flow of change. Imperial historians are especially reluctant to see the American Revolution in exceptionalist terms or as a major and incomparable historical event. Revolutionary Americans created an empire, different from the British Empire, "but an empire nonetheless." The new US empire was a continuation of the British Empire, but with an increased emphasis on using war, settlement, and trade to increase territorial expansion and Native American dispossession. This means that "many of the changes scholars once made synonymous with the revolution started much earlier or were completed much later or both."[88] New forms of imperialism in the United States were very much like the old imperialism, characterized by "land hunger, profit seeking, and eagerness to exploit new resources."[89]

Plus ça change, plus c'est la même chose in short. It has become a commonplace that the result of the American Revolution was just a continuation, in only slightly different form, of British imperialism so that "the colonists' truly revolutionary act was to break from Europe in order to set up their own violent empire." Such statements lead to a depressing view that the major consequence of the American Revolution was that it was "a revolution that gave rise to a virulent empire in which war's disruption followed by the quickening pace of colonialism outweighed gains made by subaltern groups during the revolutionary settlement."[90]

The leading historians of the American Revolution support such conclusions. Alan Taylor, for example, finds little that was transformative about an American Revolution that he sees as an event mostly about imperial rule. The transformations he sees are that the Revolution increased racial distinctions that associated freedom with whiteness; provided for stronger state formation that advanced white settler interests; and accelerated westward expansion and attacks on Indigenous occupation of settler-desired land in the American interior. The Revolutionary Settlement, he suggests, provided freedom and prosperity for Patriot victors but delayed the resolutions of major contradictions in the founding, notably slavery, that eventually "provoke[d] a new civil war, even bloodier and more destructive than the revolution."[91] Serena Zabin is similarly unimpressed with the results of an American Revolution characterized by imperialism. For her, the American Revolution is "not a proud story," as it was "the foundation for the creation of a neo-imperial United States, and we live today in the long shadow of that history." "In every direction," she concludes, "the view is bleak."[92]

Younger historians have an even harsher verdict on the American Revolution. Rashauna Johnson, for example, argues that because of the settler victory of the British Empire in the 1780s, "the early United States was a racialized nation, produced and reproduced through empire." She contends that nationalism, racism, and empire-building were fundamentally related principles that led to dire consequences for enslaved and Indigenous people.[93] Her view echoes the views of the many scholars who see in the ideology of settler colonialism that the United States was a settler empire that adopted the "logic of elimination" of Native Americans.[94]

So too historians studying the development of the American state in the early republic find imperialism a useful concept to analyze a state that, through the exigencies of wartime mass mobilization, was surprisingly strong and had augmented its capacity through war making, which compelled it to use that increased capacity to develop an efficacious state.[95] Gautham Rao argues that the federal government was a strong state when the subject was Indigenous peoples. Rao has examined the federal government's relationship with Indigenous peoples as part of what he calls an imperial state, or what was a vison of statecraft that cohered around an ethos of systematic governance. He argues that "the early federal government's imperial aims and practices picked up where Britain's came to an unexpected halt," and that "one empire gave way to another as an array of officeholders and administrators collected taxes, expanded national communities, planned roads, carried out military expeditions, and performed other tasks that would be crucial to the rise of an American empire"—all in pursuit of expanding that empire through territorial acquisition at the expense of Indigenous land rights.[96]

Matthew Lockwood has a particularly harsh view of the impact of the American Revolution on world history. He frames the American Revolution as the start of an authoritarian backlash throughout the institution of the British Empire. He argues that a revolution in favor of liberty in America initiated "a reactionary revolution in the wider world, inflicting new suffering and new restraints on people for whom freedom and independence were not available," with the "hard lessons learned from the American Revolution" for the empires of France, Spain, and Britain being that independence needed to be imposed with a more authoritarian emphasis. The American Revolution underpinned Britain's rise as an imperial nation: "the war forced Britain to think about its empire in new, more centralized, hierarchical, authoritarian ways, allowing Britain to tighten its grasp both at home and in its far-flung possessions." Indeed, he suggests, "Britain's survival of the French Revolution and the wars it spawned owed much to the counter-revolutionary measures it had already undertaken in the years between 1776 and 1789." In short, Britain experienced a Thermidorean reaction to revolution a decade before France did, especially if we focus on the violence of this imperial civil war in which ordinary people had their world turned upside down. Doing this gives a "veneer of haloed respectability" to an imperial counterrevolution that "was in reality a nasty, bloody, confused and chaotic era."[97]

Thus, we could see the creation of a second British Empire between 1790 and 1830 as the work of an "aristocratic reaction," with the imperial regime as statist, militaristic, authoritarian, and agrarian, with trade playing second fiddle to security issues.[98] This view, however, overplays the devastating consequences of the American Revolution and underplays the liberating influence of the event on people in the Age of Revolution.[99] What is correct is portraying Britain as a counterrevolutionary nation in the 1780s and 1790s. The French Revolution alarmed many in Britain in its attacks on established institutions, like the church, the aristocracy, and the monarchy. Edmund Burke's denunciation of the French Revolution found a ready audience in 1790–91. Burke combined sensationalist polemic with systemic analysis, idealizing the French *ancien régime* while lamenting the hallmark of the French Revolution, which he felt was its unstoppable energy, threatening to destroy not just property but all habits of respect and deference that in his view constituted a functioning society. He argued that an excess of liberty always led to license, license to anarchy, and anarchy to despotism.[100] The political response to the French Revolution on the part of William Pitt the Younger was to back down on reform, notably stopping the abolitionist movement in its tracks. Pitt also started to worry about subversion at home and the risks associated with making war abroad. Britain's ruling elite thus exhibited enormous anxiety about the infusion of French republicanism into public culture and believed that any concession to radicalism would lead to French-style social disorder.[101]

It was a little different in the United States. At first Americans were highly enthusiastic about the French Revolution, seeing it as validation of their own revolt and similar in kind to the American Revolution. Some Americans, notably Thomas Jefferson, a committed Francophile, retained their enthusiasm for what the French were doing throughout the 1790s and into the 1800s. Yet, as in Britain, the execution of Louis XVI in 1793 and the excesses of the Terror under the Jacobins in 1794 changed many opinions in America. The meaning of the French Revolution became entwined in the quarrel that Americans had among themselves over the direction of the American Revolution as the decades passed from 1783. Americans belonging to the Federalist Party (heavily concentrated in the northern states of New York and New England) were convinced that the radical popular and egalitarian principles of the French Revolution threatened to corrupt Americans and turn American society into a wild and licentious democracy. Revolutionary France, consequently, was a scapegoat for all that conservative Americans felt disturbing about democracy in the new American republic.[102]

An Imperial World

The period of the American Revolution is often thought of as the first event in a half-century Age of Revolution, but the period we cover, from the 1740s to the 1790s, is just as accurately an age of imperialism. Let's have a brief outline of the empire in which Americans, West Indians, and, after 1760, Canadians and Bengalis lived to give some idea of the imperial dimensions within which contemporaries moved. We also note that the British Empire was just one of several empires competing in the Atlantic world. The British Empire was mostly an Atlantic empire before the American Revolution, but it was not entirely based in the western hemisphere. Britain had a significant colonial possession—its most valuable one in the eyes of most imperial politicians based in London—in the neighboring island of Ireland, as well as control over the Channel Islands resulting from the conquest of England by the Normans in the eleventh century. It also had small but geopolitically vital possessions in the Mediterranean—Gibraltar and Minorca. It did not have imperial territories in Asia and Africa, but it was increasingly drawn into these regions through state support of commercial corporations specializing in overseas commerce, notably the East India Company in Bengal, Madras, and Bombay, and the Royal African Company and its successors (both companies and private traders) in West Africa. Moreover, the empire expanded remarkably because of the Seven Years' War, to include an imperial presence in large parts of South Asia and Senegambia in West Africa. These possessions had been acquired almost randomly over many centuries, from the Channel Islands in the eleventh century to Ireland in the thirteenth century to acquisitions in the Atlantic in the seventeenth and eighteenth centuries. There was a suitably diverse set of arrangements by which possessions were ruled and had a constitutional relationship to Britain. All were under the rulership of the king of England, who after 1535 also became king of Wales and who ruled Scotland independently from 1603 and as part of the union of Great Britain from 1707. He (or she—it was under a female monarch, Anne, that the union of Scotland with England and Wales happened) was also the king of the colony of Ireland, which was officially a kingdom, with its own parliament, over which the British Parliament was sovereign, and its own administration, subject to oversight from London. The monarch presiding over this set of possessions was the ruler of "a composite monarchy with both contiguous and overseas components."[103]

But the British did not move in a world of their own making. It was a period of intense imperial competition that had lasted between Britain, France, usually Spain, and occasionally the Dutch Republic for a century since the Glorious Revolution of 1688 and the Dutch conquest of England and Wales. We do not spend much time on this imperial competition, though it is central to chapter 6, which looks at the American Revolution as a global war between 1778 and 1783, involving conflict between French and Spanish Empires as well as war in North America between Patriots, Loyalists, and British soldiers and sailors. But a few comments are in order on how a war conducted in a world consumed by imperialism was affected by those imperial currents.

In some respects, the idea that this was an age of European imperialism par excellence was not commonly expressed at the time. Linguistically, the British were more imperially minded than their European rivals, with the English envisioning Britain as an empire as early as Henry VIII's break with Rome in 1533. In Spain, however, as late as the 1750s, it was uncommon for Spaniards to see their overseas colonies as part of an empire, while in France no one used the word "empire" until the end of the eighteenth century.[104] As it became more common to think "imperially," the nature of empire changed. From the 1750s, European empires that were various and diverse came increasingly to resemble each other. It was not just in Britain but in France and Spain that statesmen came to see centralized control as desirable. Empires moved toward conformity. In large part this conformity came from the ultimate purpose of empire seen from metropolitan centers: its role was to sustain balances of power in Europe. The Seven Years' War intensified this trend toward imperial conformity and toward a reduction in imperial diversity. With conformity came expansion, especially in the British Empire but also in the French Empire.[105] Britons broadened their horizons to look at colonization in the Pacific Ocean and came to see the vitality of the African slave trade as a reason to be particularly interested in solidifying their position in West Africa.

That does not mean, however, that there were not numerous points of tension between European empires. Spain had complaints against France, such as where the boundaries were between Saint-Domingue and Santo Domingo in the western Caribbean and whether France would move from its base in Louisiana to threaten Spanish North Mexico. It was much more concerned about what the British were doing, such as where they fixed the boundaries between British Georgia and Spanish Florida, the obstruction of long-standing Basque fishermen's fishing expeditions in Newfoundland, and the incursions made by British colonists in cutting mahogany on the Mosquito Shore. Britain, in turn, seethed over Spanish ships in the Caribbean suspected of smuggling.

Nevertheless, while empires were powerful, they were not all-powerful but "entangled." That meant that empires were connected not just by imperial structures but by "an array of interconnected processes . . . some national in character, others having more to do with cosmopolitan phenomena such as race, religion, commerce, gender and law."[106] Colonial borders were porous, allowing rampant smuggling.[107] War in the Caribbean meant a frequent exchange of colonies between empires and a loose attitude toward imperial belonging. Loyalties to empires were often transactional—the empire providing the best benefits might get the most committed loyalty. Working out the contours of imperial subjecthood was to be an urgent issue in places like Grenada and Quebec.[108]

Our book looks at all these places as part of a dynamic, evolving, and always contestable imperial framework from the 1760s to the 1780s. It starts with a chapter on the Seven Years' War (1756–63), discussing how it evolved, how it was an imperial war, and how the victories in many imperial theaters of war, notably in India and Canada, but also in the West Indies, shaped and conditioned the policies described in chapter 2. Chapter 2 is a crucial chapter in the book. It outlines the imperial choices made in the 1760s by the British government trying to govern and bring under order a more diverse and globally wide empire that extended from Ireland to Africa to the Atlantic and to South Asia. Chapters 3 and 4 step back from the immediacy of events and policies in the mid-century British Empire and look at two underlying features of imperial expansion in the first half of the eighteenth century. The British Empire was increasingly devoted to the liberty of an increasingly large number of assertively British, aggressively expansionist, and decidedly ideological settlers in North America. It was also an empire as committed to coercion as to liberty, both of Indigenous peoples perceived to be getting in the way of settler dominion and of enslaved people, envisioned as essential to making Britain and its white Protestant subjects prosperous. Moreover, the white Protestants who rebelled against Britain in the Thirteen Colonies in 1776 and the white Protestants in places like the West Indies and Ireland who stayed loyal were assertively British in their cultural habits, social mores, and political orientations. They had a fervent belief everywhere before 1776 that they were as British as anyone living in Scotland, Wales, or England. These beliefs—a set of assumptions we can label as Anglicization—were very important both in shaping imperialism before, during, and after the American Revolution and in provoking imperial subjects' shock at metropolitan Britons treating them as second-class and often non-British subjects.

We hope to convince readers of this book of the utility of seeing the

American Revolution as an imperial event, and of the necessity for a full understanding of this topic to study not just those places that rebelled against Britain and created a new American republic but the many places in the empire that did not rebel. That is key to chapter 5, on the loyal colonies. Chapter 6 expands on the imperial perspectives outlined in chapters 3 and 4 by examining how the tensions of empire played out in the Americas, and to an extent elsewhere, between 1776 and 1783, especially in the years after French and Spanish entry into the War of American Independence from 1779, when the conflict became truly a war between empires and for empire. Our concluding chapter, on consequences, argues that the end of one kind of empire in North America, through the creation of a new republic in the eastern seaboard, far from ended the importance of imperialism on the continent. We ask whether the new United States of America was an empire in new form (we contend the answer is mixed: in some ways it was, but otherwise it was quite a different beast from the colonial empire it replaced). We also assess how the British Empire quickly adapted to the greatest defeat in its long history but, in adapting, changed the nature of its imperial mission. Imperialism and revolution went together in the British Atlantic world.

PART ONE
Causes of the American Revolution

HOW DO WE ASSESS WHAT WERE the causes of the American Revolution? A formulation we have found useful is that put forward by Lawrence Stone on the causes of another Atlantic revolution. Stone, writing about the seventeenth-century English Civil War, adopted a typology of "long term" (or "preconditions"), "short term" (or "precipitants"), and "immediate" (or "trigger") causes in which the relative weighting of factors might vary over time. He made a sharp distinction between long run, underlying causes—"the preconditions, which create a potentially explosive situation and can be analyzed on a comparative analysis"—and immediate, incidental factors—"the precipitants, which trigger the outbreak, and which may be non-recurrent, personal and fortuitous." Stone's actual interpretation of the causes of the English Revolution has been largely discredited by "revisionist" historians of the English Civil War, who have pointed out that there is a marked absence between cause and effect in the various "causes" that Stone put forward.[1] Nevertheless, his typology is one that helps to place different types of causes into balance and may, as Stone provocatively argued, dispose "of the objections of those historians whose antipathy to conceptual scholarship takes the naïve form of asserting the uniqueness of each historical event."[2]

Early American historians have adopted variants of the typology that Stone suggested to explain the causes of the American Revolution, albeit without direct reference to the differences between long-term, short-term, and immediate causes that Stone illuminated. Bernard Bailyn, for example, put forward his republicanism interpretation as a long-term cause to explain why colonial discontent in the 1760s turned into revolution in the 1770s. He argued that the rise of the assemblies—a common explanation in the 1960s about why the American Revolution occurred—was not a sufficient explanation because "it does not make the dynamics of the Revolutionary movement intelligible—it does not provide a basis for understanding what impelled it forward at the time and place it moved forward."[3]

Bailyn contended that without a set of beliefs which he termed "republicanism," colonial discontent could never have turned into fully fledged rebellion. His argument is supported by how ideologies of republicanism seldom were as prominent in the West Indies as they were among North American colonists, even when West Indian thinkers shared much of the political assumptions that were current in North America—a fact that helps to explain why opposition to imperial actions in the 1760s was less intense in the Caribbean than in North America.[4]

How does an imperial approach help us understand better the causes—preconditions, precipitants, and triggers—of the American Revolution? An imperial approach has many advantages, as outlined in the introduction to this book. But it also has some explanatory disadvantages. The long history of empires, the fact that "British and American history happened under imperial skies" and that "we live in a world that empires have made," with the modern world "riddled with the memories, aspirations, institutions, and grievances left behind by [the British] empire," tends to suggest the importance of continuity rather than change as a force in human history.[5] An emphasis on imperialism in the context of the American Revolution makes it hard to see how this event could ever have happened. The British Empire was effective and the white people within it were prosperous and happy, if often resentful that the benefits of the empire they professed to love were extended to people they disliked, like Catholics in Quebec, Indigenous peoples in the Ohio Valley, and even Bengalis. British Americans found what happened in 1776 to be mysterious, given the harmony that had existed at the conclusion of a glorious war, the Seven Years' War. Indeed, some North Americans, like Benjamin Franklin, were so enamored of empire that they supported before the Seven Years' War a strengthening of imperial bonds so that the American colonies might have the same place in the empire as did Scotland post-1707. As late as 1768, Franklin was "fully persuaded" that a union of America like that of Scotland with England and Wales was "best for the whole," commenting "that though particular parts might find particular disadvantages in it, they would find greater advantages in the security arising to every part from the increased strength of the whole."[6]

Our account supports change being less important than continuity in the era of the American Revolution. We show that while imperial reform in the 1760s and 1770s may have failed badly in the Thirteen Colonies that broke away to form the United States, it generally succeeded elsewhere, in looking at the "empire as a whole."[7] Only half of Britain's American colonies joined with the Thirteen Colonies in rebellion, and revolutionary agitation in support of American Patriots was relatively limited (though not non-existent) in Scotland, Wales, England, and Ireland. The British Empire did not fall because it was divided from 1783. Indeed, it flourished as never before as an empire that historians now think bore more continuity with the pre-1783 empire than differences from it.[8]

It is interesting to reflect that if an interest in empire—with the tendency to stress continuity—is currently fashionable, it comes at a time when historians are increasingly reluctant to see what used to be termed "revolutions" as being periods of sudden transformative change.[9] English history is especially allergic to notions of revolutionary change, with few of the events traditionally thought of as signaling early modern historical breaks—the English Reformation; the English Civil War; the Industrial Revolution—now treated as being defined by sudden and revolutionary change.[10] It is hard to imagine revisionist historians writing an account of the English Civil War in the confident way Lawrence Stone did over fifty years ago, explaining how social and economic changes in Tudor and Stuart England caused a revolution. They tend to steer away from seeing long-term causes of this revolution or even accepting that it had any causes outside historical contingency.[11]

Historians of the American Revolution, who two generations ago had an "abiding preoccupation with the causes and consequences of the American Revolution," are now as reluctant as English historians to see the American Revolution as a transformative revolution or to worry about what caused it.[12] They—like us—are allergic to monocausal interpretations of the origins of the American Revolution, as so "many of the changes that scholars once made synonymous with the Revolution started much earlier; or were completed much later; or both."[13] Historians of the American Revolution resist being placed into interpretative schools, declaring that "the new paradigm is that there is no single paradigm," suggesting that it is not the duty of the historian "to clarify the past" but to provide more complicated narratives that show a "willful quest for messiness."[14]

So, do we have a view on what caused the American Revolution? That is not our object, of course. We are interested in the event's imperial dimensions rather than in providing an analysis of how the American Revolution arose and ended up in conflict. Our first four substantive chapters after the introduction, however, provide lots of information which is useful for understanding how the American Revolution came about. Like most historians of this event, we prioritize the Seven Years' War as pivotal in creating the conditions through which the imperial reforms which so annoyed North Americans were deemed necessary. The Seven Years' War was also important in establishing new ways of thinking about empire and new models for Britain to exploit its colonial possessions that came about from the territorial expansion of Britain into Bengal, Canada, Senegambia, and the eastern Caribbean.[15]

The opportunities and complications arising from the Seven Years' War led to parallel imperial policies throughout the British Empire, which are outlined in chapter 2. What is clear is that while the imperial policies implemented in the empire had distinct similarities, how they were received varied dramatically in various parts of the empire, with much the worst response being in New England while the response in the West Indies was restrained. Two chapters correspond to the "precipitants" (chapter 2) and "triggers" (chapter 3) in Stone's typology—the events that led directly to the Declaration of Independence and the War of American Independence.

We do not follow Stone blindly, however, as we do not accept his assumptions, drawn from the heyday of social history, that social and economic changes led to revolutionary situations. Thus, we place "preconditions" after "triggers" to suggest that these preconditions did not cause revolution but provided the context through which the imperial reforms had to operate. The British Empire in the Atlantic was an empire of slaves and settlers, living in uneasy tension, at least in North America, with substantial populations of Indigenous peoples. But while changes in colonial society undoubtedly played a part in causing the Revolution and certainly shaped how the Revolution developed as it did, this did not mean that such changes were pivotal to causing a revolution. They were not. What the extraordinary expansion of colonial British America in the eighteenth century did was to generate "striking differences in demography, political economy and aspirations for territorial expansion across the colonies" that "created complex challenges for colonial governance that lay at the heart of Britain's imperial crisis."[16]

These challenges, however, were not insuperable. The British Empire was a remarkably resilient and flexible institution. The crises in the entire history of the British Empire and Commonwealth that led to colonial separation were relatively few: the United States in the 1780s; Ireland in 1921; India in 1947; and South Africa and Rhodesia in the 1960s. Usually, British imperial possessions stayed imperial or at least attached to Britain in some form, often for centuries. The British Caribbean, for example, has been part of the British Empire and the British Commonwealth since the 1620s; Canada since 1759; Australia since 1788; and New Zealand since 1840. And just because the Thirteen Colonies were growing ever more populous and increasingly rich in the first half of the eighteenth century, revolution was neither inevitable nor even likely—rich and happy places are not the obvious candidates for abrupt social and political change. That is particularly true when we consider that it was British officials, not colonists in British America, who were the agents demanding change, first on the western frontier, and then in the combustible port cities of Boston, Philadelphia, and New York.[17]

If our first four substantive chapters point to a principal cause of the American Revolution, connecting preconditions with triggers, then we opt for the American Revolution being a countercyclical event, a crisis of imperial *integration* that the British state could not handle. Or more precisely, it was a crisis of imperial integration that could not be handled by the British state with respect to the Thirteen Colonies.[18] Everywhere else, imperial policies fostering a stronger integration with the aims of the central government while maintaining economic prosperity, social harmony, and political quietude tended to work. Imperial integration is closely associated with themes of Anglicization—the idea that free white settlers increasingly oriented themselves and their societies around British values and social and economic assumptions, in which demographic and economic growth and the birth of an Anglicized consumer culture provided mechanisms whereby rich colonists could emulate successfully British genteel culture.[19] Ironically, as North Americans became more recognizably British in how they behaved, thought, and looked, it created imperial tensions as settlers came to believe that Britain was intent on destroying the developing Anglicized society that colonists had worked so hard to create. Colonial opposition to British acts in the 1760s was based around colonial adherence to "fundamental English rights and the British constitution," which "underscored the English-speaking Atlantic's growing political unity."[20]

The paradox of imperial integration was that the rapid transformations in British American life which occurred during the first half of the eighteenth century, making settlers receptive to social and economic change, were accompanied by a remarkable political conservatism. What worried American Patriots was the changing nature of British actions when they wanted to cling to old ways, "particularly their continuing adherence to seventeenth-century English political culture"—notably their memory of resistance to what they considered a tyrannical monarchy under Charles II and especially under James VII and II—and their lack of recognition of the sovereign authority of Parliament.[21] In short, "the crisis leading to the American Revolution revolved around the implications of ordering space in new ways and trying to bring rule to unruliness, to untangle entanglements, and to disconnect the connections that made the Atlantic system as dynamic as it was."[22]

Yet what we must keep in mind is the divided nature of responses to attempted reforms of European empires. These conflicted responses suggest that it was the Thirteen Colonies which were unusual in their resistance to imperial reforms. If we examine other responses to European imperial reforms, the reform process was both universal and accepted. There were, of course, significant exceptions, the reaction in the Thirteen Colonies being especially consequential. Colonists in other European empires, exposed to centrally driven reforms in the 1760s, also protested vociferously and sometimes violently to how they were being treated by imperial administrations and resisted attempts to implement reform of colonial institutions and structures without consultation or approval from local elites. In the same year of the Stamp Act, in 1765, for example, colonists in Quito in the Spanish Empire's viceroyalty of New Granada also protested government changes to taxation, leading to riots and then rebellion. In May 1765, the people of Quito attacked and destroyed government premises and, in riots that convulsed the city for several months, nullified royal government. These "rebellions of the barrios" were like North American Stamp Act riots but led neither to permanent networks of opposition to imperial actions, as in the northern cities of British North America, nor to any stop in processes of Spanish imperial reform.[23]

However, the reform processes that occurred everywhere in Europe and European empires were usually met with acceptance, if not enthusiasm, by colonists. Saint-Domingue, the wealthiest colony in the Atlantic world, provides an instructive case study. White colonists were not passive recipients of French reforms: when they did not like them, as in a prolonged dispute over taxation and a requirement that whites needed to serve for extended periods in colonial militia, they made their displeasure known and thwarted imperial desires. But when they were able to influence the reform process, as in new laws that enhanced white supremacy in the colony and reduced the political standing of wealthy free men of color, they enthusiastically supported them so that race, rather than class, became the primary criterion for social and political status. France proved itself especially good at imperial reform. It reconceptualized its reduced post-war empire into being an empire of trade based on sugar and slaves; reorganized the defense of the colonies; asserted the consolidation of royal authority; and rationalized laws governing trade. It did so either as part of a coherent "imperial" program or, more often, as ad hoc responses to issues that arose in complex colonial settings. The result, nonetheless, was a successful rethinking of imperial administration and increased centralization of imperial authority which encouraged the Saint-Domingue economy to grow while reform impulses from the center advanced white settler power and wealth.[24]

One major advantage of taking an imperial approach is that it cuts across the usual ways in which the developing crisis in British America is treated, which is to see all events through a nationalistic lens. For instance, the existing literature on the taxation crisis within the British Empire after 1763 which led to the Stamp Act does not engage with the financial reforms of the Austrian monarchy or the bankruptcy of the French monarchy, both of which influenced what Britain was trying to do. Similarly, little has been written on the connected expansion of the Dutch financial market and the growth of the European slave trade in the immediate aftermath of the war, which shaped the massive expansion of slave trading within the British Empire in the 1760s. On the contrary, the imperial reform movements started everywhere in Europe in the aftermath of the Seven Years' War, including in states without an Atlantic border, such as Russia, Austria, and Prussia, were closely interlinked. Indeed, "the massive wartime mobilization of economic and financial resources profoundly destabilized the financial foundations of European monarchies" and "intensified a continental political economy debate from which administrators at every level drew inspiration." Everywhere in Europe and its empires, the cost of the Seven Years' War "created tensions between the governments and the governed that were not easily remedied, as swelling public debts led to excessively unpopular reforms and the rocky reconfiguration of imperial states." It also provided advantages to some individuals, notably transatlantic slave trading merchants in the British and French Empires, who continued after the end of the Seven Years' War to take advantage of the increased need that financially burdened states had for their services.[25]

One of the wealthiest men in France, for example, the Bordeaux merchant Abraham Gradis, abundantly benefited from the confidence of the principal minister, Étienne François de Choiseul, by signing provisioning contracts with the ministry of the navy. He extended his activities during the war into providing enslaved people to Saint-Domingue in the booming 1760s. Similarly, the London merchant Richard Oswald, who supplied troops with grain on the German battlefield, prospered during the war and gained further prominence in the following years and formed part of a formidable trading partnership of London-based merchants who invested heavily in the fast-developing and commercially lucrative slave colonies in the eastern Caribbean taken by Britain from France after the 1763 Peace of Paris. There were winners as well as losers in the reconfiguration of empire in the 1760s, and many of these winners concentrated their activities on those parts of the British Empire that remained reasonably happy with imperial reforms in the 1760s.[26] The nature of the reform process in the Spanish, French, and British Empires was that all looked more like colonial empires by the end of the 1760s than each had done at the end of the 1750s. As François-Joseph Ruggiu notes, "each empire came to see colonial trade as crucial to the European balance of power; each had massive security problems; and each had to reform or coerce settlers' allegiance," leading in each empire to more authoritarian modes of government and rationalized imperial systems.[27]

Britain was in a stronger position than most European states to make imperial reforms, despite its massive wartime debts.[28] It did a decent job of making those reforms work outside the Thirteen Colonies, as chapter 3 outlines. Britain, like France, had realized that British America, especially the West Indies, was particularly important to the imperial economy and that Ireland and Canada could become part of a coherent imperial "system." It was still working out in the 1760s where India fit into this picture. Its actions in the "other" colonies we are so concerned about in this book showed an imperial system that largely worked—authority was becoming centralized in London; imperial abuses such as smuggling were being remedied; and crucial actors, such as the transatlantic slave trading merchants who dominated imperial trade, were being encouraged. The general failure of reform efforts in the Thirteen Colonies before 1776 should not mask how well many reform movements were working elsewhere in the British Empire.[29]

ONE

The Seven Years' War and the New Empire

THE SEVEN YEARS' WAR WAS THE pivotal event that transformed the mid-eighteenth-century British Empire. One of the problems with treatments of the Seven Years' War as a precursor of the American Revolution, however, is that such accounts have a decidedly teleological character, with the Seven Years' War as mostly important for what came later.[1] But the Seven Years' War was much more than just the prelude to the American Revolution. It was a massive event, the most significant war in the eighteenth century, much more so than the less global and more parochial American Revolution.[2]

That so many accounts of the American Revolution assume the opposite—the American Revolution as more important than the Seven Years' War—betrays an overly American-centric set of assumptions about these conflicts. It also downplays the imperial dimensions of the Seven Years' War, which was later dubbed a mighty war for empire and even a world war.[3] The Seven Years' War affected the standing of the British Empire throughout the world as well as being a war about Britain's place in Europe. It was fought on multiple fronts, from Europe to the American interior, to the Caribbean, to Africa, to the Philippines, and to South Asia. Britain's victory over France as confirmed in the Treaty of Paris of 1763 resulted in the British Empire becoming significantly more global, with its multifaceted character causing problems for a British elite inexperienced in how the world worked and slow to understand how events in one part of the world, such as the problems of the East India Company in India, could have an impact on other parts of the empire. The British governing elite had a narrow knowledge of events outside Britain, indeed outside southern England, and were out of their depth in managing a complicated global empire. American Patriots were similarly unprepared to adapt their worldview to the reality of Britain after 1763 having global imperial preoccupations that did not always include the Thirteen Colonies. As one historian argues, the global war that occurred between 1756 and 1763 "forced Britain's governing elite to confront what they came to conceive to be their American problem: the weak governance of Britain's dependencies seemed to render the colonies incapable of defending themselves or of making an adequate contribution to Britain's efforts to defend them." The American problem was accompanied by a "similar Irish problem, a West Indian problem, and a problem with the East India Company in India."[4] In this chapter, we explore how the Seven Years' War and its aftermath affected not just the Thirteen Colonies that later rebelled but the whole of the British Empire—an empire largely reshaped and to an extent created by the reverberations from this great conflict.

A Narrative of the Seven Years' War

The Seven Years' War started in North America, emerging from growing tensions between the British, French, and Indigenous peoples in the pays d'en haut region of the Great Lakes and the Ohio Valley.[5] These tensions had been simmering since the inconclusive end of the War of the Austrian Succession and the Treaty of Aix-la-Chappelle in 1748. The tensions escalated in the early 1750s, leading to what is considered the traditional start of the war from a skirmish in the Ohio Valley between a young Virginia militia officer, George Washington, and the French general Joseph Coulon de Villiers du Jumonville on May 28, 1754. The origins can be tracked back even further. The conflict arose because of the activities of a leader of the Miami people, called Memeiska. Memeiska participated in disputes and fighting with the British in 1752 in the small Anishinaabe village of Pickawillany. It was this fighting that formed the backdrop to the Battle of Jumonville Glen in 1754, where Washington's "assassination" of Jumonville caused a diplomatic uproar in Europe.[6]

Yet even though the war started in North America and the North American theater was at the forefront of imperial attention during the war, the main theater of the war was in Europe. It was there that the battles were biggest and most consequential. Britain's major objective was in maintaining and improving its place within European geopolitics, with imperial concerns envisioned as mostly important as far as they advanced Britain's ambitions in Europe. William Pitt famously declared that he would conquer America through victory in Germany. As Daniel Baugh notes, "the ultimate object of statesmen in London ... was to maintain and increase security, power and influence in Europe." Prestige came from Europe, not from empire, and what dominated politics in the eighteenth-century British Empire revolved mostly around how much it needed to actively intervene in European affairs to protect its national as well as its imperial interests.[7]

The financial costs of the war were immense for European participants. Austria was virtually bankrupted, while the cost of servicing war created debt in the 1760s in France that was around two-thirds of annual revenue, or twice the level of 1753.[8] It is hardly surprising that Britain, also burdened by debts incurred on fighting and winning a global war, when it looked across Europe and assessed the physical and financial devastation of the Seven Years' War, felt the increasingly rich American colonies could pay more for colonial defense. Britain considered how little in aggregate the Seven Years' War financially had cost them. That assumption that the colonies had not provided their financial share for the cost of the war was true for some colonies, such as New York, Maryland, and Virginia. It was not true, however, for New England, which had provided large numbers of men as soldiers and spent considerable sums on their military contribution to the war. These colonies enlisted eight and a half times as many men as Virginia, although Virginia's white population was about the same as the region's, while New England recruited four and a half times as many men for the war than the whole of the wealthy slaveholding South.[9]

All the European states involved in the Seven Years' War had to cope with its massive costs, which far exceeded the costs of the previous war, the War of the Austrian Succession. For Britain, which spent £161 million, as opposed to £96 million for the previous war in the 1740s, one of the major concerns was its cost. Beginning with the government of Robert Walpole, Britain had advantages over France in dealing with the war as it had a financial system that enabled the government to borrow money and to finance a national debt thanks to the Bank of England, a stock market, wealthy merchants, a robust parliamentary system, transparency in public accounts, and an ability to expand taxation so as to sustain British credit. Nevertheless, the cost of the war was a severe challenge. Public debt ballooned from £74.6 million in 1756 to £132.6 million in 1763, by which time it took up a sobering 186 percent of Britain's national income.[10]

The amount of public debt accumulated because of war stimulated European-wide debates over political economy and the role of the state in promoting agriculture, industry, and trade. It also occasioned debate over whether the prestige of empire was worth its cost. William Knox, for example, thought that the debt Britain had incurred put Britain at a disadvantage to its great European rival because, though defeated, France's "want of credit preserved her from a great increase in debt and the loss of her ultra-marine dominions lessened her present expenses."[11] Knox's argument was aided by France's actions in confronting the expense of imperialism in 1761 in the *Affaire du Canada,* where it accused colonial officials in New France of corruption, fraud, and war profiteering, providing a moral validation of policies it pursued of repudiating war debts. A subsequent and sustained commercial boom in France between 1763 and 1770 when the Saint-Domingue economy powered ahead suggested that the Seven Years' War was but a temporary setback in a century-long expansion of colonial trade. Indeed, one of the most important European trends in the 1760s, notably so in both Britain and France as Jamaica and Saint-Domingue became increasingly prosperous, was a massive injection of European capital into colonial economies and the Atlantic slave trade.[12]

Merchants did well after the Seven Years' War, but the British government was troubled by the immense financial burden that it was ill-equipped to carry. There was a gap between the British government's financial needs and the tools it had at its disposal to deal with those needs. It was a gap intensified by increasing public scrutiny as the social contracts in place between government and citizen were renegotiated repeatedly through global wars, creating the conditions if not for revolution then at least for change and contestation that led to revolution.[13]

The Seven Years' War was also hugely consequential in South Asia, where it was part of a much wider global crisis identified in 1974 by Marshall Hodgson as a breakdown in the great landed empires of the Ottomans, the Safavids, the Mughals, and the Makram. C. A. Bayly extended this idea of an Asian crisis into the concept of a global crisis and imperial reorientation lasting almost all of the eighteenth century.[14] Indeed, historians of South Asia see the Seven Years' War as just one of multiple wars between competing Indian powers and newly ascendant representatives of European seaborne empires, such as the British East India Company. The Seven Years' War was mostly important in India for expanding European power and laying the foundations of a bigger shift to European domination of India in the late eighteenth and early nineteenth centuries.[15]

In North America, the Seven Years' War had short-term causes—tension in the American interior—and mid-term causes, rooted in British imperialism. The former included a breakdown in Native American relationships, sustained by gift-giving, with French and British cultural brokers.[16] The latter were connected to geopolitical contestation over which European empire had seaborne dominance in the Atlantic Ocean, so that either France or Britain could take advantage of the flourishing Atlantic slave trade and plantation systems. Both Britain and France were convinced that the other nation was acting overly aggressively in defending valuable Atlantic commerce and were keen to displace the declining influence of the Dutch Republic and especially the Spanish Empire in Atlantic trade.[17]

The Seven Years' War started very badly for the British throughout the British Empire. Britain suffered a terrible defeat even before the war officially started, with the French and their Indian allies killing the British general, Edward Braddock, and routing his largely Irish troops at the Battle of Monongahela, and then it lost the island of Minorca in the Mediterranean in 1756.[18] Matters only improved after 1757, when William Pitt was given control over strategy and the British war effort by a reluctant George II who disliked Pitt for his sometimes-intemperate outbursts. The British enjoyed a remarkable run of military successes on land and at sea between 1758 and 1762. They captured Louisbourg and destroyed Fort Duquesne in Canada in 1758; conquered Quebec in 1759 and forced the surrender of Montreal in 1760; captured Guadeloupe in 1759 and Martinique in 1762; and forced the surrender of the seemingly impregnable fort of Havana in 1762.[19] In the 1763 Treaty of Paris, Britain forced France to withdraw from North America and confirmed gains of territory in the eastern Caribbean and West Africa. France was left permanently embittered about its losses. Its foreign policy for the next thirty years was based on avenging its losses by reducing Britain in Europe and the Atlantic.[20]

Understanding the Seven Years' War

The Seven Years' War was a crucial event in the eighteenth century as the first "global war." It looms large in British imperialism. It was the war during which some of the most potent symbols of British nationhood were invented, such as "Rule Britannia," and the turgid "God Save the King," which became increasingly sung to celebrate Britishness. It was also the period in which the memorial landscape of the imperial capital, London, was remade to celebrate imperial heroes, General James Wolfe and Robert Clive, Lord Clive of India, principally among them. Yet we often think of the Seven Years' War as the eighteenth-century equivalent of the twentieth-century World War I, with the American Revolution or the French Revolution as the equivalent of World War II. Nevertheless, unlike World War I, the Seven Years' War is often treated, certainly in accounts of the American Revolution, as merely a prelude to later and more important global events, even though the Seven Years' War—with theaters of action in several parts of Europe, South Asia and the Philippines, North America and the Caribbean, and even to an extent in Africa—was much more obviously a global event than what happened in the relatively concentrated geographical scope of the American Revolution.

Certainly, what is conspicuously missing from most studies of the origins of the American Revolution is an analysis of the conflict as an outcome of imperial competition between Britain and France that had not been resolved during previous wars. Britain and France were significant European imperial powers that wanted to fight proxy contests for global dominance in various parts of their empires.[21] The French in the 1740s were far from being merely passive observers of British imperial expansion, eventually provoked by small but irritating incidents in the interior parts of North America to attack Britain at its western frontier. Indeed, the French changed their foreign policy in the 1740s specifically to make the British concerned about their ability not just to keep their empire but to make safe the British archipelago.

The decision by France to fight Britain in the ways that it did in the early 1740s, in the War of the Austrian Succession, when its foreign policy was based upon the three things that the British most feared, had profound consequences in inter-imperial competition. These three things were a proposed invasion of the English Channel; a restoration of the Stuarts, as shown in French support of the 1745 Jacobite rebellion in Scotland; and the aim to conquer a North Sea port in the Low Countries, that region of western Europe historically vital to British interests. What this meant was that from the early 1740s onward, British imperial policy was made in the context of imperial competition with France in ways that had not been the case during the long Walpolean peace.[22]

In short, Britain did not "sleepwalk" into the Seven Years' War, in ways reminiscent of how the great European powers slid into war in 1914.[23] It responded to what it saw as aggressive actions by France against its vital interests, at home as well as abroad. Placing the causes of the Seven Years' War within the context of intense imperial competition between Britain and France in the 1740s makes it hard to see the war originating out of contingency only, let alone, as is so often related in histories of the conflict, as being best understood merely as a prelude to the greater conflict of the American Revolution and as an "accidental" conflagration in the American interior that soon spiraled out of control.

The end of the War of the Austrian Succession in 1748 was unsatisfactory for both France and Britain, as it left too many points of worldwide contention unsettled and unable to be resolved except through the application of force, especially in the two areas of contention in the Ohio Valley and southeast India. Moreover, an even greater point of contention that exacerbated tensions between the two countries was in Europe, especially in George II's homeland of Hanover. Britain found itself troubled by its relations with another European empire, the Holy Roman Empire, where the geopolitical system erected by an earlier generation was in a state of terminal despair.[24] Just because the Seven Years' War started in America and had long-term consequences in that region does not mean that it did not have deep European and wider imperial roots. We might see the start of the war as Britain's and France's mutual fear of each other, leading each to start a preemptive war with the other for defensive reasons, notably the need to defend imperial global interests.

There were also internal reasons within Britain propelling war, some of which came out of the imperial expansion of the first half of the eighteenth century. Historians have had a sea change in how they write about the 1750s: it is no longer seen as a period of political stability, calm, and confidence. The War of the Austrian Succession was expensive, with a great increase in the national debt, while the inconclusive peace had done little to solve imperial rivalries. The demobilization of 80,000 soldiers and sailors exacerbated social and economic dislocation, unemployment, and crime. Coinciding with a crime wave that occurred in England between 1749 and 1753, the years before the Seven Years' War were ones "of deep anxiety, if not panic, about the state of the country and its capacity to continue a war that everyone feared had been abandoned only temporarily."[25] Another historian sees the early 1750s as a time "marked by a deepening sense of national malaise, stimulated by xenophobia . . . , exacerbated by imperial rivalries and tinged by sharpening anti-aristocratic sensibilities."[26]

In short, this was a decade when Britain experienced one of its periodic moral panics, because growing prosperity in the "industrious revolution" had given poor people more money, some of which they spent in conspicuous consumption and in enjoying themselves too obviously and too publicly. It felt to elite Britons that the nation was unraveling. Hanoverian stability was a delicate project. Party politics had not disappeared even if Tories were weak at the national level and the Whig supremacy was becoming entrenched at the local level. Whigs had many doubts about Tory allegiances and remembered that the shock of Jacobite rebellion in 1745 was not that long ago.[27] The dreadful military results of the Seven Years' War before Pitt took over also caused Whigs considerable concern. The triumph of the Whig oligarchy was in part due not to the virtues of Whig gentlemen but to the realization that alternatives to their political dominance might be worse.[28] It is going too far to say that the Seven Years' War was a means whereby British internal problems were solved. But it helped. It is noticeable that the accession to power of George III in 1760–61 was accompanied by great celebrations of how wonderful Britain had become, allowing George III to do what his two kingly predecessors had not had the fortune to manage—to concentrate upon matters other than the survival of the Hanoverian Protestant Succession.[29]

One such matter was imperial reform. It took a particular form in Britain but was universal in the countries that had fought the Seven Years' War, as we have noted above. In short, "by the middle of the eighteenth century, rulers and ministers wrangled over how to adapt their ways and embark on increasingly ambitious plans to modify the institutions, private and public, that held their emporia together. Though each regime set about to modify their imperial pacts, it is important to stress that they did so in response to the ways in which empires coiled together into a single, internally competitive and increasingly disequilibrated regime."[30] Britain was especially committed to a reform process, which was not surprising given its comprehensive victories after 1759. Its aim overall was to rationalize power under parliamentary authority. At least that was Prime Minister

George Grenville's ambition. He advocated a policy of extraction and austerity that one historian criticizes as narrow and cramped, illustrating "no vision and no grasp of the wider problems of empire."[31] British imperial reformers believed that colonies needed to be subordinated to the metropole and acted to implement this ambition more than did other European nations. Britain was well placed to make far-reaching and invasive reform measures because it had advantages other nations did not. Its colonial holdings were less complex than Spain's and more established than France's. Moreover, its institutional apparatus and the mechanism of the fiscal-military state gave Britain greater capacity to act and follow through on its reforms.[32]

India

The Seven Years' War also brought a new element into British imperialism that was to shape relations between Britain and the Thirteen Colonies in unexpected ways. In world-historical terms, the main change in geopolitics was a transformation of politics and empire in India because of the remarkable rise of the East India Company, especially after it had been granted in 1765 by the Mughal emperor the *diwani*, or the right to collect the huge revenues of tax in Bengal in return for financing the province's administration. Bengal was wealthy, well-managed, and had a European-friendly network of Indian merchants.[33] Despite misgivings, the East India Company was now a territorial power in India. Its new status meant greater imperial involvement in India by a British government and ruling elite increasingly economically and politically tied into the complicated affairs of the East India Company.[34]

The incorporation of the East India Company into the British Empire also provided a new model of imperial governance that had an impact on how Britain viewed governance in North America. We often forget in our obsession with how imperial conflicts in North America in the 1760s led to war in the mid-1770s that British officials were more occupied with India than with America in this period. What concentrated British minds were two things: first, the immense riches that the East India Company took out of India to augment the British state as well as individual coffers, but which led not to unprecedented prosperity, as predicted after 1765, but to imminent financial ruin; and second, the extent to which the authoritarian rule of the company over Bengalis could be a model of governance for the empire.

The East India Company had been in existence since 1600, founded like the Virginia Company as a corporation of merchants and investors who had the exclusive right to trade with Asian goods to Britain. While it was large in British terms—the biggest business enterprise in seventeenth-century Britain—it was small in the context of the trade conducted overall in India.[35] The company was an unusual beast. From the start it relied on maritime force and on establishing diplomatic relations with powerful Indian states as much as on its connections to Europe. Its relationship with the British Crown was crucial, however, to its survival. That relationship was highly contentious, in part because the company claimed "increasingly broad jurisdiction over all English subjects in Asia as well as an expanding network of coastal and island populations, their cosmopolitan Eurasian populations and the maritime space that connected them."[36] It grew into a massive power in India but always with British imperial assistance. Between 1756 and 1760, for example, Britain spent £4.5 million creating an army of 2,000 European troops and 23,000 Indian sepoys. It was rewarded with victories in the Battles of Plassey (1757) and Wandiwash (1760).[37] Yet the East India Company was never subsumed within the British state. There was always a question of who exercised sovereignty in places like Bengal—the company or the British state.[38] Moreover, in ways resembling how British officials in Indigenous territory in North America operated, the company had to consider its relations with Indian merchants and rulers.[39] As has been observed about the company, by 1765, "if Bengal had indeed become a British dominion, it was still a dominion built on British foundations and offerings for Indian participation."[40]

One problem for Britain in its dealings with India was corruption, or what was described as "Asiatic despotism." That "Asiatic despotism" involved the idea—and the reality—that East India Company officials had adopted Indian ways of cheating the company and the state for personal advantage while living the high life as nabobs, as if they were Indian luminaries. American Patriots were especially attuned to such tales of corruption. They noted how Britons living in India had slipped into tyranny, and they condemned the British government for accepting such tyranny as part of imperial relations. Arthur Lee from Virginia fulminated that "for the future, the story of lord Clive will be that of every military plunderer . . . it begins in blood and plunder, it ends in servility and dependence." Britain and its short-lived empire would "fall as Greece and Rome have fallen," having been "nurtured in the corruption and despotism of the East."[41]

India, for Lee, was the antithesis of freedom, with its abundant evidence that despotism was rife. He thought it was entirely the wrong model of governance to impose upon liberty-loving British subjects in America. Nevertheless, imperial statesmen realized that they could not avoid involvement in Indian affairs and in the ramifications of East India Company politics in Britain, no matter how mired in corruption Bengal and Madras were. The financial rewards of Indian empire were too great. Moreover, if Britain departed, its absence would be filled by France, whose natural affinity, it was presumed, for tyranny and universal monarchy would be advanced because "the remedy was to establish a benevolent autocracy accountable to parliament which would be able to curb the excesses of Europeans and to protect the Company's provinces from Indian mercenaries."[42]

Britain very quickly got used to India. It helped that the East India Company was extraordinarily influential in British elite circles from the mid-eighteenth century onward and that the company was careful to manage its affairs with government in ways that soothed imperial fears. The British government was aware of the company's political power and knew it could cause problems domestically if not assuaged by various concessions. Increasingly, it was the East India Company, not the American colonies, which was the model that worked best for imperial rule. The company was more docile, for a start, than American colonists, and it accepted, unlike Americans, the authority of Parliament in all respects. The East India Company, however, quickly disappointed its supporters. Its rule in India was fraught. In the 1760s, the company faced lengthy war in Madras, pursued policies that resulted in a devastating famine in western Bengal in 1769–70, and had systems of governance and finance that were so chaotic that the company was only saved from bankruptcy in 1772 by the British government lending it millions of pounds.[43]

Canada

The other big consequence of the Seven Years' War was an expansion of British empire in Canada following the Conquest of Canada after the Battle of Quebec in 1759 and the subjugation of Montreal in 1760. Incorporating Canada into the empire posed many problems, as we will outline in our treatment of the 1774 Quebec Act, but it was done in an imperial environment that was different to that which pertained in the Thirteen Colonies. Canada was "another British America," marked by "an early and strong state presence that preceded British settlers, weak colonial governance relative to the metropolitan bureaucracy, colonial governments subservient to parliament [and] with powerful metropolitan-based commercial interests."[44] Even before the Seven Years' War, Britain's northernmost territories exhibited in their governance the kind of imperial political control and lack of local autonomy that Patriots feared Britain wanted to implement in the Thirteen Colonies in the 1760s. Britain had economic interests in Newfoundland from the sixteenth century and in the American interior following the establishment of the Hudson's Bay Company in 1670 with a monopoly over trade in minerals and especially furs. It traded extensively with Indigenous peoples in the vast drainage area of Hudson's Bay and Prince Rupert's Land. Formal colonization, however, did not occur until 1713, when Britain acquired Nova Scotia in the Maritimes as a colony from the Treaty of Utrecht. The Treaty of Utrecht also confirmed British rights to fish in Newfoundland and furs and minerals in the Hudson's Bay region.

Colonization sputtered in Canada until the Conquest of Canada in 1760, which added Quebec to the British Empire. Canada had a European population in 1763 of just under 100,000 people, of whom 8,000–9,000 lived in Nova Scotia and another 8,000 in Newfoundland, with the rest, mostly French Canadians, in Quebec. Its economic importance to empire was greater than its demographic presence, as the Newfoundland fisheries and furs obtained through the Hudson's Bay Company were valuable commodities. Slavery existed in Montreal but the number of enslaved was small, mainly Indigenous rather than African, and its economic impact was minimal.[45] External interests were more significant than elsewhere in North America because Quebec was dominated by a military governor and a hand-picked council of like-minded cronies operating outside an established judicial system, and the state had a powerful presence. London merchants used their political influence in the metropolis to establish rules about fish and fur in ways that often constrained political and economic development.[46]

The power of metropolitan authority in the region was seen most graphically in 1749 when Arthur Dobbs, a Westminster politician with an interest in imperial matters who was a principal critic of the Hudson's Bay Company, forced a public inquiry into the company's affairs. Dobbs thought that the Hudson's Bay Company was dilatory in finding the fabled Northwest Passage and was failing in not establishing British settlements in Indian territory that might drive a wedge into French colonization.[47] Dobbs failed in his attacks on the Hudson's Bay Company, as the 1749 inquiry vindicated the company's policies. What the inquiry did show, however, was the primacy of the state in shaping Canadian development. Representative institutions were weak and few in number, and imperial officials believed that colonial autonomy was a decided impediment to what they wanted to happen, which was to make policy unburdened by having to explain themselves to colonists. The state in Newfoundland, Nova Scotia, and Quebec was strong from inception, with no assemblies and strong gubernatorial authority. Colonial rule was made with one eye on not repeating what were believed to be the mistakes of colonization in seventeenth-century New England, where state intervention had largely been absent. After the American Revolution, in the Canadian colonies Britain took the view that it could extend the practices by which it ruled French Catholics to the governing of white Protestants.[48] The Board of Trade distanced itself from New England customs by formulating imperial policies that led to strong executives, weak assemblies, minimal local government, and the pacification of settler ambitions through the cultural toleration of diverse colonial groups under the benevolent gaze of powerful governments.

That authoritarian tendency continued after the Conquest. Quebec remained a French society under British military occupation without an assembly or rights available to new British settlers.[49] Nevertheless, many settlers flocked to Nova Scotia despite the lack of rights available to them. It provided abundant land, acquired by the state by seizure from Indigenous peoples. Nova Scotia experienced a land boom between 1764 and 1768 when immigrants, mostly from North Yorkshire and some from New England, took up 3.5 million acres, increasing the population to 17,000–18,000 people. How this land was distributed was revealing. Britain favored settlement through the granting of large estates in Nova Scotia (a system also employed in the Spanish-ceded colony of Florida) to influential Britons who then recruited immigrants privately to own or lease parts of these estates. One such man was Lord Egmont, who tried to establish a neo-feudal society in St. John, in the Maritimes, in the same way an earlier generation of aristocrats had established neo-feudal fantasies in places like early seventeenth-century Maryland.[50]

In short, the history of British imperialism in the Canadian colonies before the 1770s demonstrates a different model of colonization from that which took place in the rest of British America, one shaped by the contours of imperialism as developed in the early eighteenth century more than by settlement in English America in the seventeenth century.[51] Its territorial extent, in contrast to its demographic presence, was huge, extending from the Atlantic Ocean to the Rocky Mountains, most of which land was not part of colonial government and was controlled by a large population of Indigenous peoples. Its settler population was small, and most Europeans were either seasonal workers in the Newfoundland fisheries or cultural brokers to Indigenous peoples in the Canadian interior. Canada was thus both an empire of settlement and an empire of extraction through the exploitation of the area's rich natural resources. The British state believed it had an interest in the profits from these extractive industries. The 1749 inquiry into the Hudson's Bay Company had established that the company, and by extension other colonial enterprises in Canada, had to manage its affairs in ways that were consistent with the public interest and with a willingness to submit its management to parliamentary oversight. Metropolitan involvement in imperial affairs in Quebec and Nova Scotia might have been "incremental, reactive and unplanned," while "colonial governors had few long-term policies for managing a diversifying empire."[52] But the general direction was clear. If Nova Scotia was another model of British America, it was one that was congruent with the plans that the British government imagined would take hold everywhere in the empire in the 1760s. That was even more the case in Quebec. The emergence of liberal democracy was a long and convoluted process in Canada, only really happening in the tumults of the 1840s.[53] It showed that the Thirteen Colonies were increasingly out of step with an imperial policy in which territorial expansion was not especially associated with settlement by Europeans but with a concern over extracting wealth through engagement with Indigenous peoples and with control exercised through company rule.

British Imperial Policy after the Seven Years' War

One of the great mistakes that the British made after the Seven Years' War was to fail to recognize the extent to which the settler colonies in British North America were different from other areas of imperial presence, as settlers in these areas saw themselves as being attached to Britain by ties of consanguinity. Indeed, the North American colonies were closer to Britain than were Scotland and Ireland, where rebellion against the English was frequent—no such rebellions against imperial authority occurred in North America in the first half of the eighteenth century. There was no excuse for such ignorance on the part of the British; Benjamin Franklin had made this point with especial clarity as the revolutionary conflict started. As Franklin insisted, the links that connected Britain to British settlers in the Americas were those of fraternal affection and a shared sense that they were members of a common enterprise. He told Peter Collinson, "We are in your hands as Clay in the Hands of the Potter; and . . . as the Potter cannot waste or spoil his Clay without injuring himself; so I think there is scarce anything that you could do that may be more hurtful to us, but what will be as much or more so to you." British vitriol against their fellow countrymen left him bemused. He could only resort to sarcasm: "The gentle terms of republican race, mixed rabble of Scotch, Irish and foreign vagabonds, descendants of convicts, ungrateful rebels etc., are some of the sweet flowers of English rhetoric, with which our colonists have of late been regaled. Surely, if we are so much their superiors, we should shew the superiority of our breeding by our better manners!"

Franklin could not believe that Britain would do what it threatened, not only because by attacking American settlers it was engaging in obviously un-British, tyrannical behavior, but because he reckoned the British chances of success in imposing tyranny were small. Once he was convinced that America had "no favours to expect from the Ministry; nothing but submission will satisfy them," he knew that North Americans would fight. Otherwise, they would suffer "the most abject slavery and destruction." With both sides on the "high road to mutual enmity, hatred and detestation," "separation will of course be inevitable." Asked by friends in 1766 about what made Americans loyal before 1763, he told them: "They were governed by this country at the expence only of a little pen, ink, and paper. They were led by a thread. They had not only a respect, but an affection for Great Britain." Once the bonds that linked Englishmen in America with Englishmen in Britain were dissolved, then the British Empire, as he knew it, would be dissolved. "America," he told David Hartley, a British parliamentarian, "will not be destroyed: God will protect and prosper it. You will only exclude yourselves from any share in it."[54]

The East India Company and the Takeover of India

The attempt to introduce more direct metropolitan control and to extract more revenue from the colonies was especially apparent in India. We cover India within the empire in more detail elsewhere but can note that "in the 1760s and 1770s, while an empire in America was disintegrating, an empire was being consolidated in eastern India." That empire was "an entirely different kind of regime . . . claiming an absolute sovereignty for Britain." India was governed through the East India Company, a commercial corporation with its own army, navy, and officials. It had traditionally administered its own affairs and governed without significantly involving Parliament. In 1767, the same year the Townshend Duties and a bill to augment the size of the army in Ireland were passed, the home government began to intervene more directly in the affairs of the East India Company. In contrast to its intentions in Ireland and America, Britain was not trying to enlarge its claims of authority against a colonial elite, but against company directors, agents, and stockholders. This action proved to be much more controversial in Parliament than were affairs in America.[55]

Events in India resonated throughout the British Empire. What placing the American Revolution in imperial context helps to show is how events in India could influence events in America. The Boston Tea Party, for example, was a central event in the coming of the American Revolution. It serves as a case study of how an imperial perspective deepens familiar tales. Tea, of course, was one of the great imperial commodities—grown in China, bought by the East India Company, transported to Britain, and then re-exported throughout the empire, including to Boston. Generally, the event is described in American-centric terms, with the sending of tea to America an act of provocation, "a ministerial scheme to trick Americans into acceptance of taxed teas."[56] But in regard to Britain, "it would have been extremely unlikely that an event sparked by a debate over the nature of imperial taxation, about a commodity produced in China, purchased with specie from India, aiming to benefit an institution that had suddenly come to rule over the wealthiest region of the world, would focus so narrowly on North American issues."[57] And it didn't. What Britain was interested in was how lowering taxes on tea in America (and thereby increasing the likelihood those taxes would be paid) might help the stricken East India Company.

That distinction was lost on Americans. They were hugely hostile to the East India Company and to British imperialism in India. John Dickinson (1732–1808), an influential political pamphleteer, argued that a corrupt British ministry hoped to support a broken East India Company by the ruin of American freedom and liberty, lambasting the company as a vile institution that for years had "levied war, excited rebellions, dethroned lawful princes, and sacrificed millions for the sake of gain" and now "cast its eyes on America, as a new theatre whereon to exercise their talents of rapine, oppression and cruelty." He thundered that "We are not Sea Poys, nor Marathas, but British subjects, who are born to liberty, who know its worth, and who prize it high."[58] Americans believed that the intentions of British ministers were despotic. In India, the land of despotism, they could fulfill their wicked intentions; in the colonies, the land of freedom, they were resisted. Colonists saw the East India Company as infected by "Asiatic despotism." It was a glaring example of the cozy corruption in high places that justified Americans' growing republican beliefs. The company, in short, was the preferred tool of a predatory state.[59]

There was some truth to one of the conspiracy theories of the North Americans who were outraged at attempts to make equivalences between their situation and the situation of conquered Indians in Bengal. Imperial officials preferred dealing with the East India Company to recalcitrant and bumptious colonial Americans. It was in many ways one model of how empire should work, according to Britons wanting to organize the American empire on new grounds. The East India Company was a compliant partner of the British imperial government. It was willing to yield its autonomy over local rule in ways that no American colony was prepared to do. It was also prepared to submit to imperial reforms that were impossible to implement in America. British officials could not help comparing an India "where empire in the sense increasingly envisaged by British opinion was being increasingly successfully made" and a recalcitrant America, full of imperial subjects who refused to accept that they were subjects who would easily accede to the imperial and parliamentary will.[60]

The increased imperial attention given to India after 1760 led to a

Shah 'Alam, Mughal emperor (1759–1806), conveying the grant of the *diwani* to Lord Clive, August 1765. Painting by Benjamin West (1738–1820), c. 1818. (Paul Mellon Center for Studies in British Art)

development that proved unfortunate for British-American relations. British officials, to their cost, ignored Franklin's warnings about the need to distinguish between white "Britons" living overseas and non-white or non-Protestant subject peoples.[61] Franklin's warnings were ignored. Building on assumptions that began to be formulated in the 1740s, the British, in a spirit of "cosmopolitan authoritarianism," increasingly refused to differentiate between white fellow citizens and non-white subjects.[62] An expanding imperial garrison state became more and more a feature of the post–Seven Years' War empire. The British government became more insistent in the reach of its authority and advanced the view that the duty of subjects, Black or white, was to obey rather than treat with British officials on grounds of near equality. The sensibilities of white colonists about greater imperial oversight and what they perceived as softness toward non-white and non-Protestant people were increasingly set aside, to the disquiet of white settlers.[63]

Although the policies of the 1760s may have been disjointed, they had common origins.[64] Dreams of imperial reform had been apparent before, in plans put forward by colonial administrators, William Blathwayt in 1701 and Martin Bladen in 1721 and again in 1739. Administrators from the 1750s, however, were more inclined than their predecessors to regard themselves as inaugurating a more rational and efficient system of imperial government influenced by the principles of the Enlightenment. Their thinking was not devoid of the more positive and humane ideas that we associate with the Enlightenment. It included limited Catholic Emancipation and greater concern about the treatment of Indigenous peoples. The reforms of the 1760s were much less ambitious, for example, than the centralizing policies of James II with the Dominion of New England (1686–89).[65] But these plans, designed to deal with a greatly expanded empire in which the Thirteen Colonies were just a part, were very disturbing to white colonists brought up in previous understandings of empire in which they were considered full citizens of Britain.

Officials, moreover, contemplating a debt-ridden empire where they had many more responsibilities as imperial managers than in the 1740s and 1750s, knew that the cost of empire was likely to rise with the major territorial acquisitions of the Seven Years' War, including the Canadian colonies, the Northwest Territories, East and West Florida, the Windward Islands, Tobago, Senegal, and Bengal. Many of these possessions contained large foreign populations which needed to be absorbed and defended, making elites fearful about how they would be defended in case of war or internal revolt. William Pitt the Elder echoed Franklin in believing that the growing wealth of the colonies and India meant that the large debt that existed in 1763 was sustainable and an acceptable cost of imperial victory, but it was harder for more conventional statesmen, alarmed at how much debt the British state was carrying, to act so blithely in financial matters.

Imperial Consequences

If the causes of the Seven Years' War are more complicated and more consequential than usually depicted, so too are the consequences of the conflict multifaceted. It is remarkable how often the end of the Seven Years' War is not seen as Britain's greatest eighteenth-century triumph, initiating, as it did, a century-long period of global dominance, but is depicted instead as a "crisis," where the fruits of victory proved too much for a state unused to such dominion over vast territories and huge numbers of people. In short, the extent of British victory had made Britain so proud and insensitive to others that it saw itself as invincible and powerful enough to go it alone in the world, breeding great resentment among European powers already predisposed to wish Britain harm.

Political divisions also operated within the Thirteen Colonies, which were not as united in 1763 as they were to become by 1776. New Englanders, for example, had more reason than most North Americans to resent the British government for its perceived indifference to New England efforts in securing victory for Britain in both North America and the Caribbean after the transformations of British war strategies by William Pitt the Elder from 1757.[66] Virginians (and Jamaicans) paid little in money and even less in men for British victory. That was not true in New England. Massachusetts and Connecticut provided 65,060 men to the British war effort, or 50.8 percent of all provincial enlistments. They were reimbursed for these recruitments—Connecticut leading the way with 89 percent of its expenditures of £241,340 being returned to it. But they still made a major contribution to the costs of the military in North America. Mainland assemblies spent £2,568,248 on soldiers, with the Treasury returning only £1,068,769 in the form of reimbursements.[67] New Englanders, who not only put large forces into the field in North America but suffered considerable war casualties, felt they were major contributors to imperial success in the Seven Years' War. Massachusetts provided most of the soldiers from North America who achieved one of the greatest and most unlikely triumphs of British arms in the Seven Years' War, the conquest of Havana in 1762. That victory was a major achievement but came at the cost of a massive loss of lives, mostly from disease. Memories of the sacrifices that men from Massachusetts made in Cuba played a significant role in shaping attitudes toward Britain in that colony and added to the resentment people there felt toward what they perceived was a mother nation ungrateful to its loyal and suffering subjects.[68]

Provincial Americans were brutalized by the war. The British army was a harsh institution. Soldiers from New England were horrified by how the army treated its rank and file. Punishments for military infractions were severe, with men regularly inflicted with lashes so copious that they were a death sentence. It seemed to many colonists who came from places where slavery was limited and relatively benign, such as New England, that the British army was willing to treat white men as if they were enslaved.[69] They also disliked the vanity and superciliousness of British officers and the profanity and irreligiosity of British soldiers and sailors. Many of these British soldiers, of course, had no roots in the Americas. One effect of the Seven Years' War, notably in upstate New York, was a policy of land distribution to discharged British soldiers, making them the front line between Indigenous peoples and settlers but also committing them to the colonies. It was a policy especially followed in Nova Scotia. The fourteen new townships established during the Seven Years' War in that sparsely populated colony (after the expulsion of the Acadians) were full of soldiers from Massachusetts and Connecticut: 7,794 by 1764.[70]

Of course, the enormous acquisitions that Britain made during the Seven Years' War caused problems of adjustment for imperial statesmen after 1763. All the acts reshaping empire in 1764 and 1765 replayed the difficulties of 1756–57 rather than the achievements of 1758–62. If we employ a counterfactual to imagine a different settlement after 1763, we can think of what might have happened if Britain had extended the lessons of victory by continuing to do as William Pitt had done to win the war rather than to embrace projects stimulated by the fear of defeat. Instead of devising an unpopular Stamp Act to get more taxes out of the colonies, which would, in any event, not have been enough to do more than raise a small proportion of the costs of maintaining a British army in America, it should have retained Pitt's subsidy policy which may have stimulated at less cost a larger voluntary response from the colonies. Certainly, colonies which knew that they required a strong state presence and considerable imperial protection, such as Jamaica in the aftermath of Tacky's Revolt in 1760–61, were prepared to pay more in taxes in the 1760s than they had done in the 1750s.[71]

In short, Parliament and George III's ministers kept trying to address the problems of 1756–57 between 1764 and 1766 by ignoring how Pitt had solved such problems through his wartime system of spending lots of money on troops and subsidies. Pitt's extravagances horrified more sober politicians, who fretted about the debt that Britain was forming. It was not unreasonable to worry about the national debt, as the interest alone on the national debt was often close to 50 percent of total taxation income and Britain was already the most taxed nation in Europe other than Austria.

Moreover, resistance to increased taxation was growing in Britain. Yet despite gloomy talk from Pitt's opponents that the national debt was unmanageable, the financial reforms of the previous half century meant that Britain could fight an expensive war without ruining itself. It is easy, however, to criticize men of limited ability and limited perspective for getting things wrong in unprecedented circumstances. There was a consensus in the British ruling class about what policies should be employed in respect of increasing imperial integration. Everyone, for example, supported the principle of absolute parliamentary supremacy over the assemblies of the colonies, and no one accepted the American view that their assemblies were the equivalent in authority to the British Parliament. General John Burgoyne (1722–92), for example, argued that regardless of which party in England fathered the rebellion, "all parties nursed it into manhood."[72]

If we take a less American-centric view of the American Revolution than is normal, then we can see the age of the Atlantic revolutions in the British Empire as starting outside the Thirteen Colonies, in the years of imperial triumph between 1759 and 1762, rather than at the customary date of 1763. In these years, Britain acquired a global empire that betokened lasting geopolitical and economic dominance for the small European set of islands. The major events of this period happened outside the Thirteen Colonies, and the great imperial heroes, like General James Wolfe and Robert Clive, Lord Clive of India, made their reputation in this new empire. Britain acquired Quebec, meaning that it now had massive holdings north and west of its existing American possessions. It also achieved a dominance it had never had before in Bengal with the acquisition of the *diwani,* or rights to tribute in that rich province. Indeed, James Vaughn argues that the second British Empire began on August 12, 1765, when the extractive riches of India fell into Britain's grip.[73] And perhaps the most remarkable triumph of the Seven Years' War came in the Caribbean in 1762 when imperial and American troops besieged and took the seemingly impregnable citadel of Havana in Cuba, creating unprecedented tremors throughout the Spanish Empire, as the Spanish realized that their American possessions were suddenly vulnerable.[74] It was in the "other colonies" that the empire to come in the nineteenth century evolved—one divided between settler societies, like Australia and Canada and to an extent Ireland and South Africa, and extractive societies, such as the new colonies of the British West Indies in the southern Caribbean taken in the first years of the nineteenth century, as well as colonies in Asia and Africa.

Rebalancing Britain and France

The most important benefit to Britain of the Seven Years' War was the permanent weakening of the French imperial state so that it thereafter never matched the British Empire in strength and spatial breadth. France tried its best to restore its imperial position, as can be seen in its actions in support of American Patriots in the 1780s and in its aggressive expansionism during the French Revolution and the subsequent Napoleonic Wars, but it never recovered in the later eighteenth century what it had lost in the single year of 1759. The second major benefit of British victory was to show that the governmental transformations of the early eighteenth century, creating what we generally characterize as the fiscal-military state, had worked brilliantly in enabling Britain to defeat a more populous, wealthy, and powerful European rival. British victory came primarily from its ability to fight war efficiently and effectively across four continents, meaning that British victories over France came not from "military prowess, technological innovation or diplomatic skill" but from "overwhelming financial superiority." War was "a question of money, not men, since money could always be used to hire men and Europe was full of mercenaries willing to serve a reliable paymaster."[75] Britain's financial reforms made the state very agile. It was able to enormously expand the size of the British army from 1757, using well-paid foreign auxiliaries and giving subsidies to American colonies in return for provincial troops, so that "vast sums, in short, were found to pay for a global war effort, and this must surely be counted as a major achievement." Britain spent large but was able to borrow easily enough from the City of London to pay its way. In 1763, it borrowed £12 million at 4.8 percent interest, having borrowed in 1756 £2 million at 3.4 percent interest.[76]

The effects of British victory were positive in Britain. British victories made British people highly patriotic. The good feelings established after the end of the Seven Years' War reflected the benefits that victory brought to Britain, a nation secure under the political control of a confident landed elite that faced no serious challenges to its oligarchical rule, which was defended by the greatest navy in Europe, making invasion from the English Channel in support of rebellious movements such as Jacobitism implausible. Britain's most troublesome region—Scotland—had been brought firmly under control and was becoming a vital partner to England in imperial activity. Moreover, economic transformations resulting from industrialization had begun to make Britain wealthier than it had ever been before and accentuated its geopolitical and financial advantages over other European nations. One sign of British confidence was a renewed interest in speculation in imperial schemes to an extent that had not been known since the unsustainable South Sea Bubble of 1720. The areas where speculation was most obvious were in Grenada and the Windward Islands, India, Florida, and Maine. They were not in the Thirteen Colonies. These new areas saw speculative booms in the early to mid-1760s, and while no boom was sustainable, leading to mighty crashes in 1772–73, the amount of money invested in the new parts of the empire was substantial enough to make many people rich and British society wealthier overall.[77]

In short, the Seven Years' War was a "culmination" of Britain's transformation into an imperial nation. It was the triumphal conclusion to processes that had been occurring since the Glorious Revolution of 1689. The old paradigm of the running of the empire between 1713 and 1763 as based upon "salutary neglect," in which Britain turned a blind eye to what colonists were doing, does not hold when "we think the empire whole."[78] Between 1690 and 1763 Britain developed a workable imperial "system" in which component parts of its empire were treated differently according to imperial conceptions of their value to Britain rather than with the same rules applying to each part, irrespective of local circumstances.[79] Whereas in many British North American colonies the imperial state had a limited presence, there was another British America in Canada, Florida, and most of all in parts of the West Indies, where "the state had considerable presence, acquiring new territory through conquest and state-funded exploration."[80] From the First Maroon War in 1739 through to the end of the Second Maroon War in 1796, for example, white Jamaicans accepted a vigorous imperial state and high taxes as the price they needed to pay to keep themselves safe in a colony surrounded by the colonies of other European empires and with an enslaved population that posed an existential threat to settlers.[81]

The Seven Years' War looks different if it is seen in imperial terms as an event that was more important than the American Revolution. It involved much of the world rather than primarily Atlantic America. It was a war which had the full-hearted support of all the existing white Protestant subjects of empire rather than dividing that group internally. It also looks different if it is seen as a culmination of and justification for the previous half century's imperial policies rather than the initiation of a crisis that led to imperial disaster. It is difficult to see the statesmen of the 1740s and 1750s who shaped Britain's imperial policy as being notably hopeless. There is no reason we need to accept the judgments of statesmen in the 1760s and the historians who study them, successfully impressed upon the historical literature as those judgments may be, that men like the Duke of Newcastle and his monarch, George II, who were important in the 1750s, were poor politicians. These were the men who won, with William Pitt, the great war for empire that transformed imperial politics in the 1760s. The Seven Years' War raised issues that proved exceedingly difficult to solve, but it elevated Britain to a position of global power that it had hitherto never even imagined. And no one in 1763 believed that part of this imperial edifice would soon come crumbling down.

TWO

British Imperial Policy

IN 1760, THE LONG-SERVING BRITISH monarch George II died. He was aged seventy-seven and had been on the throne since 1727. He was replaced by his young grandson, George III, aged twenty-two. It was more than just a dynastic shift; it suggested a very different British orientation to the world. George II was extremely concerned about the fate of the land of his birth, Hanover in Germany, over which he ruled as an activist monarch. George II was as much a European monarch as one presiding over the British Empire. George III, by contrast, was born in Britain and stayed in that country (indeed, in just the southeastern metropolitan corner of England) his whole life, "glorying," as he said, in "the name of Britain." He was very much an imperial monarch, coming into his reign in an auspicious period, a year after the "annus mirabilis" of 1759, when British forces won stunning victories in India, America, and the Atlantic, and a few months after the greatest slave rebellion to date in British imperial history had rocked Britain's wealthiest West Indian colony, Jamaica. He was the head of a worldwide empire that was much larger and more important than that which had been inherited by his grandfather.

We can see Britain as an imperial nation in the magnificent coronation of George III on September 22, 1761. The coronation of a new monarch involves a symbolic expression of a nation's hopes and fears. George's coronation, involving one climactic moment after another, from having Handel's "Zadok the Priest" as the musical centerpiece (as it has been at every coronation since 1727) to the crowning of the king to the singing at the conclusion of a bathetic "God Save the King" and the "Te Deum," was full of symbolism. What distinguished this coronation from its predecessors was its imperialist iconography. War motifs were prominent, as befitted a nation embroiled in a major conflict with France. But imperialism was referenced more than war, since "at the height of the first truly global war, there were rich opportunities to convey a confident, patriotic message of British imperial triumph under a reinvigorated British monarchy."[1]

One positive result of George III's accession is that the hitherto divisive conflict between British and Hanoverian interests disappeared. George III had little interest in Hanover, where he had never been. He also came to the throne at a very propitious time. He was the first monarch in centuries to ascend the throne with his legitimacy to rule uncontested. And he became king when Britain's relations with the wider world and their imperial success in arms meant that "Great Britain displayed her power and influence beyond what she had ever done, in the most shining periods of history."

George's horizons, however, were narrower than the empire over which he presided. He saw himself as a patriotic Briton, which in the politics of the 1760s meant following a Tory blue-water colonial naval strategy. It also meant abandoning European entanglements, especially in Germany where George III distrusted Frederick, the ruler of Prussia. He also disliked William Pitt, the architect of victory in the Seven Years' War, and replaced him with his former tutor, the Scottish aristocrat the Earl of Bute, who was often satirized in caricatures as a "boot" and was popularly associated with the tyrannical House of Stuart. George III and his ministers withdrew from Europe, abandoning allies such as Prussia (Frederick never forgot this). Meanwhile, France was determined to avenge its humiliation in the Seven Years' War. That desire for revenge governed its foreign policy toward Britain for the next sixty years, so that "once again, Britain was baling out of a European war at the expense of her allies. Britain was, in strategic terms—at least in terms of strategic self-perception—an island again."[2]

Hubris had overcome common sense when Britain needed its European allies most, as it now had a massive global empire to defend and pay for. Trouble was apparent very soon: controlling this vast empire would be difficult. Ireland was roiled by a rebellion of Catholic agrarian poor, the Whiteboys, between 1761 and 1765; Pontiac's War of 1763-65 was a violent rebellion of Indigenous peoples against British policy in the western American interior; Jamaica was aflame with an intense constitutional dispute between the assembly and the governor; and India was both a wonderful opportunity for financial gain and a cornucopia of geopolitical issues which an avaricious, profit-oriented East India Company kept on inflaming. And at home the libertine rake and radical Whig antagonist of the king, John Wilkes, was creating havoc in the politics of London.[3]

A distinctive feature of great power politics in Europe during the 1750s was that overseas territories became the main sites around which the balance of power played out, making places like Acadia or the Ohio Valley important when they had previously occupied virtually no attention among European statesmen.[4] In France, Spain, and Britain, political anxiety about trade and interest in the overseas territories during the Seven Years' War began to converge, helping to create an imperial perspective in which the relationship between such territories and the metropolis needed to be rethought. The relations of the three empires to their overseas territories, roughly unchanged during the 1730s and 1740s, took a deliberately divergent path after 1763. Specifically, "the European kingdoms reorganized the links with their overseas territories in three key areas: the organization of their defense; the consolidation of royal authority; and the laws governing trade. It is not clear if these reforms were linked to a coherent 'imperial' program or were a simple addition of measures concerning different parts of the government. But they were everywhere preceded and accompanied by intense reflections both outside and inside the state bureaucracies."[5] A crucial question for each empire was how to sustain the loyalty of settler populations as imperial reform was contemplated. The American Revolution showed just how badly this went wrong in the British case. But it was not just the British Empire that became "colonial" in the 1760s. Each European empire wanted to make the most of expansive and growing colonial trade; each needed to solve massive security problems; and each had to maintain the support of settler populations. The reform efforts did not all coincide together temporally, with Spanish Bourbon reforms taking much longer than the French and British reforms, but they were all structurally similar.[6]

Americans tended to think that George III's constitutional authority resembled that of their governors, who could exercise their prerogative more easily than the British monarch. But, in fact, George III in 1760 was a modernizer and was like other European monarchs who were planning imperial reform. He was not the avatar of reactionary royalism that he became in the latter part of his reign. He was remarkably fluent in the scholarship on the Law of Nations, and was better acquainted with the works of Hugo Grotius, Thomas Hobbes, and Samuel Pufendorf than almost any of his subjects.⁷ His reading helped him formulate policies for ruling an empire of heterogeneous peoples. He was especially well read in the writings of Montesquieu, including Montesquieu's pioneering antislavery position. Indeed, George III was an early abolitionist, even though those sentiments faded dramatically over time as he realized the contribution that West Indians made to imperial coffers through custom taxes on plantation produce. His abolitionist views were precocious—no abolitionist in England would draw as heavily on Montesquieu until Granville Sharp in 1769.⁸ Alas, George III's youthful modernizing tendencies declined over time. His vision did not keep up with the evolution of the Law of Nations while he was preoccupied with his kingly duties. His vision of the Law of Nations thus remained a product of the Montesquieuean moment of the 1750s and did not develop over time.

The American Revolution proved crucial in George III losing his status as a "very model of a modern monarch for other kings, emperors and even presidents across the globe." George III appreciated the portent of the American Revolution for the end of the *ancien régime* in Europe, and he "used every means to defend the empire against revolutionaries whose victory he believed would annihilate the national greatness of Britain."⁹ He had many virtues, but these were of a private man rather than those of a public figure. He was a devoted family man, extremely conventional in his views and prejudices, and while personally quite cosmopolitan in his tastes had no experience of other countries or any feeling for the many peoples and areas he now ruled. His mental boundaries were drawn by his narrow sense of the world. In short, his failure to understand Americans and Atlantic empires was one of imagination.¹⁰

George III was no tyrant, as much as Thomas Jefferson tried to paint him as one in his inflammatory Declaration of Independence in 1776. Indeed, before 1774 North Americans wanted him to be more tyrannical, believing in time-honored fashion that he was being misled by his ministers. They also misunderstood his position in Britain, one that was shaped by the constitutional settlement of the Glorious Revolution and by the circumstances in which the Hanoverians ascended the throne. The Glorious Revolution had secured the authority of Parliament over the Crown in deciding how money was raised and spent. George III was careful never to challenge this essential reality of British politics. Americans thought that George III had a great deal of prerogative rights that he could exercise without contradiction. That was not the case. Of course, George III was not powerless. He appointed the prime minister, the most significant of the political powers remaining to the monarchy. Nevertheless, his choices were confined to supporting men in office who were able to command majority support in Parliament. In the case of America, he did not instigate the colonial policies that triggered the American Revolution, although he did support the fateful decision to send an army of 10,000 troops to America in the aftermath of the Seven Years' War. This was when he was a political neophyte under the influence of his former tutor and prime minister the Earl of Bute. Otherwise, he followed the advice of his ministers, on whom initially he was a restraining influence, at least until the Boston Tea Party in 1773. For the first decade of his reign, he was more concerned about domestic stability than imperial and overseas considerations.[11]

The Parallel Initiatives of Imperial Policies

In the 1760s and early 1770s, British policy toward America was part of a series of parallel initiatives throughout the British Empire. Indeed, the causes and intentions of these policies are more comprehensible when understood in a broader imperial context. The Thirteen Colonies were part of a mid-eighteenth-century imperial system and not necessarily the most important part. The importance of various parts can be seen graphically in the rank and prestige of the government officials appointed to various overseas imperial possessions. Rank was something the Georgians cared deeply about, with dukes ranking ahead of earls, earls ahead of barons and baronets, and peers and titled people well above those without titles. The importance of Ireland was clear. The people sent to govern that island were senior aristocrats who were important players in English political life. In the 1750s, three dukes—Dorset, Devonshire, and Bedford— were lords lieutenant of Ireland, followed by the Earl of Halifax, the principal architect of colonial policy under the Duke of Newcastle, and William Pitt. Every lord lieutenant in the period of the American Revolution was a peer, usually a duke or an earl, and if they were not an earl, they were, like George, Viscount Townshend, lord lieutenant between 1767 and 1772, connected to the most significant politicians in England and Wales.[12]

By contrast, governors in the Americas came from less elevated social positions. The few who were peers tended to be peers whose status was compromised, such as James Murray, Lord Dunmore, the governor of New York and then Virginia, who was the descendant of a family indicted for being Jacobites in the 1745 Scottish Rebellion. The low regard in which Dunmore was held can be seen in George III's refusal to accept Dunmore's daughter, Lady Augusta Murray, marrying his sixth son, the Duke of Sussex. West Indian governors were of greater status than those in the Thirteen Colonies, as reflected in the high salaries they were paid. They were sometimes baronets, like Sir Henry Moore of Jamaica (later New York) and Sir William Trelawney, a much-loved governor of Jamaica in the early 1770s.

In mainland North America, governors were often not of high status at all. They were either landed gentlemen in search of a job who were foisted upon colonial citizens or prominent colonists like Thomas Hutchinson of Massachusetts, William Franklin of New Jersey, or Cadwallader Colden of New York. These governors seldom commanded popular support. They found it difficult to walk a steady line between upholding royal authority and evincing a commitment to colonists' interests and mores. They were inadequate defenders of metropolitan goals whenever those goals differed from local opinion. The standing of governors was not helped by the customary practice of men appointed as governors sending deputies to act in their place. Virginia, for example, was the most lucrative and prestigious governorship in North America, but it was not until Lord Botetourt came to Virginia in 1770 that the colony was led by the man appointed as governor rather than someone to whom the governor subcontracted his duties.

It was policies rather than people, however, which were the main problem creating strife between Britain and the North American colonies in the 1760s. The imperial policies that precipitated the revolutionary crisis were shaped by seven different governments between 1760 and the outbreak of the American Revolution. Rapid cabinet turnovers prevented colonial agents and merchants from developing relationships with the different government ministries.[13] Governance was disjointed and unsystematic, with new colonial policies often gratuitous and unnecessary, addressing issues that were no longer relevant and creating "real problems by compelling colonial legislatures to do what so far they had all done voluntarily."[14] Britain failed to repeat the previously successful subsidy and voluntary assessment method of raising revenues that had served well in the Seven Years' War.[15] After 1763, the problem of an uninformed and uncoordinated imperial policy was exacerbated by the waning influence of the Board of Trade. It ceased to correspond directly with the colonial governors, together with losing the right to make representations to the Crown and the ability to appoint colonial officials. After the influential presidency of Lord Halifax (1748–61), there were nine successive presidents of the Board of Trade in less than ten years, while a myriad of different departments had responsibility for colonial affairs, including the Treasury, the Customs Board, the Commissioners of Customs, and the impotent Plantations Committee of the Privy Council.[16]

The policies of British government toward its empire in the 1760s and early 1770s were frequently introduced at the behest of different government departments and interest groups. Examples include the 1764 Sugar Act (or Revenue Act), which was enacted partly in response to the demands of the merchants and planters of the West India lobby and by the Commissioners of Customs.[17] The attempts to prevent the printing of paper money in the colonies were similarly intended to answer to complaints about inflated colonial currencies from merchants in Britain. The 1764 Quartering Act, designed to permit the billeting of troops in public buildings, was motivated by requests from the War Department and army commanders whose troops had suffered from the lack of proper barracks in America during the Seven Years' War. These imperial policies were "a series of pragmatic responses to administrative problems."[18]

There was, indeed, a lack of coordination in implementing colonial policies. Following the passage of the Tea Act in 1773, Frederick North, Lord North (1732–92), and the Treasury failed to inform the secretary of state for America, William Legge, Earl of Dartmouth (1731–1801), the Board of Trade, and colonial governors regarding the sailing of the East India ships for America. In the same year the Coercive Acts were passed, in 1774, to punish Boston for its insubordination in throwing tea from imperially approved ships into Boston Harbor, the Quebec Act, though developed over the course of seven years and unrelated to the Coercive Acts, was also passed, without forethought as to the possible ramifications in America. There were only a small number of politicians actively thinking about imperial problems and solutions on the grand scale, such as the Earl of Shelburne, Lord Halifax, and William Knox. Otherwise, government ministers increasingly failed to consult with the most knowledgeable colonial department: the Board of Trade.[19] They "were not seeking to establish an imperial 'system' as such ... they often had neither the time nor the inclination to attempt to make connections with the broader scheme of things." They were content to make piecemeal changes.[20]

Nevertheless, common themes to these policies existed, especially when seen in the context of parallel metropolitan intervention throughout the British Empire. In the aftermath of the Seven Years' War, Britain made a concerted attempt to reform the empire, increase revenues, regulate trade, improve defenses, and strengthen metropolitan control. Its ambitions were reflected in the rising number of imperial officials.[21] The royal governors and imperial officials were political appointees whose views reflected the mindset of Britain and its distrust of colonial rights.[22] Power was highly devolved within the British Empire, with "the empire resembl[ing] a rabbit warren of differing arrangements passed under different monarchs all for different reasons to address different problems."[23] British authority was increasingly token, with real power held by the colonial assemblies—not the governors. The Thirteen Colonies already enjoyed considerable autonomy.[24] In the 1760s, Britain attempted belatedly to strengthen central government throughout the British Empire.

Ireland

The new imperial policies in America and the West Indies in the 1760s were like those implemented in early eighteenth-century Ireland. In some ways, however, Ireland fits uneasily into the imperial paradigms of the first half of the eighteenth century. Ireland was more an *ancien régime* society, as in provincial France, than like an American colony.[25] The Irish Parliament was subject to more direct control from London than the assemblies of North America, Bermuda, Nova Scotia, the Bahamas, and the West Indies.[26] In accordance with Poynings' Law (1494), it was only permitted to meet after the proposed legislation for a forthcoming session had been approved by the British-appointed Irish Privy Council and then by the king and Privy Council. Similarly, the Declaratory Act of 1720 asserted the supremacy of Britain's Parliament over Ireland and made the British House of Lords its final appellate court. As a conquered country, Ireland lacked the right to make changes to its laws and constitutions, which conflicted with the view of the native elite who thought of themselves as settlers with all the rights of Englishmen. Consequently, colonial elites considered Ireland to be a dreadful example of imperial misrule.[27]

Such fears were not unfounded. Ireland was often a model of governance used by imperial officials in other colonies. In the late 1670s, for example, the Lords of Trade had tried to subject Jamaica and Virginia to Poynings' Law. In the 1720s, Jamaica was so nervous about its constitutional status and the possibility that it might be classified as a conquered colony (it had been seized from the Spanish in 1655 and then made into a royal colony in 1660) that the assembly agreed to pay a perpetual revenue of £8,000 per annum toward the cost of imperial government. As late as 1765, imperial administrators like Governor Francis Bernard of Massachusetts urged Britain to adopt the system of administration in Ireland for America.[28]

Nevertheless, despite these formal constitutional restraints, Britain was very cautious about exercising formal authority over internal Irish matters and in practice often sought the agreement of the Irish Parliament before initiating any policy. It did not attempt a direct tax upon Ireland.[29] In common with the governors of Virginia, the lord lieutenant did not even reside in Ireland until George, Viscount Townshend, removed there in 1771. In the mid-eighteenth century, Irish government was conducted by a cabal of local politicians, known as the undertakers, who were rewarded with sinecures and patronage in return for managing the Irish Parliament for Britain. After 1767, in common with North America, Ireland was drawn increasingly into the affairs of empire under the lord lieutenancy of Viscount Townshend. As chancellor of the Exchequer in Britain, his brother, Charles, simultaneously championed a vision of empire as less an assemblage of regions and societies than a coherent and consolidated "system" and introduced the Townshend Duties to develop this vision of empire.[30]

In common with North America, the British government in the 1760s became more active in the affairs of Ireland. From 1767, at the behest of Britain, George Townshend attempted to increase the number of British troops funded by the Irish Parliament. An act of Parliament from 1699 required that 12,000 British troops be funded and supported in Ireland, which the government now proposed to increase to 15,235. Previously, 2,000 of the 12,000 troops were stationed abroad at Irish expense, but this was to be increased to 3,000, while the domestic force would increase from

10,000 to 12,000.[31] About a third of the domestic peacetime British army was stationed in Ireland, which had the largest system of barracks, distributed throughout twenty-five locations, of anywhere in Europe except France. Resident army officers were as numerous as lawyers and beneficed clergymen.[32] In 1765, Britain had introduced a rotation scheme for army regiments throughout the empire to end a tradition in which they had served in one post, such as the 38th Regiment of Foot, which had spent fifty-seven years in Antigua between 1707 and 1764. The policy was symbolic of Britain becoming more active in the affairs of its colonies. The plan of exchange, however, was hampered by the much smaller size of peacetime regiments in Ireland compared with Britain. This was the pretext for the increase in the number of troops. As in America, Britain justified the expense, arguing that Ireland had lower taxes than Britain.[33]

George Townshend's initial failure to secure a vote for the augmentation of troops led to a more direct system of imperial government in Ireland.[34] He attempted the conventional approach of going through the undertakers, but they demanded various guarantees including that the troops not be used for service outside the country. Furthermore, they rejected a money bill on the grounds that it had not arisen from the House of Commons, causing Townshend to prorogue the Irish Parliament for the first time since 1692.[35] Dispensing with the services of the undertakers and redistributing patronage, Townshend succeeded in obtaining a more amenable Irish Parliament in 1771. The difficulties that he had confronted, however, forced him to become the first resident lord lieutenant of Ireland. His successors were to continue the tradition of residence, taking control of the patronage system and governing more actively from Dublin Castle. Lord North, significantly, saw the rejection of the money bill and the prorogation as part of a broader imperial problem in which "the vast bodies of British territories must have a head," a superintending power in the British Parliament.[36]

India

The attempt to introduce more direct metropolitan control and to extract more revenue from the colonies was also apparent in India, where a new kind of empire was emerging. India had been governed through the East India Company. It was a commercial corporation with its own army, navy, and officials. It had traditionally administered its own affairs and governed without significantly involving Parliament. In 1767, the same year as the Townshend Duties and the bill to augment the size of the army in Ireland, Britain began to intervene more directly in the affairs of the East India Company. In contrast to what it was trying to do in Ireland and America, Britain was seeking to enlarge its claims of authority not against colonial elites but against the East India Company directors, agents, and stockholders. These efforts proved much more controversial in Parliament than did affairs in America.[37]

The East India Company was privately owned and had chartered rights like some of the colonies in America. Its investors were determined to defend its privileges, and it had a more powerful lobby in the House of Commons than did colonists from America. Furthermore, questions related to government oversight of the company played into domestic politics, since many of the company's shareholders, proprietors, and directors were also members of Parliament. Indeed, the pro-government and opposition factions within Parliament were replicated in the company itself. If it tried to assert greater control, the government risked arousing fears traditionally held by opponents of the Whig Oligarchy rulers (termed Country Whigs) about the growth of royal power. These Country Whigs were concerned that the government might exploit the company's wealth as patronage for the Crown and its ministers to bribe and totally corrupt Parliament. It was precisely such fears that later helped bring down the Fox-North administration in response to the East India Act (1783). In contrast to its dealings with America, the government always acted in consultation with the East India Company. The ministry, sometimes through the Treasury Board, gave advanced notice to the directors of its intention to bring the affairs of the company before Parliament. It invited recommendations and it negotiated with the company before submitting bills to the House of Commons. In common with Ireland, however, it had to resort to manipulating support through patronage and its policies were vigorously contested, especially within the company Court of Proprietors.[38]

During 1767, Parliament conducted an inquiry and subsequently passed three acts affecting the management of the East India Company. In so doing, it acted "in a manner which had no parallel since the end of the preceding century and which made it certain that still more sweeping measures were to come." In 1766, after the repeal of the failed stamp duty in

America was passed and Parliament voted to reduce the land tax in England, the Chatham ministry showed its determination to extract revenue from the newly acquired territories in Bengal "to the exclusion of all other aspects of the Indian problem." The ministers debated whether to claim all the revenues from the new territories as rightly belonging to the Crown or simply to draw a share of the income. They were also divided as to whether to proceed by negotiation or by diktat.[39]

The ministry opened its campaign with an inquiry led by the absentee Jamaican planter William Beckford. He was opposed to the monopolistic trading rights of the East India Company and advised voters in 1767 to "Look to the rising sun. . . . Your treasury coffers are to be filled from the east, not the west." In response to the company's attempt to raise its dividend and without even awaiting the outcome of the inquiry, the government passed an act to cap dividends paid to stockholders at 10 percent and imposed an annual payment of £400,000 to the Treasury. George III regarded such a measure as "the only safe method of extracting this country out of its lamentable situation owing to the load of debt it labours under." The measure was limited to two years, which made further government intervention inevitable. In 1769, the Grafton administration negotiated a five-year renewal of the annual revenue of £400,000 from the East India Company. It agreed to suspend the payments if the dividends fell below 6 percent. It permitted a half-percent increase in the existing dividends and limited future increases to no more than 1 percent per year. The company was required to lend surplus cash at 2 percent to the nation, which meant that it had to submit its accounts to the Treasury. To ensure that trading was not overlooked in favor of revenue collection, the government required that the company continue current levels of exports from Britain to India. By the end of 1769, "it would not have required much perspicacity to foresee the end of the Company's independent political existence."[40]

Early in his administration, Lord North indicated to Lord Clive of India that "the very critical and dangerous situation of our possessions in India will probably make it necessary to bring them under consideration of Parliament." Apart from some minor reforms of administration in Bengal, Britain had neither attempted to reform the governing structure of the East India Company in Britain nor to regulate the affairs of the company in India. Britain necessarily became involved because of the critical state of the finances and administration of the East India Company, which was made worse by an international credit crisis in 1772. The company proved incapable of self-regulation and was in severe debt owing to the increased cost of defending and administering its expanded territories. Lord North believed the company to be of "too great a consequence, considered in a commercial light, not to call our attention to its welfare."[41] It was too big to fail. Its hand was further forced by public revelations of corruption among company officials and servants. In April 1772, John Burgoyne, the general who was to be defeated at the Battle of Saratoga (1777), called for a Select Committee to inquire into what he described as "the most atrocious abuses that ever stained the name of civil government" and insisted that the government must "hold up the mirror of truth to the Company." His initiative succeeded in stifling government plans, including a judiciary bill that North had developed to encourage self-regulation in association with the company. The Select Committee thereafter degenerated into a trial of Lord Clive. Distrustful of such dramatic public exposure and fearful of members who wanted to enlarge government powers, North opted for his own Secret Committee and was still intent upon resolving the issue in cooperation with the company. By October 1772, the company was close to bankruptcy and North decided to introduce legislation in Parliament.[42]

By 1773, North was adamant that there would need to be a quid pro quo with major reforms in return for a government bailout. He argued that the economic problems were interlinked with the mismanagement of the company. Despite much opposition from the Court of Proprietors of the East India Company, he successfully obtained passage of three acts whose main emphasis was upon reform, with extracting revenue a secondary aim. Although a temporary stopgap, the acts represented a compromise which endured through the American War of Independence. They consisted, first, of what in America became known as the Tea Act, which granted the company a license to export tea to North America without paying import duties in Britain. This aimed to make the East India Company more solvent while simultaneously raising more tea duty in America, where it led to the Boston Tea Party.

The second act and centerpiece of this legislation was the Regulating Act, which gave the government authority to appoint a governor-general and a four-man council in Bengal, together with a chief justice and three justices of a new Supreme Court. It gave the directors longer terms in office while raising the qualifications of stockholders to vote in the more recalcitrant Court of Proprietors. The new system undermined any advantage in stock splitting by which proprietors might have attempted to increase their leverage within the company. A leading figure in the East India Company and an MP, Lawrence Sullivan, believed that the act would result in state control and thought Lord North "the boldest minister the realm had been blest with since the days of Oliver Cromwell." Indeed, "the motives for such changes had some affinity with designs to strengthen the position of the governors and councils in American colonies."[43]

The final act provided a loan of £1.4 million. It was made conditional upon restricting dividend to 6 percent until the loan was paid, after which it could only be raised to 7 percent until the total debt was reduced below £1.5 million. The company was also required to export £287,000 worth of British produce and manufactures to India. It was prohibited from accepting bills of exchange for more than £300,000 from India without permission from the Treasury. In short, "while it is difficult to discern any direct connexion between American and Indian policy, it is nevertheless possible to see ministers attempting to exert a much stronger degree of control over British overseas affairs during the 1760s and 1770s."[44]

Canada

Britain was also active in making policy in the Canadian colonies with the passage of the Quebec Act in 1774. It was an enlightened act. There was indeed a question among the Patriots in the Thirteen Colonies and the opposition at home as to why Britain would be so lenient toward French Catholics while pursuing what they regarded as a hostile policy in America. In Grenada in the Caribbean and Quebec in Canada, the British attempted to assimilate the French population with terms that were much more favorable than those granted to Catholics in Ireland and even to those in England.

The Quebec Act foregrounded an issue simmering in the background of British imperial policy, which was the place of Catholics. The precedents of bringing Catholics into the empire were highly negative. American colonists, notably in New England, were strongly committed to the idea of Protestant internationalism. Colonists in British America were enthusiastic participants in what they saw as a worldwide, apocalyptic duel between a Protestant interest and what they derided as the Roman Catholic alliance with France in a quest for an absolutist world order.[45] Those prejudices were applied to one of the more shameful episodes in early eighteenth-century British imperial history, the expulsion during the Seven Years' War of 11,500 French-speaking Catholic Acadians from the Maritime provinces of present-day Canada. Their land was taken from them and given to New England and Scottish immigrants. The message was that Catholics were only welcome in the empire if they converted to Protestantism, although the mistreatment of Acadians was as much due to their continued loyalty to France as to their unwillingness to give up their Catholic truth. Lord Halifax exclaimed that the children of Acadians "should be taken from them and educated in the Protestant religion, by which means they at least, however stubborn their parents might prove, would have become good and usefull servants."[46]

In 1763, the problem of how Catholics could fit into the empire re-emerged. The imperial (though not colonial) attitudes to the new empire's multiplicities of peoples and religions had softened. One reason was the Acadian removal during the Seven Years' War, which even as it was occurring was viewed as an inhumane disaster. A more practical reason was based on necessity: the numbers of Catholics in Quebec were too large for removal to work, and in Grenada the disparity between the numbers of whites and the numbers of Blacks in a thriving plantation society meant that any white planter was useful in expanding imperial control, even if that planter was a French Catholic. Moreover, French planters had more at stake than the Catholics of Acadia did in accepting British sovereignty because otherwise they would have to give up their substantial wealth. Patriotism was a major problem for the French in the West Indies, where on several occasions French planters found it easier to hide their religious orientations than to give up on plantation-derived wealth.[47] In addition, hostility toward Catholics in Britain, which had reached a fever pitch during and after the Jacobite crisis in Scotland in 1745, had reduced considerably by the end of the Seven Years' War in 1763.[48] Some imperial statesmen, such as the Earl of Rockingham and the Earl of Shelburne, believed that Catholics could and should be assimilated, and that this process of assimilation required some initial accommodations. As William Knox wrote in his apologia for the Quebec Act in 1774, it was essential not to repeat the sectarian problems of Ireland.[49]

In Canada, the British initially tried to impose their legal system and courts upon the French. The Stamp Act (1765) discriminated against French Catholics by charging punitively high rates on foreign publications and newspapers that were written in the French language.[50] It was only gradually, over seven years, that the government shifted to an assimilative policy first tried out in the Caribbean island of Grenada.[51] The governor of Grenada was instructed to allow French Catholics to vote for members of a new elected assembly, and to be able to serve as assemblymen if they renounced allegiance to France and to Catholicism. Grenada was explicitly intended to serve as a blueprint for later policies in Quebec. The lawyer for the Crown observed that the situation in Grenada was "materially connected with the consideration of what is fit to be done in the Government of Canada, where His Majesty has a greater number of new subjects under the same predicament."[52]

The results were disturbing for later policies in Quebec. The proposals for assimilation of French Catholic planters caused consternation among strongly anti-Catholic British planters. They argued that "the very existence of the constitution of Great Britain," and therefore of those of its colonies, depended on "the support of the Protestant religion and the colony from the councils and offices of the nation, all enemies of their persuasion." British planters withheld taxes, producing a state of virtual paralysis. Their spirited resistance to Popery and to what they considered to be inappropriate uses of the Prerogative was welcomed in the anti-Catholic heartland of Massachusetts. It formed a foretaste of New Englanders' complaints about the Quebec Act in 1774.[53]

The Quebec Act granted freedom of worship to Catholics and restored the tithes of the Catholic Church. It permitted French Catholics to hold office and allowed for the continuance of French civil and commercial law, dispensing with trial by jury in civil suits. What disgusted Protestants in the Canadian colonies and Americans in New England was that it made no provision for an elected assembly but instead concentrated power in the hands of a governor and council. The Anglo-Protestant community in Quebec—the Old Subjects—numbered 2,000 out of the total estimated population of 75,000. There were about 110 Protestants in Quebec City, the population of which numbered around 10,000. The act was primarily aimed at winning the loyalty of the French priests and gentry in the expectation stated by its primary advocate, Governor Guy Carleton, that "the Common People are greatly to be influenced by their Seigniors."[54] In ret-

The Thistle Reel, 1775. In this print the cartoonist mocks Lords Bute, Mansfield, and North, government ministers who played a leading role in passing the Quebec Act of 1774. (Library of Congress, Prints and Photographs Division)

rospect, it marked an important step toward Catholic Emancipation in the empire, with the first Catholic Relief Act in Britain and a related bill in Ireland happening in 1778, as well as similar legislation made later in Scotland.[55] It was one of the unsung successes of Lord North that he managed to persuade Parliament, the cabinet, and even the strongly anti-Catholic George III to acquiesce in the unprecedently tolerant Quebec

Act. George III regretted his acquiescence in 1774. He later opposed the plans for Catholic Emancipation in Ireland put forward by William Pitt the Younger in 1801. He argued that it controverted his coronation oath as defender of the Protestant faith.[56]

Opponents of the act routinely pointed out that the Quebec Act gave Catholics in the empire more rights than in Britain. It confirmed to people worried about the creep of colonial Popery that Britain had decided that a French Catholic colony could not become part of the British Empire, no matter the extent of assimilation to British ways, if most of the population felt their religion made them inferior subjects. Anglo-Protestants regarded the act as a violation of their right to trial by jury and representation through elections. They noted that since 1759 little had been done to implant the Church of England or to implement British legal systems in the colony.[57] Furthermore, the government of Quebec included the territories of the Northwest in America which were variously claimed by Virginia, Maryland, Pennsylvania, Connecticut, and New York.

The Pacific

The Seven Years' War also saw Britain move into another area of the world where it could develop an empire, the vast reaches of the Pacific Ocean. For the first two centuries of European intrusion into the Pacific, the region was dominated by the Spanish, to the extent that the Pacific was commonly thought of as a Spanish lake. English interest in the Pacific was predatory—a means to capture Spanish galleons and gain American silver. It also attracted adventurers such as William Dampier, who escaped from a miserable existence as an overseer on a Jamaican sugar estate to circumnavigate the world in 1697, writing a best-selling narrative about what he had done. Sporadic interest in the Pacific then followed, but the financial disaster of the South Sea Bubble in 1720 led to the Pacific dropping from British attention for nearly twenty years. Some interest was reignited by Commodore George Anson's world trip of 1739, saved from complete disaster by the capture of the Acapulco silver fleet containing unbelievable quantities of silver, which made Anson extraordinarily rich and underpinned his successful naval career.[58]

A few enthusiasts boosted the prospects of imperialism in the Pacific, though they were few and not very influential. John Campbell boasted that if Britain could explore, exploit, and settle the still unknown but presumably existing great southern continent, then this settlement of Terra Australia would likely result in a colony "as Rich, as fruitful, and as capable of Improvement, as any that have been hitherto found either in the East Indies or the West."[59] Alexander Dalrymple thought that the economic benefits of Pacific exploration would be immense, especially if the great southern continent contained, as he thought, millions of people wanting to trade with Britain. He enthused that trade with this putative continent would be sufficient "to maintain the power, dominion, and sovereignty of BRITAIN by employing all its manufactures and ships."[60]

British expansion into the Pacific did not start before the end of the Seven Years' War. After the Peace of Paris in 1763, Britain sent four expeditions in the 1760s to the Pacific—in 1764 under John Byron, in 1766 under Samuel Wallis, in 1767 under Philip Carteret, and, most famously, in 1769 under James Cook. These were missions that combined exploration and a search for profitable trade with science and the pursuit of useful knowledge. They were very influenced by previous American colonial experience and were continuations of the westward movement of settlers into the American continent. The British explorers in the Pacific had learned much from 150 years of settler colonialism in North America. They had learned that it was easier to achieve one's aims by treaty rather than through force. They cultivated Indigenous go-betweens to ease their ways into local societies. In Tahiti, Samuel Wallis relied upon Purea, a high-born chieftainess with an agenda of her own, to gain a foothold in the island. James Cook followed the same path and cultivated a young man called Tupaia in 1769 and Omai in 1772, each of whom came with him to Britain. Omai became a cultural sensation, presented in court, lionized by the fashionable, and famously painted by Joshua Reynolds.[61]

The Seven Years' War shaped all these expeditions in another way. They were a means of continuing in peacetime the competition between Britain and France that had gone on in wartime. France's expedition in 1766 under Louis-Antoine de Bougainville was designed to replace lost markets and territories. Britain also wanted fresh markets and territories to pay for its war debts and to maintain its war winnings while forestalling any advantage now sought by a defeated France.[62]

Nevertheless, expansion into the Pacific was not a major consideration for the British. It was essentially a gamble. If Britain found the rumored great southern continent, then it might gain substantial wealth. Otherwise, it could justify its investment by saying that British expeditions advanced science and helped in the training of seamen. Its trips to the Pacific also involved a new first encounter between the British and a set of Indigenous peoples who resembled in many ways Indigenous peoples in the Pacific Northwest.[63] Pacific exploration was heavily influenced by Enlightenment ideas, and it was stressed by British officials that Natives needed to be treated at all times with humanity and respect and that nothing was to be done in regard to colonization without their consent. But the actual process of encounter brought Indigenous peoples great problems. The introduction of venereal disease, alcohol, and firearms brought a depressing train of consequences to the Pacific islands—the usual troika of sickness, demoralization, and depopulation.[64]

Senegambia

One way of appreciating the novelty of Britain's imperial policies in the 1760s, and how they were fashioned out of attempts to deal with an empire that was now global rather than mostly Atlantic, is to look at where colonization was new, such as Britain's acquisition of Senegambia. It was conceived of as a way of integrating politically what had already been integrated commercially, through the slave trade, connecting Africa with goods from India and providing enslaved people to the Caribbean.[65] The problem for the British in Senegambia in 1763 was like that in the Middle Ground of Indigenous–settler relations in the American interior. British traders were notable for their avarice and were thought of by imperial officials as self-interested and unpatriotic.

In a review of how the governance of this new colony was to be done, carried out in the mid-1760s under the direction of the major imperial theorist Charles Townshend, an imperial policy based solely on trade was argued not to generate the kind of political oversight essential for the dignity of British power. Townshend and others wanted to align commercial development with political oversight. Britain was no longer willing to give state support to private commercial concerns and let those commercial companies run things under their own control, on the model of the East India Company in the early eighteenth century. The reforms made to the East India Company after 1765 convinced them that the new model established in India could be transferred to West Africa, with the added advantage of there being no established company to deal with and where commerce and politics could be brought under an authoritarian government. Senegambia, therefore, was more important as an imperial experiment than it might seem, with reverberations throughout the empire, including in the settler colonies of North America.[66]

British officials were influenced in Senegambia by what imperial officials did elsewhere. They were especially informed by the withdrawal of the management of diplomatic relations with Indigenous peoples in North America from colonial officials and its placement in the hands of the Indian Department. They also noted the passing of parliamentary acts in 1773 and 1784 that increased the extent of parliamentary sovereignty over the East India Company's rights to the *diwani* in Bengal.[67] It was a bellicose reading of the purpose of the British Empire, in which the interests of merchants were subordinated to the concerns of the state. Officials in Senegambia, where there was no settler population and where the colony was entirely extractive in nature, felt that the model they should follow was what had been attempted in India. Merchants would not be allowed to disrupt ambitious but unrealizable plans to make Senegambia a plantation society producing gum through enslaved labor on the model of plantation societies in the Caribbean. These plans were an indication that the new empire was to be more centrally controlled, on the model of the Spanish Empire, with a more resolute application of parliamentary sovereignty over imperial affairs.[68] The changing nature of the British Empire can be seen in Senegambia, India, and Canada as the idiom of a maritime and commercial empire, once paramount, gave way to a more authoritarian language in which power, rather than commerce, served to delineate the contours of British policy. The British believed their powers to be almost limitless in "a Country which has now become an essential object of British policy. By our conquest there . . . we are in a manner absolute masters where before we were entire strangers."[69]

The reality was very different. As Britain was to find out to its cost in the twenty-one years between 1763 and 1784—the year when British control over Senegambia limped to its sorry end—Britain was not the master of the imperial situation. Colonial governance was not helped by a series of very poor senior leaders and by the disease environment in Senegambia, which decimated white populations. The dread demography of the region meant, unsurprisingly, that there was a distinct unwillingness on the part of British migrants to move to West Africa to develop plantations. Disease and low migration from Europeans to Africa made dreams of establishing a settler society in Senegambia illusory. The major problem, however, that imperial officials faced was that Britain was never fully in control of the colony. It depended for its authority to be recognized on carefully worked-out negotiations (or "palavers" in the language of West Africa) between imperial officials and the West African elites who oversaw affairs in the region. These African elites rejected the assumptions undergirding British imperial policy in Senegambia. They wanted trade and economic expansion without having to endure any political management of their affairs. The failure of Senegambia after 1763 "shows how imperial officials could imagine an imperial order which was entirely at odds with the realities of power on the ground. . . . More than a site of commodity exchange, Senegambia was a site of political and ideological reconceptualization that intimately reflected the priorities of British imperialism in the eighteenth century."[70]

The British Caribbean

Many of the imperial policies imposed in America also applied to the British Caribbean. There were differences though. The Caribbean had a deserved reputation, especially in Jamaica, for contentiousness, both in its local politics and even more so in how it interacted with the imperial government. Contrary to how the West Indies behaved in the later 1760s and early 1770s, when it was more quiescent than the North American colonies, its imperial relations were often stormy before the Stamp Act. During the Seven Years' War, for example, in 1757, Parliament formally censured the Assembly of Jamaica for its combustible relations with Governor Charles Knowles—the first time any colonial assembly had been censured. In 1764, British customs reforms adversely affected the Spanish bullion trade in Jamaica.

The islands already paid regular taxes to support the metropolitan government, and since the Restoration, Barbados and the Leeward Islands had paid the imperial government a 4.5 percent duty, which amounted to an annual income of £40,000–£50,000. Between 1764 and 1774 the Windward Islands also paid the duty. Jamaica had granted a perpetual £8,000 per year toward the cost of imperial government by a local revenue act in 1728. Since the 1730s, Antigua and Jamaica voluntarily paid high annual subsistence allowances toward the maintenance of local garrisons of the British army. After Tacky's enslaved rebellion in 1760, Jamaicans also started to pay local stamp duties. Unlike the Stamp Act and Townshend Duties, however, none of these other revenue payments were the result of legislation by Parliament.[71]

However, in a trend reflected throughout the empire, Britain began to treat the islands more favorably than North America due to their less confrontational approach to paying imperial taxes and their greater leverage through the absentee West India lobby in Britain. The Sugar Act of 1764 revived the Molasses Act of 1733, reducing duty on foreign molasses going into North America. Unlike the previous legislation, however, it was more rigorously enforced, thereby discriminating against the cheaper sugar and molasses of the French islands to the benefit of the British Caribbean. The Sugar Act showed the power of the West India lobby in London and was resented in the northern colonies. John Adams argued that every New Englander saw their interests sacrificed to satisfy the superior interest of the West Indies in Parliament.[72] As the first overt imperial tax raised by Parliament, the Sugar Act ruptured relations between the West Indies and North America, though, contrary to what North Americans believed, the act imposed some boundaries on West Indian planters, even if these borders were overall confined to Caribbean commercial interests.[73]

Nevertheless, this was not the case with the Stamp Act. It imposed the greatest tax burden on the islands rather than on the mainland, with clauses specifically discriminating against them. Britain allocated more stamps to the islands than to North America. On the other hand, the 1764 and 1766 Sugar Acts favored the islands over North America, aiming to prevent illicit trade in molasses with the French West Indies, and in 1766 Britain granted free ports to Jamaica and Dominica. The Townshend Duties were imposed on both the British Caribbean and North America: Jamaica and the Lesser Antilles imported and paid duty on an average of 30,000 pounds of tea per year between 1773 and 1775.[74] Yet the islands negotiated specific exemptions from the act, such as not being subject to the Boston Board of Customs and the vice-admiralty courts, which were given jurisdiction only for the thirteen North American colonies as well as

Florida, Bermuda, the Bahamas, and Newfoundland. The British Caribbean remained subject to the jurisdiction of the English Board of Customs. In another example of inconsistent treatment, when for eighteen months in the 1760s Jamaica refused to pay the army subsidies and defied an order of the Privy Council, it received no punishment. Nor did Ireland, where there was a similar situation. But for the same cause Parliament suspended the New York Assembly in 1767. In *Campbell v. Hall* in 1774, the Windward Islands won their case against the use of prerogative powers to the 4.5 percent duty, after the settlement of their constitution. In the Taxation of the Colonies Act in 1778, Parliament declared that it would not impose any tax, assessment, or duty for raising revenue in the colonies in North America and the Caribbean. It yielded to the colonial contention that this was the exclusive right of their elected assemblies. Although it was a failure as part of an attempted peace proposal with America, it benefited the British Caribbean.

A New Set of Imperial Policies

The causes of the more authoritarian tendency in policy making toward America are more comprehensible when understood in the broader context of the British Empire. If indeed there ever was a period of "salutary neglect," which we think would only have applied, and then in limited ways, to several North American colonies in the Long Peace of the 1720s and 1730s, it was no longer an option after 1763, with the growing recognition of the commercial value of the colonies and the territorial expansion which followed the Seven Years' War. The colonies were too important to leave alone, even if we ignore the incessant demands that Ireland placed upon the metropole. Colonial commerce in North America and the Caribbean, for example, had increased from one-twelfth to one-third of the total trade of Britain. Bengal alone had a population of some thirty million and was the richest province in India. It was necessary to adjudicate between French and English legal systems in Canada, and Mohammedan, Hindu, and English systems in India. The British had to establish the boundaries of the territories of the new Northwest in America and were in the process of colonization in the Pacific and into Senegambia in Africa. Tighter control was also necessitated by changes within Britain, meaning that "there is a profoundly important sense in which the American Revolution can only be understood by placing it in a series of crises occasioned by the growth and change of English political institutions."[75]

The British state in the 1760s was expanding, becoming more militarily powerful and more authoritarian. The government of the early eighteenth century had been highly devolved, leaving much discretion to the localities both within Britain and throughout the British Empire. The traditions, customs, and common law were major influences upon local political practice, while metropolitan authority over the localities was often negotiated. This situation changed as members of Parliament increasingly turned to statute law and to parliamentary intervention. Except for the Currency Act in 1751, the British cabinet had not involved Parliament in its attempted reforms of the empire during the 1740s and 1750s. The increased pretensions and activism of Parliament in all spheres was to have great significance for America.[76]

The centralizing trends throughout the empire are significant in understanding the causes of the American Revolution. For much of the twentieth century, it is remarkable that American historians regarded the constitutional arguments of the Patriot cause as little more than a rhetorical pretext because they accepted the view of the British government that "the constitution was what Parliament declared it to be." Imperial historians sometimes dismissed the opposition to taxation on the grounds that the taxes were insignificant and that the real cause was that the colonies were outgrowing the imperial economic system and the confines of the monopoly of the metropolitan market. Progressive historians saw the ideological and constitutional claims of the colonial elites as largely a front for their desire to seize power. Even in the 1970s and 1980s, the republican school of historians did little to erase such a view by giving the impression that the motives for rebellion were based upon conspiratorial and paranoid fears that arose from a republican literature which treated any form of power as potentially tyrannical.[77]

In defense of the British government, it is not self-evident that there was real tyranny in America in 1776. The term, of course, is relative depending upon how we define tyranny, but it signifies a system of arbitrary, violent, and oppressive government. Before Lexington and Concord (1775), the British government made very little attempt to use force, not least because it acknowledged the right of the colonial civil courts to bring trials against military personnel. In the bloodiest pre-war incident known as the

Boston "Massacre" of 1770, the commanding officer and eight soldiers were tried for shooting and killing five civilians; the court found two of the soldiers guilty of manslaughter, for which the sentence was commuted to branding.[78] The policies of Britain were vexatious and cumbersome, but were they so oppressive as to constitute a tyranny? After all, and in response to colonial protests, by 1770 Britain had repealed the Stamp Act and all the Townshend Duties except the tax on tea. In addition, Lord North made other significant concessions by relaxing the currency rules and the Western Proclamation of 1763. Britain was far from being a tyrannical power regarding its colonial possessions.

The broader context of British policy throughout the British Empire, however, shows that colonial concerns were far from groundless and that there was indeed a dramatic change in the system of government from 1763. Of course, the theory of parliamentary sovereignty put forward by George Grenville had antecedents dating to the English Reformation.[79] In short, changes in imperial governance in the eighteenth century were both gradual and sudden. The concept certainly became more fully evolved because of the Revolutionary Settlement of 1688–89, which required that the Crown summon Parliament at least once a year to vote on the Mutiny Acts for extending the existence of a lawful standing army. In addition, in the eighteenth century, Parliament sat regularly and passed increasing amounts of legislation, often initiated by private members. In domestic politics, it became involved in social policy and began to systematically collect data to guide its decisions.[80] The government increasingly preferred to legitimize its policies by legislating through Parliament rather than using proclamations and the authority of the royal prerogative.

Nevertheless, although the British Parliament had formally asserted supremacy over the Irish Parliament by the Declaratory Act of 1720, no consistent tradition existed about theoretical claims of parliamentary supremacy over America. The writings of seventeenth-century jurists were conflicting and often only allowed for direct intervention in the affairs of conquered colonies. Although the Board of Trade wanted Parliament to intervene in colonial affairs in the 1720s, the involvement of Parliament in the internal affairs of the colonies was very limited. Colonial policies were more typically enacted by royal prerogative. Furthermore, the Board of Trade had previously shown considerable flexibility in the enforcement of legislation and willingness to compromise.[81] Its role in colonial affairs was primarily limited to the regulation of trade with the Navigation Acts (1651, 1663, 1673, and 1696), the Iron Act (1749), and the Hat Act (1732). It was only from mid-century that it began to assert its theoretical supremacy and to become less responsive to colonial interests. Until the 1760s "there was little concentrated thought on the nature of imperial sovereignty," even though there was a "slow, nearly imperceptible creep of parliamentary supremacy across the Atlantic."[82] First published between 1765 and 1769, Sir William Blackstone's *Commentaries on the English Laws* was the most authoritative source on the question of the sovereignty of Parliament. With the exception of conquered territories like Ireland, Blackstone regarded parliamentary authority as limited in the colonies to occasional and extraordinary circumstances, while he believed that the name of a colony ought to be specifically mentioned for parliamentary acts to be enforced.[83] Nevertheless, absolute sovereignty was an unspoken assumption which embodied "attitudes to authority and state formation which were of ancient origin and which were widespread within England."[84] Indeed, the common good was predicated on the idea of an absolute source of power and authority. Regardless of the merits of the debate, the lack of well-defined constitutional boundaries between the authority of the central government and the rights of the colonists was a fatal flaw in the composition of the empire.[85]

In the 1760s, the government of George Grenville was the first to attempt a direct tax in America and the British West Indies, an expedient not even attempted in Ireland. Grenville claimed that what he was proposing was intended to regulate trade, which is why violators were prosecuted by the vice-admiralty rather than the common-law courts. In fact, Parliament in the 1760s was making new claims with the concept of colonial "virtual representation," which was advanced by Thomas Whatley in response to colonial opposition to the Stamp Act. The government of the colonies had hitherto been conducted through negotiation. Britain traditionally accepted colonial customary rights, common law, and local constitutions. It was a federalist system with multi-constitutions.[86] Although imperial politicians later claimed that power could not be limited and divided, it had in practice been divided for much of the colonial period in America.

The implication of absolute parliamentary authority was that the colonists had no rights, and their constitutions had no validity other than what was acknowledged by a metropolitan legislature in which they had no representation. It conflicted with colonists' long-held view that their constitutional traditions and precedents protected their internal affairs from intervention by Britain. This "settler political theory" was asserted with remarkable uniformity by mainland settlers as early as the 1670s and 1680s when faced with the threat of direct metropolitan intervention in the affairs of New England and Virginia.[87] Britain's insistence upon absolute supremacy left the colonies no room to maneuver, other than by making an appeal to the king to intervene over the authority of Parliament. Reflecting on the causes of the war in 1778–79, William Knox, an undersecretary of state in the American Department, wrote that "the Claim of unlimited unrestrained Jurisdiction in Parliament has alarmed and terrified them."[88] It was essential for the colonists to defy the taxes and other internal policies to prevent a precedent for much higher taxes and greater intrusion in the future. It is true that the taxes were light, and the indignities minor compared with modern ideas of tyranny, but the colonists rebelled against a very real latent potential for tyranny if they had permitted new constitutional precedents to be established. The issue of tax escalated into a debate about the power of Parliament as the ultimate source of authority in the British Empire.[89]

The sheer volume of new policies and metropolitan involvement was greater for North America than the rest of the British Empire and reflected the growing importance of this region to Britain. It legitimated the Patriot narrative in the Declaration of Independence that "a long train of abuses and usurpations pursuing invariably the same Object evinces a design to reduce them under absolute Despotism," and bolstered the claim of "a history of repeated injuries and usurpations, all having in direct object the establishment of an absolute Tyranny over these States." The opposing British and Loyalist narratives were correspondingly far less persuasive in their claim that the Patriots were delusional and that the real threat of tyranny was posed by a few unscrupulous revolutionaries.

Such a conclusion, of course, does not validate the old conspiracy theory that there was a deliberate plan of tyranny against British North America initiated by George III and Lord North. They were not tyrants, and their belief in parliamentary sovereignty was shared even among opposition parties that continued to be mostly concerned with the powers of the Crown and protecting the Revolutionary Settlement of 1688–89. Indeed, those who today argue that the best policy would have been to continue past practices and maintain the status quo ignore the extent to which the problems posed by the aftermath of the Seven Years' War required solutions which could only be effectively coordinated by a central government. This included the treatment of Indigenous people, whether the inhabitants of India, the Caribs in St. Vincent, or Indigenous Americans. The cost of the empire at the conclusion of the Seven Years' War exceeded the resources of Britain. It is also useful to remember that the former Thirteen Colonies were themselves forced to adopt in the 1780s a more central government, although based on a broader consensus.[90]

So, what sort of empire was Britain dealing with in the 1760s? It had changed because of the Seven Years' War. It was now a global empire. That the British Empire was much more global than before this war is crucial to understanding the imperial complexities that both gave great opportunities to Britain for wealth and global influence and also threw up problems, notably in North America, that had not been so evident before 1756. The British Empire was a more complicated place to deal with. The pre-1763 British Empire was one concentrated on the Atlantic—from Ireland close to the British mainland, to Bermuda in the Atlantic, to the Caribbean and to North America. After 1763, the British Empire extended spatially from Ireland to the South Pacific, with significant nodes in an enlarged North America that now included Canada, in the Caribbean with new colonies in the Windward Islands, in Africa, and in the Pacific. Imperial policies had to make sense in all these very different regions of the world. This wider global empire and its complicated imperial policies also needed to be applied in an Atlantic empire committed to slavery more than ever, and with a powerful, growing, and wealthy settler population full of white Protestants fervently determined to assert their British identity as a people accustomed to exerting a great deal of autonomy over the control of their own affairs.

THREE

Empire of Coercion

ONE OF THE MORE WELL-KNOWN anecdotes about the importance of the West Indies to the British economy in the eighteenth century is the story of George III driving in a carriage with his prime minister, William Pitt, near Weymouth. The monarch met a very pretentious equipage, with many outriders in grand liveries. When George III learned that the carriage belonged to an absentee planter from Jamaica, he turned to Pitt and exclaimed, "Sugar, sugar—hey?—all *that* sugar! How are the duties, hey, Pitt, how are the duties?"[1]

The story is no doubt apocryphal. One does not imagine that a British monarch ever has shared the same carriage as his or her prime minister. It is also vague as to time. The context suggests the anecdote comes from the 1780s when William Pitt the Younger was prime minister, but it could conceivably come from the early 1760s when the prime minister to the new monarch, George III, was William Pitt the Elder, though that would presume a degree of closeness and familiarity between the monarch and his chief minister which famously never existed.[2] What the story does suggest, however, is the centrality of sugar and by extension the British Caribbean to British economic prosperity and British commitment to empire in the eighteenth century. This chapter argues that what contemporaries wrote at the time was correct: the plantations were universally supported within Britain until late in the eighteenth century because they provided wealth and geopolitical advantages to Britain that fueled metropolitan prosperity and security. Understanding the significance of slavery in an empire of coercion is crucial for understanding the contexts of imperial policy laid out in the previous two chapters. One reason Britain began to focus so much on trying to reorganize its American empire in the aftermath of the Seven Years' War is that slavery-derived wealth had become so conspicuously important within the British and the imperial economies.

The Wealth of the Plantations

That sugar and the West Indies were vital to British economic and geopolitical interests was axiomatic in the reigns of George III's predecessors, George I and George II, from 1714 to 1760, at least to the few Britons who thought about imperial matters. If sugar and the West Indies were central to the value of empire to Britain in the first half of the eighteenth century, then so too was slavery particularly important. The whole basis of West Indian wealth was due to the labor of the millions of slaves imported from West Africa to work on British West Indian plantations. It meant that before the American Revolution, the British Empire, one focused mostly on England's seventeenth-century acquisitions in the western hemisphere, was an empire devoted to and dependent upon slavery. To be sure, the eighteenth-century British Empire in the Atlantic was not solely an empire of slavery. It also involved extensive relations with the very numerous Indigenous peoples of North America and a smaller number of not unimportant Indigenous peoples living, like those in most parts of North America, outside the direct control of European governments, in places like St. Vincent and Dominica.

Overall, plantations and slavery were the most conspicuous and most conspicuously successful feature of the first British Empire as it developed in the early eighteenth century. Indeed, "It was slavery that made the empty lands of the western hemisphere valuable producers of commodities and valuable markets for Europe and North America. What moved in the Atlantic in these centuries was predominantly slaves, the output of slaves, the inputs of slave societies and the goods and services purchased with the earnings on slave products."[3] The plantation sector was the most dynamic part of the New World economy before 1800, with rates of economic growth that corresponded well to ratios of economic growth in industrializing Britain and the United States, exhibiting strong productivity gains after the establishment in Jamaica and the Leeward Islands in the early eighteenth century of the large, integrated plantation system which had transformed Barbados in the third quarter of the seventeenth century.[4]

The large, integrated plantation system, in which all functions of production were conducted on the same property by dint of a labor force of hundreds of enslaved people of African descent, growing and harvesting crops, notably sugar, for a British market, was a brilliant Caribbean innovation. It was "as modern as it was repugnant," an economic transformation of the Greater Caribbean environment that proved to be one of the best eighteenth-century expressions of the agricultural capitalism that transformed British agriculture in the seventeenth and eighteenth centuries. In short, it was "the manipulation of a complex agro-industrial technology, an integrated trade network, and a brutal system of labour exploitation."[5]

We can dismiss ideas that the plantation machine contained within its workings the seeds of its own destruction even though the system was always challenging for planters, facing soil exhaustion in old, settled colonies such as Barbados and, more importantly, competition from more efficient producers in the French Caribbean. As time went on, though not during the first half of the eighteenth century, the extent to which West Indian prosperity was dependent upon an extremely high degree of protectionist legislation under the mercantilist frameworks of Britain was clear. Its products were given priority in the valuable British home market, which became increasingly problematic in a political economy moving toward the ideology of free trade.[6] But as long as the slave trade operated, the plantation system of the British West Indies flourished and was profitable.[7] Productivity kept on increasing, reaching per capita productivity of £29.20 in Jamaica in 1800, over three times per capita productivity in Britain. That figure demonstrated an extraordinary degree of productivity for preindustrial times.[8]

Increases in productivity in the West Indian plantation sector were most pronounced in several periods in the eighteenth century—the 1710s to the mid-1730s; the 1760s; and the 1790s.[9] Profits were correspondingly high. Average rates of profit per annum throughout plantation America were around 10 to 13 percent before 1775, a considerable increase on rates of profit in the last two decades of the seventeenth century. These rates compare favorably with other rates of return in the most profitable mercantile sectors and were much higher than in even the most advanced areas of agriculture in England, let alone in Scotland or Ireland. These rates of profit suggest an average yearly profit on enslaved persons of between £5 and £8, at a minimum.[10]

George III was right to think that investment in sugar, as well as in tobacco and other crops produced in the Americas by enslaved people, was likely to augment national coffers in Britain. The Caribbean was a central plank in Britain's growing eighteenth-century prosperity. That this was correct was a view shared by other European commentators. As Abbé Raynal commented in 1770, "the labours of the colonists settled in these long-scorned islands are the sole basis of the African trade, extend the fisheries and cultivation of North America, provide advantageous outlets for the manufacture of Asia, double perhaps triple the activity of the whole of Europe. They can be regarded as the principal cause of the rapid movement of the universe."[11] Wealth from slavery was so obvious and important, the commitment to all aspects of slavery in the Americas was so strong, and the addictive powers of sugar, and, to a lesser extent, tobacco and coffee, were so overwhelming to the sweet-toothed European, that it was hard to imagine a world in which slavery did not exist. It took an enormous leap of imagination for British imperial theorists to conceive of an empire before 1790 that could flourish without slavery at its heart.[12]

Slavery and Imperial Policy

Such leaps of imagination occurred late in the history of British imperialism, starting only tentatively after the end of the Seven Years' War. At the start of the eighteenth century, imperial theorists may not have been united on all things.[13] But everyone was agreed that plantations and slave labor were essential to any notion of imperial growth. John Oldmixon, for example, in his comprehensive *The British Empire in America* (1708), argued that "A labourer in our American colonies is of more advantage to England though out if it than any 130 of the like kind can be in it."[14] Significantly, Oldmixon saw little distinction in political terms between colonists and the British metropolitan subjects of Queen Anne. Like Edward Littleton from the 1660s, he argued that the colonies must be treated as they had been in the early seventeenth century, as "a part of England" rather than places comprised "of foreigners and aliens."[15]

One of the principal supporters of the plantation system was the colonial enthusiast, Board of Trade member, and political philosopher John Locke. He was convinced that America was the solution to England's future prosperity. It could be a repository for England's unwanted people, and it could cultivate staple products via slavery in places like South Carolina, where Locke was an important projector. His views in support of greater commitment by England to slave labor were influenced by English ethnocentrism. Land in America, he claimed, would be one hundred times more valuable if cultivated by Devonshire farmers (for whom he seems to have had an especial attachment) than any other ethnic group. What was needed to make these farmers productive in the New World was access to enslaved people. Locke stressed the multiplier effects of slave-produced plantation labor. Increases in colonial agricultural production would create manufacturing jobs in England and would support maritime employment.[16]

The Bristol-based merchant, radical Whig, and Protestant dissenter John Cary, an important imperial ideologue of the late seventeenth and early eighteenth centuries, was direct and blunt about the economic benefits of slave-based imperialism.[17] He strongly supported the Atlantic slave trade and was a vehement opponent of the Royal African Company's monopoly over the importation of Africans to the Americas. He was especially critical of the low volumes of enslaved captives sent to the thriving West Indian islands. He argued that the company stifled a desirable enlargement of the slave trade and an enriching of the merchant classes of Bristol and London. He declared that the slave trade was "a Trade of the most Advantage to this kingdom of any we drive, and as it were all Profit," as it cost little to enter and provided enslaved people through whose work "great Quantities of *Sugar, Tobacco, Cotton, Ginger* and *Indigo* are raised." The trade was the English equivalent of Spanish silver mines, with Jamaica "a Magazine of Trade to *New-Spain* and the *Terra Firma,* from whom we have yearly vast Quantities of Bullion imported to this kingdom both for the Negroes and manufactures we send them."[18]

The West Indies' principal crop, sugar, was highly praised. Sir Dalby Thomas declared that "the pleasure, glory and grandeur of England" had been advanced "more by sugar than by any other commodity, wool not excepted."[19] Writers began to claim that the plantations were central to the very essence of the nation. Joshua Gee in 1720 claimed that "If we take a view of our own Kingdom we shall find our Trade and Riches came but very slowly till our Plantations began to be settled, and as they throve, our Trade, and Riches increased, our Lands rose in Value, and our Manufactures increased also."[20] The hack writer and empire-booster Malachy Postlethwayt extended Gee's theme: "Since we have established colonies and plantations our condition . . . has altered for the better, almost to a degree above creditability. Our manufactures are prodigiously increased, chiefly by the demand for them in the plantations, where they at least take off one and a half and supply us with many valuable commodities for re-exportation, which is as great an emolument to the mother kingdom as to the plantations themselves."[21]

The most sustained argument in support of the importance of trade with the West Indies in the early eighteenth century as a foundation for British prosperity came from the polemicist William Wood, a leading representative of merchants in the slave trading ports of London, Bristol, and Liverpool. His most important book, *A Survey of Trade* (1718), was much reprinted. His ideas were very influential with the British prime minister Robert Walpole, who favored policies that supported British overseas trade. Wood had lived in Jamaica and spoke with authority about the Caribbean. He considered Jamaica "the most valuable plantation belonging to the Crown" and "an inexhaustible mine of treasure to their Mother Country" because it "produc[ed] commodities indispensably necessary to this part of the world."[22]

No one was in any doubt that the value of the sugar colonies depended upon African labor and that slavery made the empire work. Wood concluded that "the labour of negroes is the principal foundation of our riches from the plantations" and that "Negroes are the first and most necessary materials for planting from whence it follows that all measures should be taken that may produce such a plenty of them, as may be an encouragement to the industrious planter."[23] Daniel Defoe, in his inimitable way, put the importance of enslaved labor clearly and succinctly, if in overstated fashion: "No African trade, no negroes; no negroes, no sugars, ginger, indigoes etc; no sugars etc, no islands; no islands, no continent; no continent, no trade."[24] In short, the freedom that colonists found in America and the wealth that the Americas brought Britain were underwritten by bondage.

The Harshness of Black Bondage

Black bondage was accepted as unproblematic because it did not involve the mistreatment and overworking of Europeans but merely of Africans, who were people Britons did not feel any obligation toward. Britons had no doubt that the Caribbean was a sink of iniquity and a place for exploitation rather than an area containing societies which deserved to be nurtured and engaged. The Grub Street writer Edward Ward excoriated Jamaica as being "As Sickly as a Hospital, as Dangerous as the Plague, as Hot as Hell, and as Wicked as the Devil, Subject to Tornadoes, Hurricanes, and Earthquakes."[25] The most wicked thing about the island, from our perspective certainly but also from people at the time, was how badly enslaved people were worked and how viciously they were punished. The West Indian slave regimes were incredibly brutal. Whites' severity toward Blacks was justified, it was argued, by Blacks being, as they were described as early as 1661 in the first slave code passed in Barbados, "an heathenish, brutish, and an uncertaine, dangerous kinde of people."[26] Hans Sloane, a beacon of Enlightenment thought and the founder of the British Museum, reflected Jamaican and British attitudes in this period toward Africans in his acceptance of cruel punishments being meted out to "disobedient" enslaved people. He justified "Gelding, or chopping off half of the Foot with an Ax" as far as "these Punishments are sometimes merited by the Blacks, who are a very perverse Generation of People, and though they appear harsh, yet are scarce equal to some of their crimes."[27]

Many of these anti-Black sentiments percolating in British thinking came from the Caribbean, where writers admitted that the essence of slavery was fear and the constant recourse to terror. Historians James Knight and Charles Leslie argued in the 1730s and 1740s that extreme violence was necessary against a people who were "sullen, deceitful [with a] Refractory Temper," meaning that Jamaica's deserved reputation for a brutality so extreme that "No Country excels them in a barbarous Treatment of Slaves, or in the Cruel Methods they put them to death" was acceptable "given how impossible it were to live amongst such Numbers of Slaves, without observing their Conduct with the greatest Niceness and punishing their Faults with the utmost severity."[28] These sentiments were also shared by metropolitan Britons. Defoe, a key contributor to establishing Britain's imperial identity, especially in the iconic *Robinson Crusoe* (1719), even though he never traveled to the Americas, encapsulated hostility to Africans in his novel *Colonel Jack* (1722).

The novel was set in Virginia around the turn of the eighteenth century and followed the fortunes of a London pickpocket turned into an indentured servant who then became an overseer on a large Chesapeake tobacco plantation. Jack began his career by treating Africans gently and with deference to their humanity. He soon learned, Defoe explained, the error of his ways as enslaved people laughed at him and took advantage of his seeming softness. The English, Jack declared, might be thought tyrannical, in the ways that Leslie was to later claim for Jamaica, yet that was not part of their nature but arose from managing Africans. Overseers needed, it was argued, to treat Africans badly because "it is owing to the Brutality, and obstinate Temper of the *Negroes,* who cannot be mannag'd by kindness and Courtisy; but must be rul'd with a Rod of Iron, beaten with *Scorpions* as the Scripture calls it, and must be used as they do use them, or they would rise and murther all their Masters, which their Numbers consider'd would not be hard for them to do, if they had Arms and Ammunition suitable to the Rage and Cruelty of their Nature."[29]

Slavery, moreover, was not just something that happened in far distant places and to which the British could conveniently close their eyes. Simon Newman has traced the many ways in which the British were alerted to the presence of enslaved Africans in their midst, looking in particular at the many hundreds of runaway advertisements that mentioned enslaved people in British publications. During the first three-quarters of the eighteenth century, when Newman collected 836 runaway advertisements, white Britons returning from the Americas regularly brought with them enslaved people to work as servants.[30] These enslaved servants worked in most ways as if they were domestically born servants, but the fact that they remained chattel was obvious and important. What also differentiated Black servants from white servants was that they were used as objects of display, most notably in portraits where their Black skin was pointedly contrasted to the alabaster skins of rich English women. They were demeaningly portrayed as luxuries for the amusement of the elite, often with clear signs that they were people who were owned by others, as in a portrait of the Jacobite James Drummond, Duke of Perth (c. 1700), where a small boy is pictured with a silver collar around his neck, or in a group painting of the Duke of Devonshire, his brother, William, and Elihu Yale (1708) with an enslaved servant in attendance.[31]

The standard legal ruling, by Sir Philip Yorke and Charles Talbot in 1729, was that enslaved people coming from the West Indies to Great Britain or Ireland remained enslaved.[32] Blacks in Britain were not just visible in many ways but were usually identified as being enslaved, as in the case of Pompey, who in 1704 ran away from Rotherhithe near London and who could be identified by the "Iron Collar around his Neck." Paul Moon was advertised as a runaway in 1723 and was noted as a twenty-year-old "Negro young Man" with African scarification, and as wearing a dark coat, with waistcoat and plush breeches, as well as "a Steel Collar about his Neck with his Master's Name ingrav'd upon it."[33]

In short, you would have had to be determined not to see slavery, in an eighteenth-century Britain where slavery was extremely visible and obvious. And Britons were not deliberately looking away from slavery. They understood the link between West Indian trade, the sugar they consumed, and the enslaved people who suffered and died to satisfy British wants. The waspish son of the prime minister, Horace Walpole, wrote scornfully in 1750 of "the British Senate, that Temple of liberty and bulwark of Protestant Christianity . . . pondering more methods to make more effectual that horrid traffic in selling Negroes."[34] Britons saw, but kept quiet, so that "contemporaries who were prepared to scream out against Louis XIV's use of Protestant galley slaves were mute on the lot of ever-increasing numbers of plantation slaves." They saw Africans and enslaved Blacks all around them, in many parts of England and Scotland. It meant that there was no excuse for ignorance of the slave trade: it was knowingly sustained by economic opportunism and racial stereotypes.[35] Indeed, when Britons did come to think about the ubiquity of West Indians and their slaves in eighteenth-century Britain, they tended, like the early abolitionist Granville Sharp and even more so the prosecutors defending the enslaved man James Somerset in the famous *Somerset* case of 1772, to couch their opposition to Blacks in Britain in distinctly xenophobic terms. Britain, in this view, was overrun by Blacks, callously brought into the country by their selfish West Indian owners, and these Blacks were corrupting the morals of the poor. Sergeant Davy, arguing the prosecution case in *Somerset*, called, for example, for a law against bringing slaves to Britain because otherwise race-mixing would occur and miscegenation would result, which, he argued, "would occasion a great deal of Heartburn."[36]

Whether wittingly or unwittingly, writers on empire in the last two hundred years who have dealt with slavery in the first half of the eighteenth-century British Empire have followed the lead of the Scottish philosopher and economist Adam Smith. Smith made the first sustained challenge to the political standing of the West Indies and the first challenge to the untested assumption that slavery was vital to British imperial prosperity in *The Wealth of Nations* (1776). He argued that the colonies were a wasteful deployment of national resources that might be better employed at home. His arguments about the superiority of free labor were well ahead of his time and did not really begin to attract notice until well into the nineteenth century. Moreover, his arguments did little to affect the specific imperial policies that Britain adopted. Nevertheless, his arguments, which were economic, but which were rooted in a deep moral distaste for slavery, proved retrospectively enormously powerful, contributing to a long-standing idea, popularized by later political economists such as Karl Marx, that slavery in the Atlantic world was an inherently backward institution. His arguments helped eventually to underpin a powerful social movement suggesting that slavery was not just morally wrong but economically mistaken.[37]

Smith's objections to slavery were based on moral distaste for the practice and dislike of West Indian planters, as can be seen in *Theory of Moral Sentiments* (1759). He insisted that the conditions of slavery and the existence of the slave trade precluded "happiness," or the common good. Moreover, he ascribed Enlightenment feelings to Africans which would have seemed alien and confusing to Defoe just a generation earlier. Smith noted that "there is not a Negro from the coast of Africa who does not . . . possess a degree of magnanimity by which the soul of his sordid master is too often scarce capable of receiving." He acidly commented that "Fortune never exerted more cruelly her empire over mankind" when she entrusted Africans, whom he thought "a humane and polished people" to "the refuse of the jails of Europe . . . whose levity brutality and baseness, so justly expose them to the contempt of the vanquished."[38] Smith's dislike of Black bondage, his disdain for Caribbean and American planters, and his belief that investment in the West Indies was a serious misallocation of resources helped shape his views on the superiority of free enterprise and free wage labor over protectionism and enforced labor.

Such views have had a strong retrospective power. They rendered illusory the encomiums to the importance of slavery put forward in the early eighteenth century, given the obvious advantages of free trade as experienced by a globally dominant Britain in the mid-nineteenth century, including such things as trade in slave-produced cotton with the United States. Other factors besides slavery appeared important in studies of British imperialism and the growth of the British nation. These views of the relative unimportance of slavery in this period, however, are less common than they were. There is widespread support nowadays for the view that slavery was vital to the eighteenth-century British and imperial economy, including increased recognition of the importance of slavery in the past as percolating in popular culture. The venerable and reliably conservative *Financial Times* estimates that slave-related businesses in the eighteenth century accounted for about the same proportion of GDP as the professional and support services sector does today. That is probably an overestimation, as the share of GDP made up of plantation-related activity was probably no more than 6 percent of GDP at even a generous estimate, making the contemporary comparison less with the whole of the service sector than with the computer industry.[39] The popular historian Robert Winder exclaims that "the fortunes founded on slavery . . . shaped the structure of British life as decisively and irrevocably as had William the Conqueror's gifts of land to his favoured knights."[40]

A System Upheld by Debt

Smith argued that the wealth of the West Indies was illusory, as it was supported by vast amounts of credit supplied by British merchants, a good deal of which got wasted in frivolous expenditure on country houses, good living, and expensive politics. Thus, not only was slavery morally despicable; it was not economically desirable but a misallocation of resources that could have been better invested in more productive and less morally dubious activities within Britain. Writing in the mid-twentieth century, Richard Pares (1902–58), who, along with Eric Williams (1911–81), was the leading scholar of Britain's involvement with the West Indies, agreed with Smith that the plantation colonies were as avid in consuming capital as they were in consuming enslaved peoples' lives. Indeed, the two forms of consumption went together, as planters needed to borrow money to buy increasingly expensive enslaved captives from the flourishing slave trade. Nevertheless, Pares argued that Smith exaggerated in assuming that this meant the West Indies were just an offshoot of British capital. He noted that planters borrowed as much from local merchants as from British ones. More important, the money which funded the British West Indies came, as in the French colonies, from the planters themselves, through the large sums they made from growing plantation crops that Britons wanted to buy, and which sustained a large trade surplus with Britain and were used to finance a deficit with North America. He suggested that "the profits of the plantations were the source which fed the indebtedness charged upon the plantations themselves," drawing on the Bristol-based house of the Nevis sugar-planting Pinney family as evidence of how debt from the Caribbean leeched to Britain. West Indian money went especially to firms that were founded on little capital but which, by lending to improvident planters who were making great sums but spending even more, soon became, like the Lascelles from early eighteenth-century Barbados, extraordinarily rich.[41]

Planters got into debt principally because they needed to buy captives from the slave trade to keep up and to increase the enslaved population. These payments for slaves cancelled out more than half of the favorable balance which the plantation colonies had with Britain. Slave prices kept on advancing over time at a pace greater than the rates of profit from sugar. These increasing slave prices made the planter increasingly indebted. In formal terms, slave investment was subject to terrible depreciation. The imbalance between slave prices and productivity, however, only became a problem in the West Indies after the American Revolution and especially after the Haitian Revolution (1791–1804). The Caribbean plantations depended upon leverage so that captives destined for plantation slavery could be bought on elevated levels of credit. But such leverage only lasted while the profits of slavery were high and slave prices not so great as to cause an inflationary bubble. It is why the plantation system worked best in the first half of the eighteenth century, even though profits were higher, and productivity was greater, in the second half of that century.[42]

Racism and Empire

Pares and Williams laid down an agenda about the importance of the West Indies, plantations, and slavery that has come back into favor after a generation in which the primacy of these things to British prosperity in the first half of the eighteenth century was downplayed in favor of approaches that highlighted internal rather than external causes. Pares and Williams, the former by implication, the latter explicitly, discounted racial explanations for why Africans were enslaved by the British in the Americas. Williams insisted that the explanations for the introduction of slavery in the West Indies were entirely economic in origin. Slavery occurred, he argued, due to the cheapness of labor, not race. Thus, he believed that white supremacy did not play a part in the development of the plantation system, though it might have been important once slavery and the plantation system were in place. Indeed, he believed that "the exploitation of the slaves on plantations did not differ fundamentally from exploitation of the feudal peasant or the treatment of the poor in European cities."[43]

The evidence is against Williams. It is difficult to see that racism was "invented" in Barbados in the seventeenth century because of the implementation of a race-based slavery that was founded not on racial difference but on class. Of course, before the eighteenth century, slavery was not associated with Blackness alone, and there were many and varied attitudes within European thought about what Blackness and race meant and what their relationship was to enslavement. Those more rigid associations of Blackness equaling slavery developed over time and these meanings accentuated especially as the large plantation system became established. Yet from the classical period onward, Blackness had attached to it among white Europeans a host of negative associations: death, melancholy, and above all Satan, who was thought of as being Black. "Racist opinions about blackness," Stephen Epstein argues, "were part of Europe's share of the classical inheritance, as shaped ultimately by Christianity." Europeans were fearful of Black people and were more likely to enslave them than they were likely to enslave white people. They had these fears and tendencies well before the Columbian encounter. Europeans, in short, had a racist ideology, "sustained by science and religion, that was well prepared to grasp any new opportunities to invent an even more racist slavery."[44]

That more racist slavery was evident in Barbados around 1660 and in the rest of the West Indies by 1700. The solidification of the plantation system in Barbados by the 1690s or 1700s led to a significant new theme in British thought on Black people, which was the development of whiteness, and hence also Blackness, as a means of indicating ethnic identity. "Whiteness" started to be used legally not as a physical descriptor but as a means of identifying people who had European ancestry and no African ancestry. In short, the language of race began to shape ethnic identification, making it clear that anyone with Black skin who became Christian, unlike in the seventeenth century, would remain enslaved. White supremacy was thus codified in the Caribbean before being translated to Britain, eliminating the possibilities for Black people to become in any way legally equal to whites.[45]

It would be untrue to state that colonization in the American South and the Caribbean created racism. But it reinforced ideas of white supremacy and expressed those ideas in novel ways. Free Blacks and enslaved Christians were crucial to this process because "as Blacks recognized the significance of Protestant baptism and sought to secure more rights, slave owners responded by protecting their property and redefining the justification for servitude by race rather than by religion."[46] Of course, the relationship between race and empire was never neat or clear cut. But it was a crucial relationship, for "the story of how race was naturalized, made part of the ordinary, is both linked to and overflows from that of the Empire." Race and whiteness were connected, if only because "for nearly all imperialists, the British race was an exclusively white one."[47]

The Williams Theses

When we discuss the importance of slavery in the eighteenth-century empire, we come quickly to an evaluation of the famous theses of Eric Williams. Williams highlighted how slavery, especially in the West Indies, was fundamental to the economic prosperity of Britain in the first half of the eighteenth century, undergirding every aspect of imperial policy and imperial ambition. His foundational work, *Capitalism and Slavery,* has dated surprisingly little in the eighty years since its first publication in 1944, even in its tone, which is the aspect of historical writing on this subject that often makes work seem outmoded between generations of historical writing. But its reception has waxed and waned over time. By the turn of the twenty-first century, the interrelated set of theses in Williams's work had been relegated to being thought of as interesting, but not proven, arguments that had a large element of overstatement about them.

The role of slavery in creating wealth in eighteenth-century England was relegated to a second-order issue when considering how England developed in the eighteenth century. The myopic nature of English historiography meant that British and imperial perspectives were often discarded in accounts of industrialization firmly focused on England, while Williams's most contentious claim, that West Indian wealth was essential for the accumulation of capital that fed into industrialization, was ignored or even patronized. The prevailing interpretation of the causes of the Industrial Revolution were internalist: it occurred because of what was happening in England from the late seventeenth century, with coal, energy, and the leviathan of London far more important as drivers of economic development than overseas trade and the contributions of slave-generated commerce. Another interpretation is that relatively high male wages in England forced entrepreneurs to seek technological solutions to substitute for expensive labor costs, while the arrival in large quantities of Indian textiles, used to fund the Atlantic slave trade in West Africa, forced manufacturers to match the quality of Indian textiles through developing cottons and calicoes that suited European and African tastes.

The same process also occurred for North America, the most dynamic area for British exports, where demanding American settlers were a massive market for British goods, but only if those goods met American tastes. Perhaps more influential than any of these interpretations has been the argument that British institutions favorable to the rule of law and the protection of private property created in the aftermath of the Glorious Revolution of 1688–89 and the after-effects of the late seventeenth-century scientific revolution, as well as the Enlightenment belief that knowledge should be used for entrepreneurial ends, were what triggered Britain's industrial rise. These themes were also advanced as explanations for British contributions to the "Great Divergence" that led to the West overtaking the East as the wealthiest and most dynamic section of the world economy around 1800.[48]

Recently, however, the arguments put forward by Williams have had a renaissance, with renewed appreciation for the strength of his arguments where he is most convincing—the centrality of slavery and the plantation system to British wealth and imperial geopolitics in the first half of the eighteenth century. His British near contemporary Richard Pares connected finance, trade, and war in an early conceptualization of the fiscal-military state, and produced a pioneering case study of a West India fortune created in Nevis and translated into British wealth that fits excellently into the new emphasis, in such things as the Legacies of British Slave-Ownership project from University College London, on the lasting ways in which British institutions and individual wealth had a West Indian origin.[49]

The reasons behind the renewed popularity of a historiography last prominent in the mid-twentieth century are complex and are connected to contemporary politics as much as with changing historical fashion. But three findings are influential. Wealth derived from Africa and Asia was pivotal in British economic development, a process that was evolutionary rather than revolutionary, and was highly connected to an "Industrious Revolution," in which demand factors, such as British (and African) tastes for Indian fabrics fueled consumption.[50] Overseas trade is especially important in such developments. It was not just imports coming into Britain that were important in increasing consumption and economic growth. Exports of manufactured goods to the rapidly growing and extremely prosperous residents of British North America brought about a range of positive effects for the British economy.[51]

And the multiplier effects of slave-related economic activity on the industrial and financial infrastructure of eighteenth-century Britain is increasingly appreciated, with slavery vital to developing industries such as copper, iron, and guns.[52] Plantation profits played a crucial role in making the fiscal-military state of the eighteenth century a success with consumption taxes gained from plantation produce helping to redistribute wealth from taxpayers and government creditors to merchants and manufacturers, especially in emerging industrial regions such as Lancashire, a region heavily dependent upon Atlantic trade. Further, the plantation trade stimulated process, product, and financial innovations that in effect created hothouse conditions for the encouragement of entrepreneurial activities.[53]

These arguments are backed up by empirical data which prove how the polemicists in the early eighteenth century were right in arguing that the wealth of the plantations based on slave labor was essential for British growth. If we accept, as we should and as contemporaries insisted, that the colonies were politically and economically integral to the spatial limits of Britain, then colonial wealth added massively to British prosperity. British America accounted for 34 percent of total British imperial wealth in 1774, with the wealth of the plantations comprising 21 percent. If we add the per capita wealth of plantation America, including the value of enslaved people, as a component of personal wealth, to that of England and Wales, then per capita wealth increases by £11.62, or 22 percent. If Scotland and Ireland are included in such calculations, then per capita wealth drops by £12.30. Thus, the wealth of America was sufficient to make up for the economic loss that England suffered by including within its realm the three Celtic kingdoms of Wales, Scotland, and Ireland.[54]

What this data suggests is that the most profitable part of the most dynamic sector of the eighteenth-century economy was hidden in plain sight: slavery and the slave trade. It is appropriate that we bring slavery and the slave trade from the shadows into its rightful position as central to British society and economy. We can see its importance in Thomas Truxes's authoritative survey of the overseas trade of British America. Citing Pares, who wrote that "colonization and empire-building are above all economic acts undertaken for economic reasons and very seldom for any others," Truxes argues that "without the slave trade and chattel slavery, the overseas trade of British America could not have existed in the form—and on the scale—that it did."[55]

The importance of the Caribbean to British society and economy was more than just its financial contributions. The plantations were a new economic form which connects more to the hyper-capitalism of today than to what we might think of as traditional merchant capitalism. Plantations were postmodern because they replaced "labor" as a factor of production with "capital" in the form not of robots, as today, but of enslaved people. Commodification was thus a key contribution of the plantation system to models of capitalist development: "plantations operated in a relatively free market, employed advanced management and agronomic techniques and raised funds for their extremely capital-intensive operations through complex global credit relations."[56]

Slavery and the American Revolution

In summary, the first half of the eighteenth century was the sole period in British history where state and popular support for the plantation complex, a complex reliant completely upon slave labor, was unwavering. Planters enjoyed healthy profits, an efficient slave trade, favorable legislation in Britain, and minimal public opposition to slavery. They were treated with great favoritism in an empire in which they not only enjoyed advantageous conditions but were supported by the powerful British navy. Britain facilitated colonial leaders' access to imperial power brokers and metropolitan merchants and cultivated a political system that systematically favored colonial commerce. It used its state power to protect slavery in the courts at a time when most Britons were either comfortable with or indifferent to the system of racial domination that sustained planter rule and enabled plantation wealth.

Although vested interests diverted capital and enterprise into rent-seeking activities, as early as 1700 and through to the American Revolution, the success of the American plantations and their ability to advance mercantile profits in Britain were noticeable. In addition, planters' capacity to provide desirable products like sugar and tobacco to make life more enjoyable for British people made them valuable parts of a flourishing empire. Moreover, the multiplier effects that helped transport links and manufacturing capacity to be improved while increasing useful knowledge and sustaining the political power of ruling elites showed that mercantilism worked. The highly performing plantation economies lifted British prosperity and laid down long-term social and economic advancements that made the Industrial Revolution not only possible but increasingly likely. It is hardly unusual, therefore, that William Pitt the Elder could declare in the mid-1750s that sugar planters should be thought of in the same way "as the landed interest of this kingdom," it being "a barbarism to consider them otherwise."[57]

Pitt's comments cast light on an issue that has become a matter of contention in the contemporary United States, due to the remarkable success of the *New York Times*' 1619 Project in reshaping the historiographical agenda about the historical importance of slavery in the United States, including in the colonial period. Its principal claim is to insist that the true start of American history should be in 1619, with the arrival of the first African enslaved people to Virginia, rather than its customary dating to the Declaration of Independence on July 4, 1776. Making slavery a more central theme in American history is a laudable and desirable aim, though scholars of the pre-revolutionary British Atlantic world have emphasized the importance of slavery as a fundamental institution shaping a great deal of what happened in early America for many years. It was a capitalist world, with slavery as a major driver of economy, society, and politics, for "Capitalism made the Atlantic World go around, from the ships that moved people and goods from one coast to another, to the silver dug from the mountains of Mexico and Peru and minted with coins, to radically commodified labor in the form of enslaved persons forcibly transported from distant places and turned en masse to producing commodities from which their alienation was total."[58]

Where the 1619 Project has been most controversial among historians is the role assigned to slavery in the coming of the American Revolution.[59] As Daryl Michael Scott writes: "If race has been identified almost everywhere in the American founding among professional historians, it is also true that few professional historians or the public have accepted that slavery was even a tertiary cause of the American Revolution."[60] An imperial perspective allows for a wider understanding of this issue, one based on the close interplay between Britain, the Caribbean, and West Africa in the provision of enslaved people to the mid-eighteenth-century plantations. We support the idea of the American Revolution as a counterrevolution but not in the terms that have been expressed about it being a counterrevolution in support of maintaining slavery.[61] White Americans, especially slaveholders, it is argued, became irate when they learned that Blacks had forged an informal alliance with the British because of Lord Dunmore's notorious proclamation in 1775 that enslaved people who left their masters to join British forces would gain their freedom.[62]

The truth was that Britain was committed fully to the institution of slavery, as much if not more so than slaveholding Patriots in North America. Indeed, for many Americans, including Thomas Jefferson, who launched an angry tirade against Britain's policies in regard to the slave trade in *A Summary View of the Rights of British America* (1774), British commitment to the continuation of the Atlantic slave trade was a principal point of contention between the Thirteen Colonies and the imperial government.[63] Jefferson was a leader in a campaign against the continuation of the Atlantic slave trade to Virginia, believing from his brief and unhappy experience as a slave trader that participation in the slave trade was a means whereby Britain ensnared people like himself in debt. Jefferson and other wealthy and established planters had ulterior motives, however, in opposing the slave trade. As Virginia governor Francis Fauquier argued in 1762, "old Settlers who have bred great Quantity of Slaves, and would make a Monopoly of them by a Duty which they hope would amount to a prohibition" were waging a class war against "the rising Generation who want Slaves." What Americans felt about defending slavery thus depended very much upon their personal perspectives and perceived self-interest.[64] Britain paid little attention to Jefferson's strident arguments that stopping the Atlantic slave trade would be economically beneficial because the West Indian slave trade was extremely lucrative and essential for the prosperity of a region in which enslaved people working on sugar plantations suffered terrible health. Virginia was but a small player in a British slave trading system focused on the Caribbean.

The British West Indies required large numbers of enslaved people to maintain and grow their plantations, as was outlined above. Britain provided such enslaved people in substantial numbers, with the size of the Atlantic slave trade increasing remarkably in the years immediately preceding the American Revolution. The annual number of enslaved Africans boarding British-flagged ships rose from just under 5,000 in the late seventeenth century to over 33,000 in the third quarter of the eighteenth century. By this time, Britain was the latest national carrier of slaves across the Atlantic, ferrying 43 percent of all Africans ensnared in the Middle Passage. Some of these carriers came from North America, notably Rhode Island, although American involvement in the slave trade was hampered by the fact that Americans had few trade goods, with the partial exception of rum, that Africans wanted and that could persuade them to sell captive Africans into transatlantic slavery.[65]

Indeed, British involvement with the slave trade only increased as abolition—a movement of limited to no importance before the 1780s—developed. The slave trade peaked in 1799 and 1800, when Britain transported over 48,000 enslaved people per annum.[66] British Atlantic slaving especially flourished during the period before the American Revolution. Between 1763 and 1775, Britain transported 391,635 enslaved people to their colonial possessions. The trade ramped up in the years before the Declaration of Independence in 1776, with 164,395 enslaved people transported between 1771 and 1775 and a remarkable 69,668 enslaved people in 1774 and 1775.[67] If Americans doubted British commitment to expanding Atlantic slavery, these figures should have reassured them.

There were, of course, people in Britain who were fervent opponents of slavery, like the London activist Granville Sharp. Nevertheless, "Sharp worked tirelessly against the institution of slavery everywhere within the British Empire after 1772, but for many years in England he would stand nearly alone."[68] The most important early abolitionists lived in the Quaker heartland of Philadelphia, such as Anthony Benezet, John Woolman, and Benjamin Lay.[69]

British imperialists went in other directions, however, than those advocated by the tiny group of early abolitionists. Britain showed little interest after 1763 in developing new settler colonies in North America and concentrated on establishing plantations in the southern Caribbean. The big money went to areas suitable for slave-based plantation development. British commitment to slavery was almost total, meaning that "slavery in the British Empire survived the American Revolution because the British government wanted it to do so."[70] The slavery interest was extremely powerful and in 1763 its influence was at its peak. Many officials, moreover, who shaped the British Empire's post-war policy had interests in or connections to the West Indies or to the slave trade or slavery and thought that one way to personal fortune and imperial influence was to get involved in land speculation and building plantations.[71]

Britain's Hostility to Non-Whites

Britain matched its commitment both to slavery and to settler interests by actions as much as by deeds. It was perfectly capable of protecting white people—whose prejudices it shared—against "Merciless Savages and Domestic Insurrectionists." As William Knox, one of the rare early abolitionists with American experience, lamented, it was "most reproachful to this country that there are more than five hundred thousand of its subjects for whom the legislature has never shown the slightest regard."[72] Indeed, "to detect a new climate of humanitarianism in responses to the problems posed by the incorporation of new subjects is probably to claim too much, although it is undeniable that concern for non-British peoples featured increasingly both in official rhetoric and in public debate."[73] That concern, however, was only apparent when non-British peoples behaved submissively and acknowledged British power. When they resisted, Britain dealt with such resistance extremely harshly.

An imperial approach allows us to see how the British state met and surpassed in its ferocity toward Indigenous peoples and enslaved people the worst excesses of white supremacist North American settlers. If North American settlers were worried that British attitudes toward slave rebellion were too accommodating, then what happened in the great Jamaican slave rebellion of 1760 should have eased those worries. The Jamaican slave revolt was the greatest challenge to imperial rule from non-white British subjects until the Sepoy Rebellion of 1757. Led by Wager, or Apongo, an enslaved person, reputedly once a prince in Dahomey, thousands of enslaved rebels in several parts of the country exploded into rebellion in April and May 1760, burning plantations and killing sixty whites. The rebellion was put down with difficulty by a combination of white militia, British armed forces, and Maroon allies of the British. The consequences of the revolt were a massive bloodletting on the part of the British. Hundreds of slaves were transported to Honduras and dozens were executed, often in grisly ways. White Jamaicans enacted a series of laws designed to control enslaved people so they would not revolt again. Their firmness succeeded—there was no enslaved rebellion that occurred in Jamaica until 1831-32. Jamaicans were convinced that if white people stood firm and united and they were willing to use excessive violence, then their security could be protected. Their actions, however, horrified Britons at home, who were scandalized by the brutality of white Jamaicans and the imperial state which supported them.[74]

In short, the British were hardly the friends of enslaved Africans. An imperial perspective makes that clear in ways that the American-centric interpretation of the coming of the Revolution central to the 1619 Project does not. It also shows that British humanitarianism in the 1760s was shallowly based. Grand claims of changing attitudes by the British to its imperial subjects that envisioned enslaved people, Indigenous peoples, and Catholics having the sorts of rights commonly enjoyed by white settlers need to be tempered by the unwillingness of imperial officials to have their authority challenged and by the general failure of efforts to make effective imperial policy toward marginal groups in the empire. In short, "the record of British governments in their dealings with the empire's new subjects around the Atlantic was one of almost unrelieved failure."[75] It was unable and unwilling to protect North American Indigenous peoples from settler depredations, and its actions in the 1760s and 1770s toward Black Caribs in St. Vincent were shameful. It demonstrated a brutal logic of cruelty toward enslaved West Indians so that the plantation machine continued to produce substantial profits at the expense of Black bodies. And its endorsement of East India Company policies in Bengal led to the disastrous, man-created famine of 1770, for which the East India Company was responsible and in which many millions of people died in what was "one of the great catastrophes of the eighteenth century, and indeed, of modern times."[76]

Moreover, any dissension against imperial dictates was met with force. Britain had a powerful army and was not afraid to use it to keep its empire of coercion secure, and, as in Pontiac's War of 1763-65 and in the Black Carib War of 1772-73, to keep Indigenous pretensions in check. Subversive doctrines could not be allowed to spread from one part of the empire to another. Subjects needed to be reminded, as the House of Commons resolved in 1763, that "true liberty" required a "due veneration for the legislative authority of the kingdom and a perfect obedience to the law."[77] Authoritarianism was bred deep into the fabric of imperial life. Britain's encouragement of the brutal coercion of enslaved people and Indigenous peoples to further imperial aims were evidence that the iron fist of Britain could always be drawn from any soft glove. An empire of coercion was not a gentle empire.

Slavery was an institution that brought the British Empire together in the eighteenth century. Britain relied upon slavery for a considerable proportion of its wealth, while those parts of British North America where slavery was not well established, such as the northern colonies, were integrated into the plantation system through trade with the Caribbean. Ireland and Scotland were similarly connected to slavery through their trading relationships with British America, as were Senegambia and Bengal, which provided people (Senegambia) and cotton fabrics (Bengal) that helped sustain the Atlantic slave trade.

An imperial perspective highlights just how much slavery integrated the empire prior to 1776. It helps us understand why perceptions of how important the plantation colonies were inspired plans to reform and "improve" the enlarged and increasingly profitable, if troublesome, Atlantic possessions after the Seven Years' War. Slavery did not "cause" the American Revolution. If anything, transatlantic slavery was an institution that provided unity to diverse imperial possessions. The conflict between the British Empire and white settlers in the Thirteen Colonies was a conflict that arose between polities that were in the main friendly to slavery—abolitionism hardly existed in the British Atlantic except in pockets of Quaker politics in Philadelphia—and thus the American Revolution was a very different event in regard to slavery than what happened in the split between North and South in the 1850s, leading to the Civil War. That does not mean that slavery was unimportant. Far from it. Slavery shaped almost every aspect of the empire in the mid-eighteenth century, making it a classic precondition of revolution, not causing it but influencing imperial policies about how the empire needed to be reformed so that the British Atlantic of West Indian and North American colonies could provide even more wealth and even greater geopolitical strength in a world of European empires all dependent upon transatlantic slavery for prosperity and power.

FOUR

Settlers and Indigenous Peoples

WHITE SETTLERS WERE BECOMING increasingly powerful in America in this period. The most important fact about eighteenth-century British North America was the remarkable growth of the power, wealth, and influence of an expanding and expansive British North American white population—a fact which set these colonies apart from the British West Indies, where the demographic growth of the white settler population was anemic, though the advance of the total population, due to the extraordinary in-migration of enslaved people through the Atlantic slave trade, was strong.[1] The first half of the eighteenth century in British America "was a period of extraordinary growth . . . in terms of the volume and value of all colonial trades and in the territorial, demographic, economic, social, political and cultural development of the American colonies." New colonies were established in Georgia, the Virgin Islands, and Nova Scotia, while Britain "consolidated and extended [its] areas of effective occupation in all the older colonies." Metropolitan writers started to take notice of this growth and how valuable the colonies were becoming, noting that "their welfare became a prime consideration in the state's decision to invest heavily in imperial conflicts with France and Spain between 1739 and 1763." Victory in the Seven Years' War advanced expansion and reinforced the value of this area of the world to Britain, with nine new Atlantic and one African colony being added to the British Empire beginning in 1763.[2]

The most dramatic expression of settler growth was in the demography of British North America, which was transformed in the eighteenth century. In 1700, the total population of Europeans (Britons, French, and Spaniards) in their empires in North America was less than 330,000. The Indigenous population was between 1.4 and 1.6 million people, many of whom, such as the 189,000 Indigenous people in the Great Plains, 221,000 in California, 175,000 in the Pacific Northwest, and 160,000 in the subarctic, lived lives entirely separate from European settlers. In 1700, 85 percent of the people living on the North American continent were Indigenous. If we add the 147,000 people (mostly Black) living in the British West Indies, the Indigenous percentage drops to about 78 percent.[3]

In 1800, however, the situation was reversed. The Indigenous population was still substantial—about the same as Scotland's population within the British Empire—but had declined by over 30 percent to one million. Meanwhile, the settler population of America, the overwhelming majority of which was in the new nation of the United States, had multiplied to a remarkable 5.6 million. Thus, the percentage of people in North America who were Indigenous in 1800 was 15 percent, the same percentage of Americans who were European in the 1700 population. If we added the West Indies to this population mix the Indigenous share of the total population in the region would have been about 12 percent.

The increase in population was among both whites and Blacks in North America and among Blacks in the West Indies. In 1700, the white population of British America was 266,200, of whom 234,000 (88 percent) lived in North America. In 1750, the white population had increased to 1,235,000, of whom 1,190,000 (96 percent) lived in North America. By 1770 that population had soared to 2,290,400, of whom 2,251,400 (98 percent) lived in North America. The Black population had increased dramatically as well, from 146,000 in 1700 to 537,000 in 1750, and to 901,000 in 1770.[4] In 1750, slightly more Blacks lived in the West Indies than in North America; by 1770 slightly more Blacks—almost all of whom were enslaved—lived in North America than in the Caribbean—where the great majority of Blacks were enslaved but where there was a growing population of free people of color.

The North American Black population was quite different from that in the West Indies. Few Blacks in North America by mid-century had been born in Africa and brought to the region by the Middle Passage. North America, alone of slaveholding societies in the Atlantic world, had a naturally increasing enslaved population. By contrast, the Black population of the British West Indies, reflecting a dreadful demography where the population suffered a natural decrease of between 2 percent and 3 percent every year, was mostly African born, with population increases dependent on a vibrant and ever-growing Atlantic slave trade. A high proportion of

Black deaths came from malaria and fevers, but an appreciable number also occurred from malnutrition, overwork, and mistreatment, especially on sugar plantations.[5] The overall trend in the Black population, however, was growth. By 1770, the number of Blacks in British America approached the number of Indigenous people, while the number of whites was significantly larger than either population.

The older colonies were by the mid-eighteenth century extensively settled, with most Indigenous peoples reduced heavily in numbers and even more so in influence. The areas of confrontation between settlers and Indigenous peoples had moved much further west than in the seventeenth century, to the Ohio and Mississippi Valleys.[6] Population figures were high and were increasing in every region of British America except in the British Caribbean, where horrific mortality rates among both Blacks and whites kept population increase dependent on migration through the Atlantic slave trade.[7] In North America, the population increased by 23 percent between 1750 and 1770 in New England, by 23 percent in the Chesapeake, by 23 percent in the Middle Colonies, and by a remarkable 38 percent in the Lower South. The Conquest of Canada from 1759 added 120,000 people to the settler population of British America, including many French Catholics in Quebec.

By 1760, British North America contained 1.6 million Blacks and whites, most living in well-populated communities in river valleys and among cultivated land. The area they lived in was increasingly thought of as a single continent, extending from Nova Scotia to South Carolina. Central to this vison was the Ohio River Valley as key to white settlement in the American interior, so that "whichever imperial power could take control of its rivers and integrate colonial settlement in a single, defensible whole might drive out the others."[8] This new continental geographic understanding was revolutionary in its implications. As Thomas Paine observed, "there is something absurd in supposing a Continent to be perpetually governed by an island."[9] Settlers considered it their inviolable right to occupy and develop all of North America, including land occupied by Indigenous peoples.

It was the peopling of British North America that caused this geographical expansion and continental integration. The demographic filling in of spaces on maps meant that this expansion can be seen as a "system" that grew out of "a geographic space tied by trading concerns and defined by the rivalry of states that did not have the capacity to project power effectively." Geographic integration that was dependent upon population growth meant that "regions that had been isolated from Atlantic markets became embedded in them, and entrepots emerged that were regional nodes bound up into broader Atlantic networks."[10]

Such a description suggests a peaceful integration around processes of modernization, but, in fact, this movement of peoples, goods, and ideas started conflict, not least during the Seven Years' War when fighting over the Ohio River Valley showed how vital that region was for the future expansion of both the French and British Empires. An even greater area of conflict was to emerge between growing British influence in the American interior and the consolidation of Indigenous power in the American West. Indigenous sovereignty prevailed everywhere across the trans-Mississippi West. It was only with the establishment of the new American republic after 1800 that this large-scale Indigenous power was challenged by aggressive settler colonialism. At mid-century, however, Indigenous power was usually unchallenged outside major centers of European population.[11]

Benjamin Franklin and Population

The growth of the European-descended settler population led to a famous and notorious pioneering tract in political economy, written in 1751 and published in 1760, Benjamin Franklin's *Observations on the Increase of Mankind*.[12] Franklin (1706–90) was a fervent imperialist before becoming a reluctant Patriot in the late 1760s. He was an inveterate American booster who imagined an imperial British North America with a glorious future as the population and economy of the mainland American colonies multiplied over time. He attributed the massive population increase of his native Pennsylvania to the ability of young Americans in the northern colonies to marry early, and thus have large families, because they had easy access to abundant and cheap land. That land, Franklin omitted in saying, came from Indigenous Americans, meaning that Native American dispossession through the relentless push of settler colonialism was central to Franklin's vision of future American prosperity. Early marriages in an age without effective contraception meant lots of children. Good nutrition and excellent health meant that most of those children would survive to adulthood. In these circumstances, natural population increase was bound to be strong, with families of six or more children common.

Franklin also argued that the incidence of marriage was more frequent in British North America than in Britain. It was certainly more frequent than in the British West Indies, a region that Franklin disparaged for its appalling demographic data, which he attributed to the malign effects of slavery. Franklin was not alone in denigrating the West Indies as morally unsound and economically unstable, even as the British Caribbean entered a period of prolonged economic prosperity. The rich sugar colonies of the British West Indies were, according to Bostonian James Otis, "a compound mixture of *English, Indian* and *Negro*," ruled over by tyrants who liked nothing better than "to whip and scourge the poor Negroes according to their own brutal will and pleasure."[13]

Not all these white American children came from regularized marriages. Colonists came increasingly to reject the idea that sex was only possible during courtship or in marriage. Illegitimacy rates soared in colonial North America from the middle of the eighteenth century, as did rates of venereal disease. They were even higher in the Caribbean, which had a sexual culture all its own, with, among whites, infrequent marriage, extraordinarily high rates of illegitimacy, and considerable female sexual agency, and, between white men and Black women, high rates of sexual violence including rape.[14] Franklin welcomed the loosening of sexual mores, which is not surprising since he himself had an illegitimate son, who went on to become the governor of New Jersey. He mocked older attitudes that condemned illegitimacy as immoral. He wrote a witty tract about a Connecticut woman called Polly Baker who was repeatedly brought before the courts for having illegitimate children. Polly was unrepentant. She defended herself, in Franklin's ventriloquist voice, by stating that instead of being punished for sexual irregularity, she should be commended for bringing into the world white children who added to the population and were future workers, increasing American wealth.[15]

Franklin's analysis contained an explicit racism. The aim of an American population policy, Franklin believed, was to increase the number of white people while reducing the number of Black and Indigenous people. Franklin was one of the first advocates of an ideology of whiteness and white supremacy, although in this respect he was following attitudes expressed and then put into law in Jamaica following a highly damaging enslaved revolt in 1760.[16] Whites were superior, in his view, to inferior African, Native American, and German populations. Franklin derided German settlers as "Palatine Boors" and "Aliens," asking why they should be allowed to "establish their Language and Manners to the Exclusion of ours." He complained that America, through the immigration of "swarthy" Europeans and "the Sons of Africa," was becoming full of "Blacks and Tawneys," when it should have been thinking of ways of "increasing the lovely White[s]."[17] His racist views reflected his geographical position in Pennsylvania. Over 90 percent of the population of Canada and the American North were European-descended, compared with 40 percent in the American South and under 10 percent in the British West Indies. The result of rapid population growth in British America, Franklin asserted, was a rebalancing of the relative importance of the colonies as against Britain. This development spelled no geopolitical dangers for Britain, Franklin thought, because all of these white Americans would be firm defenders of empire. Franklin believed that "there is not a single native of our country who is not firmly attached to our King by principle and affection." That affection was presumed to be long-lasting and permanent.[18]

Franklin did hint, however, at a significant division between Britain's Atlantic possessions. The northern colonies, he argued, would continue to grow, and prosper without Britain doing anything, due to the power of strong demographic growth in a country where abundant land made high standards of living very achievable. It was in these colonies that Britain, Franklin insisted, should devote its attention, as the rewards, in respect of the "Increase of Trade," were likely to be greatest. Accurately predicting the future, he saw the northern colonies surpassing the plantation colonies in wealth and power as its population surged, which, of course, is the history of the United States in the nineteenth century. He proposed reducing the expenditure on defense in the plantation colonies and wanted Britain to stop pandering to the interests of overmighty West Indian planters. An early abolitionist, living in the abolitionist heartland of Philadelphia, Franklin foreshadowed Adam Smith in seeing slavery as diverting resources from worthwhile and sustainable long-term goods. Slavery, he argued, was economically problematic and morally indefensible.[19]

All this was in the future. What people noticed most was that North America's demographic growth meant the colonies were going to be increasingly valuable to Britain. Franklin's views were echoed thirteen years later by the richest man and largest slaveholder in Maryland, the center of British immigration to the colonies in the years immediately before the American Revolution. Charles Carroll of Carrollton exclaimed that "the growing population of the colonies, increased by such a considerable influx of newcomers, bids fair to render British America in a century into the most populous and of course the most potent part of the world. I fancy many in England begin to entertain the same opinion."[20]

Standard of Living

Franklin's rosy summary of settler demographic prospects, free from any Malthusian warnings that rapid population growth would advance the chance of famine, has been partly confirmed by recent studies of the standard of living of white Americans in the middle of the eighteenth century. American incomes were high—equal, or slightly superior, to those in England—but these incomes bought a great deal more of a reasonable basket of commodities necessary for comfortable living than was possible for the average English person. Most of these advances in colonial income occurred before Benjamin Franklin was born, in a sustained economic boom between 1650 and 1700—the years, not coincidentally, when the switch to African chattel slavery and large-scale plantation agriculture occurred. By 1700, the plantation South was the richest place in British North America, with real income per capita (for both whites and Blacks) of £18.30 per annum in the Upper South and £24.30 per annum in the Lower South, more than the £11.50 per annum in Britain and appreciably more than the £7.70 per annum in New England and £10.10 in the Middle Colonies. Income growth, however, was slow between 1700 and 1774, with the average real income per capita increasing from £13.10 per annum in 1700 to £15.60 per annum in 1774, just slightly less in that year than the £15.70 per annum in Britain. Growth was strongest in the Middle Colonies and New England, where the gap with the South slowed over time, as real income per capita stayed constant in the Lower South and declined in the Upper South.[21]

Significantly, American wealth was distributed equally, even if servants and enslaved people are included in the figures. Egalitarianism increased among whites as the population of the egalitarian frontier grew much faster than less equal coastal America. Overall, however, the Thirteen Colonies were probably more inegalitarian in 1774 than in 1700, due to the substantial rise in the Black population, with most Blacks living at or a little above subsistence level.[22] In contrast to British North America, eighteenth-century Jamaica (the only West Indian place to date where a standard of living analysis has been attempted) was highly unequal. Indeed, it was the most unequal place on earth, if we look at inequality as marked by Gini coefficients. Whites received all the wealth of the island, with large planters and transatlantic merchants receiving so much income from sugar and slavery that they were easily the wealthiest people in the British Empire. The overwhelming Black majority population, on the other hand, was worked brutally and was kept, even in good times, at a standard of living that was below subsistence levels. When tough times arrived, enslaved people did not have enough to eat, they lived in inadequate houses, and they were dressed in rags. They were so poor that they starved to death, which added to the mortality rates brought about by working in the harsh environment of a sugar plantation.

The gap between the wealth distribution in Jamaica and that in the Thirteen Colonies helps explain how these two parts of the British Atlantic world were drifting apart in the mid-eighteenth century. A quite different situation concerned Canada. The addition of Quebec to the British Empire reduced average imperial wealth in the Americas. The residents of French North America may have had real wages less than three-quarters of the wages of people in New England, the poorest region in British North America, primarily due to high seigneurial taxes and low levels of immigration, though wages increased considerably after the Conquest in 1759 as the Quebec economy expanded quickly.[23] Thus, an imperial perspective shows both increasing wealth and inequality, if the West Indies is assessed alongside North America, and a reduction in wealth, once Canada is included.

The Imperial Economy

Colonial economic growth by per capita income may have been slow and steady, but what is most impressive around mid-century is the increase in the scale of American trade. English exports to North America increased tenfold between 1701 and 1705 and again between 1771 and 1775. Over that seventy-four-year period, exports to the West Indies grew by 444 percent, North American exports to England increased by 535 percent, and West Indian exports to England grew by 515 percent.

By the mid-eighteenth century, the trade between British America and England was very substantial. Exports to England, the vast majority of which came from the plantation colonies, amounted to £3,679,790 in 1761-65, of which just 6.6 percent came from the northern colonies. That figure had increased to £4,724,570 a decade later in 1771-75, with 9.2 percent of exports coming from the northern colonies. Imports from England were not as large but were also considerable, at £2,065,210 in 1761-65 and £2,870,126 in 1771-75, with the majority (62 percent) going to the northern colonies. If we just look at the balance of trade with England, then it was highly in favor of England in respect to trade with North America and strongly in favor of the West Indies in that sector of the trade.[24] The colonists also engaged in extensive trade with Ireland and Scotland. Irish exports to British America peaked at £556,400 between 1769 and 1772, with imports similarly amounting to £526,850.[25] Trade data for Scotland and the West Indies have yet to be compiled for the colonial period, but Scotland exported £236,570 to British North America between 1771 and 1775 and imported goods worth £535,100.[26]

These figures are indicative of the growing wealth of British America over the course of the eighteenth century. To take Jamaica as one example: the colony's wealth increased from £4,833,734 in 1722 to £10,338,236 in 1754, and to £27,680,517 in 1778.[27] By 1774, British American wealth was rapidly approaching that of the metropolis itself. English wealth was £278 million, or £42.3 per capita. British American wealth was equivalent to 58 percent of the wealth of England, or 37 percent of the combined wealth of England and British America. Wealth in British America was heavily concentrated in the plantation areas, especially the West Indies. The plantation colonies contained wealth amounting to £104,358,000, which was 64 percent of the total wealth of British America. Non-plantation America, which included the northern colonies and much of the piedmont areas of the southern colonies, was not insubstantial at £57,688,000, but was not much more than the £51,926,000 of the much less populated West Indies. The wealth of plantation America was seen most clearly in the individual wealth of white people. People in non-plantation areas had slightly more wealth per white capita, at £46.20 per person, than the £42.10 per white capita in both England and Wales. Wealth in the southern colonies was higher, at £92.70 per white capita and a still high £54.70 if Blacks are included in these figures. Wealth was especially high in the Lower South at £420 per white capita and of a different order altogether in the British West Indies, where 45,000 white people had an average wealth of £1,042.50.[28]

West Indian wealth was especially high in Jamaica and was likely also extremely high in the small eastern Caribbean islands of Grenada, Nevis, and St. Kitts, though figures are not available for these colonies. The outlier was Barbados, where a comparatively large white population had wealth only one-fifth the amount of average wealth in Jamaica. In 1774, the recorded personal wealth, excluding real estate, of the ten richest Jamaicans who left wills and inventories was £246,872, compared with £101,308 for the ten richest South Carolinians whose wealth was inventoried after they died in that year. South Carolina, it should be noted, was easily the richest colony in British North America. Yet there were four rich Jamaicans—headed by the London Lord Mayor, William Beckford, who had much of his assets held in Britain but who also left £81,621 in Jamaica, mostly in the form of 1,356 enslaved people valued at £70,713—who were considerably wealthier than South Carolinian Peter Manigault, easily the richest man in British North America who died in 1774. No one in the northern colonies approached that amount of wealth, with the wealthiest man in Philadelphia who died in 1774 having an inventoried estate of £8,336 and the wealthiest man in New England having an inventoried wealth of £4,188.[29]

Not surprisingly, merchants in Britain, Ireland, and the northern colonies of America tried to access the wealth of the West Indies through trade. The sugar colonies and the southern mainland colonies that exported rice and tobacco were classic staple colonies. They grew tropical goods for sale in Europe, using the labor of oppressed African slaves, who gained little themselves of the wealth that they produced for others. Sales of tropical products provided money for buying more enslaved people from Africa and for purchasing European manufactures, either for advancing plantation productivity or for purposes of consumption. The staples approach emphasizes the expansion of a land-abundant and labor-poor region that was driven by the expectation of potential rents from the cultivation of a staple for sale in the metropolitan economy.[30]

The West Indies, however, increasingly depended upon imperial economic protection.[31] The protection afforded West Indian sugar planters led to a serious distortion in the Atlantic economy and caused problems in the American colonies where settlers outside plantation economies felt that they were paying for the wealth of much richer colonists.[32] It was high differential tariffs on sugar that preserved the British sugar market for British West Indian suppliers, meaning that Britain consumed a third of all sugar imported into eighteenth-century Europe. Protection, however, kept

British sugar prices artificially high and dependent on the strong political power of the West India lobby in England.

The British were high-cost producers, unable to compete without protection in a free market with the rapidly growing output of French Saint-Domingue. French trade to the West Indies grew more rapidly than the British trade, and French merchants dominated the re-export trade of sugar within Europe and the trade of coffee to northern Europe.[33] The northern colonies, by contrast, operated according to a different model, one we can term the Malthusian approach, characterized as such because it was driven by population growth. The presence of these Malthusian colonies is what distinguished the British Empire from its competitors. It became the principal market for diversified manufactured exports from Britain.[34]

This process was the "Americanization" of British trade, with Britain moving from a wool export trade to Europe to selling abroad a diversified set of manufactured products. The rapidly growing population of British North America demanded British imported goods. If exports to the Americas disappeared and the resources used in their manufacture were left idle, the reduction of British income would have been about 8 percent of national income and about one-quarter of manufacturing output.[35] The growth in American trade was thus central to the beginnings of modern economic growth, usually associated with the first cotton textile factories in the Industrial Revolution. It coincided with a reorientation of British foreign trade away from Europe toward British America.[36] While plantations were certainly important in advancing British economic growth, as sugar made up 11 percent of English imports between 1699 and 1701 and 19 percent between 1772 and 1774, increasingly, what was transformative was England's own agricultural revolution and the large amount of manufactures sent by England to satisfy the consumer demands of a wealthy and growing British North American settler population. By 1772–74, English exports of manufactures to the Americas, at £3,9881,000, was appreciably greater than the £2,684,000 of mainly plantation imports.[37] The British Empire was singular not in having slave plantations, something shared with other empires, notably the French, but in having a large market of settlers for British goods.[38]

How did the northern colonies, with their miniscule exports to Britain, pay for all these manufactures? They did so by providing goods, like livestock, fish, lumber, candles, ironware, and building supplies, to the West Indies. The northern colonies' economies evolved so that the residents' purchases of European products were financed by the sale of services, timber, and foodstuffs to the Caribbean. These exports supported the West Indies' specialization in staple production, and without them the islands would have struggled to find affordable temperate commodities, as was the case for Saint-Domingue, which did not have a place comparable to New England to supply it.[39]

The West Indian trade was especially important in New England, where "trade with the Caribbean . . . was the most dynamic sector in New England overseas trade in the period after the War of the Austrian Succession." It fostered a powerful merchant class and a strong shipbuilding industry and came from a deliberate choice made by Boston merchants in the mid-seventeenth century to favor developing trade with Caribbean slave economies.[40] That trade grew exponentially after 1750, quadrupling between the 1750s and the early 1770s until the share of New England's exports traveling to the West Indies was 64 percent in the early 1770s, more than to any other region.[41]

We can better understand this inter-imperial trade through an in-depth case study of 5,227 entrance and 4,620 clearance records from British naval office shipping lists for Kingston, Jamaica, between 1752 and 1769.[42] Jamaica was a powerful regional hub within the large British Atlantic economy, an economy in which North America, Ireland, and West Africa figured as important hinterlands. We cannot disentangle one imperial region from another, as by mid-century the economy of British America was highly integrated. The enormous profits made in West Indian plantation production only occurred because of supplies and provisions shipped by mainland North American colonists. The American Revolution promised to break this delicate system apart. The Barbadian planter George Walker, speaking to the House of Commons, listed the ways in which different regions played distinct roles in supplying the islands. "North America," he concluded, "is truly the granary of the West Indies."[43] We can make a similar observation about inter-island slave trading, an activity which supplemented the much larger Atlantic slave trade by distributing African enslaved people from the Caribbean to the British mainland colonies.[44]

The reality of the colonial British American economy, and to an extent its politics, as a "system" was understood by a few officials prone to systematic thinking from the 1740s onward. A remarkable set of documents produced in the 1740s by Robert Dinwiddie (1692–1770), surveyor-general of the southern colonies from 1739 to 1748 and lieutenant governor of Virginia between 1751 and 1758, provides "a snapshot of Britain's American and West Indian colonies during the 1740s," a period in which imperial rivalry with France and Spain was an urgent concern in London and in the colonies.[45] Dinwiddie saw the colonies in a wide perspective, valuing New England for its large population of men of military age who could be employed, as they were in the 1740s in unsuccessful sieges of Cartagena and again in 1762 in the occupation of Havana, in imperial military adventures. He assumed that British America was an integrated whole, showing that both plantation and non-plantation life were important and complemented each other. Dinwiddie put figures to his analysis, with New England and Jamaica the regions he thought most valuable to the empire, with shipping especially important for the former and plantation crops vital to the latter.

Dinwiddie concluded that the trade of America was "of inestimable value to the Nation of Great Britain," but he warned the Board of Trade, the Duke of Newcastle, and the prime minister, Henry Pelham, that Britain needed to pay attention to the expanding military and commercial strength of France. Overall, however, he saw the colonies as "a grand Source of Britain's Opulence," which were making "vast Progress," due "to the Blessing of Heaven," and, more concretely, to the "universal industry of the Planters, to the singular Felicity they have of framing their own laws, and to the generous Credit constantly indulged to them by the Merchants here."[46]

Indeed, by the time of the American Revolution, British export trade was not just "Americanized" but "globalized," oriented around the twin economies of providing manufactures to North American settlers and producing cottons, which were used as trade goods to purchase enslaved Africans for the West Indian plantation trade, as "presents" to secure the alliance of Indigenous peoples, and as commodities to satisfy a wealthy and growing North American settler population. Indeed, the British trade system in the second half of the eighteenth century was a "diamond shaped" integrated economy, connecting, through the commodities of cotton and sugar, the trade systems of South Asia, West Africa, Western Europe, and the Americas. Changes in demand and consumption in the Atlantic created new markets for textiles from India, meaning that increasingly the Indian and Atlantic worlds were closely integrated.[47] The global nature of British trade by the early 1770s, as the Industrial Revolution kicked off, within an imperial system with African, Asian, European, and American components meant that an enormous amount was at stake for Britain when the empire imploded into war and rebellion in the mid-1770s. It is possible that, in the absence of expanding colonial markets, the home market would have provided compensatory demand.[48] That is unlikely, for "without colonies, British revenues from exporting would have been reduced, but it is inconceivable that revenues would have fallen by an amount commensurate with the colonial market's actual share."[49]

Losing an imperial war therefore was likely to have severe economic consequences, consequences which were masked in retrospect by the fact that early industrialization proved such a boost to the British economy. The British knew this because they had the French example from the Seven Years' War immediately in front of them. The loss of Canada and Louisiana meant that France had a huge problem in provisioning and protecting its booming colonies in the West Indies, notably Saint-Domingue. To keep its plantation machine humming, the French were forced to rely on smuggling from New England. It was in the interest of empires in the age of mercantilism to maintain closed systems, as "much of the emergence of the Atlantic world took place in the context of state policies intended to hold a mercantilist grip on as large a share as possible of the newly explored overseas territories and trade routes, and to minimize the impact of outsiders."[50] Britain's settler revolt in the Thirteen Colonies thus was likely to break down this closed system and to accentuate an imperial crisis, as George Walker intuited in 1776. British defeat confirmed Walker's fears: it was a serious threat to other parts of the empire, which depended on settler purchases of British exports as well as exports of North American commodities. An integrated but closed system was extremely vulnerable in times of geopolitical disorder.[51]

The Effect of Growing Settler Power on Indigenous Peoples

The people most threatened by the growth of the British settler population and its wealth in the second quarter of the eighteenth century were Indigenous peoples. Native American power was still very strong even in places where Indigenous peoples had been battered by settlers for a century and a half, on the Atlantic coast and indeed in the whole eastern half of the continent. It would seem to be a place impossible for Indigenous peoples, a dead end against overwhelming settler power. The result of the Seven Years' War exposed Indigenous peoples in the East to a new unipolar world dominated by Britain. It was hugely challenging and led eventually to a lasting loss of land and autonomy. But Indigenous peoples in the East persevered, holding significant power bases east of the Mississippi well into the nineteenth century.[52]

Indigenous peoples, however, were fighting a losing battle against the remarkable demographic growth of the European settler population. By the 1750s, 1.5 million British colonists lived in mainland North America, outnumbering any other single group, whether Indigenous, French, or Spanish. The 1750s marked the moment of demographic transition, when newcomers first outnumbered Indigenous peoples.[53] Most Indigenous peoples in the areas where Europeans were pressing hard to settle saw colonists as a bigger threat to them than a distant king. This helps explain why so many Indigenous peoples supported Britain rather than American Patriots in the American Revolution.[54] They were right. American forces killed between two and four times as many Indigenous people during the War of American Independence as British and colonial forces did during the Seven Years' War and Pontiac's War combined, destroying Indigenous towns from the Carolinas to New York and devastating the Ohio Valley.[55] The American Revolution in Indian Country, where Indigenous peoples waged their own war of independence, mostly against American colonists, was a race war marked by an undistinguished destruction of all ages, sexes, and conditions in which the primary motivation for American colonists was to encroach on Indigenous land.[56]

As General Thomas Gage argued, no matter what boundaries Britain made to separate Indigenous peoples from settlers "the Frontier People are too Numerous, too Lawless and Licentious ever to be restrained." That meant, as Irish fur trader George Croghan argued in the extraordinarily violent Shawnee War (or Lord Dunmore's War) in western Virginia in 1774, that the "frontier people had too great a spirit . . . for killing Indians," a "spirit" which incensed Indigenous peoples. A deputation of Delawares, Munsees, and Mahicans in 1771 told three colonial governors that "unless you can fall upon some method of governing your people who live between the Great Mountains and the Ohio River, and who are now very numerous, it will be out of the Indians' power to govern their young men, for we assure you the black clouds begin to gather first in this country."[57]

Indigenous survival in the areas where settlers were numerous relied upon accommodation, which was nowhere better represented than by the Catawbas, a smallish confederacy located in the North Carolina piedmont. The Catawbas were able to maintain their territorial boundaries against Europeans until the early nineteenth century, thus demarcating limits for English colonialism in the Carolinas. They found it easy to repel Europeans—whom they derisively termed "nothings"—but in any event solidified their position in relation to the British Empire through a series of strategic alliances with the Carolinian colonies. The Catawbas were less concerned by European incursions than by the threat posed to them from the powerful Iroquois, or Haudenosaunee, confederation, hundreds of miles to the north. The Iroquois were an imperialist power who dominated the eastern woodlands of eastern North America, mainly through skilled diplomacy rather than through military might. They posed more of a threat to the Indigenous peoples of the southeast than did Europeans. The battles for power were between Cherokees, Creeks, Choctaws, and Chickasaws, with the Creeks being the most successful group in gaining some form of superiority over other tribes. The Native southeast was a violent battleground, a militarized landscape where lethal microbes, new technologies of killing, and colliding colonial interests fueled local wars. Southeastern Indians kept fighting and killing each other not so much because they were vulnerable to external European forces but because they remained so powerful.[58]

Central to Indigenous power relations with Europeans in the East in the first half of the eighteenth century was skilled diplomatic maneuvering by individual groups between different European powers. Negotiated interactions as much as conflict and colonialism in what historians working in the troubled Great Lakes region have termed a "Middle Ground" strategy shaped how Indigenous peoples framed their relationship with European empires. It was through relationships such as intermarriage that Indigenous peoples and Europeans moved to a state of relative equality in a dynamic fur-trading world where the balance of power was often in flux. Fur-trade marriages, for example, were ways for Europeans and Indigenous peoples to make alliances and were cemented through Indigenous customs and formalized by European trading companies or churches.[59]

These communities were relatively new polities, few of which had

Agostino Brunias (c. 1730–96), *Pacification with the Maroon Negroes*, 1780. Depicting the end of the First Carib War in St. Vincent, in 1773, this painting was converted to an engraving and misleadingly titled in Bryan Edwards, *An Historical Survey of the Island of Saint Domingo* . . . London: printed for J. Stockdale, 1801. (Brown Digital Repository, Brown University Library)

existed one hundred years prior and which were amalgams of survivors, refugees, and war captives that were produced by violent transitions in the late seventeenth and early eighteenth centuries.[60] Peter Wraxall from New York argued in mid-century that "to preserve the Ballance between us and the French is the great ruling Principle of the Modern Indian Politics."[61] A French official in the pays d'en haut region near the Great Lakes argued in 1736 that Indigenous peoples made "a treaty not to kill one another, and to let the whites act against each other" because, as another French official claimed, "through the jealousy of these two nations [the British and the French] these tribes may live independent of, and draw presents from both."[62] That was possible for the many Indigenous groupings who lived between competing imperial powers but was more difficult for Indigenous

Agostino Brunias (c. 1730–96), *Linen Day, Roseau, Dominica—A Market Scene*, 1780. (Yale Center for British Art, Paul Mellon Collection)

peoples who lived within the borders and under the direct political authority of British colonies, as in New England and the tidewater Chesapeake. They lived precariously, only occasionally able to preserve their landholdings from British settlement. English and then British colonists had proved that they were relentless in using their numerical advantages to diminish Indigenous rule, as they did, for example, in genocidal wars in the 1670s in Massachusetts against the Wampanoags.[63]

The Haudenosaunee and Creeks were not the only aggressive imperialist Indigenous powers. The Comanches had become by the late seventeenth century a formidable equestrian warrior nation. By the early eighteenth century, they were starting on their expansion into the southern Great Plains, including Spanish New Mexico and what is today northwest Texas. They initially challenged sparse Spanish colonial power and then moved into British-controlled areas. Their rise to imperial greatness was marked using extreme violence against Indigenous rivals. They stayed in power, however, through adroit diplomacy and the judicious application of trade goods. They became the dominant Indigenous group in the southwest by the mid-eighteenth century, bringing—through force and authoritarian rule—peace and prosperity in the region and incorporating bordering Indian tribes as allies and dependents.[64]

In the area west of the Great Lakes, in present-day Minnesota and South Dakota, a confederacy of the tribes of the Sioux people, the Očéthi Šakówin (or Seven Council of Fires), became a colossal force that controlled a vast territory from the upper Mississippi to the Missouri Valley. One of these peoples in the Očéthi Šakówin confederacy, the Lakota, was beginning to rise to power as "an expansive, constantly transmuting Indigenous regime that pulled numerous groups into its orbits. By the early nineteenth century, it had marginalized and dispossessed its rivals—both Indigenous and colonial—and commanded the political, social, and economic life in the North American interior for generations."[65] We should not exaggerate, however, the dominance of the Comanche and Lakota in the far West, which was not, after all, a major theater in the American Revolution. Their imperial supremacy was short-lived, lasting for not more than two generations. Even at the height of their imperial expansion the West contained numerous groups that often fought with each other. Moreover, both groups were badly affected by disease, with the Comanche population declining by 50 percent between 1780 and 1820.[66]

The enduring presence of Indigenous power in several parts of North America does not mean that the defeat of the French in the Seven Years' War did not make a massive difference in Indigenous-European relations. Pontiac's War of 1763-65, a remarkably successful pan-Indian war against the new British regime, is unimaginable without the disappearance of France from the Great Lakes region. The cost of this war, coming on top of the expense of the Seven Years' War, reinforced the British imperial state's determination that settlers needed to pay some of the costs of placating Indigenous peoples and that new taxes upon colonists were necessary.

The Seven Years' War was decisive in changing power relations in the interior. By removing the French presence in continental North America, it lessened the ability of Indigenous peoples and the British to ease the pressure of a growing colonial population on Indian land. The Seven Years' War saw a dramatic shift in the patchwork character of British imperial policy, where a conciliatory attitude toward Indigenous peoples, born of the desire to thwart the French, was replaced by the British behaving like conquerors. They treated Indigenous peoples with massive disrespect. Jeffery Amherst, Lord Amherst (1717-97), exemplified this new attitude, as he believed that there was no need to foster good relations with Indigenous peoples and that they needed to be governed, not coddled. The result was increased violence and war, such as the brutal Cherokee War in South Carolina in 1760-61, provoked when Governor William Henry Lyttelton (1724-1808) stopped the practice of gift-giving and imprisoned Cherokee leaders. As commander-in-chief of the British army in North America, Amherst responded to Indigenous violence by adopting strategies of total warfare, burning villages, destroying Indian fields, and executing Cherokees to reduce them to total submission.[67]

At the stroke of a pen in 1763, North America's imperial map was redrawn. New France and Louisiana were gone and Indigenous peoples in the southeast, Great Lakes, and Ohio Valley lost most of their political leverage. They were forced to negotiate with a British Empire that was now determined to rule them, in the manner of Lord Amherst, rather than treat with them, as Sir William Johnson (1715-74), the British superintendent of Indian affairs, had done.[68] Indigenous peoples like the Odawa, from the confluence of Lakes Michigan and Huron, were unable to use the diplomatic strategies that had worked successfully for a century, which was to play the French and the British off each other.

Instead of diplomacy, Indigenous peoples in the Great Lakes region turned to war. If Pontiac's War was a military defeat, it was an Indigenous political triumph. Britain was forced to restore gift-giving. It agreed to make no further settlements west of the Appalachians in the Proclamation of 1763. This concession appalled settlers, but it was a decision that recognized the reality of Indigenous power. The proclamation was never intended to be permanent. It was a "temporary expedient to quiet the minds of the Indians."[69] But the proclamation formed a radical departure from established practice. It adopted a new attitude to the dispersal of land, usually taken from Indigenous peoples in North America but also from French Catholics in Canada and the West Indies. It forbade private subjects from purchasing land directly from anyone other than the Crown and its agents. Any negotiations with Indigenous peoples were now seen not as private transactions within a land market but as a part of treaties between sovereign powers. The Proclamation of 1763 stripped colonies of the right to develop land previously granted to them by earlier kings than

George III, which was a violent change to a long-established set of fundamental customs and practices that resembled in its effects Henry VIII's seizure of land owned by Catholic monasteries between 1536 and 1540. It led to a considerable constitutional revolution. It was now the Crown that governed new territories, not imperial agents such as companies, and this was accompanied, disturbingly for existing settler colonists, by the Crown adopting imperial policies like those in Ireland, where representative government was denied until a population was deemed suitably amenable. Given that white subjects in places like Quebec and Grenada were French Catholics and thus outside the realm of Protestants, that transition was unlikely to ever occur.[70]

It worked badly, leading to more racial violence, more seizing of land, and growing white anger and resentment, culminating in settler violence, such as in western Pennsylvania with the Paxton Boys, a murderous vigilante group, forcing the Pennsylvania government to act against Native Americans on the frontier.[71] Indigenous power, however, was ebbing in the face of the extraordinary and relentless expansion of settler population and property. For the moment, Britain did not have an inland empire but remained a maritime power, focused on the Atlantic world. But that moment was not to last. Settler revolt in the American Revolution and the continuing growth of settler America while the Indian population and its power declined foretold a future recalibration of power relations in favor of settlers in all of British North America and the infant United States.[72]

Before the Seven Years' War, the western interior, while far from being a peaceful kingdom, was "a veritable Rabelaisian world of multiple cultures, languages, ethnicities, faiths and races" where, for example, Mohawk communities in the Hudson Valley, New York, lived usually harmoniously with Europeans.[73] The 1760s put an end to this Rabelaisian world. Continuous pressure on Indigenous land, sporadic but frequent explosions of violence, and obvious imperial weakness in a region where Britain could not control its white subjects helped both fuel a sense of white entitlement to Indigenous lands and end Indigenous willingness to coexist with settlers. The Quebec Act aggravated matters by extending Quebec's southern border deep into the Ohio Valley, where many land speculators lost land to which they believed they had legitimate deeds.[74]

By 1776, the poor policy choices of Britain had helped make the West more ungovernable and more costly to maintain than in 1763.[75] Indigenous peoples tried in time-honored fashion to play one empire off another, which is something the Choctaws, Chickasaws, and Creeks in the South and Shawnee and Delawares in the North attempted to do.[76] But such strategies failed against a settler empire willing to see nation-building and settler colonialism as complementary. Their attitudes in the Revolutionary War were shaped by their imperial experience. George Washington, for example, drew from his experience in the Seven Years' War to adopt highly destructive policies designed to sop Indigenous resistance, crushing them by targeting fields and villages, the places women congregated in, and by encouraging plunder and revenge. That revenge included sexual violence by American troops.[77] Adding to Indigenous woes was a familiar killer—disease. Thousands of Indigenous people in the far West through to the Hudson Bay died in a massive smallpox epidemic between 1779 and 1782.[78] The imperial hubris of the revolutionary period spelled troubled times for America's Native inhabitants—times that only got worse with the establishment of the United States.

Scotland and Ireland

One of the ironies of the American Revolution is that before 1763, settlers in the Atlantic world were among the least problematic of British imperial subjects. The title of most problematic imperial subjects in the first half of the eighteenth century went undoubtedly to the Scots, especially Scottish Highlanders. They took command of that title from the Irish, who had been at the forefront of conflict in the empire in the sixteenth and seventeenth centuries when colonial violence against Catholic Irish people was so vicious as to amount to genocide.[79]

Scotland is peculiar in Britain's overseas expansion as being not only a region colonized by England but also a colonizing region itself. By the second half of the eighteenth century and into the nineteenth century it was an enthusiastic supporter of empire and a major beneficiary of imperial-created wealth, notably from India and the West Indies.[80] Scotland had been part of English colonization even before it became part of Britain. It sent 30,000 Presbyterians to settle plantations in Ulster in what was the biggest migration from Britain in the seventeenth century. That Scots were eager imperialists is hardly surprising. They built in Ulster on a long tradition of trading, sojourning, and settling in the Baltic, Scandinavia, and the Low Countries.[81]

Yet Scottish incorporation into the British Empire was difficult. Many

Scots did not accept the Union of 1707, denouncing it because it was an event orchestrated corruptly by Scottish elites and forced on Scotland after both the disaster of a failed colonization effort in Darien on Panama in the 1690s and the economic travails of famine in Scotland in the mid-1690s.[82] Dissatisfaction with union with England was aggravated by the replacement of the Scottish Stuarts with the Hanoverians in 1714. It led to two major rebellions in 1715–16 and 1745–46 by Scots, mostly from the Highlands, against Hanoverian rule and in support of the heirs of James VII and II. These rebellions failed, but they were massive shocks to the British state and the most serious challenges in the eighteenth century by British subjects to monarchical rule before the American Revolution. Jacobites, as the rebels were called, especially after 1745, were put down with great ferocity. That ferocity, however, was matched by serious reform in the Highlands, through economic modernization by "improving" agricultural practices by large landlords, and by recruiting their highlanders into the British army, where they fought alongside colonists in the Seven Years' War.[83] In a precursor of what George Grenville and Lord North tried to do in North America in the 1760s and 1770s, the Earl of Hardwick used legal radicalism to effect a "Scotch reformation." He abolished ancient Scottish acts and insisted on vesting judicial power fully in the Crown and Parliament.[84]

Scotland was a troublesome part of the early eighteenth-century British Empire, brought into it as a fully constituent partner through a combination of coercion and collusion. Scots became fully incorporated to such an extent that their contribution to the empire stands out as disproportionate.[85] That incorporation was more difficult for the other troublesome province of Britain, Ireland, with its large and always potentially rebellious population of dispossessed and resentful Catholics. The biggest potential risk to British security in the eighteenth century was always Ireland rather than Scotland. Ireland was a colonized country, more so than Scotland or Wales, with most of its Catholic population repressed by the Protestant Ascendancy. As a result of its colonization, Ireland was always a powder keg of potential rebellion and the obvious means of entry for any French military force wanting to invade England, as became very clear in the French Revolutionary and Napoleonic Wars.[86] Somewhat surprisingly, Ireland was relatively quiescent before and during the American Revolution, even despite Ireland's rural Catholic majority having a dire standard of living that resulted in a devastating famine in 1740-41, killing perhaps 13-20 percent of the population.[87]

It is hard to fit Ireland within eighteenth-century models of colonization, but it was a colony, even if it lacked some of the features that we usually think of as marking eighteenth-century colonialism, such as extreme temperatures and exotic produce. One of the most incisive evaluations of Ireland as a colonial society was made by the great Anglo-Irish satirist Jonathan Swift. His *A Modest Proposal* (1729), where he made the outrageous suggestion of using poor Irish children as roasted delicacies for the Protestant Ascendancy, is the most magnificent satire in British and Irish literature. It is usually read as a generalized critique of European imperialism, given how often Swift compared the Irish poor to Native Americans. But the target of Swift's fury was not English oppressors as much as Ireland's predatory ruling class, who Swift felt were complicit in Irish subjugation. He asked pointedly at the end of *A Modest Proposal* that "Landlords have at least one degree of Mercy towards their Tenants."[88] Swift's satire "was a distinctly Irish critique of a distinctively Irish process of reconquest and recolonization." It was less condemnatory of colonization than is sometimes thought. Swift did not challenge Ireland's social or political order or entertain the idea that Gaels might have some redeeming features to make them part of civilized society. His aim was to attack the Protestant Ascendency for their backwardness in not adopting ideas of agricultural improvement. He approved of settler colonialism if it led to making the land (and its inhabitants, like Indigenous peoples and Irish Catholics) productive and stopped settlers from going native and thus failing to bring a just and progressive social order to Ireland. The Irish were poor due to settler laziness and indifference, in Swift's view, not because of English colonial rule.[89]

Ireland was as much a settler society as was the Thirteen Colonies, not least in Protestants showing "a shocking callousness toward the native inhabitants of the land they were colonizing."[90] In the 1760s, under the authoritarian rule of Viscount Townshend, Ireland's colonial status became more pronounced, as we have noted above. Townshend was determined that Ireland would be ruled from London, rather than from Dublin. Thus, at the same time that Britain was trying to refashion its relationships with British America to increase metropolitan control over its colonies, the same process was occurring, and with more success, in Ireland.

Resistance in Ireland

Ireland was quiescent in the first half of the eighteenth century, with no major rebellions such as in 1641 and 1798. It demonstrated some signs of prosperity as it benefited from increased trade across the Atlantic, with colonial trade amounting to about 8 percent of total Irish exports in the early eighteenth century. Transatlantic trade increased in the half century before the American Revolution, accounting for about 10 percent of total exports between 1732 and 1756 and 16 percent between 1756 and 1776. America took 40 percent of Irish beef, between 55 percent and 76 percent of its pork, and by the 1770s 21 percent of its linen.[91]

Ireland was quiescent only, however, in relative terms. The island simmered with potential discontent, and it remained painfully poor, with most of its rural Catholic population perpetually on the edge of starvation. It suffered recurrent crises of subsistence, and its overall economic growth was slow, even in a period of low demographic growth and an out-migration of 100,000 between 1700 and 1776 to North America.[92] Ireland had severe famines in 1726–29 and most seriously in 1740–41. In the latter famine, the death rates were enormous, with estimates suggesting that between 13 percent and 20 percent of its population, or 310,000 to 480,000 people, perished in the frozen winter of 1740–41.[93]

Unsurprisingly, there was a pervasive sense of malaise in Irish writings from the early eighteenth century onward. People dwelt obsessively upon British statesmen putting obstacles in the way of progress, such as not allowing until 1731 Irish merchants to import non-enumerated goods from the Atlantic colonies, making commodities like sugar and tobacco very expensive compared with prices in Britain. Irish Protestants thought of themselves less as masters of their realm than an oppressed people with no equality allowed to England. As Thomas Bartlett argues, "in self-defense, Irish Protestants formulated a defense of their rights as the English-born-in-Ireland which they pitted against metropolitan condescension, its oppressive agents, and their colonial theory." It meant that "English Imperialism was combated by 'Protestant' or 'colonial' nationalism."[94]

To a limited degree, Protestant resentment against England in this period, when political turmoil was less than in the bloody seventeenth century, gave Protestants some sympathy for their Catholic co-residents because "although Ireland's religious strife was never far from the thoughts of people on both sides of its confessional divide, enterprising Catholics in Dublin and the kingdom's ports found ways around the Penal Laws, leasing and profiting from land that they were legally barred from owning, moving into trades and occupations where landownership was not necessary and converting—sometimes nominally—to Protestantism."[95] One indication that Catholics were being slowly accepted into imperial polities was an increasing willingness to exploit the manpower the British state could find in Ireland to staff the British army. The Seven Years' War started the process of Catholic armed enlistment, and it was made permanent by the American Revolution. The American Revolution thus challenged the religious and political foundations upon which Catholic exclusion rested. In 1774, an alternative oath of allegiance was devised for Irish Catholic soldiers. For many Americans, such willingness to accept Catholics into the British army was yet another sign of British perfidy.[96]

Toleration of Catholics by Protestants went only so far. Protestants remained fiercely conscious that they lived in a country with a large Catholic majority, chafing under a long history of conquest and punitive legislation. Catholics remained a threat to Protestant control, even if they were not actively opposing such control. Protestant distrust of Catholic intentions overwhelmed any resentment toward British authority. The Catholic population was badly treated. The Earl of Chesterfield, a former lord lieutenant, wrote in 1764 that "the poor people in Ireland are used worse than negroes by their lords and masters."[97] They faced systematic discrimination through Penal Laws which restricted landownership, education rights, and what occupations they could enter, even though after the 1720s there was not much effort to put the Penal Laws into effect. That leniency was due less to increased tolerance than to the declining necessity for such legislative restrictions as Catholics were squeezed out of landownership. In 1641, Catholics owned 59 percent of Irish land; in the 1680s that had reduced to 22 percent; and in 1703 it was just 14 percent. By the 1770s Catholic landownership reached a probable record low of 5 percent, though this comes from anecdotal rather than firm evidence. The Catholic landowning class had virtually disappeared in a century of Protestant Ascendancy.[98]

The Catholic Irish were not African slaves, even if their lives were harmed by British colonization in ways that replicated what was happening among Africans in the Caribbean. The rural Catholic Irish were mostly peasants and retained a measure of independence over how they lived their lives. Their working conditions were poor but nowhere near as terrible as on West Indian sugar plantations. The relative advantages they had over enslaved people in their work and standards of living were reflected in healthy demographic increase. But the Catholic Irish were like enslaved West Indians in one important respect. They were excluded from a rights-based culture and from entitlements to a limited form of social welfare. The rural Irish poor were remarkably exposed to the full pressure of a rapidly developing market economy. In this respect, Irish Catholics fit into models of settler colonization, being structurally similar in many ways to American Indigenous peoples.[99]

And like the enslaved in the West Indies, Irish Catholics resisted their oppression. They were strongly Jacobite in sentiment, but circumstances did not cohere sufficiently for them to join Highland Scots in colonial rebellion in 1745. Resistance, instead, was localistic and based around rural agrarian grievances. Ireland experienced waves of agrarian protest starting with the Houghers in western Ireland between 1711 and 1712, during which time peasant rebels targeted livestock, destroying thousands. The most significant agrarian protest came in the 1760s with the Whiteboy movement. It started in southern Ireland and intensified between 1769 and 1775, moving east and north. The Whiteboys were agrarian rebels in a traditional European mold, less revolutionaries than conservatives believing in a moral economy of reciprocity between landlords and tenants. They were prepared to act in pursuit of clear but narrowly defined aims when the moral economy of reciprocity was threatened. These aims included reducing high food prices, resisting enclosures, and opposing the reduction of common land. They were not especially violent. Only fifty people died in Whiteboy attacks between 1761 and 1790. Their objects were more often property and livestock than people. Whiteboy tactics—oaths, uniforms, marching on agreed targets, "houghing" (cutting the Achilles tendons of livestock)—"reinforced peasant solidarity and communal values against the landlords . . . [which] created the mechanisms of a revolutionary and rebellious culture that had a lasting effect on subsequent movements, but until the 1790s neither rebellion nor revolution was the aim."[100]

As traditional protests that were very much in the early modern pattern of rural rebellion, the Whiteboy attacks were dangerous to established state and church order but did not pose an existential threat as did the slave revolt that occurred in Jamaica in 1760, a year before Whiteboy agitation began. Whiteboys never attempted to overthrow established order but sought pragmatic solutions to distinct problems. Rural activism was often violent and personally directed, but it derived from a distinctive understanding of what tenants and the rural poor were entitled to. It was non-revolutionary resistance, in short. The poor and the weak had "a pragmatic acceptance of the existing social hierarchy even at times when grievance became acute enough to warrant the risk of engaging in social protest."[101] Nevertheless, the Whiteboys were put down with ferocity, with eighty-five executions, including some for acts of treason, under legislation passed in 1765 which increased sharply the number of offenses that could result in execution. The pattern of repression in Ireland stands out as legally extreme. It betokens how the British Empire was prepared to use an iron fist to control others, be they Caribbean slaves or Irish Catholic rebels, in ways that were not envisioned in dealing with white Protestant North Americans.[102]

The British Empire in 1763 was remarkably diverse, as we have seen in the last two chapters, and was becoming increasingly so. Before 1763, British officials largely contained such diversity within an imperial system that was flexible enough to accommodate digressions from imperial intentions while being strong enough to crush rebellions, as in Scotland in 1745 and Jamaica in 1760. It contained resistance against colonial rule in Ireland and among Indigenous peoples in the American interior so that the rule of Protestant settlers of European descent could be maintained. The British Empire was overwhelmingly successful in the first half of the eighteenth century, at least by its own definition.[103] That definition was largely framed in economic and geopolitical terms—how did a growing British Empire, especially the slave and settler colonies in the West Indies and British North America, serve the interests of a metropolitan government? It formed a closely integrated system, in which textiles went from India to West Africa so that European traders could purchase enslaved Africans, who then labored in harsh conditions in the West Indies and the American South to produce commodities for the northern colonies and for Britain and Ireland, all facilitated by trade in provisions and goods sent by British North America to keep plantations going in the Caribbean. The trick for imperial statesmen, in the context of a greatly expanding slave system in the plantation colonies and the remarkable growth in population, wealth, and power of the North American settler colonies, was to keep all the pieces of this complex system of an empire that ranged from Scotland and Ireland in Britain to colonies in the Americas, Asia, Africa, and eventually the Pacific together in ways that satisfied a demanding group of colonists. There were indications that this empire could be integrated in ways that Britain desired through what has been described in the last two chapters, where the British Empire from the Seven Years' War onward was bound together, and increasingly so, over the defense of African slavery; the increasing profitability and global reach of Atlantic commerce; and the willingness to acquire for settlers the lands of Indigenous peoples in North America and the West Indies, Bengalis in South Asia, and Catholics in Ireland. The next chapter shows how this trick of imperial integration was achieved in many colonies, even if the system fell apart in the Thirteen Colonies by the mid-1770s.

PART TWO

The War and Its Effects

IN WHAT WAYS DOES THE American Revolution matter as an historical event? The historian E. H. Carr's claim that "all history is the history of causes" elides what is just as important in historical explanation: the evaluation of consequences, or effects, in historical events.[1] Thus, we are interested as much in what the American Revolution meant, or, better, how it is represented within the history of imperialism, as we are concerned about the causes of this world-historically important event. Representation involves a relationship between past and present, seen as a temporal chain of events on the one hand and as an interpretation that gives meaning to these events, charging it with norms and values, on the other.[2] Consequence might be causation's forgotten sibling, but it involves both the intended and, more interestingly, the unintended results of human actions, which, in this case, led to an imperial war between Britain and nearly half of its American colonies. It resulted in the creation of the United States and a reconfigured British Empire in the 1780s. Our main argument is simple, though explaining all its permutations is complicated. We argue that we understand the American Revolution better if we place it in an imperial context. We also argue that imperialism remained central to how the American Revolution came about; how the resulting war was fought; and what happened after 1783 for both the British Empire and the United States of America.

These three chapters that follow—on the loyal colonies; on the War of American Independence as a global and imperial war; and on the imperial futures that unfolded from the 1780s—deal with both causes and consequences, in a manner that suggests alternative ways of looking at the American Revolution and counterfactuals about an empire that did not have to break up in the way that it did. What is distinctive about our approach in these three chapters is that we emphasize how successful Britain was in many aspects of this imperial conflict. Of course, success is relative and is also not what historians tend to measure—what is success and in what ways and with what results?

Overall, the American Revolution was not Britain's finest geopolitical moment. The loss of the Thirteen Colonies was an unprecedented disaster for Britain, the greatest single catastrophe in Britain's entire imperial history. America was an especially dynamic part of a growing empire, and its loss was keenly felt. It brought down a powerful government, the North administration, which had lasted in power for twelve years before Yorktown; it provoked such a crisis for George III that he contemplated abdication; it fostered a disturbed political environment in which three short-lived administrations quickly followed each other; and it led to a popular reform movement demanding changes in parliamentary practice that eventually, by 1832, transformed the nature of government in Britain.[3]

Crucial to our analysis of the American Revolution as an imperial event is that we avoid single-factor analysis in assessing its causes and consequences. We depict the events around the American Revolution as polyvocal, uncoordinated, and with many cross-cutting vectors of intention and conflict. This means that we can avoid describing the events between 1763 and 1787 as "successful" or a "failure," depending on perspective. As one historian argues in describing another revolution, "we don't say of an ocean storm, a solar flare or sixteen days of heavy snowfall that they 'succeeded' or 'failed'; we simply measure their effects." What is true for natural events is just as true for political conflicts—success or failure is less important than meaning and representation.[4]

Many Britons tried to shrug off what had happened to the empire with the loss of the Thirteen Colonies. Richard Price (1723–91), the most committed supporter of America in Britain, lamented in 1785 that "during the war the cry was that our essential interests depended on keeping the colonies. Now it seems to be discover'd that they are of no use to us." The American Patriot Silas Deane (1738–89), living in London in 1783, argued that "the loss of America is already forgotten except in some party debates and writings, and there the principal question is, whether on the whole, it be a loss."[5]

Naturally, such sentiments belied the deep unease which accompanied the sole eighteenth-century defeat Britain suffered in its imperial wars. Nevertheless, there was an element of truth to this robust British approach to imperial defeat and to global geopolitics. If we take our perspective to be the empire in its entirety, Britain managed its imperial policies from the 1760s to the 1780s better than might be thought if we only considered its relations with the Thirteen Colonies. Only a minority of British American colonies joined in rebellion, and Britain kept the tinderbox of Catholic Ireland from exploding in sympathy with American Patriots. Most colonies stayed loyal. As we argue in chapter 5, on the loyal colonies, what needs to be explained is not why so many white colonists stayed loyal. Loyalty was the default option; what needs to be explained is rebellion.

Loyalty was what British ministers expected when they initiated imperial reforms in various parts of the empire in the 1760s. They assumed, for example, that all colonies in which slavery was the primary social and economic institution would stay loyal, as colonists would be too afraid of slave rebellions and were too dependent on British troops to risk making grand assertions of liberty. It was an immense surprise when slaveholding colonies such as Virginia, Maryland, the Carolinas, and Georgia supported fellow colonists in Boston, where slavery was minimal.[6] Similarly, British ministers assumed that Irish Protestants would never rebel when surrounded by a majority hostile Catholic population.[7] There were critical differences between Ireland and the West Indies—the imperial possessions most likely to support American rebellion—and North America, as we explain in chapter 5. They were fundamentally happy with British imperial trade policies and liked the protection against internal enemies afforded them by the British military.[8]

The loss of the Thirteen Colonies did not stop Britain's surge to unprecedented imperial expansion after 1783, though it diverted imperialism into new directions. In the colonies which remained in the empire, imperialism became notably more authoritarian and centralized than earlier in the eighteenth century. Britain felt that what it had done in these "other" colonies justified that expansion and showed loyalty to the empire in a good light. We can see this recovery of Loyalism as a positive force in Britain's self-image in American-born Benjamin West's portrait of John Eardley Wilmot (1709-92), the Loyalist claims commissioner. West's painting contained some pointed allegorical messages. Its background shows a diverse range of Loyalists after the American Revolution, from royal officials to ordinary farmers, women, Black people, and, at the center, a Native American man who shelters wartime victims and who reaches out his hand to Britain. As an historian comments, "it is hard to imagine a more straightforward image of an inclusive British Empire that had managed to mint moral capital out of its wartime defeat."[9]

Britain also managed to do better in the War of American Independence than its catastrophic defeats in North America would suggest, if, once again, a wider imperial context is considered, whereby British defeat at Yorktown in 1781 is compared with British naval triumph in the eastern Caribbean in 1782 at the Battle of the Saintes. The role of foreign allies of America, notably France, in securing victory for America, France, and Spain in North America in 1781, considered alongside an imperial conflict where Britain retained all its imperial possessions outside the Thirteen Colonies in the Peace of Paris in 1783, is our theme in chapter 6. Britain's loss in North America resulted from the war becoming global in 1778, meaning that Britain had to fight on multiple fronts without having sufficient soldiers, sailors, and ships to do so.

If we think of the war, especially in its crucial early years, when America fought alone against Britain, as akin to a counterinsurgency campaign, such as that fought by Britain in Malaya in the 1950s or by America in Vietnam in the 1960s and 1970s, then British performance was poor.[10] But if the war is viewed as an imperial war, British performance was better. Britain in the last years of the war was concerned with preserving Britain's remaining imperial assets in the Caribbean, Europe, and South Asia. It achieved what it wanted to achieve. Chapter 6 traces how it accomplished this quite remarkable feat, in the face of considerable pressure from its European imperial rivals, notably France. France made considerable gains in the American Revolution at the expense of its traditional European rival, Britain, but at massive long-term cost, with its debts from the war making a major contribution to the tumults that began in 1789 and which became the French Revolution.[11]

What would have occurred in world history and the history of the British Empire if alternative possibilities had happened? How different would eighteenth-century history have been if Britain had solved its American problem and the Thirteen Colonies had stayed in the British Empire, or if Britain had defeated the American Patriots, or if more colonies in the Atlantic world had joined Americans in rebellion? All these possibilities are feasible, if we run the tape of history in other ways.

Of course, thinking such things puts us into the realm of constructing counterfactuals or imagining historical causation differently. Entering the realm of counterfactuals is fun if futile, although doing so helps to expand the range of how we conceptualize an historical event and work out what factors are more important than others.[12] Usually, counterfactuals are found wanting. The great imperial historian Lawence H. Gipson argued in the mid-twentieth century that the American Revolution only happened because Britain won the Seven Years' War and thus removed from North America "the Gallic peril," which before the 1760s had kept British colonists quiescent. John Murrin, however, cast doubt on Gipson's thesis by showing that such a counterfactual interpretation depended upon a host of problematic assumptions and crucially did not take seriously colonial grievances arising between 1763 and 1775.

As we argue, maintaining the imperial status quo after 1763 was impossible when Britain faced significant fiscal challenges that encouraged it to pursue more interventionist policies, at home and in the empire, which provoked dissatisfaction. It was not, moreover, just the British who saw the need for state reform in the 1760s—the French, Spanish, Austrians, and Prussians also saw the Seven Years' War as a spur to change.[13]

One plausible counterfactual, however, is that Britain might have been able to overcome its issues in North America because, as we explain in chapter 5, it did do so effectively in the loyal colonies. If the British had solved their problems in North America as well as they did in Ireland and the Caribbean, then the issue that would have ultimately divided the empire would not have been the relatively minor grievance of taxation without representation but the major dividing line between Atlantic colonies—slavery and whether it should continue or be abolished. The revolution that occurred in late eighteenth-century Britain was the abolitionist movement to abandon the Atlantic slave trade. It is likely that this movement would have developed even if there had been no American Revolution, though undoubtedly it would have had different characteristics if the slaveholding section of the British Empire in the Americas had remained unified. Slavery threatened the stability of the United States from its foundation and led, of course, to its second civil war, over the place of slavery in American life, between 1861 and 1865.[14]

We mention counterfactuals because one reading of our work is that it gives support, as we outline extensively in chapter 7, to views that the American Revolution did not matter very much. One could read our work as suggesting that the American Revolution in its imperial aspects did not initiate revolutionary change, but continued patterns of colonialism and imperialism that were well established before the American Revolution.

This assumption of continuity over change was not, of course, how participants in the American Revolution saw this world-historical event. American exceptionalists from the 1780s until today have insisted that the break with Britain was genuinely radical, overturning traditional interpretations of hierarchy and social order and instituting a republican government that was something new under the sun. The American Revolution, in this reading, was not just a revolution but was also an important way station toward modernity. David Ramsay, in the first historical treatment of the American Revolution in 1789, declared that it started "an Era in the history of the world, remarkable for the progressive increase in human happiness!"[15] The old monarchical regime was gone, to be replaced by republicanism and this, people at the time thought, was massively consequential.[16]

Thus, the American Revolution had revolutionary aspects, if we consider a revolution to be something that initiates a new horizon of possibility and a sense that time itself is accelerating into a better tomorrow. That sense of time expanding made the French philosopher Abbé Raynal argue that the American Revolution was a Novus Ordo Seclorum (a new order of the ages) where "the present is about to decide upon a long futurity" so that "All is changed" as "a day has given birth to a revolution."[17] The Connecticut minister Ezra Stiles proclaimed in 1783 that the United States would be an example to the ages: "this great American revolution, this recent political phenomenon of a new sovereignty arising among the sovereign powers of the earth, will be attended to and contemplated by all nations."[18] The American Revolution may not have had the global impact of the French Revolution, but it had transformative aspects, not least in cultural practices, which historians argue were the fulcrums for the creation of revolution. Some of these changes took a long time to develop, waiting another generation to flower fully, but they were durable changes that altered patterns of everyday life and the nature of politics, including the politics of empire.[19] It seemed to American Patriots, reflecting on generational change emanating from the American Revolution, that the Revolution was indeed revolutionary. John Adams (1735-1826) wrote in 1818 that "its effects and consequences have been awful over a great part of the globe," demonstrating "radical change in the principles, opinions, sentiments and affections of the people."[20] It marked a caesura between old hierarchies and the creation of a modern, liberal, and democratic world.

Readers of this book are unlikely to be convinced entirely by what the second American president contended. We show that what remained after the end of the American Revolution was something very old: imperialism. It survived the American Revolution largely intact. The Age of Revolutions was also the Age of Empires. In short, America's Revolution was Britain's American War: "it was a series of fateful moves in the high stakes chess game of the European great powers and a chapter in the entangled history of a vast and growing empire."[21] The changes in British imperialism that resulted from Britain's loss in America in the 1780s were subtle rather than abrupt. The loss of America combined with the Industrial Revolution to eventually lead to a reordering of the British Empire, but this process was slow and was only complete at the end of "the imperial meridian" in the 1830s.[22]

The British Empire did not experience a "swing to the east," as an earlier generation of historians suggested. The East (or India) had been firmly established and the areas under the control of the East India Company were highly valued by Britain well before 1776. Meanwhile, Britain remained significantly invested, as we argue in chapter 7, in developing its slave-based Atlantic colonies well into the nineteenth century.[23] Elements of an old empire and those of a new one existed for many years, and it is hard to see how one coherent system of empire gave way to another without accepting that the change was gradual and never complete. The first British Empire did not die in 1783. Moreover, the ideological example of a republican America did little to change either British imperialism or British politics. The political reform movement that began in England after the loss of America was more backward looking than influenced by the ideas of the Age of Revolution. It reaffirmed traditional "Country Whig" principles from the early eighteenth century, in which Englishmen sought the independence of Parliament from the executive of the Crown, and thus was more about disputes over prerogative than preludes to democracy.[24]

The United States, also, retained much of its imperial heritage in its new republican form. It remained an economic dependency of Britain well into the nineteenth century, if less so than Britain's actual colonial possessions, such as Canada and Australia. It retained its unchallenged political independence. It could therefore pursue policies of economic nationalism, even to disastrous effect, as in the War of 1812.[25] Britain's proportional slice of America's economic pie amounted to just 5 percent of capital stock increase in the early nineteenth century. It would have been more if the United States had remained within the British Empire.[26]

But the United States was deeply affected by imperialism and continued to act as an imperial power well after its 1788 creation. Its commitment to empire is most evident in the United States' uneasy relationship with Indigenous peoples, which was even worse than what Indigenous peoples had experienced within the British Empire before the Peace of Paris in 1783. Indigenous peoples were not enamored of the British who were so flush with victory in the Seven Years' War that they had behaved after 1763 with extraordinary arrogance, peremptory diplomacy, and quick resort to violence.[27] The British Empire was no friend to Indigenous peoples at any time in its history, and the effects of British imperialism on nonwhite peoples only got worse in the late eighteenth and early nineteenth centuries than it had been around the middle of the eighteenth century. The late eighteenth- and nineteenth-century experiences of Aborigines in Australia, the San people in South Africa, and, as we discuss in chapter 7, the Kalingos in the eastern Caribbean were uniformly terrible, showing the harsh hand of British attitudes toward Indigenous peoples on land Britain wanted for itself.[28]

Yet for most Indigenous peoples in North America, American settlers—and the government they formed in 1788—were even worse opponents than the British. The United States was built on a culture of frontier racial violence and Indian hatred that was heightened during the American Revolution. The American Revolution proved a disaster for Indigenous peoples. And the end of the war led to terrible results for Indigenous peoples who were previously part of the British Empire, as Britain abandoned its Indian allies in the 1783 Treaty of Paris, giving to the Americans Indian land east of the Mississippi River, which the British did not actually own themselves.[29]

The end of the American Revolution thus did not end violence in Indigenous country. That violence was conducted through the practices of empire that had been learned by settlers before and during the American Revolution and then refined and made government policy in the last decades of the eighteenth century. White settlers "asserted the right to use violence in support of a civic order they believed to have been forged in the crucible of the American Revolution" which "required the displacement and deracination of Native Americans."[30] The United States felt it had to act as an empire in its ongoing and disastrous relations with Indigenous peoples because the War of American Independence had left the new nation heavily in debt. Its only asset on the creation of the United

States as a nation-state was the Indigenous land that Britain had unlawfully taken from Indians and illegally given to Americans. Indigenous peoples fought back fiercely against American imperial aggression, obliterating in 1791 the United States' nascent army.[31] But the inexorable growth of settler populations and their repeated violation of Indigenous peoples' rights meant that Indigenous peoples were forever failing to win the continuing fight for independence. From an Indigenous perspective, Jefferson's empire of liberty was built on Indigenous lands at the expense of Indigenous liberties and was justified by a systematic and sustained assault on Indigenous ways of life.[32] Having won its independence from the British Empire, the United States created a different kind of empire, turning a blind eye to settler violence and illegal actions while governing its own colonial territories. Our study concludes with an appreciation of how important imperialism was after as well as before and during the American Revolution.

FIVE

The Loyal Colonies

IN THE AFTERMATH OF THE Seven Years' War, Britain pursued a series of parallel authoritarian policies throughout the British Empire. We have treated these extensively above. These various initiatives represented a concerted attempt to make reforms across the empire to increase revenues, regulate trade, improve defenses, and strengthen metropolitan authority. This raises the obvious question as to why the colonies reacted differently to such intervention in their internal affairs and why some colonies remained loyal during the American Revolution. A collective consideration of all the colonies can enable us to debate and rank the causes of the American Revolution. This chapter therefore traces and explains the different responses of the colonies to the imperial crisis. It examines the implications of the responses of the "loyal" colonies for our understanding of the causes of the rebellion in America. The most relevant and analogous comparisons are those of North America with Ireland and the West Indies. In contrast, few insights can be gained from comparisons with the very different situation of the colonial possessions of the East India Company or of Quebec and Nova Scotia or Senegambia—places without the settler populations of white Protestants that were in Ireland and the West Indies.

What we are doing is not an attempt to offer a grand thesis about the causes of the rebellion but rather to propose that an imperial comparison offers historians a tool with which to evaluate and even reconcile competing interpretations of the American Revolution. Our argument is that the empire largely held together outside the Thirteen Colonies during the years of imperial conflict and global war. Loyalty to the empire prevailed, even though the policies pursued by Britain during the American Revolution often occasioned dissent in the so-called loyal colonies of Quebec and Nova Scotia, Ireland, and the West Indies.[1]

Quebec, Nova Scotia, and Support for Americans

In the Thirteen Colonies, the Patriots believed their cause to be that of all the empire and anticipated support from other colonies. Nevertheless, they only made repeated efforts to enlist support in Quebec and Nova Scotia, not elsewhere in the British Empire. On October 26, 1774, at the conclusion of the last day of its final session, the First Continental Congress sent an "Address to the Inhabitants of the Province of Quebec." Written by John Dickinson, it appealed to British settlers in Quebec and Nova Scotia on the grounds that they were being deprived of the rights to which they were entitled: representative government, habeas corpus, trial by jury, freedom of the press, and free land tenure without obligatory duties to the government. It invited them to join in union and send their own delegates to the next Continental Congress. The address amounted to eighteen pages, compared with a couple of long sentences sent to other colonies in British America.[2] The same month, the Massachusetts Provincial Congress voted to send an agent to open relations with Quebec and Nova Scotia and later to open and establish an intimate correspondence and connection with Quebec "for and on behalf of Massachusetts." On February 21, 1775, the Boston Committee of Correspondence sent a letter to "the Inhabitants of the Province of Quebec" encouraging them to send delegates to the Second Continental Congress to bring "great Reputation and Weight to the Common Cause."[3]

The American Patriots continued to include Quebec and Nova Scotia of the Atlantic colonies in their dreams of a large North American republic. The Articles of Confederation included Quebec alone of the other twenty-six colonies in British America, although Benjamin Franklin had included Ireland in his first draft in July 1775. The attempt to enlist Quebec and Nova Scotia was not limited to political overtures but involved a military offensive beginning in 1775. The revolutionaries regarded it as a liberation campaign. In January 1776, the Continental Congress created two battalions of Canadian troops who styled themselves "Congress's Own" and who were the only regiment to serve directly under Congress. As late as 1782, George Washington was contemplating another campaign against Quebec and Nova Scotia. Franklin tried again to incorporate Quebec and Nova Scotia in the negotiations of the peace terms with Britain in 1783.[4]

Canadians remained immune to American calls to join them in rebellion. Throughout the British Atlantic, however, there were self-described Patriots who gave overt support to the American Revolution. There was minority support in Canada, not least among some of the English-speaking British Protestants (Old Subjects) and French inhabitants (New Subjects) in Quebec and Nova Scotia.[5] Protests by French Canadians were significant and long lasting and were only stopped by strong action when Governor Guy Carleton imposed martial law. The first statue of George III to be defaced, in fact, was in Quebec. Among Old Subjects such as Thomas Walker, an English merchant who had spent ten years in Boston, there was "an extremely active and energetic minority" who openly favored the American Revolution and who corresponded with the American commander Benedict Arnold. The Old Subjects were particularly unhappy to be deprived of their traditional rights as British subjects by the Quebec Act.[6] Only Montreal and Quebec were to have their loyalties tested by the approach of the Continental Army. General Robert Montgomery, commanding the invading force, was initially confident that he could find as many volunteers as he could afford to pay among the inhabitants of Montreal.[7] Indeed, at first, the army was welcomed in the Richelieu Valley. As late as the withdrawal from Quebec in late 1776, there was support for the invasion of Benedict Arnold.[8] The revolutionaries were hostile toward Catholicism, which had been apparent in their reaction to the Quebec Act as expressed in the Suffolk Resolves of September 9, 1774, in Massachusetts, rejecting the Coercive Acts, and the address to "Friends and fellow subjects" in Great Britain by the Continental Congress in September and October 1775.[9]

Like the British in America, the American Patriots overestimated the potential for support in Quebec and Nova Scotia. They conspicuously failed to find allies among the priests and seigneurs who were beneficiaries of the Quebec Act, whose generous provisions for the French elite were denounced by the Continental Congress. In Montreal, priests even denied absolution to Patriot supporters of the Continental Army. When Ethan Allen thought that he could enter Montreal unopposed, he was "shocked to see that an armed force was emerging from the city instead of a friendly welcoming committee," which consisted of only thirty-four British soldiers with two hundred citizen volunteers, 60 percent of whom were Canadians. Many of the Old Subjects were Loyalists, despite their opposition to the Quebec Act. Edward Antill, a Canadian officer in the Continental

Army, admitted that the Canadians were "not to be depended upon." Prudent Lajeunesse, a French Canadian visiting Philadelphia, reported that the letters of Congress "made little Impression, the common People being generally unable to read"—an overstatement, as French Canadians were well informed about political events from having letters and newspapers read aloud in taverns and other places.[10]

As with the British in America, the very presence of the army alienated potential support by their pillaging, forced requisitions, and indiscipline. With the loss of momentum following the capture of Montreal, it became apparent that the invading army was too small and insufficiently resourced to have much chance of success. As soldiers besieged Quebec, Colonel Moses Hazen warned General Philip Schuyler that loyalties were shifting and that seven-eighths of the better sorts of people were Tories who "would wish to see our Throats cut and perhaps would readily assist in doing it."[11] That was unlikely, as most wealthy merchants were Americans and, possibly, if they had been able to under the constraints of martial law, might have supported the American cause.[12] If the French Canadians disappointed the Americans, it was also apparent that they were far from zealous in their support of Britain. David Wooster, a Connecticut general, compared them to Indigenous peoples, "fond of choosing the strongest party." They often seemed indifferent and unwilling to do militia service. In contrast to the expectation of the home government and colonial officials, they were not easily influenced by the French Canadian elite of seigneurs and priests.[13]

Bermuda

Bermuda was the most overtly Patriot of the other colonies in its support of the American Revolution. The Tucker family, who had relatives and commercial ties in South Carolina and Virginia, was the most prominent family on the island in support of the cause. Colonel Henry Tucker (1742–1800) led the only group of delegates representing one of the colonial assemblies from outside the thirteen mainland colonies to petition the Second Continental Congress. The petition presented on July 11, 1775, sought exemption from the embargo and explained that the island's numerical inferiority prevented them from giving substantial reciprocal assistance to "the noble stand made by [the] . . . patriotic sons for the liberties of America." While in Philadelphia in 1775, Tucker negotiated with Benjamin Franklin to send gunpowder in exchange for the lifting of the embargo. After a covert operation to seize the gunpowder at St. Georges in Bermuda, the gunpowder was shipped to Charleston, where it was used in the defense of Fort Moultrie against Admiral Sir Peter Parker (1721–1811). According to the island agent in London, many assemblymen and even councilors were involved in the seizure.

In late 1775, Captain Abraham Whipple (1733–1819), who has traditionally been alleged to have played a major role in the burning of the *Gaspee* in 1772, invited five of the nine members of the island council on board his ship to celebrate the seizure and wrote that they "were hearty friends of the American cause, and heartily disposed to serve it." The island also shipped salt, vital for preserving food for the army, and small ships made from light cedar wood to America. In response to another petition to Congress in 1776, the island received shipments of corn and other food supplies principally from Delaware, Maryland, North Carolina, and Virginia. In April 1776, Silas Deane visited the west end of Bermuda and similarly thought that "the people of this island are zealous in the American cause and appear willing to do everything in their power to promote it." Indeed, such was the extent of their sympathies and illicit trade with the rebel colonies that Britain mounted a naval blockade and deployed troops in Bermuda in 1778 and 1779.[14]

Nevertheless, Bermuda never openly questioned the sovereignty of Parliament. Like the British Caribbean, its political disputes were about the prerogative powers of the governor and the Crown, not Parliament. In common with other island colonies, Bermuda's petitions continued to express loyalty to the king after 1774. Even the Tucker family was split in its attitude toward the American Revolution. The island paid the duty imposed by the Stamp Act (1765) and only began to protest when the stamped papers were rejected in America. They similarly paid the Townshend Duties. They were reliant on food imports, however, meaning that the prospect of famine was an important influence in their decision to petition the Continental Congress. Their earlier sympathy for the Patriot cause became more equivocal with the influx of Loyalist refugees, such as the Goodrich family of Virginia. In common with Antigua and Tortola in the British Virgin Islands, Bermuda began to arm merchant ships as privateers against America. They successfully preyed on shipping in the

Chesapeake. Thomas Jefferson's first concern as governor of Virginia from June 1779 was to intercept these privateers, which, he complained, represented as great a threat to Virginia as Lord Dunmore had in 1776. In retaliation Congress revoked the island's exemption from the embargo, although it made some exceptions for individuals until finally revoking any such privileges in May 1781.[15]

Ireland and the West Indies

The most analogous of the other colonies to the thirteen mainland colonies were Ireland and the British West Indies. This is because they also had elected governments and similar political ideas to North Americans about their capacities as white Protestants whose English heritage entitled their governing colonial elites to the same rights as Englishmen, though they did not adopt the republican ideology so common in the northern colonies. They regarded their elected colonial legislatures as critical to the protection of their freedom and constitutional rights. Indeed, in some cases they not only anticipated but were ahead of constitutional theory in America. As early as 1460, the Irish Parliament had claimed legislative autonomy from Britain. In 1651, the Assembly of Barbados denied parliamentary sovereignty, over a hundred years in advance of writers in America. In 1692, the Irish House of Commons claimed the sole right to initiate money bills and levy taxes. In 1698, William Molyneux's pamphlet *The Case of Ireland's Being Bound by Acts of Parliament in England, Stated* denied the right of the English Parliament to legislate for Ireland.[16] Molyneux continued a tradition of earlier writers like Patrick D'Arcy and Molyneux's father-in-law, William Domville, who similarly insisted on the autonomy of the Irish Parliament.[17] Based on historical precedents and natural rights theory, Molyneux's pamphlet was condemned by the House of Commons in London as "of dangerous consequence to the crown and people of England by denying the authority of the king and parliament of England to bind the kingdom and people of Ireland." In the weekly *The Censor, or, The Citizen's Journal* in Dublin (1747), Molyneux's argument was revived by Dr. Charles Lucas, while the case also found a caustic advocate in the writings of Jonathan Swift.[18] Long before the nonimportation committees in America, there were appeals for an economic boycott and the promotion of home manufactures in Ireland against Britain.[19]

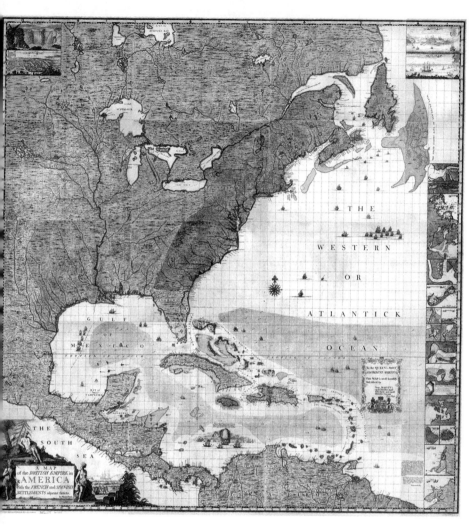

Henry Popple, composite map of the British Empire in America. London: Henry Toms and R. W. Searle, 1746. (Library of Congress, Geography and Map Division)

Despite the parallels, Ireland and the British West Indies did not join the American Revolution. One view often expressed by contemporaries, and later by historians, was that rebellion was impractical in the Caribbean, given its very large enslaved majorities. The Caribbean was not inclined to break away from imperial rule at any time in its eighteenth- and nineteenth-century history. With the great exception of Haiti, the islands were the last colonies in the Americas to gain independence from Europe. Cuba was the last Spanish colony to become independent in the Americas.

It was not until 1962 that Jamaica and Trinidad became the first Caribbean colonies to gain independence from Britain. Although the term is studiously avoided, there are still European colonies in the Caribbean.

The loyalty of the planter and merchant elite in the British West Indies, however, was not simply due to physical impediments in the era of the Revolution. Before 1776, there was nothing to prevent the islands from publishing pamphlets in support of the Patriot cause in America. How can we explain that no Jamaican participated in the exchange of some 1,178 pamphlets debating the relative merits of the imperial issue on either side of the Atlantic? Only three authors in the British Caribbean wrote about the Stamp Act. They were all from Barbados, where they defended the compliance of the island with the stamp duties in ways that provoked a hostile rebuke from John Dickinson in Philadelphia. The islands had printing presses and articulate writers who produced a volley of literature against metropolitan interference in the slavery system. But they were mostly silent about North American grievances. Furthermore, they did not create intercolonial correspondence committees, sons of liberty organizations, or nonimportation associations, or engage in a petitioning movement.[20]

There were also alternative strategies of opposition that West Indian planters failed to pursue. The Stamp Act riots in St. Kitts and Nevis belie the notion that whites in the British West Indies were incapable of even token opposition to imperial policy. These riots were major in proportion to the size of the free population. They occurred despite the islands' dependence on the British sugar market, despite having the highest proportion of slaves in British America, and despite a powerful military presence in the region. Furthermore, the assemblies of the British West Indies demonstrated that the planters were very capable of defending their interests and defying imperial government in local prerogative disputes like that of Jamaica under Governor William Henry Lyttelton.[21] After the American war, the planters developed various strategies in opposition to antislavery policies, which they had conspicuously failed to use earlier.

The reactions of the British West Indies and Ireland to the outbreak of the American Revolution consequently had much in common.[22] There were significant parallels in the views held by Ireland's Protestant population and by West Indian legislators. Before 1775, elites in both Ireland and the British West Indies tended to avoid discussions of the constitutional merits of the imperial crisis. At the same time, local constitutional issues about royal prerogative powers often overshadowed the fundamental issue of the sovereignty of Parliament and pivotal events in America. As the imperial crisis loomed, these colonies attempted to remain aloof and tried to avoid blaming either side.[23]

The divergence of the British West Indies, Ireland, and the thirteen mainland colonies of America, outlined above, was anticipated by actions in the West Indies in the 1760s. West Indian planters and merchants, for example, not only supported the Sugar (Revenue) Act of 1764 but campaigned for higher duties on sugar and rum after that act had been passed. Although the Stamp Act of 1765 imposed a greater financial burden on the Caribbean than on North America, Jamaica and Barbados paid stamp duties—in contrast to all the mainland colonies. The submission of the largest and most populous islands was mocked by mainland Patriots, who regarded any payment of imperial taxes as an acknowledgment of parliamentary authority to tax the colonies and therefore a fatal precedent. Stamp Act riots in St. Kitts and Nevis only occurred after threats of what amounted to an economic boycott by the mainland Patriots. The Leeward Islands had little choice but to resist because they imported most of their food from North America. They risked a famine and the associated danger of a slave rebellion if they complied with the Stamp Act. Unlike in North America, tensions in Ireland and the West Indies did not mount to a climactic breakdown between their respective legislatures and the lord lieutenant and governors in the 1770s. On the contrary, there was unusual harmony. There were no committees of correspondence, economic boycotts, or sons of liberty.[24]

Ireland and the British West Indies were less strident in their ideology than the mainland Patriots. Like the American Loyalists, Irish elites objected to imperial taxes, but they believed in obedience to authority. Furthermore, they preferred to stress commercial and practical rather than constitutional objections to imperial policies. West Indian elites shared more in common with contemporary political leaders in Ireland and opposition leaders in England than they did with revolutionaries in America. Leaders like Henry Grattan (1746–1820) and Henry Flood (1732–91) in Ireland, Charles Price (1708–72) in Jamaica, and Sir John Gaye Alleyne (1724–1801) in Barbados sought to direct the internal affairs of their colonies and to obtain local autonomy *within* the British Empire: "they spoke the same language of law and politics, but not for the same ends" as the

Francis Wheatley (1747–1801), *The Dublin Volunteers on College Green, 4th November 1779*, 1779–81. (National Gallery of Ireland)

Americans. They wanted only to reform, not to dissolve, the empire.[25] They believed that the benefits of their membership in the empire outweighed the advantages of independence.

As with the opponents to government policy in England, West Indians and Irish only attempted to intervene in American politics to avert a crisis in 1774–75, when relations between the Thirteen Colonies and Britain had reached a point of no return. They did very little to assuage the competing parties before that time. The most radical statement was a petition from Jamaica in December 1774. It repudiated parliamentary sovereignty over the internal affairs of the colony. It is often cited as crucial evidence to support the contention that only the threat of coercion or the impracticality of a revolt prevented the islands from joining the mainland colonies. One historian likens the petition to the Declaration of Rights, while another describes it as "a ringing endorsement of the emerging colonial view of the distribution of authority within the empire."[26] Both the timing and content of the petition, however, make it suspect as evidence of British West Indian support for the American Revolution. It was passed after the announcement of the nonimportation and nonexportation resolutions of the Continental Congress, which would have serious implications for the economy of Jamaica.[27] It was not the climax of a cumulative opposition movement in the islands but rather a spontaneous reaction to the threat of losing their trade with North America and the associated danger of a slave revolt caused by famine. The Jamaican Assembly simultaneously renewed its request "in the most forcible manner" for more troops from Britain. Moreover, the members voted their usual additional subsistence for the two regiments that garrisoned Jamaica. The day that they passed their controversial address, they voted five hundred pounds for the military hospital at St. Jago de la Vega. According to one local merchant who was sympathetic to the revolution, "the Sentiments so Nobly Expres'd by our Assembly . . . in their Address to the Crown [were] . . . by no means the general sense of the People," and the majority of Jamaicans gloried in the downfall of America.[28] In December 1775, Jamaicans led all the islands in sending a declaration of loyalty to the king in which they also requested more troops. George III replied by publicly expressing his pleasure at the dutiful behavior of the Jamaican Assembly.

Before 1775, "Irish Protestants were divided between a minority of vociferous Patriots who proclaimed their support for the colonists, a more traditional and conservative body which instinctively supported the mother country's assertion of its authority, and a third section of opinion, which continued to hope that some compromise would avert a conflict which seemed increasingly likely."[29] In February 1775, the merchants of Belfast sent a petition to Britain warning of the economic crisis that would result in the event of a war in America. There was, indeed, a minority who supported America. In July 1775, the club of free citizens in Dublin toasted "Our fellow subjects in America now suffering persecution for attempting to assert their rights."[30] Sir Edward Newenham (1734–1814), who was an MP representing the county of Dublin, built a tower in 1776 dedicated to George Washington on his estate, Belcamp, in Raheny, whose inscription partly read, "Oh, ill-fated Britain!"[31] Such reactions were far from common and largely predated the signing of the Declaration of Independence. In October 1775, for example, both houses of the Irish Parliament voted to send a loyal address to the throne formally condemning the "rebellion" in America. Although opposed by a determined minority in the House of Commons, the address passed by a majority of ninety votes to fifty-four. The following month Ireland agreed to send 4,000 troops for overseas service but refused to replace them with German mercenaries offered by

Britain.[32] Ireland would become an important hub for recruits and supplies for the British army in America.

Irish and West Indian Opposition to War

Despite the number of Ulstermen who had emigrated to America in the 1760s, "the attention given by the Belfast patriots to transatlantic events was no greater than one might expect to find at a similar gathering in Dublin."[33] Nevertheless, Presbyterians were the most prominent opponents in Ireland of the war in America. In November 1776, a new edition of Molyneux's *Case of Ireland* significantly appeared in Belfast.[34] At the same time, "the Catholic community remained divided between prosperous landed and commercial interests anxious to assert their loyalty to the house of Hanover, and the bulk of the population whose long-standing hostility towards the existing political order showed no sign of waning.... The Irish political nation would support the crown in its efforts to suppress the American rebellion, but not without considerable misgivings."[35]

The Anglo-Irish and West Indian elites did not subscribe to the conspiracy theory that Britain was systematically attempting to impose tyranny on America. They did not speak the republican language of equality nor of virtue to claim moral superiority over the mother country. In Ireland, the results of the general election did not "support the view that any significant patriot sentiment had occurred among the electorate." After the American Declaration of Independence, it became even less common for anyone outside of the "core of radical patriots" to express their support in Ireland or the British West Indies for America. This was apparent in the municipal politics of Dublin and in the press coverage in Ireland.[36] In the British West Indies, the assemblies sent petitions of loyalty to the home government. The legislatures of Tobago, Grenada (the second largest sugar-producing colony in the British Caribbean), and the British Virgin Islands specifically denounced the rebellion in America. In a reversal of a 1775 petition critical of Britain, Grenada conceded that the mainland colonies had suffered "oppression" but that their sufferings did not "justify the proceedings of the revolted provinces." It expressed regret at the "violent and unjustifiable proceedings of the people of those Colonies [who] ... forced your Majesty to the painful necessity of reducing them to a proper obedience by Coercive means."[37]

Nevertheless, there was increasing opposition in Ireland and the West Indies to a war that brought economic hardship without benefits, with considerable opposition expressed about the embargoes imposed to prevent exports to America.[38] Planters and merchants in the Caribbean had nothing to gain and much to lose from conflict between Britain and America, since the war exposed them to the threat of foreign conquest and to large-scale insurrection. They felt themselves neglected and defenseless. British military resources were overstretched in a global struggle against France (1778), Spain (1779), and the Dutch Republic (1780). On the eve of the war with France, there were only 8,871 troops in Ireland instead of the regular peacetime garrison of 12,000.[39] For much of 1779, there was an invasion scare in Ireland, but the real objective of the French was in the Caribbean, where they captured Grenada and St. Vincent. In both Ireland and the Caribbean, the fears of the political elite were justified by a rise in acts of resistance among the Catholic or enslaved majority of the population, who used the crisis for their own struggle against oppression.

In the Carlisle Peace Commission of 1778, the British offer to give up the claim to tax America removed a major constitutional issue that resonated in Ireland and the British West Indies. Similarly, the French alliance with the United States turned the war into a traditional patriotic struggle against a Catholic power, which posed a security threat to both the British West Indies and to Ireland. It quieted critics, especially among the Presbyterians, who took an early lead in the formation of independent Irish Volunteer companies that were armed groups aiming to protect Ireland from an invasion by France. These voluntary military units were a substitute for a militia or government-sponsored independent companies whose formation was prevented by the state of public finances and earlier opposition by the home government. Although portrayed by some as a sinister challenge to government, "such initiatives were regarded as commendable efforts by loyal and well-disposed individuals to fill the vacuum which had been created by government's financial inability to embody a national militia." The development was reported in a matter-of-fact manner and "with complete equanimity" by the Earl of Buckinghamshire (1723-93), the lord lieutenant of Ireland, to Lord George Germain (1716-85). With the entry of Spain into the war in July 1779, the Volunteer companies continued to grow, comprising as many as 60,000 armed men by mid-1780.[40]

As the elite leadership in Ireland and the West Indies became weary of the war between 1779 and 1780, periods of political stalemate occurred between the lord lieutenant and the Parliament of Ireland and between the colonial governors and assemblies in the British West Indies. Lord North attempted to appease Irish opinion by making major concessions, beginning with the passage of two Free Trade Acts (1778 and 1779) and a Catholic Relief Act (1778), the transfer of the cost of the troops sent from Ireland to Britain, and the repeal of a clause in the Test Act (1704), which had precluded Presbyterians from full political participation. Nevertheless, the Irish Volunteer movement became overtly political in an implicit attempt to intimidate the British government. They wore uniforms of scarlet, green, blue, and orange, which they began to insist should be made from homespun. They supported the Patriot campaign to secure the legislative independence of the Irish Parliament, which was achieved with the repeal in 1782 and 1783 by Britain's Parliament of the 1720 Declaratory Act and the Renunciation Act. These measures helped to remove many of the earlier colonial constitutional objections and might have succeeded in America in the 1760s. In Ireland and the West Indies, growing criticism of the war was apparent, but this was not synonymous with support for the rebellion.

The parallel was not with the Patriots in America but with opposition parties in Britain. If there seemed to be a quasi-revolutionary mood in Ireland, the same was true of Britain with the Wyvill Association Movement (1780–85), a petitioning campaign for social and political reform in England, and the massive Gordon Riots in London (1780).[41] Indeed, the rhetorical opposition to the war in Ireland and the West Indies was more restrained than in England. The Irish and the West Indians expressed their frustration in practical terms relating to cost, economic impact, and failure to gain military advantage rather than in ideological opposition to the war. Despite their misgivings, Ireland and the British West Indies contributed significantly toward the cost of defense, and their representatives continued to vote addresses of loyalty to Britain.

Critical Differences with North America

The reluctance of the elites in Ireland and the British West Indies to support the thirteen mainland colonies reflected critical differences with North America. In the case of the British West Indies, the most fundamental cause of these differences was their commitment to producing sugar, which made these island colonies economically dependent on Britain. For most of the eighteenth century, the island colonies were unable to compete with the price of rival French sugar, due to differences in economies of scale with Saint-Domingue alone producing more sugar than the entire British Caribbean. So great was the price differential that British West Indians rapidly lost their market share to the French in both Europe and North America. Only the monopoly of the British market enabled them to flourish. Hence, while the mainland colonies were outgrowing the imperial economy, the island colonies were increasingly dependent on the discriminatory duties that guaranteed their monopoly of the home market. Their inability to compete extended beyond sugar and was a cause of friction with the North Americans, who preferred to purchase cheaper molasses from the French West Indies. The West India lobby clashed with the North American interest over the Sugar Acts of 1764 and 1766.[42]

The Navigation Acts had many negative implications for Ireland. Unlike North America and the British West Indies, Ireland did not enjoy free trade with Britain or even with the British colonies in the Atlantic. Nevertheless, the major source of growth in Irish trade was with Britain and the West Indies. Exports grew by two-thirds between 1770 and 1775. Cork was a major Atlantic port, larger than Glasgow. Furthermore, a variety of different products accounted for this expansion, including grain and provisions. By the end of the 1720s, linen accounted for over half of Irish exports to England. In 1696, free access to the home market had been granted to linen, which was "the very condition for its expansion." The major source of overseas demand for beef was in the West Indies. In the meantime, trade—primarily in butter and dairy products—contracted with the rest of Europe.[43]

Ireland was integrated into what was called the "Irish triangle," where American ships carried flaxseed to Ireland and then loaded supplies for markets in the British Caribbean, exchanging those supplies for sugar, rum, and molasses for the American mainland. When it all worked properly, the vessel returned to Philadelphia or New York to start the flaxseed cycle once again. The trade was substantial, with exports to America between 1761 and 1776 averaging £112,946 and imports from America averaging £112,411. The American Revolution saw that trade dramatically decline, with exports to America dropping to £73,605 and imports to a mere £19,908 between 1777 and 1780.[44] During the American Revolution, the restrictions on Irish trade were lifted, beginning with woolens to the colonies in 1778 and followed by woolens and glass to England in 1779. The prohibition on the import of foreign hops was removed in 1780.[45] Indeed, while official trade largely collapsed, smuggling allowed reasonably impressive amounts of American produce to enter Ireland, such as tobacco from Dutch St. Eustatius and Danish St. Thomas, and most of all from British Tortola.[46]

The Anglo-Irish and the West Indian elites were fearful of rebellions among, respectively, the majority Gaelic-speaking Catholic population in Ireland and the majority Black enslaved population in the Caribbean. Protestants were less than a quarter of the population of four million in Ireland, while whites comprised less than a tenth of the half-million people in all the islands of the British West Indies except Barbados.[47] Furthermore, these minorities were unevenly distributed, which meant the disparity was even greater in rural areas. In Ireland, Protestants made up less than one-eighth of the population in Galway, one of the few areas of the country where Catholic gentry managed to survive, like the Blakes of Ballyglunin.[48] In some parts of the west, Protestants were outnumbered nineteen to one and in the south by four to one.[49] The Penal Laws discriminated against Catholics, restricting their civil, economic, and religious freedom, including prohibiting them from bearing arms (1695) and from voting (1728). Indeed, "Irish political and demographic realities were such that a large standing army, which might indeed pose a threat to liberty in other circumstances, was essential for the very existence of a Protestant state in Ireland. The same consideration rendered the formation of a militia . . . impracticable under Irish conditions."[50]

But we should not overstress how paranoid Protestants were about Catholics. The Catholics "were feared more for their numbers and their poverty than for their religious principles," but we should note the increasing "ease with which, at least in their recorded comments, Irish Protestants generally ignored the Catholics around them," which "could be interpreted as evidence of growing Protestant confidence," based largely on the threat of coercion.[51] The recognition by Irish and West Indian elites of the importance of physical force was reflected in their attitude toward the British army, which differentiated them from their counterparts in North America. In Ireland and the British West Indies, Protestant and planter elites needed the army not only for protection from foreign attack but as a police force. In the 1760s and early 1770s, there was an ever-present danger of rebellion from below, which was apparent during the agrarian Whiteboy and Hearts of Steel insurrectionary movements in Ireland and frequent slave uprisings in Jamaica, as noted previously. St. Vincent and Dominica in the Caribbean faced an additional threat from the Black Caribs, leading to a war in St. Vincent in 1772.

In contrast to Americans, neither the West Indian planters nor the Anglo-Irish wanted to rely on militia to defend themselves from insurrection. Unlike American assemblies, the Irish Parliament and the British West Indian assemblies voluntarily contributed toward the cost of maintaining and supporting the British army. Beginning in the 1730s, Jamaica and Antigua paid annual subsidies toward the army that doubled the normal rate of pay to compensate the troops for the higher cost of living in the Caribbean. These payments were a reaction to the First Maroon War in Jamaica, which reached a climax in 1731, and a suspected slave conspiracy in Antigua in 1736. The planters did not expect the army to defend them effectively against foreign attack, for which they depended on the navy. Instead, they regarded the army as a vital instrument of white control over the majority Black population, which the assemblies frequently called the "internal enemy." As the Jamaican Assembly explained in its address on behalf of the Americans in December 1774, "week and feeble as this colony is, from the very small number of white inhabitants, and its peculiar situation, from the encumbrance of more than two hundred thousand slaves, it cannot be supposed that we now intend, or ever could have intended, resistance to Great Britain."[52] The Irish Parliament had objected to the augmentation bill of 1767, but only because it was expected to pay for troops deployed outside of Ireland.

In Ireland and the British West Indies, troops were distributed in interior posts with a clear view toward policing the countryside. They were not there principally for defense against foreign attack. The real threat of rebellion throughout the rest of the empire was from below, whether among the majority Catholics or Protestant tenant farmers in Ireland, enslaved people in Jamaica, Indians in Bengal, or French Catholics in Quebec and Nova Scotia. These were not illusory threats. The potential had been demonstrated in Jamaica in slavery revolts, such as Tacky's Rebellion in 1760, the only fortuitously foiled Coromantee risings in the mid-1760s, and the large-scale and only accidentally discovered Hanover plot in 1776. There were simultaneous agrarian risings among the Protestant

Whiteboys, Oakboys, and Steelboys in the 1760s and 1770s in Ireland. The danger was dramatically demonstrated in Ireland by the Great Rebellion of 1798 and in the Caribbean by the Saint-Domingue Rebellion (1791–1803). Unlike settlers in America, Irish and West Indian elites additionally were concerned by the continued threat posed to their security by France and Spain.

Ideologies of the Dominant Minority and Causes of the American Revolution

West Indian planters and Irish elites had much in common.[53] Their connection to Britain was reinforced by absenteeism among the planter elite in the islands and major landowners in Ireland. This trend increased in the decades before the American Revolution.[54] The historiography of both regions currently plays down the significance of absenteeism, but contemporaries regarded it as a fundamental flaw that strengthened colonial dependence on Britain. In Ireland, "a third of the lay peerage seldom or never took their places in local society," while absentees accounted for an eighth of all rents to landlords in the 1770s. Absenteeism was high in the Leeward Islands, where most of the sugar plantations were owned by absentees in islands like St. Kitts. Nevertheless, it has become apparent that absenteeism was much more limited than conventionally believed in Jamaica. The island once had many more large plantation houses than was hitherto appreciated, which is again indicative of the presence of elite planters, although the homes of absentees were much grander in England.[55] Absenteeism was even lower in Barbados than in Jamaica. The problem of absenteeism, however, extended beyond the leading planters to include public officeholders, clergymen, and army officers.[56] It created an ethos of wanting to return "home," which was intensified by the horrendous disease environment and high mortality rates in the Caribbean. Of greater significance in the islands was the tradition of planters sending their children to schools and colleges in Britain. More than half the members of the Assembly of Antigua in 1763–83 had been educated in England. The proportion was actually much higher, as the lists are incomplete and often nonexistent. Even in Ireland, barristers were expected to have spent time at the Inns of Court in London. Patriot leaders like Henry Flood and Henry Grattan often completed at least some of their education in England.

In addition, there was a "lack of a substantial yeomanry" and middling people in both Ireland and the British West Indies. This was an observation made by George Washington on visiting Barbados, which had the highest proportion of whites in the British West Indies. Charles O'Hara (1740–1802), an Irish landowner who would later gain fame for having surrendered Lord Cornwallis's sword at Yorktown, wrote about the stark division between "gentlemen farmers and cottage tenants who were the lowest species of slaves." He argued that the country needed a substantial class of yeomanry.[57] This would have precluded a consumer revolution on a transforming scale as occurred in America, where the experience of engaging in economic embargoes was fundamental in building ordinary people's support for revolution in British North America.[58]

In contrast to America, the franchise was limited in these colonies owing to the exclusion of the votes of the Black majority in the Caribbean and the Catholic majority in Ireland. The vote of one planter in St. Kitts determined the election of five candidates in 1773. In Ireland, an estimated one hundred voters controlled two-thirds of the seats of the House of Commons. After 1692, Roman Catholics were prohibited from sitting in the Irish Parliament. For much of the eighteenth century, about 80 percent of the total male population was debarred from voting because of religious and property qualifications.[59] Sharing power was not an option. In Ireland in 1800, the leaders of the Ascendancy opted for union with Great Britain rather than admit Catholics to the Irish Parliament.[60] In the British Caribbean, all the assemblies ultimately chose to dissolve themselves in favor of direct government rather than permit free Blacks or people of color to vote and become members of the legislatures. The only exception was Barbados and the Bahamas, which had the highest proportion of whites.[61]

The examples of Ireland and the British West Indies allow us to debate and prioritize competing explanations relating to the causes of the American Revolution. Some factors cited as fundamental causes for rebellion were also present in colonies that did not rebel. At the very least, this would allow us to argue that such factors were necessary, but not sufficient, conditions. In *American Slavery, American Freedom,* Edmund Morgan famously argued that the presence of slavery made whites more vigilant of their own freedom and made them willing to embrace ideas of equality. He claimed that it was slavery that "enabled Virginia to nourish representative government in a plantation society, slavery that transformed the Virginia of Governor Berkeley to the Virginia of Jefferson, slavery that made the Virginians dare to speak a political language that magnified the rights of freemen, and slavery, therefore, that brought Virginians into the same commonwealth political tradition with New Englanders." This was the reason planters were some of the most eloquent proponents of liberty: "The very institution that was to divide North and South after the Revolution may have made possible their union in a republican government."[62]

The presence of slavery, however, is also used to explain the continued loyalty of the British West Indies to Britain. In reviewing Morgan's book in the *William and Mary Quarterly,* Richard S. Dunn thought Morgan's "analysis of Virginia invites comparison with the British West Indian sugar islands," which Dunn believed showed the limitations of the central theme of *American Slavery, American Freedom.* According to Dunn, "What gives the West Indian analogy pertinence for the eighteenth century is that the Caribbean slaveholders did not become libertarians or republicans. On the contrary, they evolved a peculiarly narrow, selfish variant of traditional elitist politics. This raises questions about Morgan's connection between white freedom and black slavery." The same observations might be made about claims that the dependence on tobacco and the credit crisis before the war explain the Revolution in Virginia, since the British West Indian economy was similarly dependent on a single crop and was severely affected by the credit crisis of 1772. It is possible to reconcile these different claims for the role of slavery or debt, but only by invoking other influences. In the case of slavery, we need to discuss how the differences in the relative proportion of enslaved people within the respective societies is significant, which may explain the conundrum of why their presence might have caused planters in the islands to remain loyal and those in the southern mainland colonies to rebel.[63]

Quebec and Nova Scotia, Ireland, and the British West Indies pose a particular problem for the powerful case made by proponents of ideological, legal, and constitutional explanations of the American Revolution. These loyal colonies had radical traditions of political ideology, customary rights, long-established local constitutions, and elected assemblies. The comparison is often dismissed on the grounds that their elites simply could not rebel for practical reasons, but this ignores the extent of their willing compliance and even denunciation of the American Revolution. The opposition parties and radicals in England exhibited much more sympathy for the Patriots and were more vocal in their criticism of the British war for America.

Slavery and Loyalism

An imperial perspective on the American Revolution is valuable in giving a wider context to one of the more contentious issues in the contemporary historiography about the American Revolution, which is the role that slavery played in encouraging southern slaveholders to join their New England counterparts in rebellion in 1775–76. Recent studies of the causes of the American Revolution have placed more importance than in the past on slavery as a galvanizing cause of rebellion. Robert Parkinson sees a determination to rebel against Britain so as to preserve slavery from what he argues was an incipient abolitionist British imperial nation. This "common cause" of the Revolution, he argues, being the result of "racial fear," was even more important in uniting colonists than the common cause of outrage over taxation and issues of representation that is usually cited.[64] He thus contests Christopher Brown's comment that "most [people] in revolutionary America cared much less about the problem of slavery than the few abolitionists at the time and the many historians who have written about them since."[65] So too has Woody Holton, in a monograph on the coming of the American Revolution in Virginia and in a general survey of the American Revolution, stressed the extent to which American colonists were increasingly convinced that Britain was undermining slaveholders' power to command their enslaved property, thus leaving colonies exposed to slave uprisings.[66]

Holton places a great deal of emphasis in his argument upon the notorious proclamation by Virginia's governor, Lord Dunmore, on November 7, 1775, threatening Patriots with the specter of state-sponsored emancipation of enslaved people and servants who were promised freedom if they ran away from masters in rebellion against Britain. Perhaps 1,000 enslaved people answered Dunmore's call and were organized into an "Ethiopian regiment," whose uniforms proclaimed, "Liberty to Slaves." Enslaved Americans' defiance of their owners has been argued to have helped push the colonies toward independence. Gary Nash argues that Patriot fears of rebelling and rampaging freed slaves helped persuade Congress to raise a continental army so that Britain would abandon plans to encourage and exploit southern slave insurgencies.[67] "The slaves' insurgency," Woody Holton comments, "played an important role in persuading Dunmore to ally with them and thus in prodding white Virginians further along the road to independence."[68] Dunmore's Proclamation outraged Virginians, pushing some previously reluctant elite planters, such as William Byrd III, from neutrality to patriotism. The proclamation may have had more of an effect on elite planter opinion than did the Coercive Acts. The South Carolina Patriot Edward Rutledge thought that it would "more effectively work an eternal separation between Great Britain and the Colonies,—than any other expedient which could have been thought of."[69]

Fear of slave insurrection has also been argued to have pushed South Carolina toward rebellion. Enslaved men, such as Jeremiah, executed for conspiracy in 1775, started rumors that Britain intended to free enslaved people who ran away from masters, frightening whites that "if a real slave revolt crystallized around the apocryphal story of a British army of liberation, British statesmen might indeed be drawn into an alliance with the slave rebels."[70] Historians have argued that slavery was a vital impulse in the decision for revolution in South Carolina, noting how fears of slave conspiracies that surfaced increasingly in 1775 and 1776 helped turn a potentially Loyalist colony firmly into the Patriot camp, as planters came to believe that rebellion was a way of protecting slavery from a British government insufficiently attentive, in the view of planters, to threats of slave insurrection.[71]

There was some evidence in the mid-1770s that a few British politicians thought that the politics of slavery could be used to British advantage to quell rebellion in ways that mirrored the thinking of Dunmore in 1775 and 1776. William Henry Lyttelton, ex-governor of South Carolina and Jamaica and well-connected to British statesmen through family links, made a notorious speech in the House of Commons on October 26, 1775, just a few days before Dunmore made his proclamation, where he argued that the southern colonies could be separated from the northern colonies if Britain sent troops, including enslaved soldiers and free men of color, to South Carolina and Georgia. These colonies, he argued, were so paralyzed by fear of slave insurrection that a few imperial soldiers would bring them into line, as colonists, Lyttelton believed, would do anything to avoid a situation where "the negroes would rise and embrue their hands in the blood of their masters."[72]

Lyttelton and Dunmore, however, were conspicuously unsuccessful politicians who were not well respected by their peers. Lyttelton's motion to raise white and Black troops to serve in South Carolina and Georgia was easily defeated, and he was condemned by some MPs for having suggested using enslaved people against whites in ways that were shameful and which impugned the honor of Parliament. Almost no one in Britain cheered Dunmore in 1776, and Britons were equally unenthusiastic about a similar proposal made in 1778 by General Henry Clinton offering freedom to runaway slaves. Both were seen as unworthy actions for a civilized nation to take. Britain was very careful not to confront white colonial racial prejudices, most of which British statemen and other white Britons shared. The British army did little to end slavery in large part because it did not want to do so as an institution that itself owned many enslaved people. We can see the army's attitudes toward enslaved people in the ways it employed Blacks in its ranks. When Blacks assisted military operations, they were generally confined to non-fighting roles.[73]

The problem with an American-centric argument about slavery's role in causing the American Revolution is that arguments explaining how slavery made slaveholders embrace revolution can be made just as easily to explain why slaveholders stayed loyal to Britain. The conventional explanation for why Jamaica did not rebel in 1776, for example, is that it could not rebel due to slavery. Its commitment to that institution and Jamaica's geographical position as a British island in a hostile Caribbean ocean surrounded by French and Spanish enemies meant that it relied on British troops to an extent that was unparalleled elsewhere in British America.[74] Jamaica itself made this argument in its 1774 petition to the Continental Congress, in which its writers declared support for revolution but lamented, using a customary rhetoric of political helplessness developed over many years of being acutely aware of their vulnerability to internal and external attack, that their colony was so "weak and feeble" that it could not "now intend, or ever have intended, resistance to Great Britain."[75]

It is easier to see Britain and its armed forces as the guarantors of slavery rather than its antagonists. Although Britain was developing an abolitionist community, in the 1760s the number of abolitionists was pitifully small and was mostly confined to a very small Quaker religious community. The number of people who benefited from slavery and who supported the slave trade and the slavery interest was very large and immeasurably larger than the tiny number of abolitionists. Britain did not become an abolitionist nation until, at the very earliest, the late 1780s.[76] Indeed, if we look at slavery from an imperial rather than an American perspective, American concern about Britain undermining slavery in the Americas is wildly misplaced. It was, as we have argued, an empire of coercion. Britain was very prepared to use force to defend slaveowners and protect slavery. Britain in the 1760s was unreservedly committed to the preservation and expansion of the Atlantic slave trade, slavery, and the plantation system.

Of course, the politics of slavery shaped decisions to stay loyal or rebel because slavery was so fundamental to social and political relations everywhere in the British Atlantic, especially in plantation societies. And the particularities of slavery were very different from place to place. The growth of a naturally increasing enslaved population, for example, in the American South, which meant that southern colonies were not reliant on the Atlantic slave trade for the continuation of the plantation system, gave them a freedom of action in relation to slavery that was denied to colonists in the Caribbean, where the slave trade was vital to maintaining enslaved populations. It is hard, however, to see slavery as a principal cause for joining or not joining revolution in any colony. Proslavery revolutionaries had little reason to expect that Britain would not continue its wholehearted support of slavery whatever other issues divided Britain from the Thirteen Colonies. Slaveholders in Virginia might have been annoyed at Dunmore's rash proclamation and it may have tipped some reluctant revolutionaries into supporting rebellion. But the balance of British actions showed considerable support for slavery throughout the 1760s and 1770s.[77]

Colonists had other reasons to stay loyal to Britain besides their views on slavery. Jamaica, for example, was instinctively Loyalist. Its white population was largely British born, its elite links with Britain were greater than any other colony's, and it had a hostility to New England that was notably fierce, making settlers there indifferent to what was happening in Boston in 1774 and 1775. In addition, it welcomed British troops both on grounds of security and because Jamaica's white culture was oriented strongly around military culture.[78] White Jamaicans identified firmly with Britain rather than with North America. In mid-1776, the Jamaican overseer Thomas Thistlewood approvingly recorded a toast in favor of British military success in New England: "John Hartnole's wish to the No: Americans. Cobweb breeches, hedgehog Saddles, jolting Horses, Strong Roads and tedious Marches, to the enemies of Old England."[79] Thomas Iredell angrily disinherited his North Carolina nephew, James, in January 1775, "for having taken an oath of Allegiance to Congress in violation of your first to this Country."[80] Slavery united the rebellious and loyal colonies; other things divided them, meaning that the common cause was not racial fear and worry over slave insurrection.

In the other Atlantic colonies, there was no sudden shift in their political ideology in 1776. Quebec, Nova Scotia, the West Indies, Bermuda, and Ireland did not embrace republicanism. They believed in liberty but thought of it in traditional hierarchical terms, defining rights narrowly as privileges associated with property and corporations, preferring a traditional rhetoric of customary rights and privileges rather than abstract universal rights. They did not speak the language of equality and individual rights. They did not appropriate the republican language of virtue to claim moral superiority over the corruption of the mother country. They did not attempt to widen the franchise or disestablish state religion. They wanted as much autonomy as possible, but within the British Empire.[81]

The example of the loyal colonies highlights the problem of single-factor analysis in which insufficient consideration is given to context and to other influences on decision-making. Although there are notable exceptions, social, religious, economic, and constitutional explanations are often pitched against one another.[82] There are always a variety of ideas and precedents available to historical actors. This is not to deny the importance of ideas but to acknowledge that choices are inevitably affected by self-interest, emotions, class, social conditions, and relative situations.[83] This is important even in explaining the phenomenon of the Loyalists or Tories in the Thirteen Colonies, where at least a fifth of the population are thought to have supported Britain.[84]

The American Revolution was also a civil war in which some 19,000 Americans fought for the British. The Loyalists shared many of the same constitutional beliefs as the Patriots. Indeed, they regarded themselves as the true defenders of American liberty. They were privately critical of metropolitan policies like the Stamp Act. Martin Howard of Newport, Rhode Island, was the only Loyalist pamphleteer in America who attempted to defend the stamp duties.[85] Loyalists were strong proponents of liberty and constitutional government after the war, when some 70,000 Loyalists moved to other parts of the British Empire. Lord Dunmore found himself battling the Loyalists in the assembly in the Bahamas as he had once done with the Patriots when he was governor of Virginia. The politics of the Loyalists was similarly adversarial for British officials advocating constitutional reform in Quebec and Nova Scotia. The difference between the Loyalists and the Patriots in Canada was that the Loyalists did not accept that there was a British tyranny in 1776. They usually regarded the pretensions of the Patriots to political power as a greater threat to their liberty than Britain. Loyalists opposed armed resistance. They feared republicanism and anarchy more than the sovereign claims of Parliament. We need to remember, however, that Loyalists were not a unified category. They were split politically. For every Loyalist who campaigned in the early nineteenth century for representative government, there were others who were confirmed Tories and receptive to authoritarian government. The character of Loyalism in Canada after the American Revolution has attracted much attention in Canadian historiography, but what is clear is Loyalists' strong and ongoing commitment to imperialism, before and well after the American Revolution.[86]

In other words, decisions and choices cannot be explained exclusively in terms of ideological and constitutional beliefs without reference to a multiplicity of other factors that caused people to make different choices both within America and in the other colonies of the British Empire. A comparison with the other colonies offers a way to adjudicate between the different schools of thought and to qualify the role of different factors in relation to one another as causal explanations of the American Revolution.

SIX

The War of Empires

THE GLOBAL SCALE OF THE IMPERIAL dimensions of the American Revolutionary War is best appreciated from the perspective of Britain. In the late nineteenth century, it was described by Sir John Seeley as a continuation of a second Hundred Years' War with France.[1] Like the Seven Years' War (1756-63), it began in North America and spread to India, the Mediterranean, Europe, Africa, and the Caribbean. Unlike the Seven Years' War, however, the American Revolutionary War was not waged in Europe. It was a war about empire and was fought primarily in imperial domains. In this chapter, we concentrate on the imperial dimensions of the War of American Independence from 1775 to 1783, meaning that we pay attention not just to the war in North America but also to armed conflict in other parts of the world in which Britain had imperial interests. We do so to show that the War of American Independence was significant not just for the birth of the American republic in the 1780s but for recalibrating the British Empire in what was Britain's first major loss in the second Hundred Years' War with another major European imperial power, France.

Europeans in this imperial war were concerned with restoring the balance of power on the continent to reverse the devastating British victories of the Seven Years' War. British resources were overstretched in America with the outbreak of war against France (1778), followed by Spain (1779) and the Dutch Republic (1780), while much of the rest of Europe formed a hostile League of Armed Neutrality (1780). Even Sweden sent a small army in support of America. European support for America, however, was critical long before the outbreak of war between Britain and France in 1778. Britain paid the price between 1778 and 1783 for its arrogant actions in the aftermath of the Seven Years' War in 1763, when its statesmen used its overwhelming success to abandon any alliance with other European states. That arrogance by the British meant that not just France but most European powers were opposed to what they considered to be Britain's dangerous global imperial pretensions. In short, Britain was undermined in global geopolitics by its imperial hubris in the 1760s and 1770s, and was especially compromised by failing to cultivate European allies.[2]

The importance of foreign allies to the success of the American cause is best illustrated by a historiographical debate between the late Oxford historian Piers Mackesy (1924-2014) and University of Michigan professor John Shy (1931-2022) about whether the British could have won the American War of Independence.[3] Partly because they were both friends and former army officers, albeit in different national armies, it was a very amicable debate and has thus largely escaped notice. Despite its obscurity, it is an important historical argument about the war because it probes the very essence of why Britain lost the War of American Independence and does so using themes essential to studies of imperialism and imperial conflicts.

Piers Mackesy wrote a detailed account of the British side where his thesis is obscured by the richness of the detail provided in over five hundred pages of dense description. His comprehensive coverage of all the theaters of the war gives the impression that he was attributing the British defeat to their commitments elsewhere in the world in their war against France, Spain, and Holland. However, he was actually arguing that the war was winnable and that it was lost by the inadequacy of the British commanders in America rather than by the complexity of imperial global entanglements. Britain was fighting a war on many fronts, as befitted a global imperial power, but, Mackesy insisted, it had the capacity in the 1770s and 1780s to do so, if only it had benefited from leaders able to grasp the imperial dimensions of the conflict. He clarified his view in a short essay in which he absolved the politicians of responsibility and blamed the military leadership, maintaining that the generals were good tacticians but poor strategists.[4]

His interpretation, however, was contested by John Shy, an important historian of the military aspects of the Revolutionary War. Shy was informed by American experience in the Vietnam War. In his introduction to a second edition of Mackesy's book, Shy related that during World War II Mackesy's father, Major General Joseph (Pat) Mackesy, was blamed by Winston Churchill for the failure of an early attempt to create a beachhead in Europe by landing at Narvik in Norway.⁵ The shame was compounded when in his war memoirs Churchill again accused Mackesy's father of having undermined the campaign by his paralysis. Mackesy rehabilitated his father's reputation in two articles repudiating some of the more exaggerated claims against his father. He also refuted charges of cowardice attributed to Lord George Germain, the so-called coward of the Battle of Minden in 1757, accusations which followed Germain throughout the American Revolution. Even though this aside might seem at first a superfluous detail, Shy suggested that Mackesy was obsessed with the role of leadership for overtly personal reasons, which he prioritized over what Shy thought were more significant causal factors in the failure of the British in revolutionary America.⁶

In a later preface to a revised edition of his essays on the American War of Independence, Shy acknowledged that his perspective had been influenced by the contemporary Vietnam War just as Mackesy's interpretation was connected to his father's experiences in World War II. Shy compared the dilemma for the British to the problem Americans faced in Vietnam as to whether to fight a limited war against civilians or to use terror tactics. As with Vietnam, he argued, the very presence of an army from overseas contributed to the continuing alienation of the population in America. He regarded the Patriots and militia as an American version of the Viet Cong. He particularly focused on the problems of the war in the South. Aware of parallels to Vietnam, Mackesy believed that the British hit on a potentially winning counterinsurgency strategy in the South by using the army to reconquer territory and support the Loyalists, with a view to organizing the latter as a militia to police the civilian population and suppress the Patriots. Shy argued, however, that in the American South the British lost support because they were unable to contain the brutality of the Loyalists and they themselves resorted to ruthless repression in the campaigns of Colonel Banastre Tarleton (1754–1833), whose British Legion caused havoc and committed war crimes in vicious fighting in South Carolina during 1780–81.⁷

The Vietnam War was lost by some of the most experienced and intellectually impressive civilian and military commanders in the history of the United States. Lyndon Johnson's cabinet was composed of men who had belonged to the "Camelot" administration of John F. Kennedy, leaders of industry, like Robert McNamara, and academia, like Arthur Schlesinger, Jr., brought into government to shine their brilliance upon government policy. Shy briefly mentioned that the British leadership was quite able. Whatever their faults in leadership, strategy, and tactics, British leaders were the best and brightest of their day. Indeed, the parallels to Vietnam can better be shown through the lens of the British than through the American perspective in the American Revolutionary War.[8] A recent study of the remarkable Howe family, who provided in Richard, the commander of the British navy, and in William, the leader of the British army for three vital years of conflict, two of the most important British military leaders in the war, shows how, just as in Vietnam, the best and brightest of eighteenth-century aristocratic English families were placed in positions of great responsibility in America where, in general, they performed with distinction.[9]

Counterinsurgency

Shy's determination to place the American Revolution within a wider context of counterinsurgency which connected the American Revolution to contemporary events was ahead of its time, but it also harkened back to older treatments of the American Revolution as the unexpected and unhappy result of the imperial Seven Years' War. The British fought what today would be called counterinsurgency warfare of the type more recently fought by the United States in Afghanistan, where withdrawal after the longest war in the nation's history was similar to its decision to cut its losses in Vietnam.[10] Shy later called Mackesy's *The War for America* a classic, and in a review he paid tribute to the book for putting the war in a global context and helping us see it from the perspective of the British. Nevertheless, he felt that Mackesy had missed the reasons for the British defeat by focusing on the defects of British army and naval commanders.

The British have been similarly unsuccessful fighting counterinsurgencies in the twentieth and twenty-first centuries.[11] While the reasons for defeat are multiple and varied, several common factors for failure include popular support for revolt, war of attrition, difficulties of terrain, size of the army, supply logistics, and ultimately the political decision of the occupying power to withdraw. Nevertheless, domestic support and unconventional military tactics are not sufficient to explain Britain's defeat.

The Mackesy-Shy debate illustrates another essential factor in the success of the Patriots, and for historical counterinsurgencies, which was foreign support of American "rebels" (as the British saw Patriots). One common factor in imperial wars is that the occupying power is often unable to challenge outside assistance without risking the escalation of the war elsewhere. This was the case of the Americans in Vietnam, who were unwilling to bomb North Vietnam for fear of angering China, and in Afghanistan, where the Taliban had bases in neighboring Pakistan, which was an ally of the United States. Piers Mackesy used one of the few examples of British successes in fighting a counterinsurgency, which was in Malaya, now Malaysia, in 1946–48. He cited this war to show that the British could have defeated the United States. The Malayan War, however, was an aberration, first because the British were fighting an ethnic minority (the Chinese) who lacked support among the general population, and second, because the insurgents had no foreign support. It was still a long and brutal war.[12] Nevertheless, it illustrated the crucial role played by domestic support and foreign allies as a condition for the success of a colonial rebellion.[13]

Indeed, Ireland in the late eighteenth century serves as an even better example of successful counterinsurgent warfare by the British than does Malaya. Britain kept control of the island through a large troop presence that could be easily reinforced and, crucially, by the absence of sustained support for Irish rebels from France and Spain, as had been the case in America. Furthermore, the Irish Loyalist population enjoyed superiority of arms and was not on the defensive like their counterparts were in America. Indeed, great powers rarely completely lose a war against a small country or a terrorist group. They simply give up because of the expense and the loss of public support. This is what happened to the United States in Vietnam and Afghanistan. It is what happened to the British in the War of Independence. After Yorktown, their main army was still intact in New York and Quebec. They still held major cities, such as Charleston and St. Augustine, but the political will to continue evaporated, as the opposition began to gain majority support to end the war in the House of Commons.

France and Support of America

For the American Patriots, European support was crucial to the successful outcome of the Revolutionary War. It influenced events long before the formal entry of France as an ally of the United States in 1778. As early as

1775, Europe, especially France, provided vital military experience, funding, armaments, and protection to privateers, critically restricting British options in waging war in America. To allay French concerns that the war in America was merely a prelude to a British attack on the French West Indies, Britain only partially mobilized its military forces in America and the Caribbean in 1775. The government was careful not to provoke an arms race or antagonize France. This explains why Britain failed to mobilize fully its navy at the beginning of the war, despite the recommendations of the first lord of the Admiralty, the Earl of Sandwich (1718-92). The result was that the British navy was comparatively weaker against a resurgent French fleet than it had been in the Seven Years' War or was to become in the French Revolutionary and Napoleonic Wars.[14]

The British fleet was consequently too small to support the army, suppress privateers, escort convoys, and blockade America. Furthermore, the navy was instructed by Britain not to intercept French ships carrying munitions and supplies to America from Europe. From the beginning of the Revolutionary War in 1776, France, Spain, and Holland illicitly provided gunpowder, loans, and military equipment to the Continental Army. In addition, French ports in Europe and the Caribbean gave sanctuary to rebel privateers, most famously John Paul Jones (1747-92), whose raids forced the British navy to introduce a convoy system for merchant fleets, deflecting naval ships that might otherwise have been used to blockade America.[15]

France provided vital armaments and supplies, such as those sent through Roderigue Hortalez et Compagnie, which was an ambitious ploy arranged by the playwright Pierre-Augustin Caron de Beaumarchais (1732-99). The company was capitalized with a payment of three million livres negotiated by the Comte de Vergennes, the French foreign minister, in association with private investors and the court of Spain. The shipments were critical given the absence of saltpeter to make gunpowder in America. In October 1776, Beaumarchais signed a contract with Silas Deane, one of the American commissioners in Paris, to send 1,600 tons of muskets, cannon, and military supplies to the United States.[16] The first arms arrived at a critical time in New England in the spring of 1777 to help repulse the invasion force from Canada led by General John Burgoyne. Had America not received muskets and ammunition from France, it would have been impossible to inflict more than a stalemate on the British at

Saratoga later that year. Militiaman Caleb Stark claimed that "Burgoyne would have made an easy march to Albany."[17] Spain similarly used a commercial company as a front, Gardoqui & Sons, based in Bilbao, to ship arms, ammunition, cloth, and military equipment funded by the Spanish Royal Treasury. The company funneled goods through Havana, Cuba, and New Orleans, sending three hundred muskets to New Orleans on the pretense that they were destined for the Louisiana Fixed Infantry Regiment. They were transferred in New Orleans to Oliver Pollock (1737-1823), an unofficial representative of the United States, who later obtained a Spanish loan to fund the expedition of George Rogers Clark (1752-1818) in Illinois country in June 1778.[18]

The importance of foreign support for the American revolutionary cause is best illustrated in the extraordinary case of St. Eustatius.[19] Situated among the northern Leeward Islands, Dutch St. Eustatius was less than five miles long and two and a half miles wide. It was an infertile rock which owed its considerable wealth to its status as a free port. During the American Revolution, it became the chief source of gunpowder and supplies for the Continental Army. It was the primary conduit of trade between Europe and the mid-Atlantic states and New England. There was an average of seven to ten ships arriving on the island every night and regular fleets of ten to thirty sail. In 1780, some 80 percent of ships entering the ports of Philadelphia and Baltimore arrived from St. Eustatius.[20]

St. Eustatius prospered during the Revolutionary War. Trade with the North Americans was "so general and done in so publick a manner, as to be no secret to any person in the West India Islands." It included the sale of guns, rifles, and ammunition that were imported from France and the Austrian Netherlands. Some 235 American ships visited the island between 1776 and 1777. Such was the importance of the island that it attracted agents appointed by the Continental Congress, including the resident agent, Samuel Curzon, and a frequent visitor, William Bingham, the agent for Martinique. Abraham van Bibber, an agent at St. Eustatius representing the state of Maryland, enthused that he was "on the best terms" with the governor, who expressed "the greatest desire and intention to protect a trade with us." He described how "our flag" flew every day in the port aboard visiting merchant ships and privateers. Until 1777, Virginia had also used Bibber, whom it then replaced with John Ball, an aide to his relative George Washington. The agents of the Continental Congress in

Europe found it safe to send their mail home via St. Eustatius. By September 1777, the island was so notorious for supplying the rebels that the password of General John Burgoyne's troops at the Battle of Freeman's Farm was "St. Eustatius."[21]

On November 16, 1776, Fort Orange in St. Eustatius fired what is regarded as the first foreign salute of the flag of the United States. There was an interval of hesitation after the fort received a salute from the *Andrew Doria,* one of the first four ships of the Continental Navy, which was on a mission to purchase armaments from the island and to present a copy of the Declaration of Independence to Governor Johannes de Graaff. The fort commander was uncertain whether to respond and waited to receive positive orders from the governor before dipping the fortress flag and firing a nine-gun salute. The governor afterward gave a party for the commander of the ship, Captain Isaiah Robinson, which was reported in the *Virginia Gazette.* In 1939, Franklin Roosevelt placed a plaque in the fortress to commemorate the place where "the sovereignty of the United States of America was first formally acknowledged . . . by a foreign official."

Even before the outbreak of war between Britain and France in 1778, Europeans were volunteering for service in America. They provided much needed military experience in engineering, artillery, drilling, and siege warfare, which was lacking in America. Some were idealists and volunteers, such as the Marquis de Lafayette; others were sent by the French government at the request of the American commissioners in Paris, primarily Silas Deane and Benjamin Franklin. The Polish engineer Tadeusz Kościuszko (1746-1817) joined for idealistic reasons when he enlisted in the Continental Army in August 1776, rising to the rank of brigadier general and constructing the fortifications at West Point. Appointed chief engineer of the Continental Army in July 1777, Louis Lebègue Duportail (1743-1802) was one of a second group of four engineers sent by France. He eventually became a major general and the founder of the US Army Corps of Engineers. France was regarded as the leading nation in artillery and siege warfare. The Marquis de Lafayette was enlisted by Silas Deane in December 1776 and became a leading intermediary with France. He was accompanied by Johann de Kalb, Baron de Kalb (1721-80), who died a major general in the Continental Army at the Battle of Camden. Having served under Frederick the Great, Frederick Wilhelm von Steuben (1730-94) arrived in America in December 1777 and became the drill master of the Continental Army during the infamous winter at Valley Forge. His manual and reforms are credited with turning the army into a professional force better able to withstand the British.

European Contexts: Finance and Military Support

Dutch, Spanish, and especially French gifts and loans were vital for keeping the Revolution afloat. Larrie D. Ferreiro claims that France and Spain contributed 90 percent of the arms used by the Patriots and "close to $30 billion in direct monetary aid," and that the French spent a total of "1 billion livres, about half a trillion dollars today" (2017 valuations) on their total global war effort during the Revolutionary War.[22] In late 1775, Spain sent one million French livres, along with arms and supplies, through Spanish Louisiana.[23] In May 1776, before entering the war, the French provided arms and munitions to the Patriots at a cost of two million livres, and provided another six million livres in loans in 1778.[24] Between 1776 and 1778, Spain contributed between five and eight million *reales de vellón*. In 1777, Bernardo de Gálvez (1746–86), the Spanish governor of Louisiana, sent armaments worth $77,000 to the American commander at Fort Pitt.[25] Spain provided loans of 12,906,560 *reales de vellón* and gifts of 7,944,600 *reales de vellón*. It represented the equivalent of the total annual national revenue of Spain but still amounted to only 10 percent of the gifts and loans provided by France to America.[26] In addition, John Adams secured a total of eight million guilders from the Dutch for the Patriot war effort.[27]

The French contributed gifts and unpaid loans of $5 million, as well as underwriting and guaranteeing the issue of securities in Amsterdam worth $1.8 million. They sent loans of 34 million *livres tournoises* and grants of 12 million, totaling 46 million *livres tournoises*.[28] In September 1781, the French fleet of Admiral François-Joseph-Paul, Comte de Grasse (1722–88), brought 1.2 million pesos in silver coin (equivalent to $30 million today) from Havana to pay wages to American soldiers and to procure supplies.[29] Jean-Baptiste Donatien de Vimeur, Comte de Rochambeau (1725–1807), lent his own money to enable Washington to march his army to Yorktown. Gifts and foreign loans amounted to between 6 and 7 percent of the cost of underwriting the war for America between 1777 and 1783.[30]

William V. Wenger has scaled up these estimates, calculating that aid to America amounted to the equivalent in 2010 of $69 billion from France and $16 billion from Spain.[31] His figure is based not only on gifts, loans, and credit but also on military aid, materials, shipping, troops, and naval support. American revolutionaries were close to bankruptcy at several stages owing to the failure of states to send sufficient support to Congress and the inflationary depreciation of the Continental Dollar. It precipitated a crisis in 1780, leading to the appointment of Philadelphia financier Robert Morris (1734–1806), in 1781, as superintendent of finance, with a remit to fix as best he could the finances of the Continental Congress.[32] The salaries of the army were constantly in arrears, and they famously suffered from food shortages at Valley Forge and Morristown. In the last year of the war, eighteen months after the Battle of Yorktown, the issue of arrears precipitated a near rebellion of the officer corps of the Continental Army at Newburgh. French, Spanish, and Dutch loans and gifts were vital for preventing America from becoming a victim of its own anti-government rhetoric and going bankrupt because the Continental Congress did not have the power to impose taxes in America.

Britain traditionally relied on continental allies because it had a small army relative to the major nations in Europe. The American Revolutionary War was one of the only wars in which it fought alone until it did so against Nazi Germany in 1940.[33] Britain was partly a victim of its own success during the Seven Years' War, with a series of victories culminating in the acquisition of Canada and Bengal in India. European powers believed that Britain was more of a threat to global order than France, the European nation that customarily had been most feared as especially aggressive in advancing its interests at the expense of less powerful nations.

The problem Britain faced in 1776 "owed less to the failings of Britain's own statesmen than to circumstances outside her control. British diplomacy was to be undermined principally by a fundamental shift in the pattern of European alliances and by the outbreak of rebellion in the North American colonies."[34] After 1764, Russia saw little benefit in an alliance with Britain, withdrawing from negotiations for a treaty in 1773. Austria, Saxony, Prussia, and Russia became more concerned about the balance of power in the east of the continent with the War of the Bavarian Succession (1778–79) and the first partition of Poland in 1772. Despite being an Anglophile, Catherine II of Russia (1729–96) rebuffed a personal request from George III to hire 20,000 troops to serve in North America in 1775. Nevertheless, she teased Britain with the possibility of an alliance up until 1780. Even Portugal, the oldest of allies, abandoned its pro-British policies with the fall of the Marquis de Pombal (1699-1782) in 1777.[35]

Moreover, Frederick II of Prussia (1712-86) was hostile. He regarded Britain as having abandoned the alliance with Prussia in the Seven Years' War and had little intention of ever again allying Prussia with Britain. On the initiative of Catherine II in 1780, Russia joined Denmark (July 9, 1780), Sweden (August 1, 1780), the Dutch Republic (January 1, 1781), Prussia (May 19, 1781), Austria (October 9, 1781), Portugal (July 24, 1782), and Naples (February 21, 1783) to create the League of Armed Neutrality, aimed largely at protecting neutral trade against Britain.[36] Britain tried in vain to negotiate a triple alliance with Russia and Austria in 1780. This diplomatic isolation precluded the policy of William Pitt the Elder (1708-78) in deflecting French and Spanish resources from America to fighting a war in Europe and, in his famous saying, winning America on the plains of Germany. France had been humiliated by the Seven Years' War and was intent on revenge. Its foreign policy for the next thirty years was based on avenging its losses. Britain and France were old European powers, and their first concern in diplomacy and warfare was always how their actions would affect their position in Europe.

Even William Pitt the Elder, the British statesman largely responsible for British victory in 1763 and sometimes thought of as Britain's first great imperial leader, was obsessed with improving Britain's position in Europe. For Pitt and his French counterpart, Étienne François de Choiseul, Duc de Choiseul (1719-85), colonies were the means of maintaining security and influence in Europe. Choiseul was hell-bent on revenge against France's humiliation in the Seven Years' War. Along with his counterparts in Spain, he believed that the best way to cripple Britain was to deprive her of her growing colonial wealth. Indeed, he felt that to cut Britain down to size, there needed to be a colonial revolution—a development he felt to be inevitable. To help this happen, he embarked on an extensive naval building program. As early as 1763, the French were reported to have 23,000 men serving in the French fleet and in the Caribbean.[37]

Owing to its lack of foreign allies combined with the small size of its army, Britain resorted to using unconventional forces, such as sepoys in India, Indigenous peoples in Canada and North America, Miskitos in Central America, Irish Catholics and Maroons in Jamaica, and Loyalists and Hessians in the Thirteen Colonies. Its deployment of these various forces illustrates the extent to which the fighting of the war meant a mobilization of all Britain's imperial resources and how Britain placed the war within imperial contexts. During the Revolutionary War, for example, an estimated 24,000 enslaved people served in a military capacity on land and sea in the Caribbean. The use of enslaved Africans led directly to the later creation of the largest enslaved army in the world, beginning with the First West India Regiment in 1795, which evolved from the Carolina Pioneer Corps that was evacuated at the end of the war in America.[38]

Britain's army was just too small. It not only had to garrison distant fortresses in America, such as Detroit and Penobscot, but also such farflung outposts of empire as Gibraltar, Minorca, Senegambia, Jersey, Guernsey, Antigua, Jamaica, Quebec, Montreal, Halifax, St. Lucia (after 1778), Bermuda, and the Bahamas. The East India Company competed to recruit troops and seamen to serve in India. Jeffery, Lord Amherst, predicted in 1778 that Britain would need another 30,000 troops, a total of 60,000, to conquer and occupy America.[39] The use of Indigenous peoples, Hessians, and enslaved Africans alienated opinion in America and was invariably mentioned in local declarations of independence, as well as in the US Declaration of Independence, which may have been important in the creation of a nationalist, white identity in the United States.[40]

The Navy

The British navy contended with the same problems that beset the British army. Even before French entry into the war in 1778, it was too small to cope with the demands upon it. Britain had acquired a great empire. It had not yet worked out how to defend it, especially at sea. The British navy was inadequate to the task both of blockading the east coast and supporting the army in America.[41] The blockade of the North American coastline was critical, given that the Continental Army depended on the import of supplies and gunpowder from Europe. But the navy was unable to contain rebel privateers, who preyed upon British merchant ships and were active throughout the Caribbean, the east coast of America, and the English Channel. To counter the privateers, the navy had to provide protection in the form of convoys for merchant ships. As early as August 1775, merchant ships received permission to arm themselves for self-protection. In July 1776, the navy provided escorts for ships involved in the linen trade in the

Irish Sea. In August and October, it respectively introduced escorts for the homeward-bound West India trade and the East India Company ships in the Atlantic. By January 1777, a comprehensive system of naval convoys existed for almost every branch of trade in the Atlantic Ocean, the North Sea, the Baltic, the Mediterranean, the Indian Ocean, and the Caribbean. The convoys protected shipping to Lisbon, Oporto, Gibraltar, Basseterre (St. Kitts), Kingston (Jamaica), New York, Newport, and beyond. The underwriters of insurance premiums to merchant ships often insisted that they travel with a convoy, and the premiums were cheaper for those who complied. The navy was hamstrung, however, by its inability to retaliate against neutral powers like France, Holland, and Spain, which gave sanctuary to privateers and supplied America.[42]

Marine insurers underwrote the Revolutionary War by shouldering most of the financial risks at sea. Underwriters sold policies to American privateers who preyed on the British merchant fleet and indemnified privateers when they suffered losses. When privateers prospered, they bought more insurance. These successful American captures led to spikes in Britain's own insurance rates. The marine insurance business was fundamental in shaping the American national financial infrastructure, with Philadelphia financier Robert Morris playing a prominent role. He deployed his substantial personal fortune for the cause of independence, brokering foreign loans, selling state debt, and creating the Bank of America, with the effect that "Morris's warfare undertakings should be understood to include not only the establishment of home rule but the determination of who was to rule at home."[43]

After 1778, the British were engaged not only in a war for America but in the protection of British imperial possessions in the Caribbean, the Mediterranean, Africa, India, and the Channel Islands, as well as in the defense of Britain. Eventually, Britain became engulfed in a war against five nations: France, Spain, the United States, the Dutch Republic, and the Kingdom of Mysore in India. One sign of the global dimensions of the war was that the British press focused primarily on the war outside America. Each of Britain's opponents had specific objectives that Britain was forced to counter. France, for example, aimed to expand its possessions in the Caribbean and India. Spain wanted to recover the former colonies of Minorca and Gibraltar, as well as Jamaica, the Bahamas, and Florida, and to expel British log cutters in Central America (modern Belize, Honduras, and Nicaragua). Fearful of the consequences of revolution in its own empire in South America and the Caribbean, Spain neither became an ally nor formally recognized the United States. Instead, Spain allied itself with France in the Treaty of Aranjuez of June 1779. In the middle of 1779, Spain and France even planned an invasion of England. But it was France that proved to be a major threat to the British Empire. In the Caribbean, France occupied Dominica (1778), St. Vincent (1779), Grenada (1779), Tobago (1781), St. Kitts (1782), Montserrat (1782), and Nevis (1782), leaving Britain in possession of only Barbados, Antigua, St. Lucia, and Jamaica. In 1780–81, Spain took Mobile and Pensacola in British West Florida, eventually recovering both East Florida and the Bahamas. After the Battle of Yorktown (1781), Spain and France combined to conquer Jamaica. They were stopped only when Admiral George Rodney (1718–92) brought the French fleet to its knees by his 1782 victory at the Battle of the Saintes.

A Global Imperial Armed War

The British army was spread throughout the globe with garrisons in outposts of empire from Antigua, Jamaica, St. Lucia, the Bahama Islands, and Bermuda in the Caribbean to Minorca and Gibraltar in the Mediterranean, to the Falkland Islands (Islas Malvinas), to Jersey and Guernsey in the Channel Islands, to Gorée in West Africa, and to Bombay in India. The British kept a third of their peacetime army garrisoning Ireland, which had the largest fortress and barracks complex outside of France. After 1779, the army was spread throughout North America, including in Pensacola and St. Augustine in Florida, Augusta in Georgia, Charleston in South Carolina, New York, Newport in Rhode Island, and Quebec, Montreal, and Halifax in Canada. There were inland fortresses at Forts Niagara, Detroit, and Mackinaw City in the Upper Midwest, Kaskaskia in Illinois, Manchac on the lower Mississippi, and Mobile. Exclusive of Canada, they amounted to some twenty-seven different garrisons to be supplied and supervised in North America. Moreover, the threat of attack at home during the summers of 1778 through 1780 made the defense of Britain a primary objective. In 1779, the danger of invasion in Britain was greater than at any time since the Spanish Armada in 1588. There was also a simultaneous concern about the possibility of a revolution in Ireland. In March 1781, the cabinet thought it advisable to send six regiments there.

After 1778, Britain tried to win the war in North America with fewer troops and a smaller navy than it had deployed in America in 1776. Britain discovered that it was unable to withdraw its peacetime garrisons to military zones owing to the danger of uprisings. The removal of troops from St. Vincent to Boston, for instance, helped precipitate the Carib War of 1769–73. Similarly, an attempt to remove a regiment of troops from Jamaica for service with General William Howe (1729–1814) in North America was the leading factor in a slave revolt on the island in 1776. Still in the process of embarkation, the regiment returned to quell the uprising. In Ireland, the removal of troops and concerns about foreign invasion led to the creation of volunteer forces that numbered 60,000 by 1780, which the government feared might be used against Britain. In England in early June 1780, 11,000 troops were deployed to suppress the Gordon Riots. Resulting in hundreds of deaths, the riots unfolded over six days as crowds attacked the homes of government ministers and released prison inmates while 14,000 demonstrators marched on Parliament, with some bursting into the House of Commons.[44] Between 1778 and September 1780, the proportion of British troops in America fell from 69 percent to 29 percent while there was a corresponding increase in Britain and the Caribbean. Of some 100,000 British troops in 1780, only 30,000 served in America.[45]

Indeed, after 1778, Britain sent more troops and ships to the Caribbean than to America. Henry Clinton (1730–95) assumed command of British forces in America in 1778 but was ordered to abandon Philadelphia to send 5,000 of his best troops to the Caribbean for defense against the invasion of St. Lucia, the gateway to French Martinique. In addition, Britain sent 3,000 troops to St. Augustine in Florida for an intended attack on Georgia, and 2,000 reinforcements to Canada. Clinton was ready to relinquish yet more troops should they have been required by the British commander in Canada. He had 16,000 fewer troops than the total in America under Generals William Howe and John Burgoyne. His army was insufficient by his own estimates just to hold New York. In the four years after Saratoga, Clinton received only 4,700 reinforcements from Britain to make up for the loss of 19,200 men. In addition, his naval support was proportionally reduced in favor of the Caribbean.

Only 8 percent of the British navy served in the Caribbean in 1778; that proportion had risen to 33 percent by the end of 1779. In contrast, North America was allocated 41 percent of the fleet in the summer of 1778, but only 9 percent in the summer of 1779, 13 percent in the summer of 1780, and 11 percent in the summer of 1781.[46] The cabinet even discussed withdrawing from North America to concentrate on the war in the Caribbean and the defeat of France. It had the support of George III, who thought that it would be impossible to continue the war without the wealth derived from the British island colonies in the Caribbean. Indeed, Clinton was given permission to leave New York and retreat to Halifax.[47]

The strategic implications of the troop shortage were dramatically illustrated in the disastrous decision to wage an offensive war against the Spanish in Central America in 1779–80, which led directly to the British loss of East and West Florida. This expedition aimed at the conquest of Spanish America through Central America. Since the reign of Elizabeth I in the late sixteenth century, the British had held global ambitions, in which possession of Central America offered the prospect of opening a path between the Atlantic and the Pacific. By securing possession of the San Juan River and Lake Nicaragua, Lord George Germain and Governor Sir John Dalling (1731–98) of Jamaica anticipated that a single force might divide the northern and southern dominions of Spanish America. Once in control of the river and lake, they hoped to create a chain of bases to launch an invasion of the richest provinces of Spanish America. Germain sent 3,000 troops from Britain both for the expedition and for the defense of Jamaica. Horatio Nelson (1758–1805) commanded the naval escort, the twenty-eight-gun frigate HMS *Hinchinbrook*. As in North America, the plan anticipated the possibility of fomenting insurrections among Indians, slaves, and Creoles against Spain, along with support from British settlers on the Mosquito Shore (present-day Honduras) and the Miskito Indians who were traditionally hostile to Spain. The plan even considered arming prisoners of war in Jamaica and Charleston, South Carolina.[48]

Lord George Germain declared the expedition an entire failure in which "no public benefit had been derived from the Loss of so many brave men."[49] An estimated 2,500 soldiers and sailors lost their lives. There were only ten survivors, including Nelson, from the HMS *Hinchinbrook* crew of two hundred. The assault on the fortress of San Juan claimed the lives of 1,420 troops, mostly from malaria, of the original expedition of 1,800.[50] It was one of the largest losses in life in the whole period of the American Revolution, more than the total losses at the decisive Battle of Saratoga in 1777 and only less than the approximately 7,000 French losses, over-

George III. Portrait by Benjamin West (1738–1820), 1783. (Courtesy of The Cleveland Museum of Art)

whelmingly from disease, in Saint-Domingue, when the French were waiting to prepare for an invasion of Jamaica in 1782 which never occurred. The expedition not only failed but distracted from the British war effort in North America. Colonel John Campbell, the commander in West Florida, had insufficient troops to act defensively, let alone attack New Orleans. On March 14, 1780, as the expedition turned into a fiasco, Bernardo de Gálvez, the Spanish governor of Louisiana, captured Mobile, cutting off a major source of supply to the British in Pensacola. The previous year, he had taken Manchac, Baton Rouge, and Natchez. By taking Lake Pontchartrain and Maurepas, he prevented British posts on the Mississippi River from being supplied from the Gulf. After a sixty-one-day siege that began on May 10, 1781, Gálvez, with an army of 5,500 men and a combined French

The British Lion Engaging Four Powers. This print shows a lion confronting a spaniel, representing Spain, a fighting cock, representing France, a rattlesnake, representing America, and a pug dog, representing Holland. London: J. Barrow, 1782. (Library of Congress, Prints and Photographs Division, Cartoon Prints, British)

and Spanish fleet, stormed Pensacola and the remains of West Florida.[51] The victory freed the Spanish fleet to protect the French Caribbean and enabled Admiral de Grasse to take his fleet undivided to Yorktown. Gálvez's father, Matías Gálvez (1717–84), captain general of Guatemala, recovered much of Central America for the Spanish between 1779 and 1782. In the final campaign in America, in which the Spanish fleet was joined by American vessels, a force of 2,000 men sent by Gálvez took the island of New Providence in the Bahamas in 1782. East and West Florida had not joined the American Revolution. Their retention had enabled Britain to maintain an empire in the southern part of the North American continent.

British Military Weakness

The American War of Independence was the only war undertaken by the British in the eighteenth century in which Britain did not have naval supremacy. Neither did it have a "two-power" navy able to match the combined fleets of France and Spain, whose navies proved a decisive factor in defeating the British in the Revolutionary War. For the first time since the seventeenth century, the allied naval force of France and Spain outnumbered the British and threatened Britain itself with invasion in 1779. Having invested in building up their respective navies after the Seven Years' War, France and Spain raised a Bourbon navy that exceeded the size of the British fleet by 140 ships of the line to 120 in 1767, 121 to 90 in 1779, 117 to 95 in 1780, and 124 to 94 in 1781.[52] Thanks to the foresight of the Duc de Choiseul, the French foreign minister, in the 1760s the Spanish fleet adopted the ship designs, hulls, artillery, and masts used by the French.[53] The two fleets were able to act in harmony, proving a formidable obstacle to the British navy. Their movements forced Britain to reallocate naval resources to the Caribbean, the Mediterranean, India, and the coastline of Britain to counter the increased threat of French and Spanish sea power. The Earl of Sandwich, the first lord of the Admiralty, complained that "England till this time was never engaged in a sea war with the House of Bourbon thoroughly united, their naval forces unbroken, and having no other war or object to draw off their attention and resources."[54] Like the army, the navy faced severe manning and recruitment problems. Owing to his concern about the defense of Britain, Sandwich, under Germain and George III, wanted to concentrate the fleet on the western approaches to Europe rather than send out larger fleets to the Caribbean and North America. In 1778, Britain had fifty-eight battleships in service, of which thirty-three were deployed in the Channel Fleet.[55] The naval wars after 1778 demonstrated graphically the problems Britain faced as an imperial power that had to fight on multiple fronts without the resources to do so effectively.

In short, the Royal Navy in 1778 was too small to protect convoys, to combat rebel privateers, to blockade the east coast of America, and to support the British army under Sir Henry Clinton, in addition to defending Britain, Ireland, and its possessions in Europe, India, Africa, the Caribbean, Quebec, and Nova Scotia. It also had other responsibilities. In 1779, the Navy Board assumed responsibility from the Treasury for the transportation of the army in America and the Caribbean. It provided naval escorts to replace the previous system of armed merchant ships. The cost of transportation became a major financial burden. As the army spread out and the number of garrisons increased, even more supply ships and convoys were needed. As Sandwich wrote in a memorandum to the cabi-

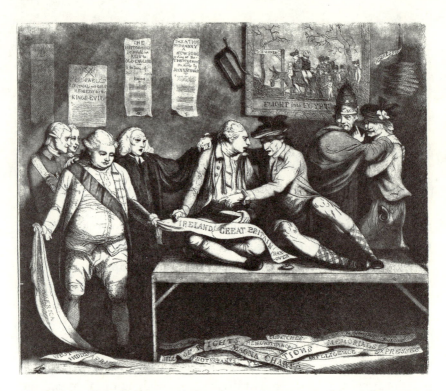

The Botching Taylor Cutting a Cloth to Cover a Button, 1779. Prime Minister Lord North depicted as presiding over the loss of imperial possessions. (Library of Congress, Prints and Photographs Division, Cartoon Prints, British)

net in September 1779, plans were pointless "without at the same time pointing out the manner of securing their success." Given the shortage of ships, it was necessary to think in terms of "not only what ought to be done but what can be done"; what might have been desirable was not necessarily feasible. Since the country had "a deep stake to play for," Sandwich reasoned that the government should husband military forces to be employed "only on those services which are of the utmost importance and that have a probability of being attended with success."[56]

In August 1780, the combined Bourbon fleet intercepted the British merchant convoys bound for the Caribbean and the Indian Ocean, taking 80,000 muskets, 1,350 seamen, and 1,255 troops, and capturing fifty-nine of the sixty-three vessels off Cape St. Vincent. It was a severe setback for the beleaguered Royal Navy attempting to defend Britain's large empire. The convoys had a very light naval escort. It was Britain's largest single

The horse "America" throwing his master, George III. Westminster: Wm. White, August 1, 1779. (Library of Congress, Prints and Photographs Division, Cartoon Prints, British)

naval loss in the war, with the capture of £1.6 million in gold and silver, an amount that Ferreiro estimated to be the equivalent of $17 billion in 2020.[57] In May 1781, the Spanish governor Bernardo de Gálvez conquered Pensacola and West Florida, territory for which the British naval squadron in Jamaica was responsible. The commander of the colony blamed the navy for the loss, but the admiral made the very plausible case that his fleet was already fully occupied in the defense of Jamaica, which was the most valuable and most important British colony remaining in the Americas. To compound the navy's woe, in July another Spanish fleet captured the British base of Minorca in the Mediterranean.[58]

The impact of the overextension of the fleet and the global scale of the war for a nation hugely invested in maintaining and protecting its global imperial interests is best illustrated by the British defeat at the Chesapeake Capes and the entrapment of Lord Cornwallis (1738–1805) at Yorktown in 1781. With a larger naval force in the Americas, it should have theoretically been possible for the navy to rescue the army of Cornwallis, transporting it either to Charleston or to New York. Many factors, however, conspired to make this option impossible, and the British navy was prevented by Admiral de Grasse from breaking the blockade of the Chesapeake Capes. Although there were elements of chance and misfortune in what happened at Yorktown and the Chesapeake Capes, the primary causes were the inferior size of the fleet, poor intelligence, and commitments elsewhere in the globe.

The Earl of Sandwich had built a successful intelligence system, with agents watching the great naval dockyards in France and Spain. It failed him, however, at a crucial time, with the result that the government was not informed of the size of the French fleet destined for America. He consequently did not give sufficient advance warning of the size of the enemy force to the naval and military commanders in the Caribbean and North America. Even with better information, he would have been unable to send out reinforcements. The Channel Fleet was engaged in the relief of Gibraltar, and he had to give priority to sending the few available ships he had to intercept the French Admiral Pierre André de Suffren (1729–88), who had sailed at the same time as de Grasse for the Indian Ocean.

Battles of Chesapeake Bay and the Saintes and Gibraltar

The imbalance of the naval forces was further exacerbated by the decisions of the respective commanders. Admiral Sir George Rodney, commanding the Leeward Islands Squadron, had orders to intercept Admiral de Grasse in the Caribbean and to follow him to America. He failed to do either. He was distracted with the conquest of the Dutch island of St. Eustatius, which his critics claimed had more to do with getting maximum personal financial advantage from the conquest than with advancing British imperial and geopolitical interests.[59] With the British declaration of war against the Dutch Republic in late December 1780, the navy was confronted with the additional challenges of waging war against the Dutch colonies in the Caribbean and the East Indies, intercepting Dutch convoys in the North Sea, and blockading the Dutch coast and the mouth of the Texel in West Frisia in the Wadden Sea. Before news of the declaration by the British reached the Dutch in the Caribbean in February 1781, Rodney attacked and spent three critical months plundering the island of St. Eustatius, during which time de Grasse successfully sailed into Martinique.

De Grasse succeeded in deceiving the British, who expected him to divide his fleet, sending part of it with a convoy of merchant ships to

France and leaving other ships to protect the French islands in the Caribbean. Leaving the Spanish fleet of Admiral José Solano y Bute (1726–1806) to guard the French Caribbean, he instead took the risk of keeping his fleet of twenty-eight ships of the line together. The decision increased his numerical superiority relative to the British in the Americas.[60] After capturing the British island of Tobago, de Grasse sailed via Saint-Domingue for Virginia. De Grasse spent his own money providing transports for additional French troops under the command of Claude-Anne de Rouvroy, Marquis de Saint-Simon (1743–1819) in Saint-Domingue, in an improvised plan to join the expedition to the Chesapeake and to reinforce the French troops commanded by the Comte de Rochambeau at Yorktown. His fleet at the mouth of the Chesapeake Bay trapped British ships, preventing them from carrying intelligence of the size of his fleet to New York.

Rodney made no effort to pursue de Grasse but delegated the job to Sir Samuel Hood (1724–1816). Rodney appreciated the portentous implications of the departure of de Grasse for North America and understood that de Grasse intended to make for the Capes of Virginia, "where I am persuaded the French intend making their grand effort."[61] He sent two warnings to Admiral Graves, the commander of the North American Squadron in New York. Neither message reached him in time. Blaming ill health, Rodney ordered Sir Samuel Hood to pursue de Grasse to America while he returned to Britain. He failed to make provision for the return of three British regiments from the Caribbean promised by the government to Sir Henry Clinton in 1778. Furthermore, he sent his flagship, the *Sandwich,* to be repaired in the naval dockyard in Jamaica, together with two other ships to provide an escort, the *Torbay,* seventy-four guns, and the *Prince William,* sixty-three guns. In addition, he took the *Gibraltar,* the *Triumph,* and the *Panther* with him to escort a convoy of confiscated goods from St. Eustatius to Britain. He described these ships as the finest in his fleet, justifying their removal by claiming that they were in desperate need of repair. In any case, Hood sailed for America with only fourteen ships, a reduction of the Caribbean fleet by one-third.

Rear Admiral Sir Thomas Graves (1747–1814) thus commanded the most important naval battle of the American Revolution, instead of Rodney. Following the departure of the elderly Vice Admiral Mariot Arbuthnot (1711–94), who had quarreled with Sir Henry Clinton, Graves was temporarily left in command while awaiting Arbuthnot's replacement

Nicholas Pocock (1740–1821), *The Battle of the Saints, 12 April 1782*. (© National Maritime Museum, Greenwich, London)

from England. Such was the lack of government confidence in Graves that he was due to be replaced by an officer of junior rank, Admiral Robert Digby (1732–1815). Partly because he lacked accurate information about the enemy, Graves failed to appreciate the threat, and he ignored a plea for immediate action by Admiral Hood, who had arrived in New York in command of Rodney's fleet from the Caribbean. Graves was senior to Hood and was consequently the commander of both the North American and the Leeward Islands fleets at the Battle of the Chesapeake Capes.

The naval battle between the British and French off the Chesapeake Bay was the battle that determined the fate of Lord Cornwallis and his army at Yorktown. On September 5, 1781, Graves arrived in the Chesapeake Bay with a combined fleet of nineteen ships. The rear division of his fleet was commanded by Admiral Hood, leading the Leeward Islands Squadron from the Caribbean. At noon, those nineteen British ships of the line, with a total of 1,500 guns, faced twenty-four French warships with 2,000 guns. The action lasted two and a half hours before nightfall, with only the vans of the two fleets closely engaged, so much so that at one point

James Gillray (1756–1815), *St. George and the Dragon*, 1782. Hand-colored etching portraying Admiral Sir George Rodney about to slay a "French" dragon, and, behind him, the statesman Charles James Fox. London: Hannah Humphrey, June 13, 1782. (© National Portrait Gallery, London)

they were almost within pistol shot range. Anticipating the tactics with which Nelson won Trafalgar (1805), Graves concentrated his ships to isolate and overwhelm part of the French fleet. He failed, partly due to adverse winds but primarily because Admiral Hood's Leeward Islands Squadron had no experience of sailing with the British North American fleet. This was a great disadvantage in the age of sail when captains needed to be able to anticipate the different speeds of each ship to act cohesively. The simultaneous signals from Graves's flagship to form the line of battle and close action were misunderstood by Admiral Hood and his captains because the two fleets had different signal systems, owing to the lack of standardization in the Royal Navy. Hood did not engage until it was too late. Graves did not renew action the next day because his ships had suffered too much damage. Indeed, the length of time spent repairing them in New York was to be a factor in the failure of Graves and Clinton to launch a timely rescue of Cornwallis.[62]

After the action of September 5, 1782, the opposing fleets continued to sail within range of one another for two days, while drifting over a hundred miles south at some distance from Cape Hatteras, North Carolina. In the meantime, Admiral Jacques-Melchior Saint-Laurent, Comte de Barras (1719–93), sailed into the Chesapeake Bay from Boston with another eight French ships of the line, four frigates, and eighteen transports, together with supplies and siege artillery intended for Yorktown. In what amounted to a strategic defeat, the badly damaged and numerically inferior British fleet returned to refit in New York. De Grasse's fleet joined de Barras's ships in the Chesapeake Bay where he had a total of thirty-five warships, which effectively precluded any chance of a British naval rescue for Cornwallis. The Battle of the Chesapeake Capes was the first major French naval victory against the British since the Battle of Beachy Head on July 10, 1690.[63]

Since the British fleet was outnumbered by the French, Rodney might well have fared no better than Graves in fighting the Battle of the Chesapeake Capes. The failure of the navy was due more to overwhelming demands upon it and the difficulties of defending a widespread global empire without a navy suitable for the purpose than to misfortune or incompetent commanders. Indeed, the navy had been lucky to escape defeat by Charles Henri Hector, Comte d'Estaing (1729–94), at Rhode Island and New York in 1778 and Savannah in 1779. Sir Henry Clinton reflected that the navy was outnumbered during periods of every year of his command in North America. He predicted the scenario in which a detachment of the army might be cut off by land and sea. Sandwich was aware of the deficiencies of the navy to cope with the demands upon it. He had urged earlier mobilization to better prepare for the war with France. When the French war broke out in 1778, he had wanted Britain to cut its losses and withdraw from America. He understood that hard choices had to be made in view of the limited resources available.

Consequences of American Victory

Despite the loss of the United States, Britain was successful in the later stages of the wider war against France. After Yorktown, Britain won important military successes in Gibraltar, India, and the Caribbean. At the Battle of the Saintes on April 12, 1782, the Royal Navy won one of its most spectacular victories, a triumph that would be commemorated until it was eclipsed by the Battle of Trafalgar. This allowed for a peace treaty that preserved much of the rest of the empire.[64]

In the months before Yorktown, the British fleet rapidly gained strength against the combined fleets of France and Spain. It enjoyed minor successes during 1781 against the Bourbon fleets. In January 1781, for example, British forces successfully repulsed an attempted French invasion of Jersey, capturing six hundred of the assailants, a victory which was commemorated in one of John Singleton Copley's most dramatic paintings, *The Death of Major Peirson*. In April, Commodore George Johnstone took six valuable Dutch East Indiamen in Saldanha Bay near Cape Town. When the enemy crews attempted to burn their ships, Johnstone personally led the boarding party. In the North Sea in August, Vice Admiral Hyde Parker (1739–1807) won a strategic victory against a Dutch fleet and convoy at Dogger Bank. The Dutch thereafter did not attempt to escort any more convoys in the Baltic. During the summer, another combined French and Spanish armada was thwarted in attempting an attack on Britain. In November, the British garrison in Gibraltar repelled a major Spanish assault. On December 12, 1781, Rear Admiral Richard Kempenfelt (1718–92) attacked a larger French fleet and convoy commanded by Luc Urbain du Bouëxic, Comte de Guichen (1712–90). In a daring act of bravado, Kempenfelt succeeded in taking twenty merchant ships from the French. His victory also delayed the intended Franco-Spanish invasion of Jamaica.[65]

Withstanding the longest siege in the history of their armed forces between 1779 and 1783, the British successfully thwarted French and Spanish attempts to capture Gibraltar.[66] With relief convoys breaking through under the command of Admiral Rodney in 1780 and Admiral George Darby (1720–90) in 1781, they succeeded in evading the blockade of the Spanish. In September 1782, the Spanish besiegers were joined by the French in an attempted "Grand Assault," involving a force of 35,000 men, forty-nine ships of the line, and ten newly invented floating batteries—against a British garrison of 3,500 men.[67] Forty thousand rounds of artillery were fired at the garrison, the equivalent of one every second, during an intense daylong bombardment on September 13. The siege finally ended in February 1783. It became a popular subject for history paintings, especially by American artists John Trumbull and John Singleton Copley. The latter portrayed the event in a picture the size of a wall mural entitled *The Defeat of the Floating Batteries at Gibraltar, September 1782*. The victory was bought at an enormous cost that again illustrates the problem of the overstretched resources of the British in trying to defend a global empire. The retention of Gibraltar proved to be the stumbling block in attempted British negotiations to persuade Spain to withdraw from the war in 1780. In April 1781, the Channel Fleet had sailed to relieve Gibraltar. The relief effort deflected the fleet from intercepting de Grasse when he sailed from France to Martinique, ending in his victory at the Chesapeake Capes and his blockading of the British navy from access to Yorktown.

Britain's global empire meant that its attention during the American Revolution extended well beyond the Atlantic world into South Asia. Indeed, if we look at the years of the American Revolution from an imperial perspective, losses in North America were balanced by gains in South Asia. They served as a prelude to the truly significant conquests in South Asia in the last decades of the eighteenth century—conquests in which veterans of the American Revolution participated, such as Charles Cornwallis, promoted in the peerage as Marquess Cornwallis for his triumphs in India. These victories to an extent obscured his American trials.[68] In India during the American Revolutionary War, Britain faced the combined threat of the Kingdom of Mysore and France. In 1780, Hyder Ali (1720-82), the sultan of Mysore, in alliance with France, declared war on Britain, precipitating the Second Mysore War (1780-84) and threatening the British presence in South India. The battles were on a scale that far surpassed those of America. With an army of 80,000 men, a large majority of whom were sepoys and with many of the European forces Irish Catholics,[69] and an alliance with the Maratha, Hyder Ali invaded the Carnatic between Eastern Ghats and the Bay of Bengal, the modern Indian states of Tamil Nadu and southern Andhra Pradesh, besieging British forts in northern Arcot. In September, his son, Tipu Sultan (1751-99), defeated a British force of 3,820 men near Pollilur, which had been sent to reinforce troops north of Madras. Sir Eyre Coote (1726-83), commander of the East India Company's forces and victor of the decisive Seven Years' War Battle of Wandiwash in 1760, checked the advance of Hyder Ali in the battles of Porto Novo in June, where he was outnumbered by five to one, and recaptured Pollilur in August 1781.

Beginning in 1781, Britain contended with the opening of another front in India with the outbreak of war with the Dutch Republic. When de Grasse sailed for America in March 1781, another French fleet, commanded by Admiral Pierre André de Suffren de Saint Tropez, headed to the Indian Ocean, where it prevented a British fleet from capturing the Dutch colony of the Cape of Good Hope. With his force threatening to reinforce Hyder Ali, the Earl of Sandwich had to give priority to sending a fleet to India rather than supplementing Rodney's fleet to intercept de Grasse, with implications for the British defeat at Yorktown. Hastening to seize the initiative before the arrival of the French fleet in November 1781, George Macartney, Lord Macartney (1737–1806), the governor of Madras, began a successful three-week siege of the Dutch outpost of Negapatam (Nagapattinam), whose defenders included 2,000 men. The land battle was fought to a stalemate, with Tipu Sultan defeating Colonel Sir John Brathwaite (1739–1803) at Annagudi near Tanjore, capturing a British army of one hundred Europeans, three hundred cavalry, fourteen hundred sepoys, and ten field pieces in February 1782. Tipu Sultan later recaptured Bednore and Mangalore, which the British had captured in March 1783. Despite five intense battles between 1781 and 1783, the naval war was similarly inconclusive between the French Admiral Suffren and the British Vice Admiral Edward Hughes (1716–94). In the final battle of the American Revolution of June 1783, the British began the siege of Cuddalore, which ended with news of the peace preliminaries between Britain and France. The British signed a separate peace with Mysore in the Treaty of Mangalore in 1784. The treaty restored the *status quo ante,* regarded as a defeat in Britain but one that preserved their possessions in India. They had successfully retained most of their possessions on the continent and acquired Dutch Negapatam.

The Caribbean became the main theater of military operations in the final year of the war. Lord North's government risked the defense of Britain to focus naval resources upon obtaining an overwhelming superiority in the Caribbean. The decision reflected the economic and geopolitical importance of the Caribbean to Britain, especially Jamaica. It was facilitated by the increase in the size of the navy, which was closer to virtual parity in effectiveness against the combined enemy fleets by 1782. Thanks to the adoption of copper sheathing the hulls as protection against barnacles and wood worms, the ships were able to sail more swiftly for longer periods.

The British won in 1782 what proved to be one of the most decisive British naval victories against the French before Trafalgar in 1805. On

April 12, in a passage of islands between Dominica and Guadeloupe, called Les Îles des Saintes, Rodney's superior force intercepted de Grasse's fleet, which was on its way from Martinique to join troops in Saint-Domingue and the Spanish fleet for the invasion of Jamaica.[70] With additional reinforcements, Rodney enjoyed naval superiority as his thirty-seven ships of the line faced de Grasse's thirty-three effective sail of the line and two fifty-gun ships. During the Battle of the Saintes, Rodney captured the French flagship, the *Ville de Paris,* together with Admiral de Grasse and four ships carrying the siege artillery intended for Jamaica.

The victory caused an outburst of euphoria in Britain. The memoirist Nathaniel Wraxall (1751–1831) described it as "an event which electrified the whole population of Great Britain" and later recalled that "only the enthusiasm roused by Nelson at the Nile exceeded it." Written with his characteristic bravado, Rodney's account of the victory appeared in the newspapers, ending with "may the British flag flourish all over the globe." He became the darling of the press. Contemporary satirical prints reveled in his humiliation of de Grasse; for example, James Gillray's *The Ville de Paris Sailing for Jamaica, or Rodney Triumphant* depicted Rodney standing on the back of de Grasse heading for Jamaica, and *St. George and the Dragon* portrayed Sir George as the legendary saint. Rodney was commemorated in medals, ballads, poems, ceramics, and souvenir pottery. "Rodney Forever" became a popular song heard daily that summer in the amusement park at Vauxhall Gardens in London. He was the subject of full-length life portraits commissioned from Thomas Gainsborough, Sir Joshua Reynolds, and Jean-Laurent Mosnier. Charles James Fox proclaimed the victory the most brilliant that the country had seen.[71]

Rodney was also celebrated in the British Caribbean, where his victory became a major anniversary until the Battle of Trafalgar in 1805 surpassed it. The assembly of Jamaica commissioned John Bacon, one of the finest sculptors in England, to construct a commemorative neoclassical statue of Rodney. Made of marble imported from Italy, it was the most impressive British monument of the Revolutionary War. It depicted the admiral in a breastplate and with a toga thrown over an extended right arm holding a baton. The monument was housed in a splendid octagonal temple with a domed roof, surrounded by a balustrade, topped by a copula, and flanked by two-story office buildings, which were linked to the temple by curving white colonnaded walkways. Three panels on the pedestal of the statue featured patriotic bas-reliefs of Britannia.[72]

Wraxall wrote in his memoirs that it was difficult to appreciate or imagine the effect of the news on the nation. He could not recall such emotions on any other occasion, including Trafalgar, when the joy and excitement was clouded by the death of Admiral Horatio Nelson. After seven years of war and national humiliation, the intensity of the victory celebrations reflected public relief. Britain had stood alone against France. The Saintes rescued Britain from additional humiliation with the pending loss of its other colonies in the Caribbean. Wraxall described the victory as "a sort of compensation" for the years of disgrace and the loss of America: "the country, exhausted and humiliated, seemed to revive in its own estimation and to resume once more its dignity among nations."[73]

The victory, however, did not allay fears of a Franco-Spanish invasion of Jamaica. While Rodney sailed for Jamaica in May, a Spanish force captured the Bahamas. The British therefore continued to prepare for the continuation of the war and even sent orders to Guy Carleton (1724–1808), the commander-in-chief in America, to move to the Caribbean. Nevertheless, the only significant action was the recapture of Honduras by the British in October. The peace preliminaries in Europe ended the military preparations for new campaigns in the Caribbean. Rodney's victory helped Britain obtain generous terms from France and Spain at the Peace of Paris in 1783. It enabled the British to make a separate peace agreement with the United States and Spain, and to obtain much better terms with France. The British had lost seven islands and made only one conquest in the Caribbean, but they were only forced by the terms of the peace to cede Tobago and to return St. Lucia to France and the coastal settlements along the shore of Nicaragua to Spain.

Like the United States in Afghanistan in 2020, the British could have continued their war for America. They were not totally defeated. After the Battle of Yorktown in 1781, Britain still possessed Charleston, Savannah, Penobscot, St. Augustine, and New York. It retained Canada. Three-quarters of the British army remained intact in North America. As is often the case with counterinsurgency warfare, the political will to continue the war was sapped, owing to the cost and the realization that the anticipated civilian support was lacking. In March 1782, Lord North resigned rather than risk losing his majority and facing a defeat in Parliament. Toward the end of the war, even army and navy officers began to vote against his government in the House of Commons. Nevertheless, the politicians and military leaders who lost America also laid the basis for what became known as the second British Empire, which comprised of a fifth of the global population at the death of George III. The final voyages of Captain James Cook to Australia and New Zealand occurred during the American Revolution. The convicts formerly transported to America became the first settlers of Australia.[74]

American independence would not have been possible without financial and military support from Europe. And without recognition from powerful European nations, the young country would have never achieved an independent status "amongst the powers of the earth." That independence and recognition came within the context of imperially minded European nations and empires trying to gain advantages for themselves in a world where, since 1763, British imperial power had grown dramatically. Because of the strength of European support for American opposition to imperial authority, Great Britain found itself diplomatically isolated, without an ally in a war that became a global conflict, and with a navy—which had until then ruled the waves in the eighteenth century—outnumbered by the combined fleets of America's allies. While nations looked to their interests, individual Europeans—like the brilliant Frenchman the Marquis de Lafayette (1757–1834)—were inspired by the ideals of liberty and equality expressed by the Americans to justify their revolt. The consequences of such enthusiasm would have a lasting impact on Europe and inspire sympathetic revolutions throughout the Age of Revolution.

SEVEN

Imperial Futures

THE AMERICAN REVOLUTION WAS AN imperial event, as we have argued in this book. It was an event that was not just central to the birth of the United States, foundational to the histories of Canada and several Caribbean nations, and heralding the separation of a large percentage of the population of the pre-nineteenth-century British Empire from imperial oversight. It can also be viewed usefully within imperial parameters and as part of larger processes of global evolutionary change, affecting empires everywhere in a "world crisis" that mirrors the older concept of a seventeenth-century "general crisis."[1] It is an event that thus needs to be viewed not just as an American event, with meaning mainly for American citizens, but as part of British imperial history, with global implications: "America's Revolution was Britain's American War: a series of fateful moves in the high-stakes changing arc of the European great powers, and a chapter in the entangled history of a vast and growing empire."[2]

It may have initiated the Age of Revolutions, being less a singular story of the foundation of an enduring republic in the New World than a revolution with extensive impact, "not just an isolated event but [for fervent Atlantic revolutionaries] as a beacon guiding toward revolution to come through the known world."[3] But it happened in an Age of Empire, with imperialism at least as important as revolutionary ideology in shaping the zeitgeist of the late eighteenth and early nineteenth centuries. The loss of the Thirteen Colonies did not stop, though it diverted into new directions, Britain's surge to unprecedented imperial expansion.[4]

In fact, seeing the American Revolution as a global imperial conflict, rather than within the framework of a nationalistic chronology, allows us to adjust its normal chronological markers to acknowledge its different imperial consequences.[5] Not everything to do with the American Revolution started in 1763. For example, the dates that span the American Revolutionary period in Jamaica are different from those in the Thirteen Colonies. For the latter, one might choose as important 1748, when it first became clear that a new imperial regime was intended for North America with the arrival of the Earl of Halifax in imperial office. One might then choose 1765 and the Stamp Act crisis; 1773-74 and the British Tea Party and Coercive Acts; 1776 and the Declaration of Independence; 1783 and the Peace of Paris; and 1788 and the adoption of the US Constitution. Jamaican historians, however, might instead see as important 1739 and the end of the First Maroon War; 1760 and the great slave rebellion, which nearly transferred control of the colony away from British hands; 1772 and the *Somerset* case in England; 1779 and French and Spanish entry into the war, threatening Jamaican security; 1782 and British victory at the Battle of the Saintes; and 1788, when slaveowners realized that abolitionists were a powerful force willing to attack plantation slavery and the Atlantic slave trade.

For Canada, the important dates might be 1759 and the Conquest of Canada; 1774 and the passing of the Quebec Act; 1791 and the passing of the Canada Constitutional Act; and 1812 and the defense of Canada against American invasion. Irish historians might concentrate on 1767, when George, Viscount Townshend, became a reforming lord lieutenant; and the repeal in 1782 of the 1720 Declaratory Act, giving Ireland something close to what was later called for settler colonies "Dominion status," which ceased with the Acts of Union in 1801. Historians of South Asia might focus on the granting of the *diwani*, or the rights to Bengal revenues, to the East India Company in 1765; the devastating Bengal famine in 1770; and the start of the trial for corruption of Warren Hastings in 1778, as well as Lord North's Regulating Act of 1778 and William Pitt's India Act of 1784, which respectively strengthened central government control of India, at the expense of the East India Company. For historians of England, an important date during this period would be the Gordon Riots in London in 1780.

Was the United States an Empire?

Was the new United States of America to be an empire? One thing to keep in mind when assessing this question is that the territory of the present-day United States was not contiguous with that of the early republic. The

Seven Years' War had seen the disappearance of the French Empire from continental America, but the Spanish Empire was a prominent, if not always powerful, presence in the American South and West. There were also Indigenous empires perfectly capable of contesting and, often, overcoming the imperial ambitions of the infant United States. Two such empires were those run by the Comanche in southwest America in the mid-eighteenth century, and by the Lakota in the upper Missouri Valley.

The new American republic was also a huge threat to Indigenous peoples outside these empires as American settlers pushed into the trans-Appalachian West, claiming by force Indian lands and resources, and violating treaties between the United States and individual Indigenous nations. The Comanche and Lakota empires, however, were strong and militarily powerful, and were able for some years to obstruct US westward expansion through both arms and diplomacy.[6] To an extent, these Indian empires emulated powerful Native American confederations from earlier periods of American history, such as the Haudenosaunee (Iroquois) and the Osages in the confluence of the Missouri and Mississippi Rivers.[7] The Comanche and Lakota, however, were new kinds of empires. They were not confined to defensive actions against European imperialism to prevent European intrusion into Indigenous lands but were aggressively expansionist empires that "would challenge Euro-American empires on [their] own terms and rearrange boundaries, allegiances, human fortunes, and macro-scale historical trajectories over several generations, all the way to the climactic battle on the Little Bighorn River" in 1877.[8] The Comanches, in particular, were especially successful against the Spanish Empire. They pushed deep into northern Mexico after the American Revolution, creating such havoc that they fatally weakened Mexico in the generation before US invasion in the Mexican war of 1846.[9]

The US empire, nevertheless, was a tougher proposition for Indigenous peoples to confront in the middle years of the nineteenth century than the declining Spanish Empire. That was not the case in the late eighteenth century when Indigenous military forces successfully confronted a small and ineffective US army, nearly destroying it in the Battle of the Wabash on November 4, 1791, when the US army under Arthur St. Clair (1737–1818) was defeated by warriors from the Miamis and the Delawares in the most disastrous defeat in US military history.[10] The balance of power changed in the nineteenth century. It was associated in part with demography—the explosion of white and Black populations and stasis and decline in Indigenous populations—and even more with increased US economic and political power relative to that of Indigenous peoples. The United States took increasingly drastic measures to fulfill its continental aims, leading to forced removal and numerous treaty violations. Yet we want to avoid demographic determinism, in which Indigenous peoples lost because their populations were in demographic free fall, a fact that fits only some Indigenous populations. What we still need to explain is how a national state that, although stronger than previously thought, was still too weak to rule effectively all the territory it claimed could succeed in acquiring Indigenous land when Indigenous power was still palpable, and which more obviously powerful European powers had failed to break. What seems to be the likely scenario is that Indigenous peoples were overwhelmed by a flood of settlers who drove them from their lands, reduced them to starvation, and built towns where Indigenous peoples once were, employing both violence and an ideology of on-the-ground "settler sovereignty" to justify their actions. These illegal actions were connived at by an American government which turned a blind eye to settler outrages and took actions that advanced irrevocably the pace and patterns of white settlement in lands that had once been controlled by Indigenous peoples.

One assumption about empires is that they are better at managing diversity than nation-states. That certainly is the case with religion. A previously vibrant transatlantic "Protestant internationalism" vitally linked around a shared commitment to the ideology of imperialism collapsed with the American Revolution. It was a "fracture within its heart," destroying a Protestant community that had been "a safety valve for controversy, preventing historical religious dissensions from growing into casus belli."[11] The lesson was that the empire united Protestants more than Protestants united the empire.

What was true for Protestant religion after the American Revolution was also true, to a limited extent, for white relations with Indigenous peoples. American colonists, of course, were upset by what they considered in the 1760s to be British imperial partiality to Indigenous peoples.[12] Outrage over the perceived favoring of Indigenous peoples found its most famous expression in Thomas Jefferson's notorious accusation in the Declaration of Independence that George III had encouraged "merciless savages" to promote depredations against white settlers. The westward march of Canadians into Indigenous territory was far from conflict free, but the level of conflict in Canada between settlers and Indigenous peoples was well below that in the United States. Although in Canada "the Indian experience with settlement differed only in degree rather than in kind, from the Indian experience on the American side of the border," the difference in degree was important: while "there was indeed violence and resistance in the Canadian story, it was nothing like the prolonged and bitter violence that marked American expansion."[13]

Elsewhere, however, the British Empire was not gentle in its treatment of Indigenous peoples. The East India Company's treatment of South Asians was appalling, both in its indifference to Indian welfare, as seen in the disastrous Bengal famine of 1770, when millions perished, and in its deliberate destruction of India's vibrant textile trade. Britain used its political power and economic clout to deindustrialize India so that Britain displaced India as the global supplier of cotton textiles.[14] Its treatment of Australian aborigines and South African Khoikhoi and San in the Cape Colony was marked by extreme violence, at times amounting to genocide, as in Tasmania, severe racial discrimination, and dispossession of land and resources.[15] The United States might have been the first "and most aggressive" settler colonial state,[16] but South Africa and Australia emulated US actions closely in the early nineteenth century, for "without the Revolution" to deflect British military might, "indigenous peoples after 1783 faced a challenging British Empire willing to deploy tens of thousands of its troops and tens of thousands of its subjects to establish its rule."[17]

If we truly want to dispel notions of the British Empire as likely to be kinder to Indigenous peoples and non-whites than were settlers in the early US republic, we can examine British actions to Indigenous peoples and the enslaved in the eastern Caribbean. If North Americans had any doubts about the willingness of the British to sacrifice the rights of Indigenous peoples for the desires of settlers, they only had to look at how Britain behaved in the Ceded Islands of Dominica, St. Vincent, and Grenada, from their acquisition by the British Empire following the Seven Years' War until the ferocious Second Carib War of 1795–96. The Second Carib War is outside the chronological remit of this book, but it deserves a mention because few episodes in the history of the infant United States, including Indian removal during the 1830s, matched the viciousness of the

British toward their opponents in this conflict. It was a war of extreme violence that resulted in the defeat of the Caribs (who go by the preferred name of Kalingos) in St. Vincent and the end of their centuries-long resistance to imperial rule.[18]

Europeans conventionally made what was an oversimplified distinction between what they envisaged as two separate kinds of people living in St. Vincent, both of whom they referred to as Caribs.[19] The people they called "Red Caribs" were a small remnant of an Indigenous population. They were thought of by the British as peculiarly docile, posing no threat to white settlement and therefore fit objects for scientific study as an example of a "savage" people needing benevolent protection. Most Indigenous peoples, however, which comprised a substantial population of about 5,000 in St. Vincent, were termed "Black Caribs," and were descended from Indigenous peoples and escaped African slaves. The Kalingos were a formidable people, known for their fierce resistance against any encroachment onto their lands. They also allied themselves successfully with the French from nearby islands. They insisted on their independence from British authority and on their right to large blocks of land in St. Vincent that were coveted for white settlement. They formed a major obstacle to British settlement in the Ceded Islands.[20]

The British were determined to remove the Kalingos from their lands. In the 1760s, Britain was less interested in western expansion into the Ohio Valley than in southern expansion out of the regional hub of Barbados into the eastern Caribbean and, by the 1790s, into Trinidad and northeast South America. The big money in imperial expansion in the 1760s was directed toward investment in plantations in this region. Grenada, in particular, at least before a major credit crunch in 1772, was the focus of huge financial investment.[21] It went from being a marginal colony under the French to a powerhouse of slave labor on new plantations in the 1760s. A later governor of St. Vincent felt that the scramble for land in the new islands could "only be compared with the South Sea Madness."[22] Britain's success in the Seven Years' War in the eastern Caribbean led to a rapid escalation of violence against Kalingos, culminating in a vicious war in 1772. The conflict was protracted and difficult and was justified by British planters because they argued that "Black Caribs" were free Blacks, not Indigenous peoples, and thus had no rights, as alien intruders, to Indigenous land. It provoked much criticism in Britain, leading to an embryonic humanitarianism where non-white subjects were considered to have rights equal to those of settlers. That was not a view shared, however, by the British government, whose representatives harassed Kalingos until they were forced to sue for peace on unfavorable terms in 1773. The Kalingos agreed to accept British sovereignty and to pledge allegiance to the British Crown, but they remained an unsubdued and unassimilated people, able to deter settlement on the lands they had formally relinquished. Their opposition kept St. Vincent from truly developing its plantation potential until Kalingos were expelled after the Second Carib War of 1795–96.[23]

Britain showed in the eastern Caribbean that the lesson they had learned from the American Revolution was that everyone except for white elites needed to be treated with the hard fist of Britain's powerful armed forces, replicating in this way not the American Revolution but the successful defeat of enslaved rebels in Jamaica's great slave revolt of 1760.[24] After 1783, Britain concentrated on the repression of non-whites in the eastern Caribbean. They took away the political rights of French Catholics; subjected free people of color to increasingly restrictive legal procedures; brutalized the enslaved in plantation societies devoted overwhelmingly to the production of plantation goods for profit, with little concern for enslaved welfare; and tormented the Kalingos in St. Vincent. Their repressive policies had consequences. When the Haitian Revolution exploded in the early 1790s, bringing thousands of British and French troops to the region, and after gubernatorial mismanagement provoked the Second Maroon War in Jamaica between 1795 and 1796, a massive slave revolt broke out in Grenada, led by Julien Fédon, a mixed-race French plantation owner.[25]

The revolt was a concrete manifestation of Britain's worst fears. It involved a coalition of Kalingos, French Catholics, free people of color, and the enslaved against a small and beleaguered British plantocracy. The revolt was put down by imperial troops with horrific ferocity and at enormous cost, wrecking Grenada's plantation economy for a generation and killing 7,000 people, mostly the enslaved, but also including French planters and free people of color executed by a vengeful government. Physical damage amounted to more than £3 million.[26] Slave rebellion was accompanied by a vicious war, the Second Carib War, by the British against the Kalingo people. The Kalingos, after fierce resistance, were defeated and were removed first to a dismal island prison near St. Vincent and then to the Spanish island of Roatán in the Bay of Honduras. There, the Kalingo people created a vibrant culture, but only after immense suffering at the hand of genocidal British imperialists. Of 4,476 Kalingos transported off of St. Vincent in 1796, only 2,248 were still alive in 1797. Their removal opened land for settlement and for an enhanced Atlantic slave trade: 37,000 Africans were shipped to the Windwards between 1796 and 1807. Many of these newly enslaved Africans were enlisted to drive the Kalingos from St. Vincent. Britain's retributive justice demonstrated how violently the British acted toward people who rejected their authority—they treated them as treasonable in ways that white American Patriots never experienced. The British were not prepared to suffer any challenges to the plantation prosperity of the West Indies, even after abolitionism had become a major social movement, and treated enslaved rebels and Indigenous opponents without mercy.[27]

The Rise of British Humanitarianism

Nevertheless, even if there are similarities between the treatment of Indigenous peoples in the United States and Indigenous peoples in the nineteenth-century British Empire, and despite it being clear that the British Empire was just as devoted to ideologies of white supremacy and exclusionary civic cultures promoting white egalitarianism while denying non-whites access to citizenship, the move to republican government in the young United States affected how processes of expansion occurred in different parts of the Anglophone world. For a start, the United States did not have the outward-looking humanitarianism that was so well developed within late eighteenth- and early nineteenth-century British imperialism.[28] The rise of humanitarianism mapped closely onto Britain's realization that the acquisition of a polyglot, multiethnic, and multicultural empire reinforced Christian reflection on the relations that Britons had with the distant peoples that it ruled. In short, imperial rule brought humanitarian responsibilities to Britain as well as imperial benefits. Edmund Burke made the point famously in 1783 in a speech on the East India Bill in Parliament. He argued that "all political power which is set over men ... ought to be in some way or other exercised for their benefit. ... Such rights or privileges are all in the strictest term *a trust*."[29]

The idea that the British Empire was in part a trust to protect those under its rule strongly influenced humanitarian thought, to the extent that by the 1830s it was encompassed within the discourse of the governing men of empire, performing a moral justification for imperial governance.[30] In the nineteenth-century British Empire, "territorial conquest, white settlement, commercial growth, economic development, and above all issues of slavery and the slave trade, raised questions about the ethics of economic exchange, the politics of equal rights or racial difference and the purpose of Imperial power."[31] Such links between humanitarianism and a global empire were hard to replicate in a republican nation-state. We can understand Indigenous dispossession through republicanism as easily as through imperial legacies or borrowings. That republicanism was predicated upon white egalitarianism and included racial discrimination. American refusal to incorporate Indigenous peoples into the US polity was part of the long-lived American dilemma of assimilation, whereby non-whites were aggressively "othered" and excluded from membership in the civic culture of the United States.[32] What was central to federalism was the notion that the population was homogenous, by which Americans meant white people, and ideally Protestants of British descent, so that the "federal government actively shaped settlements into republics fit for incorporation into the Union."[33] State-making required homogeneity and meant there was no room for the tolerance of diverse groups, as was characteristic of empires.

Slavery and Antislavery

It is possible to argue that the United States was like the British Empire when it came to its relations with Indigenous peoples. It is harder to make the same argument regarding slavery after the end of the American Revolution. The American Revolution had a massive impact on American and West Indian slavery because the creation of the United States split the British American slave empire in two. Most enslaved people in British America stayed within the empire after 1781, even though the proportion of Blacks in the US population reached a height in the 1780s it was never to approach again. At a stroke, the British Empire lost most of its white Protestant subjects, leaving only two economically powerful, but demographically tiny, white Protestant minorities in Ireland and the Caribbean, only one of which was committed to slavery.[34] The division of the slaveholding empire in the Atlantic proved a massive boost to Britain's first developing an antislavery movement in the 1780s, as the leading British abolitionist Thomas Clarkson acknowledged. "As long as America was ours," Clarkson wrote in 1788, "there was no chance that a minister would have attended to the groans of the sons and daughters of Africa, however he might feel for their distress."[35]

The changes in the position of slavery in the British Empire that resulted from the American Revolution can be seen most graphically in the dramatic decline in the image of the West India planter in the British imagination in the 1780s. There had always been some suspicions about the character of white British West Indians, as being tyrannical, uncouth, and somehow unmoored from standards of politeness and acceptable forms of masculinity.[36] These suspicions were allayed, however, by the immense wealth of white planters and merchants in the region and by the economic benefits West Indian commerce brought to Britain at a time when virtually no one questioned the morality of using Africans as laborers in brutal slave regimes. Observers of the British West Indies writing before the American Revolution gloried in "the immense Value, high Importance and prodigious national Benefit of the grand Source of Britain's Opulence," due "to the Blessing of Heaven on the unwearied industry of the Planters."[37]

In the 1780s, however, public opinion turned decisively against white British West Indians. Increasingly, West Indian planters were not fellow countrymen but foreigners, and even more were sexually deviant and morally outrageous hypocrites, wanting liberty for themselves but depriving the liberty of others. Abolitionists pointed out the brutality of the plantation system and its distinctive disruptive impact on the health of the enslaved. Planters were depicted in Britain as cruel, avaricious, and acting similarly in their management practices to the most callous and uncaring enclosing landlords in Georgian Britain. More significantly, they were portrayed as morally deficient, with a sexual proclivity toward Black women that was seen as deeply distasteful in a nation that had been taught by West Indians themselves to see miscegenation as a sign of moral degeneration. They were also thought of as disabled people, prone to venereal disease, who refused to do their manly duty and become patriarchs of large, legitimate families. West Indian women had, if anything, a worse reputation, as either sexually avaricious or as stupid and simpering. Their cultural decline was aggravated by cause célèbres such as the sensational trial of the owners of the *Zong*, following British sailors who had murdered 132 Africans off the coast of Jamaica in late 1781 and then claimed insurance for their losses.[38]

What is a matter of debate is the extent to which the American Revolution advanced the cause of abolition. We know that abolition became a well-supported moral cause in the aftermath of the War of American Independence. The American revolutionary generation presented the odd picture of a people heavily invested in chattel slavery proclaiming strongly against it. The Founding Fathers frequently asserted their antislavery beliefs, but George Washington was the only major figure to manumit enslaved people. Moreover, he did so only on his death and manumitted only those individuals he owned and not most of the enslaved people on his properties, who belonged to his wife, Martha.[39] The rhetoric of the American Revolution was strongly antislavery, and the northern colonies saw the first abolitions of slavery in the Anglophone world.[40]

The problem was that this set of admirable intentions against slavery did not last long past the founding of the United States. North America moved from being at the forefront of antislavery agitation in the 1760s and 1770s, under the leadership of "the Quaker International," especially in Philadelphia, to being antislavery laggards, behind Britain by the 1820s.[41] Leadership in the campaign had already moved to Britain by the 1780s.[42] American abolitionists were handicapped by the limits placed on national action against slavery in the federal Constitution and by the revitalization of slavery in the Deep South by the early nineteenth century.[43] Antislavery in America shrank into relative insignificance in the early republic. Its decline was obvious in such former powerhouses as the Philadelphia Abolition Society, which turned away from transatlantic abolitionism and the ideal of turning the United States into an antislavery republic to focus narrowly on the advancement of African Americans within the state of Pennsylvania.[44] In addition, the conflagration of the Haitian slave rebellion doused the enthusiasm of white Americans for abolition, as its radicalism went well beyond anything that any white antislavery activist was willing to contemplate. It played much better, however, among Black Americans who admired what Haitians had done by the early nineteenth century not just to end slavery in Saint-Domingue but to create a Black republic and to put the lie to notions of Black racial inferiority.[45]

Britain, of course, had a history of abolitionism that predated the American Revolution. The American Revolution "helped to inject into the domestic public and political spheres the intellectual challenges to British slavery that had accumulated during the previous half century." Those challenges had emanated from giants of the Scottish Enlightenment such as Francis Hutcheson, John Millar, and especially Adam Smith. Even more important influencers of opinion were humanitarians from the developing British evangelical movement. The most important of these evangelical antislavery supporters was John Wesley, the founder of the Methodists. He believed in Africans' shared humanity with Europeans under God and insisted that to follow Christ's "Golden Rule" meant extending "God's grace to all humankind" and thus abolishing evils like the Atlantic slave trade.[46]

Nevertheless, even if the intellectual case against slavery had been largely won among influential thinkers before the American Revolution, defining slavery and the slave trade as inconsistent with British values in an emerging era of civilization and enlightenment no matter how much wealth these activities brought to Britain, this intellectual movement had not transmuted by 1783 into a political ideology capable of delivering social change.[47] That transmutation occurred suddenly and massively in 1787. The American Revolution, however, played a role in preparing the ground for abolitionist agitation. It was critical in the development of abolitionism, precipitating a crisis of empire and of national identity out of which moves to abolish the slave trade emerged as part of a re-evaluation of Britain's international position.

The Impact of the American Revolution in Britain

Despite the birth of abolitionism as a major social movement, the American Revolution had a remarkably limited impact upon many areas of British social, economic, and political life. As an historian has quipped, "the Revolution was less of a traumatic shock to the British than a display of their capacity for losing an empire without caring very deeply."[48] Britain concentrated less on the loss of America than on the salvation of the Caribbean through the Battle of the Saintes. Britain recovered remarkably quickly from the War of American Independence. The 1780s in Britain was a decade of general prosperity and national self-confidence manifested in several investigations of imperial malpractice such as corruption in India and the brutality of the slave trade going to the Caribbean.[49] The early stages of the Industrial Revolution boosted the British economy, and the accession of William Pitt the Younger as prime minister in 1784 provided political stability. Britain came out of the war in financially good shape, in contrast to France, which had got itself hugely in debt through its intervention on the American side, famously leading to the French Revolution in 1789. The American war had been very expensive also for Britain. Britain's annual expenditure increased from £10.4 million in 1775 to £29.3 million in 1782, with the national debt doubling in this period. Taxes increased sharply, making Britain a highly taxed nation by European standards, the most highly taxed except for Austria. But the reforms to state financing that we call the fiscal-military state worked well both to raise money and to fight wars without incurring a financial crisis.[50] Britain remained in the 1780s in financial surplus, and government bonds in that decade increased by 48 percent beginning in 1784.[51]

The 1780s was a remarkable decade, in which Britain looked forward rather than backward, initiating a wide variety of reforms and improvement campaigns in the areas of public health, prisons, and the slave trade. It expanded, moreover, its imperial presence in an empire that was more, not less, authoritarian and where colonial governors tended to be military men not willing to put up with opposition from settlers, especially in Nova Scotia and the West Indies, where whites insisted on pre-revolutionary demands for local autonomy. What Britain aspired to and what it achieved by the early nineteenth century in places such as Australia, Canada, and the Cape Colony was a means whereby Britain's expanding state power could be used in "a systematic attempt to centralize power within colonial territories, to exalt the executive above local liberties and to remove non-European and non-British people from positions of all but marginal political authority." These measures were "an attempt to establish overseas despotisms which mirrored in many ways the polities of neo-absolutism and the Holy Alliance of contemporary Europe."[52] They coincided with remarkable growth in the global scope and scale of the British Empire. In just the years of 1787 and 1788, for example, Britain expanded into West Africa, the Malay Peninsula, and New South Wales, while starting to consolidate its holdings under the East India Company in South Asia.

In short, the American Revolution was quickly wiped from British memory, for "the eighteenth-century experience . . . revealed that 'imagined communities' of Britishness were parochial," as "English people could perhaps envisage a common identity with the Welsh and, often with great difficulty, with the Scots, but they failed to incorporate the Irish or colonial Americans into their idea of empire." Such assertions can also be applied to contemporary historiography.[53] Many historians depict Georgian England in an insular and exceptional fashion, portraying it as a prosperous and politically stable country, despite the loss of large numbers of people claiming to be British through the American Revolution; discontent among other British colonials in Ireland and the West Indies in the last decades of the eighteenth century; and massive conflicts in South Asia and South Africa. This is a depiction of Georgian Britain at odds with what this book is arguing.[54]

Part of this parochialism is connected to a long-standing British assumption that the British are a non-revolutionary people. It is an assumption so prevalent in British historiography that even major historical ruptures, such as Henry VIII's break with Rome in 1533; the Wars of the Three Kingdoms and the eleven-year period of republicanism in the 1650s; and the successful invasion of Britain by the Dutch ruler, William III, in the "Glorious Revolution" of 1688, are diminished so that what is stressed are the underlying continuities in English history rather than sudden changes. That the English people are non-revolutionary has a long history. The sentiment was expressed well by George Orwell, a revolutionary socialist with a love of traditional English culture, in the climactic year of 1941. He noted that "gentleness, the hypocrisy, the thoughtlessness, the reverence for law and the hatred of uniforms will remain along with the suet puddings and the misty skies. It needs some very great disaster, such as prolonged subjugation by a foreign enemy, to destroy a national culture." Further: "In England we could not have a civil war, not because tyranny and injustice do not exist but because they are not obvious enough to stir the common people to action."[55]

The historian of eighteenth-century Britain Ian Christie echoed Orwell in explaining why Britain did not have a political revolution in the Age of Revolutions. He explained England's anti-revolutionary stance by reference to England's finely graded social structure, which was held together by a multitude of shared interests and concerns; by a general hope of material advancement that gave individuals optimism for the future and a sense of place in the present; by the safety net of poor laws and a rudimentary welfare system that prevented people from falling into the destitution that occurred in other European countries; and by prosperity being general and well-spread enough to lessen the necessity of revolt.[56] Revolution, by this reading, was conceptually impossible, even when, as in the Thirteen Colonies, it was the experience of millions of people who thought themselves to be British.[57]

Yet the loss of America mattered in Britain. The war divided the British population even if did not lead to the radicalization of that population, as happened during the French Revolution. The loss of America was something felt keenly by British leaders. On November 25, 1781, Lord George Germain summoned up the courage (a characteristic many of his aristocratic enemies thought he lacked, given his court-martial for cowardice at the 1757 Battle of Minden) to visit the prime minister Lord North, accompanied by Lords Stormont and Thurlow. They told North of British defeat at Yorktown, Virginia. North's response was dramatic. He collapsed "as he would have taken a bullet in the breast." George III reacted to the news with stoic resolve, though he could not believe that three million of his subjects had chosen to abandon being under his rule. His despair was understandable, for Britain had "spent eight years waging what the staunchest supporters regarded as a 'holy war' against 'dangerous' revolutionary principles which threatened every system, religious or civil, hitherto respected by mankind" and "even moderates believed that the retention of America was essential to the survival of Britain as a great power within Europe."[58]

Britain's loss of prestige in Europe in the 1780s was keenly felt among British politicians. The experienced diplomat the Earl of Buckinghamshire lamented that he saw Europe sniggering at "this unhappy disgraced country surrounded by every species of embarrassment, and . . . now circumscribed as a human body in the last stage of decline."[59] The loss of America was the first partition of Britain and its empire since the English loss of much of France in the mid-fifteenth century. It also involved the loss of the area of the British Empire likely to be the most valuable future part of Britain's Atlantic world. It had been imperial growth, not imperial loss, which had previously been the normative experience in eighteenth-century Britain.

Who was to blame, besides Lord North, who resigned from his post as prime minister, and his ministry? For some Whig opponents of the government, the blame fell on George III. Indeed, the British monarch felt himself so responsible for the defeat in America that when he was finally forced to acknowledge American independence, he drafted a letter of abdication to Parliament. It was conceivable in the 1780s that George III could have met the same form of disgrace as Charles I (though he was never going to lose his head) or the exiled James VII and II. Ironically, however, his popularity as a monarch increased around this time, especially after he had his first bout of insanity, which endeared him to his country's people. But that revival in his fortunes was not foreseeable in the dark days of 1781–83. Just as in 1975, when the fall of Saigon in Vietnam showed that the unthinkable was possible and a small power could defeat a superpower, scapegoats had to be found, including not just political and military leaders but even the king.[60] What saved George III was that British politicians accepted that he was a monarch with limited constitutional responsibilities. The loss of America accelerated the marginalization of the monarchy's political power and its increasing importance as a symbolic representation of the nation and empire. In short, in terms of wielding executive power, George III's reign was the last hurrah of the British monarch.[61]

One lesson Britain learned from its defeat was that having no European allies, as had been the case between 1763 and 1783, was a major policy failure. The loss of America was in part the result of Britain having turned its back on Europe, and Europe taking its revenge. Britain henceforth kept the geopolitics of Europe firmly in mind as it moved to global war in the 1790s. Did it also signal a reorientation of Britain's global priorities? Vincent Harlow argued in the 1950s that there was a "swing to the east" in the British Empire, with the loss of America signaling a new empire focused on India and defined by the quest for new markets more than the creation of settler colonies.[62] Not many scholars would agree with this assessment today, given the huge expansion of settler colonization in the nineteenth century in the British Empire and the United States.[63]

Indeed, there was a "swing to the south" as much as to the east in the Napoleonic period. Even if the future of the slave trade was in serious doubt from 1788 on, that did not mean that the West Indies had become expendable. The destruction of Saint-Domingue from 1791 made the plantations in the Caribbean more valuable and encouraged Britain to send thousands of men to defend its Caribbean interests and to acquire more territories. Eventually, the British commitment to the Caribbean began to falter. The abolition of the slave trade was a blow to the plantation economy, and the abolition of slavery even more so. The abandonment in the 1840s of tariff protection for sugar left the West Indies poor and isolated. Britain was still dependent on plantation agriculture, but it was US cotton plantations that now mattered to the British economy. It was only "with hindsight, that the American Revolution was a threat to the survival of European empires around the Caribbean." The United States was the principal beneficiary of France's defeat in Saint-Domingue and in the dismemberment of the Spanish Empire everywhere in the Caribbean and North America except for Cuba. But in 1783, such American dominance was unlikely and British influence in the West Indies was strong and getting stronger: "Even without dominion over the thirteen colonies, the Atlantic retained a dominant position in Britain's assessment of her worldwide interests . . . for two or three decades after the loss of the thirteen colonies."[64]

Loyalists

An immediate problem for the British Empire after the American Revolution was what to do with the 60,000 Loyalists who had fled from the United States—8,000 whites and 5,000 Blacks to Britain; 6,000 whites and 15,000 enslaved persons to Jamaica and the Bahamas; 1,200 free people of color first to Nova Scotia and then to Sierra Leone; and over 30,000, mostly whites, to Canada. Loyalists varied immensely, from conservatives who feared that the Revolution promoted lawless anarchy harming a hierarchical empire, to people who shared the ideology of American republicanism but who opposed, usually for localistic reasons, British attempts to impose a top-down authoritarianism in new colonies.

The British world that emerged after 1783 may not have been a second empire, given its many continuities with the imperial power that had existed before 1763, but it did have a more authoritarian tone. That authoritarianism, however, was tempered by a new emphasis on humanitarianism. In the short term, the imperial government tried to mollify the other colonies and not to provoke confrontation. There was little attempt to reform the remnants and abuses of the old colonial system until after

1815. Other than the Constitutional Act in Canada (1791) and the Irish Union Act (1801), Parliament proved reluctant to intervene in the colonies, in contrast to the stream of legislation for America in the 1760s and 1770s. If ministers used the prerogative powers of the Crown, they no longer attempted to use them as a political weapon and generally demurred from interfering with the internal government of the older colonies with assemblies. The governors of these colonies continued to complain of their relative impotence. Unable to extract more revenue from the old colonies, the home government was forced to expend more upon their defense and civil government. However, rather than teaching the value of accommodation and flexibility, the American Revolution created an aversion to the colonial assemblies and large measures of self-government, in favor of the model of direct Crown rule pioneered by the Quebec Act of 1774 and the decision not to revive the old colonial system in Trinidad in 1810.[65]

In retrospect, Britain established a liberal constitutional empire committed to global expansion but guided by metropolitan humanitarianism. Britain founded a model of global liberty that was different from the liberty, equality, and fraternity of the French Revolution. It was a more limited ambition but one that was achievable, functioning as it did under a strong monarchical state and within a social structure shaped by a commitment to tradition and hierarchy.[66] We can see the interplay between authoritarianism and humanitarianism best in the place where Loyalists were most important and numerous: Canada. Most Loyalists arriving in Canada were not hostile to American republicanism as an ideology, even if such ideas were anathema to the British imperial state. Britain wanted, as it demonstrated in the Canada Constitutional Act of 1791, both to settle the issue of power between Anglophones and Francophones and to give Canadian government an authoritarian cast. It wanted "to avoid, if possible, in the government of Canada those defects which hastened the independence of our antient possessions in America . . . because no care was taken to preserve a due mixture of the Monarchical and Aristocratical parts of the British Constitutions."[67] Therefore, representative assemblies had limited powers and were governed by imperial officials able to do much more than had been the case for governors in colonial America. The aim, Lord Grenville noted in 1789, was to provide "a juster and more efficient security against the growth of a republican or independent spirit."[68]

This insistence on hierarchy and control, however, was balanced by practical concessions to Loyalists. Taxes were kept low and cheap land was made available, while merchants were given privileges, such as the right to trade with the Caribbean, from which Americans were excluded.[69] Canada was not especially democratic until well into the nineteenth century, and it remained committed to principles of white supremacy. The many Black Loyalists fleeing to Nova Scotia had a bad time, facing constant white opposition. The pressures of living as free Blacks in British North America led hundreds to move from Nova Scotia to the abolitionist-founded colony of Sierra Leone, along with three hundred destitute Blacks from Britain.[70] Canada retained many American values along with republicanism, including anti-Catholicism and racism. In its ethnic diversity, religious pluralism, and determination to fight Britain for the right to self-determination, it stayed connected to America until the Anglo-American War of 1812. The War of 1812 was "a civil war between kindred peoples, recently and incompletely separated by the American Revolution." It was only after this war that American identity was replaced in Canada by a close attachment to Britain.[71]

Increased authoritarianism in the British Empire was pronounced in British behavior in Upper Canada, Bengal, and Ireland, where an imperial revolution of government was promoted that disdained popular sovereignty, emphasized subordination and the fierce putdown of civil disobedience, and opposed constitutional change.[72] It was pronounced also in the new British colonies of New South Wales and Sierra Leone. In the former, slavery was outlawed on the arrival of the First Fleet in 1788, but the promulgator of that law, Captain Arthur Phillip, a forward-thinking despot, refused to entertain ideas of freedom for the convicts sent there. He placed the authority of the state above the liberties of the people. He argued that the convicts sent to Botany Bay in Australia, if freed but not allowed to return to Britain (that they could never return to Britain was the intention of the home secretary, the old-fashioned Whig Lord Sydney), would abuse those liberties that had been given to them. Phillip believed that such abuse of liberty had been the case in colonial America, and he was determined to prevent it from occurring in Australia.[73]

Sierra Leone was even more directly an antislavery initiative than Botany Bay. It was made a Crown Colony through the efforts of the abolitionist Sierra Leone Company in 1808.[74] Its capital, Freetown, was marked out to become the West African base of antislavery naval operations and

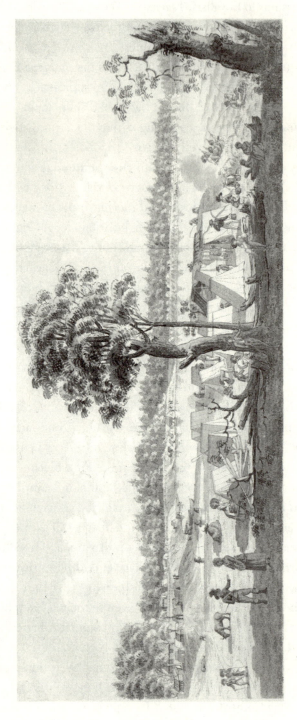

Encampment of the Loyalists at Johnstown, a New Settlement, on the Banks of the River St. Lawrence. Watercolor by James Peachey, 1784. (Library and Archives Canada, Acc. No. 1989-218-1)

Benjamin West (1738–1820), portrait of John Eardley Wilmot, the Loyalist claims commissioner, 1812. (Yale Center for British Art, Paul Mellon Collection)

the landing place of liberated Africans from ships interdicted by the British navy. The suppression campaign made leading abolitionists very rich. Zachary Macaulay amassed a fortune of over £100,000 as the leading principal of a firm with a monopoly over Sierra Leone's trade. The colony was envisioned as both a beacon of abolitionism and commercially profitable, showing that opening markets for African manufacture could overcome any financial losses from abolishing the slave trade. It was a humanitarian project embraced by abolitionist luminaries such as Henry Thornton, William Wilberforce, Macaulay, and Thomas and John Clarkson. It blended both compassion and control and was founded upon a paternalistic and explicitly racialized view of the limited decision-making capacity of Africans. The colony was decidedly dominating in tone, with the consent of the people of Sierra Leone to what happened in their land relegated to secondary importance beyond the interests of humanitarian reformers. Indeed, "the articulation and pursuit of professionally humane models of governance," as in Sierra Leone, expressed "a larger vision of global order that functioned to soften and legitimate . . . the successful projection of British power" that served the "moral expectations of an antislavery public and the material expectations of security and prosperity that defined imperial power."[75]

These authoritarian tendencies, however, conflicted with other forces. The massive migration of Britons into Canada in the early nineteenth century brought into Canada people who valued being British but who rejected British deference and hierarchy. Many Canadians, however, greatly feared the American empire they saw emerging and were wary of efforts by reformers campaigning for responsible government. Canada was a British-American democratic colony with strong impulses toward the democracy being formed in the United States, but with contested divisions about the extent to which lasting connections with British imperialism could keep it separate from its southern neighbor.[76] Loyalist Canada thus was different from the early republican United States. Loyalism had a transformative and counterrevolutionary aspect to it, strengthening beliefs in monarchy, duly constituted government, and Protestantism. Loyalists were especially concerned to defend Protestant Whig liberty against the perceived threat of Catholic tyranny, a threat much more real in religiously divided Canada than in the United States but also apparent elsewhere in the post-revolutionary empire.[77]

That renewed patriotic commitment to the British monarchy and constitution was naturally shaped by local circumstances. White Jamaicans, for example, associated their rights as free-born British subjects with their ability to buy, sell, and exploit Africans. Residents of Halifax in Nova Scotia, by contrast, focused their attentions on consent and representation, while Glaswegians emerged from the American Revolution committed to radical politics, such as greater Scottish representation in Parliament and a more determined defense of sectarian Protestantism. Loyalism also arose out of wider Atlantic contexts. Imperial leaders may have envisioned the empire as more controlled from the center and less rambunctious after the end of the American Revolution; colonial subjects did not necessarily share those ambitions. Indeed, Loyalists' "shared attitudes toward their nation and empire, their sense of loyalty and patriotism, collapsed in the face of rebellion predicated on a similar sense of Britishness" because imperial subjects "could not agree on a shared understanding of British liberty."[78]

This conflicting sense of Britishness was exemplified both in the fervent celebrations of Rodney's 1782 victory over the French in the eastern

Caribbean, when "joy seemed almost universal,"[79] and, more disturbingly, in the hugely destructive Gordon Riots in London in 1780. At least six hundred people died in these riots and large parts of London were left in ruins, including the ransacked homes of luminaries such as the politician-judge Earl Mansfield. The riots revealed a sobering fact: British Protestants had died fighting against their government's attempts to relieve Catholics while their nation was at war with the Catholic Bourbon powers, France and Spain. The Gordon Riots arose not out of parochial British concerns but out of a radical re-imagining of British Loyalism occasioned by the Franco-American war from 1778. It showed that British security was a delicate process. Loyalists professed love for the monarchy and Britain's informal constitution but could easily turn against the imperial government if that government threatened sacred British values like the Protestant cause. The events of 1688 were not yet a folk memory for the British imperial people—a fact that may not have escaped the attention of a king willing to contemplate abdication when many of his Protestant subjects chose independence over subjecthood in 1783.[80]

A Military Empire

The American Revolution made a difference to British imperialism in one important respect, which was to accentuate the military aspects of empire, both in leadership and in orientation. The British Empire in its imperial meridian in the late eighteenth and early nineteenth centuries was a curious mix of humanitarianism and authoritarianism. If you look at the British Empire from one perspective, it heralds an increased interest in reform of imperial institutions and imperial values aimed at ensuring the British Empire was one worthy of a morally upright British nation. Thus, the major reform initiatives of the late eighteenth century had strong imperial overtones, such as stopping abuses in India, as seen in the long-standing trial in the 1780s of Warren Hastings for corruption and the explosion of attention given to abolishing the slave trade. Although Britain was not willing to give to America the title of the greatest defender of freedom, the travails of war and the loss of America had encouraged many Britons to use the American Revolution as a means to reflect upon what it meant to be British and what it meant to have an empire of different subjects of different races and different experiences.

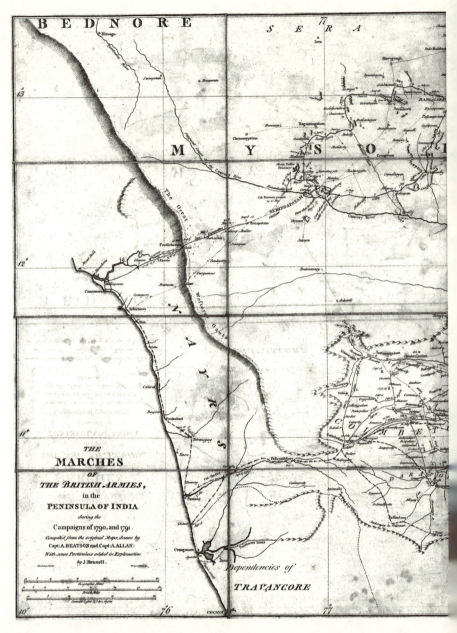

The Marches of the British Armies, in the Peninsula of India during the Campaigns of 1790 and 1791. James Rennell, cartographer. Compiled from the original maps drawn by A. Beatson and A. Allan. London: J. Rennell, February 21, 1792; Millard Filmore, collector. (Library of Congress, Geography and Map Division)

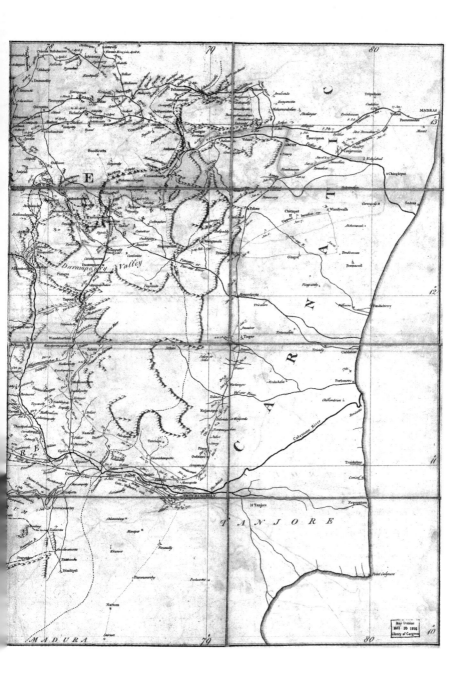

Robert Home (1752–1834), *The Reception of the Mysorean Hostage Princes by Marquis Cornwallis, 26 February 1792*, 1793. (Courtesy of the National Army Museum, London)

But if you look at the British Empire from another perspective in the 1780s, and even more so in the 1790s, a very different picture of British values and imperial objectives emerges. There was no retreat from empire after the loss of America. Indeed, imperial expansion proceeded apace, both with the establishment of Australia as a beachhead of colonization in the Pacific and with increased military action in India, which included a round of wars with the Marathas from the early 1780s and war with Tipu Sultan, the ruler of Mysore, until Tipu Sultan's defeat in 1792. In 1785, the Duke of Richmond, the master of the ordnance, undertook an ambitious plan for fortifying the British Caribbean, which led to a massive expansion of the scale of fortresses and barracks at Shirley Heights in Antigua, Brimstone Hill in St. Kitts, and St. Anne's Fort in Barbados, as well as in Grenada, Dominica, and St. Vincent. Beginning in 1795, many of these defenses were garrisoned by the First West India Regiment, the largest slave army in the world, which was an outgrowth of a Loyalist Black regiment from America, the Carolina Corps.[81]

This was very much a military empire, controlled by soldiers, many of whom had gotten their spurs in battles in North America in the 1770s and 1780s. The empire had a notably military cast after the American Revolution, especially among governors, who were invariably men with military experience. Governors in Jamaica, for example, were always military officers after 1776 until the appointment of the Duke of Manchester in 1808 (although Manchester had served in the army, his authority derived from his position as a senior aristocrat rather than any military prowess). Sir Alured Clarke (1744–1832), governor of Jamaica between 1784 and 1790, was typical of this military gubernatorial trend. Clarke was a career soldier who served in the Seven Years' War and was an important officer in the war in the American South during the American Revolution. A success as governor in Jamaica, he was then sent to Lower Canada to serve as governor between 1791 and 1793, commanded to implement the 1791 Constitutional Act. He concluded his career in India, where he combined the roles of imperial official and general, acting as both governor and commander-in-chief between 1798 and 1801, with his most important achievement gaining victory in the fourth Anglo-Mysore War in 1799.

Many military officers were influenced by their experience of service in America, such as John Graves Simcoe (1752–1806), the first lieutenant governor of Upper Canada (1791–96). The lesson they derived was that the imperial government had erred in allowing colonial elites too much power and in permitting colonial assemblies to become too powerful. In February 1786, Charles, Earl Cornwallis, was appointed to succeed Warren Hastings as governor-general of Bengal, a position he insisted upon combining with commander-in-chief of British forces in India. He led a larger army than he had commanded in America, consisting of over 20,000 men, and he defeated 40,000 troops of Tipu Sultan during the Third Mysore War (1790–92). His campaign acquired half of Tipu's territory in Mysore and paved the way for British dominance in South India. His opposition to native elites led to the racial segregation of offices, with white imperial officials and officers gaining exclusive hold of senior appointments. He debarred the children of mixed-race couples, who had previously been dominant in the administration, from holding office.

In a remarkable correspondence with Arthur Lee (1740–92), who had been a diplomat for the United States in France during the Revolution, Cornwallis wrote that he had never ceased to think that "rational liberty makes people virtuous" and that virtue makes them happy. He then proceeded to disagree with Lee about the potential for liberty in India. He asserted that the Hindus were incapable of enjoying civil liberty and that they were happier to be ruled by the British than by the Mughal emperor and his deputies. In his letters to the home government, Cornwallis stressed the need for a large European army in India. He warned that "it cannot be expected that even the best of treatment would constantly conciliate the willing obedience of so vast a body of people" with different religions and customs. His attitude reflected a growing invidious racial distinction in the nineteenth century between authoritarian imperial government in countries with a population composed of people of color and representative government in predominantly white countries. Britain was to grant increasing autonomy to countries with white majorities, such as Canada, Australia, New Zealand, and the Cape Colony in South Africa.[82]

War remained vital to imperialism after the end of the American Revolution. The history of the British Empire as it was transformed by the convulsions of the French Revolutionary and Napoleonic Wars is beyond the chronological boundaries of this book. What is obvious, however, is that these later wars were greater in global impact than even the Seven Years' War and the much more limited but still global world war of the American Revolution. War influenced empire everywhere in the aftermath of the American Revolution, but it was most important in the Caribbean and in India.

Imperialism was also very much on American minds as they contemplated how to navigate independence. It is hardly surprising that empire focused minds given that the United States was born in a colonial, revolutionary, and above all imperial age.[83] Americans in the late eighteenth century were a colonial people on the periphery of a global empire, who, under a British umbrella of economic, cultural, and sometimes political dependence, became a postcolonial people still on the global margins of an imperial world, a quasi-colonial appendage of Britain's informal empire.[84] The American republic remained an economic vassalage of the British for many years. The antebellum southern politician Henry Clay acknowledged in the early nineteenth century that the United States remained a "sort of set of independent colonies of England—politically free, commercially slaves."[85] It "was an embryonic nation-state built upon multiple layers of shared power and imperialist expansion, much of which was accomplished by subjecting indigenous peoples and by harnessing slave labour."[86]

Nevertheless, the infant and postcolonial United States was not quite an empire.[87] Thomas Jefferson wrote (albeit only rarely) of America as an "empire of liberty," but by empire he and others mostly thought that this idea symbolized how Americans had come to rule themselves and to recognize no earthly power over their freedom. "Empire" in this sense was simply another word for independence.[88] In this reading, if the United States was an empire, it was one that had explicitly rejected imperial rule, and which did not act like an empire. It did not, for example, consider Indigenous peoples or enslaved people as subjects, usually removing Indigenous peoples from land Americans coveted to desolate areas and keeping free people of color outside the bounds of citizenship. When new territories were considered for statehood, the United States actively shaped settlements for incorporation. Congress had to be convinced before a white settler population could form itself into a state that their self-government reflected the priorities of the American state.[89]

Would it have made a difference if the American Revolution had not happened? Some differences are immediately apparent, as we suggested in the start to this book and in our discussions of counterfactuals in the introduction to our part 2. The battle over slavery would have been vastly different if the slaveholding empire had not been split in two. The so-called swing to the east and the rise of the Raj after 1788 would have been less pronounced even than it was. And an Anglophone world of settlers that included an imperial America and in which industrialization was part of imperial policy and enacted in the American North as much as in Britain would have made the British Empire especially globally important.

Even without considering the counterfactual of the American Revolution not happening, or at least not starting as early as in 1776, placing postcolonial America within the story of the nineteenth-century British Empire provokes several interesting counterfactual thoughts. First, and most important, the undeniable importance of the United States as an informal appendage of the British Empire seen in capital flows, migration, patterns of trading, shipping lines, social networks, and so on shows that we need to consider "the analysis of broader systems of imperial exchange and integration (which demands a rigorous examination of America)." America "did" things for the wider project of nineteenth-century British imperialism, most graphically in the reach of the dominant commodity of the era: cotton. The growth of rival textile industries across Europe and the United States, sheltered under protective tariffs, forced the British textile trade into colonial or informal imperial markets in Asia and Latin America.[90] Indeed, "America was at once the primary source of a raw material whose finished product comprised nearly half of all British exports in the mid-nineteenth century *and* an upstart rival whose protectionism channeled British imperial expansion beyond the North Atlantic."[91] The spread of cotton coincided with antislavery, a foundation of Victorian imperialism. Antislavery was inextricably linked to transatlantic political networks, spilling beyond the Atlantic into efforts to suppress the slave trade out of Africa.[92]

America was a formidable challenge as well as a support to British imperialism and formed its own role in the British world system. America provided Britain with great wealth, but also, to residents in Britain's remaining settler colonies, was an example that might be followed. That possibility was viewed in Britain with alarm. "The formulation of white settler 'responsible government' that fostered the integration of the British diaspora, even as it developed political sovereignty, took on broad experiences from the American Revolution and federalism of Jefferson's decentralized empire of liberty."[93] The systematic colonization plans, for example, advanced by Edward Gibbon Wakefield in the antipodean colonies in the 1820s and 1830s, were very much fashioned with America as both example and warning.[94] America and Britain continued to be bound together and linked by imperialism for many decades after the end of the American Revolution.

Looking at the British Empire through an American lens and examining American republicanism with reference to the continuing vitality of British imperialism underscores the dynamism, integration, power, vulnerability, and dysfunctionalities of both empire and republic. The loss of the Thirteen Colonies did not stop, though it did divert into new directions, Britain's surge to unprecedented imperial expansion after 1783. The Age of Revolution remained the Age of Empire with imperialism at least as important as revolutionary ideology in shaping the global geopolitical reality of the period. The American Revolution was a major crisis in British imperial history. It was also indubitably shaped by the imperial context and by processes in which the various imperial possessions of eighteenth-century Britain were involved. Without understanding how the American Revolution was an imperial event, we cannot understand fully how it came about and how it was resolved.

Notes

Introduction

1. Pauline Maier, *American Scripture: How America Declared Its Independence from Britain* (New York: Knopf, 1997).
2. David Armitage, "The Declaration of Independence and International Law," *William and Mary Quarterly* 59 (2002): 39–64; Eliga H. Gould, *Among the Powers of the Earth: The American Revolution and the Making of a New World Empire* (Cambridge, MA: Harvard University Press, 2012).
3. Kermit Roosevelt, *The Nation That Never Was: Reconstructing America's Story* (Chicago: University of Chicago Press, 2022).
4. Steven Sarson, *"When in the Course of Human Events": History and Historical Consciousness in the US Declaration of Independence* (forthcoming).
5. Patrick Griffin, "Introduction: Imagining an American Imperial-Revolutionary History," in Griffin, ed., *Experiencing Empire: Power, People and Revolution in Early America* (Charlottesville: University of Virginia Press, 2017), 1–26.
6. Claudio Saunt, *Unworthy Republic: The Dispossession of Native Americans and the Road to Indian Territory* (New York: W. W. Noron, 2020).
7. Daniel Immerwahr, *How to Hide an Empire: A History of the Greater United States* (New York: Farrar, Straus and Giroux, 2019); Daniele Ganser, *USA: The Ruthless Empire* (New York: Skyhorse, 2023); A. G. Hopkins, *American Empire: A Global History* (Princeton: Princeton University Press, 2018); Sathnam Sanghera, *Empireworld: How British Imperialism Shaped the Globe* (New York: Viking, 2024); Caroline Elkins, *Legacy of Violence: A History of the British Empire* (New York: Vintage, 2022).
8. Richard Whatmore, *The End of Enlightenment: Empire, Commerce, Crisis* (London: Allen Lane, 2023).
9. John Gallagher and Ronald Robinson, "The Imperialism of Free Trade," *Economic History Review* 6 (1953): 1–15.
10. Lauren Benton, *A Search for Sovereignty: Law and Geography in European Empires, 1400–1900* (Cambridge: Cambridge University Press, 2010), 3, 6.
11. John Darwin, *The Empire Project: The Rise and Fall of the British World System, 1830–1920* (Cambridge: Cambridge University Press, 2009), xi, 3, 20.
12. Charles McLean Andrews, "Colonial Commerce," *American Historical Review* 20 (1914): 43; Vera Keller and Ted McCormick, "Towards a History of Projects," *Early Science and Medicine* 21 (2016): 423–44; Andrew Fitzmaurice, *Sovereignty, Property, and Empire, 1500–2000* (Cambridge: Cambridge University Press, 2014); and Philip J. Stern, *Empire, Incorporated: The Corporations That Built British Colonialism* (Cambridge, MA: Harvard University Press, 2023), 11–12.
13. Richard Koebner, *Empire* (Cambridge: Cambridge University Press, 1961);

Charles S. Maier, *Among Empires: American Ascendancy and Its Predecessor* (Cambridge, MA: Harvard University Press, 2006), 43; Daniel A. Baugh, "Great Britain's 'Blue Water' Policy, 1689–1815," *International History Review* 10 (1988): 33–58.

14. Peter Fibiger Bang, "Empire—A World History: Anatomy and Concept, Theory and Synthesis," in Peter Fibiger Bang, C. A. Bayly, and Walter Scheidel, eds., *The Oxford World History of Empire,* vol. 1: *The Imperial Experience* (Oxford: Oxford University Press, 2021), 1:12.
15. Darwin, *Unfinished Empire: The Global Expansion of Britain* (New York: Bloomsbury, xi–xii.
16. Stephen Howe, *Empire: A Very Short Introduction* (Oxford: Oxford University Press, 2001), 14.
17. Garry Runciman, "Empire as a Topic in Comparative Sociology," in Peter Fibiger Bang and C. A. Bayly, eds., *Tributary Empires in Global History* (Basingstoke: Palgrave Macmillan, 2011), 99.
18. Jane Burbank and Frederick Cooper, *Empires in World History: Power and the Politics of Difference* (Princeton: Princeton University Press, 2010), 3.
19. Kathleen DuVal, *Independence Lost: Lives on the Edge of the American Revolution* (New York: Random House, 2015).
20. Krishan Kumar, *Visions of Empire: How Five Imperial Regimes Shaped the World* (Princeton: Princeton University Press, 2017), 3, 475; Robert Gildea, *Empires of the Mind: The Colonial Past and the Politics of the Present* (Cambridge: Cambridge University Press, 2019).
21. Peter N. Miller, *Defining the Common Good: Empire, Religion, and Philosophy in Eighteenth-Century Britain* (Cambridge: Cambridge University Press, 1994).
22. J. G. A. Pocock, *Virtue, Commerce, and History: Essays in Political Thought and History, Chiefly in the Eighteenth Century* (Cambridge: Cambridge University Press, 1985), 125–41.
23. Adam Smith, *An Inquiry into the Nature and Causes of the Wealth of Nations,* ed. R. H. Campbell, A. S. Skinner, and W. B. Todd, 2 vols. (Oxford: Oxford University Press, 1975), 2:570, 575.
24. Whatmore, *End of Enlightenment,* xxv.
25. Whatmore, *End of Enlightenment,* 326.
26. J. C. D. Clark, "Providence, Predestination and Progress: Or, Did the Empire Fail?" *Albion* 35 (2003): 559–89.
27. Cited in Whatmore, *End of Enlightenment,* 47.
28. Colonial Office (C.O.) 137/71/227–401, National Archives, Kew, London (TNA), and *Journals of the Assembly of Jamaica (JAJ),* 16 vols. (Jamaica: Alexander Aikman, 1805), 6:634–60, 692–93. See also Richard B. Sheridan, "The Jamaican Slave Insurrection Scare of 1776 and the American Revolution," *Journal of Negro History* 61 (1976): 290–308; Michael Craton, *Testing the Chains: Resistance to Slavery in the British West Indies* (Ithaca: Cornell University Press, 1982), ch. 14; Andrew Jackson O'Shaughnessy, *An Empire Divided: The American Revolution and the British Caribbean* (Philadelphia: University of Pennsylvania Press, 2000), 151–54; Edward B. Rugemer, *Slave Law and the Politics of Resistance in the Early Atlantic World* (Cambridge, MA: Harvard University Press, 2018), 193–99.
29. Grizell to General Palmer, July 20, 1776, C.O. 137/71/238–39.

30. C.O. 137/71/71, 309.
31. Sir Simon Clarke to Benjamin Lyon, July 23, 1776, C.O. 137/71/256–57.
32. Examination of Pontack, July 28, 1776, C.O. 137/71/276–78.
33. Governor Keith to Lord George Germain, August 6, 1776, C.O. 137/71/228–29.
34. Christer Petley, *White Fury: A Jamaican Slaveholder and the Age of Revolution* (Oxford: Oxford University Press, 2018), 104–5; Michael Duffy, *Soldiers, Sugar, and Seapower: The British Expeditions to the West Indies and the War with Revolutionary France* (Oxford: Clarendon, 1987); Kit Candlin, *The Last Caribbean Frontier, 1795–1815* (Basingstoke: Palgrave Macmillan, 2012).
35. James Sidbury, "Plausible Stories and Varnished Truths," *William and Mary Quarterly* 59 (2002): 179–84.
36. Examination of Sam, July 29, 1776, C.O. 137/71/253.
37. John Grizell to Keith, July 27, 1776, C.O. 137/71/266–67.
38. Vincent Brown, *Tacky's Revolt: The Story of an Atlantic Slave War* (Cambridge, MA: Harvard University Press, 2020), 242.
39. Thomas Harrison to "Dear Brothers," August 5, 1776, C.O. 5/154 pt. 2/378.
40. Examination of Negro Adam, July 17, 1776, C.O. 137/71/234–35.
41. Examination of Pontack, July 28, 1776, C.O. 137/71/276–78.
42. John Purrier to Nathaniel Phillips, March 25, 1777, Slebech Papers, National Library of Wales, Mss. 11,485; O'Shaughnessy, *Empire Divided*, 153–54.
43. Cited in David Brion Davis, *The Problem of Slavery in the Age of Revolution, 1770–1823* (Ithaca: Cornell University Press, 1975), 398–99.
44. Lawrence Henry Gipson speaks of thirty-two colonies in *The British Empire before the American Revolution*, 15 vols. (New York: Knopf, 1936–72), 13:206; Jack Greene gives the number twenty-nine in "Introduction: Empire and Liberty," in Greene, ed., *Exclusionary Empire: English Liberty Overseas, 1600–1900* (New York: Cambridge University Press, 2010), 6. This is because they count the colonies by the number of assemblies, in which case the Leeward Islands would be considered as four colonies rather than one.
45. Whatmore, *End of Enlightenment*, 50–51; Nigel Aston and Clarissa Cambell Orr, eds., *An Enlightenment Statesman in Whig Britain: Lord Shelburne in Context, 1737–1805* (Woodbridge: Boydell and Brewer, 2011).
46. John Gascoigne, *Encountering the Pacific in the Age of Enlightenment* (Cambridge: Cambridge University Press, 2014).
47. Benjamin Franklin to all captains and commanders of armed ships, March 10, 1779, in *The Journals of Captain James Cook on His Voyages of Discovery*, ed. J. C. Beaglehole (Cambridge: Cambridge University Press, 1967), 3:1535.
48. Kate Fullagar, *The Warrior, the Voyager, and the Artist: Three Lives in the Age of Empire* (New Haven: Yale University Press, 2020).
49. Glyndwr Williams, *The Death of Captain Cook: A Hero Made and Unmade* (Cambridge, MA: Harvard University Press, 2008).
50. David E. Stannard, "Disease and Infertility: A New Look at the Demographic Collapse of Native Populations in the Wake of Western Contact," *Journal of American Studies* 24 (1990): 328–30.
51. S. Max Edelson, *The New Map of Empire: How Britain Imagined America before Independence* (Cambridge, MA: Harvard University Press, 2017); P. J. Marshall,

The Making and Unmaking of Empires: Britain, India and America c. 1750–1783 (Oxford: Oxford University Press, 2005).

52. Gordon S. Wood, *The Radicalism of the American Revolution* (New York: Knopf, 1992); Jonathan Israel, *The Expanding Blaze: How the American Revolution Ignited the World, 1775–1848* (Princeton: Princeton University Press, 2017).

53. The classic statement is Bernard Bailyn, *The Ideological Origins of the American Revolution* (Cambridge, MA: Harvard University Press, 1967). See also Joyce Appleby, *Liberalism and Republicanism in the Historical Imagination* (Cambridge, MA: Harvard University Press, 1992).

54. For American-centered narrative accounts, see Woody Holton, *Liberty Is Sweet: The Hidden History of the American Revolution* (New York: Simon and Schuster, 2021); T. H. Breen, *The Will of the People: The Revolutionary Birth of America* (Cambridge, MA: Harvard University Press, 2019); and Robert G. Parkinson, *Thirteen Clocks: How Race United the Colonies and Made the Declaration of Independence* (Chapel Hill: University of North Carolina Press, 2021).

55. Alan Taylor, *American Revolutions: A Continental History, 1750–1804* (New York: W. W. Norton, 2016); Stephen Conway, *The American Revolutionary War* (London: I. B. Tauris, 2013).

56. Trevor Burnard, Emma Hart, and Marie Houllemare, eds., *The Oxford Handbook of the Seven Years' War* (New York: Oxford University Press, 2024).

57. Edelson, *New Map of Empire*, 205.

58. Eric Hinderaker, *Boston's Massacre* (Cambridge, MA: Harvard University Press, 2017); Mary Beth Norton, *1774: The Long Year of Revolution* (New York: Random House, 2020).

59. Mark Peterson, *The City-State of Boston: The Rise and Fall of an Atlantic Power, 1630–1865* (Princeton: Princeton University Press, 2019), 298–300.

60. Mark Peterson, "The Revolution in British America: General Overview," in Wim Klooster, ed., *The Cambridge History of the Age of Atlantic Revolutions*, 3 vols. (Cambridge: Cambridge University Press, 2024), 1:177.

61. Michael McDonnell, *The Politics of War: Race, Class, and Conflict in Revolutionary Virginia* (Chapel Hill: University of North Carolina Press, 2007); Woody Holton, *Forced Founders: Indians, Debtors, Slaves, and the Making of the American Revolution in Virginia* (Chapel Hill: University of North Carolina Press, 2000); Alan Taylor, *The Internal Enemy: Slavery and War in Virginia, 1772–1832* (New York: W. W. Norton, 2013).

62. P. J. Marshall, "Britain's Imperial Problem: The International Perspective," in Edward G. Gray and Jane Kamensky, eds., *The Oxford Handbook of the American Revolution* (New York: Oxford University Press, 2013), 15–29.

63. Gonzalo M. Quintero Saravia, "The Participation of France and Spain," in Klooster, *Cambridge History of the Age of Atlantic Revolutions*, 1:269–95.

64. For a brilliant account of the British Empire in 1923, see Matthew Parker, *One Fine Day: Britain's Empire on the Brink* (London: Abacus, 2023).

65. Trevor Burnard, "Empire Matters? The Historiography of Imperialism in Early America," *History of European Ideas* 33 (2007): 87–107.

66. We, for convenience's sake, occasionally use the term "Canada" even though this term does not really apply to the situation in the 1760s and 1770s when "Canada"

was comprised of three colonies—Newfoundland, Nova Scotia, and Quebec. We do not deal much with Newfoundland in this book: an excellent account is Jerry Bannister, *The Rule of the Admirals: Law, Custom, and Naval Government in Newfoundland, 1699–1832* (Toronto: University of Toronto Press, 2014).

67. Jack Goldstone, *Revolution and Rebellion in the Early Modern World* (Berkeley: University of California Press, 1991).
68. Barbara Tuchman, *The March of Folly: From Troy to Vietnam* (New York: Knopf, 1984); Nick Bunker, *An Empire on the Edge: How Britain Came to Fight America* (New York: Vintage, 2014; London: Bodley Head, 2015).
69. Wood, *The Radicalism of the American Revolution*.
70. H. M. Scott, *The Birth of a Great Power System, 1740–1815* (London: Harlow, 2006).
71. Manuel Covo, "Economic Consequences," in Burnard, Hart, and Houllemare, *Oxford Handbook of the Seven Years' War*, 249–68.
72. George L. Beer, *British Colonial Policy, 1754–1765* (New York: Macmillan, 1907); Charles M. Andrews, *The Colonial Background of the American Revolution* (New Haven: Yale University Press, 1931); Lawrence Henry Gipson, *The Coming of the Revolution* (New York: Harper, 1954).
73. Charles McLean Andrews, *The Colonial Period* (New York: H. Holt, 1912), v–vi.
74. Steven Pincus, Tiraana Bains, and A. Zuercher Reichardt, "Thinking the Empire Whole," *History Australia* 16 (2019): 610–37.
75. Conway, *American Revolutionary War*, 5.
76. David Armitage, *The Declaration of Independence: A Global History* (Cambridge, MA: Harvard University Press, 2007).
77. Andrew Jackson O'Shaughnessy, *The Men Who Lost America: British Leadership, the American Revolution, and the Fate of the Empire* (New Haven: Yale University Press, 2013).
78. Conway, *American Revolutionary War*, 32; Jack P. Greene, "An Uneasy Connection: An Analysis of the Preconditions of the American Revolution," in *Essays on the American Revolution*, ed. James H. Hutson and Stephen G. Kurtz (Chapel Hill: University of North Carolina Press, 1973); John W. Shy, *A People Numerous and Armed: Reflections on the Military Struggle for American Independence* (New York: Oxford University Press, 1976); John Phillip Reid, *In a Defiant Stance: The Conditions of Law in Massachusetts Bay, the Irish Comparison, and the Coming of the American Revolution* (University Park: Pennsylvania State University Press, 1977).
79. P. J. Marshall, *Edmund Burke and the British Empire in the West Indies* (Oxford: Oxford University Press, 2019), 34–44.
80. Nancy Christie, *The Formal and Informal Politics of British Rule in Post-Conquest Quebec, 1760–1837: A Northern Bastille* (Oxford: Oxford University Press, 2020).
81. Jack Greene, "Colonial History and National History: Reflections on a Continuing Problem," *William and Mary Quarterly* 64 (2007): 247.
82. Patrick Griffin, *The Townshend Moment: The Making of Empire and Revolution in the Eighteenth Century* (New Haven: Yale University Press, 2017), 25.
83. Janet Polasky, "Atlantic Revolutions," in Eliga Gould, Paul Mapp, and Carla Gardina Pestana, eds., *The Cambridge History of America and the World*, vol. 1: *1500–1820* (Cambridge: Cambridge University Press, 2022), 510.

84. Caitlin Fitz, *Our Sister Republics: The United States in an Age of American Revolutions* (New York: Liveright, 2016).
85. Julius S. Scott, *The Common Wind: Afro-American Currents in the Age of the Haitian Revolution* (New York: Verso, 2018); Deirdre Coleman, *Romantic Colonization and British Anti-Slavery* (Cambridge: Cambridge University Press, 2005), 147.
86. Polasky, "Atlantic Revolutions," 511.
87. Hannah Arendt, *On Revolution* (New York: Viking, 1963), 49.
88. Edward G. Gray and Jane Kamensky, "Introduction: American Revolutions," in Gray and Kamensky, *Oxford Handbook of the American Revolution*, 68.
89. Jack P. Greene, "Colonial History and National History: Reflections on a Continuing Problem," *William and Mary Quarterly* 64 (2007): 247.
90. Michael A. McDonnell and David Waldstreicher, "Revolution in the *Quarterly*? A Historiographical Analysis," *William and Mary Quarterly* 74 (2017): 664.
91. Alan Taylor, "Expand or Die: The Revolution's New Empire," *Journal of the Early Republic* 37 (2017): 632.
92. Serena Zabin, "Writing to and from the Revolution," *William and Mary Quarterly* 74 (2017): 763.
93. Rashauna Johnson, "Settlers, Slavery and the Early Republic," *William and Mary Quarterly* 74 (2017): 235-42.
94. Jennifer M. Spear, "Beyond the Native/Settler Divide in Early California," *William and Mary Quarterly* 76 (2019): 427-34.
95. Peter Onuf, "Imperialism and Nationalism in the Early American Republic," in Ian Tyrrell and Jay Sexton, eds., *Empire's Turn: US Anti-Imperialism from the Founding Era to the Age of Terrorism* (Ithaca: Cornell University Press, 2015), 21-40.
96. Gautham Rao, "The New Historiography of the Early Federal Government: Institutions, Contexts and the Imperial State," *William and Mary Quarterly* 77 (2020): 97-128. For a counterview, see Max M. Edling, *A Hercules in the Cradle: War, Money, and the American State, 1783-1867* (Chicago: University of Chicago Press, 2014).
97. Matthew Lockwood, *To Begin the World Over Again: How the American Revolution Devastated the Globe* (New Haven: Yale University Press, 2019), 5, 6, 7.
98. C. A. Bayly, *Imperial Meridian: The British Empire and the World, 1780-1830* (London: Longman, 1989), 80-81.
99. Patrick Griffin, *The Age of Atlantic Revolution: The Fall and Rise of a Connected World* (New Haven: Yale University Press, 2023).
100. Edmund Burke, *Reflections on the Revolution in France*, ed. L. G. Mitchell (Oxford: Oxford University Press, 2009); Jennifer Mori, *Britain in the Age of the French Revolution* (Harlow: Longman, 2000).
101. Clive Emsley, "'Repression,' 'Terror' and the Rule of Law in England during the Decade of the French Revolution," *English Historical Review* 100 (1985): 801-25; Gregory Claeys, "The French Revolution Debate and British Political Thought," *History of Political Thought* 11 (1990): 59-80.
102. Gordon S. Wood, *Empire of Liberty: A History of the Early Republic, 1789-1815* (New York: Oxford University Press, 2009), 178.

103. H. G. Koenigsberger, *The Practice of Empire: The Government of Sicily under Phillip II of Spain* (Ithaca: Cornell University Press, 1969); J. H. Elliott, *Empires of the Atlantic World: Britain and Spain in America, 1492–1830* (New Haven: Yale University Press, 2006).

104. Christian Hauser and Horst Pietschmann, "Empire, the Concept and Its Problems and the Historiography on Iberian Empires in the Early Modern Period," *Culture and History Digital Journal* 3 (2014); Anna Brinkman-Schwartz, "The *Antigallican* Affair: Public and Ministerial Responses to Anglo-Spanish Maritime Conflict in the Seven Years' War, 1756–1758," *English Historical Review* 135 (2020), 1132–64.

105. Christopher Hodson and Brett Rushforth, *Discovering Empire: France and the Atlantic World from the Age of Crusading to the Rise of Napoleon* (New York: Oxford University Press, 2024).

106. Eliga H. Gould, "Entangled Histories, Entangled Worlds: The English-Speaking Atlantic as a Spanish Periphery," *American Historical Review* 112 (2007): 767.

107. Wim Klooster, *Illicit Riches: Dutch Trade in the Caribbean, 1648–1795* (Leiden: KITLV, 1998); Thomas Truxes, *Defying Empire: Trading with the Enemy in Colonial New York* (New Haven: Yale University Press, 2008); Jesse Cromwell, *The Smugglers' World: Illicit Trade and Atlantic Communities in Eighteenth-Century Venezuela* (Chapel Hill: University of North Carolina Press, 2019).

108. Hannah Weiss Muller, "Forging the Laws of Subjecthood after 1763," in Robert Olwell and James Vaughn, eds., *Envisioning Empire: The New British World, 1763–1773* (London: Bloomsbury, 2019), 57–82.

Part One. Causes of the American Revolution

1. Conrad Russell, *The Causes of the English Civil War* (Oxford: Oxford University Press, 1990); Glenn Burgess, *Absolute Monarchy and the Stuart Constitution* (London: Yale University Press, 1996); Tim Harris, "Revisiting the Causes of the English Civil War," *Huntington Library Quarterly* 78 (2015); 615–35.

2. Lawrence Stone, "Theories of Revolution," *World Politics* 18 (1966): 159–76.

3. Bernard Bailyn, *The Origins of American Politics* (New York: Knopf, 1968), 9–10. For the rise of the assemblies, see Jack P. Greene, *The Quest for Power: The Lower Houses of Assembly in the Southern Royal Colonies, 1689–1776* (Chapel Hill: University of North Carolina Press, 1963).

4. Jack P. Greene, "Liberty and Slavery: The Transfer of British Liberty to the West Indies, 1627–1865," in Greene, *Exclusionary Empire*, 61–64.

5. Danielle Kinsey, "Assessing Imperialism," in John McNeill and Kenneth Pomeranz, eds., *The Cambridge World History: Production, Destruction and Connection, 1750–Present* (Cambridge: Cambridge University Press, 2015), 7:1, 359–66.

6. Benjamin Franklin to William Franklin, March 13, 1768, *The Papers of Benjamin Franklin,* https://franklinpapers.org; Steve Pincus, "Confederal Union and Empire: Placing the Albany Plan (1754) in Imperial Context," *Journal of British Studies* 62 (2023): S589–617.

7. Pincus, Bains, and Reichardt, "Thinking the Empire Whole," 610–37.

8. C. A. Bayly, "Deconstructing the British Empire: Between Repression and Re-

form," in Peter Fibiger Bang, C. A. Bayly, and Walter Schiedel, eds., *The Oxford World History of Empires*, 2 vols. (Oxford: Oxford University Press, 2021), 2:921–40.

9. Many of the theories of historical revolution come from the 1960s. See Chalmers Johnson, *Revolutionary Change* (Boston: Little, Brown, 1966); J. C. Davies, "Toward a Theory of Revolution," *American Sociological Review* 27 (1962): 5–19; and T. R. Gurr, *Why Men Rebel* (Princeton: Princeton University Press, 1970). For the current state of play, see Jack A. Goldstone, Leonid Grinin, and Andrey Korotayev, "The Phenomenon and Theories of Revolution," in Goldstone, Grinin, and Korotayev, eds., *Handbook of Revolutions in the 21st Century: The New Waves of Revolutions and the Causes and Effects of Disruptive Political Change* (New York: Springer, 2022), 37–68.

10. Lucy Woodring, *Tudor England: A History* (New Haven: Yale University Press, 2023); Peter Marshall, *Heretics and Believers: A History of the English Reformation* (New Haven: Yale University Press, 2017); Jonathan Healey, *The Blazing World: A New History of Revolutionary England* (London: Bloomsbury, 2023); Anna Keay, *The Restless Republic: Britain without a Crown* (London: William Collins, 2023); Joel Mokyr, *The Enlightened Economy: An Economic History of Britain, 1700–1850* (New Haven: Yale University Press, 2009); Robert C. Allen, *The Industrial Revolution in Global Perspective* (New York: Cambridge University Press, 2009).

11. Peter Lake, "Post-Reformation Politics, or on Not Looking for the Long-Term Causes of the English Civil War," in Michael J. Braddick, ed., *The Oxford Handbook of the English Revolution* (Oxford: Oxford University Press, 2015), 21–40.

12. Keith B. Berwick, "A Peculiar Monument: The Third Series of *William and Mary Quarterly*," *William and Mary Quarterly* 21 (1964): 13–14.

13. Gray and Kamensky, introduction to *Oxford Handbook of the American Revolution*, 6.

14. Patrick Spero, "Introduction: Origins," in Spero and Michael Zuckerman, eds., *The American Revolution Reborn* (Philadelphia: University of Pennsylvania Press, 2016), 4.

15. Eric Hinderaker and Rebecca Horn, "Imperial Wars, Imperial Reform," in Eliga H. Gould, Paul Mapp, and Carla Pestana, eds., *The Cambridge History of America in the World*, 3 vols. (New York: Cambridge University Press, 2021), 251–73.

16. Mark Peterson, "The Revolution in British America: General Overview," in Klooster, *Cambridge History of the Age of Atlantic Revolutions*, 1:164.

17. Patrick Griffin, "The British Atlantic on the Eve of American Independence," in Klooster, *Cambridge History of the Age of Atlantic Revolutions*, 1:207; Conway, *American Revolutionary War*, 33.

18. John M. Murrin, *Rethinking America: From Empire to Republic* (New York: Oxford University Press, 2018), 162–63.

19. Craig Yirush, *Settlers, Liberty, and Empire: The Roots of Early American Political Theory, 1675–1775* (Cambridge: Cambridge University Press, 2011); Andrew Shankman, Ignacio Gallup-Diaz, and David Silverman, eds., *Anglicizing America: Empire, Revolution, Republic* (Philadelphia: University of Pennsylvania Press, 2015).

20. Eliga H. Gould, "Revolution and Counter-Revolution," in David Armitage and

Michael Braddick, eds., *The British Atlantic World 1500–1800*, 2nd ed. (Basingstoke: Palgrave Macmillan, 2009), 226; Trevor Burnard, *Creole Gentlemen: The Maryland Elite, 1691–1776* (Routledge: New York, 2002).

21. Conway, *American Revolutionary War*, 32.
22. Griffin, "British Atlantic on the Eve of American Independence," in Klooster, *Cambridge History of the Age of Atlantic Revolutions*, 1:209.
23. Anthony Macfarlane, "The Rebellion of the Barrios: Urban Insurrection in Bourbon Quito," *Hispanic American Historical Review* 89 (1989): 283–330; Allen J. Kuethe and Kenneth J. Andrien, *The Spanish Atlantic World in the Eighteenth Century: War and the Bourbon Reforms, 1713–1766* (Cambridge: Cambridge University Press, 2014), 287–304.
24. Trevor Burnard and John Garrigus, *The Plantation Machine: Atlantic Capitalism in French Saint-Domingue and British Jamaica* (Philadelphia: University of Pennsylvania Press, 2016), 154–91; Paul Cheney, *Cul de Sac: Capitalism and Slavery in French Saint-Domingue* (Chicago: University of Chicago Press, 2017).
25. Manuel Covo, "The Economic and Financial Consequences of the Seven Years' War in Europe," in Burnard, Hart, and Houllemare, *Oxford Handbook of the Seven Years' War*, 249–68.
26. Paul Butel, *Les négociants bordelais, Europe et les Îsles au XVIIIe siècle* (Paris: Aubier, 1974), 203; David Hancock, *Citizens of the World: London Merchants and the Integration of the British Atlantic Community, 1735–1785* (New York: Cambridge University Press, 2005), 239.
27. François-Joseph Ruggiu, "Empires," in Burnard, Hart, and Houllemare, *Oxford Handbook of the Seven Years' War*, 101–18.
28. John Shovlin, *Trading with the Enemy: Britain, France, and the 18th-Century Quest for a Peaceful World Order* (New Haven: Yale University Press, 2021).
29. Patrick Griffin, *The Townshend Moment*; Paul Cheney, *Revolutionary Commerce: Globalization and the French Monarchy* (Cambridge, MA: Harvard University Press, 2010).

Chapter 1. The Seven Years' War and the New Empire

1. Jack P. Greene, "The Seven Years' War and the American Revolution: The Causal Relationship Reconsidered," *Journal of Imperial and Commonwealth History* 8 (1980): 85–105.
2. Burnard, Hart, and Houllemare, *Oxford Handbook of the Seven Years' War*; Daniel Baugh, *The Global Seven Years War* (New York: Routledge, 2011). For a ranking of pre–French Revolutionary wars in the eighteenth century between France and Britain, see Brendan Simms, *Three Victories and a Defeat: The Rise and Fall of the First British Empire* (London: Penguin, 2007).
3. Lawrence Henry Gipson, *The British Empire before the American Revolution*, 15 vols. (New York: Knopf, 1936–70).
4. Marshall, "Britain's American Problem," in Gray and Kamensky, *Oxford Handbook of the American Revolution*, 17–18.
5. Fred Anderson, *Crucible of War: The Seven Years' War and the Fate of Empire in British North America, 1754–1766* (New York: Knopf, 2000).

6. Michael A. McDonnell, "North American Breakdown," in Burnard, Hart, and Houllemare, *Oxford Handbook of the Seven Years' War*, 419–36.
7. Baugh, *Global Seven Years War*, 1.
8. H. M. Scott, *The Birth of a Great Power System, 1740–1815* (London: Harlow, 2006).
9. Thomas Agostini, "'The Provincials will work like Giants': British Imperialism, American Colonial Troops, and Trans-Atlantic Labor Economics during the Seven Years' War," *Early American Studies* 15 (2017): 89–90.
10. Jan Eloranta and Jeremy Land, "Hollow Victory? Britain's Public Debt and the Seven Years' War," *Essays in Economic and Business History* 29 (2011): 101–18.
11. William Knox, *The Present State of the Nation* (London, 1768), 19.
12. Catherine M. Desbarats, "France in North America: The Net Burden of Empire during the First Half of the Eighteenth Century," *French History* 11 (1997), 1–28; James C. Riley, *The Seven Years War and the Old Regime in France: The Economic and Financial Toll* (Princeton: Princeton University Press, 1986), 36; Paul Cheney, *Revolutionary Commerce: Globalization and the French Monarchy* (Cambridge, MA: Harvard University Press, 2010); Nicholas Radburn, *Traders in Men: Merchants and the Transformation of the Transatlantic Slave Trade* (New Haven: Yale University Press, 2023); Burnard and Garrigus, *The Plantation Machine*.
13. Pernille Roge, *Economistes and the Reinvention of Empire* (Cambridge: Cambridge University Press, 2019).
14. Marshall G. S. Hodgson, *The Venture of Islam: The Gunpowder Empires and Modern Times* (Chicago: University of Chicago Press, 1974), 134–222; C. A. Bayly, *The Birth of the Modern World, 1780–1914* (Oxford: Blackwell, 2004); Muzaffar Alam, *The Crisis of Empire in Mughal North India: Awadh and the Punjab, 1707–48* (Delhi; New York: Oxford University Press, 1986).
15. Kaushik Roy, *War, Culture, and Society in Early Modern South Asia, 1740–1849* (New York: Routledge, 2011); William Dalrymple, *The Anarchy: The East India Company, Corporate Violence and the Pillage of an Empire;* Philip Stern, *Empire, Incorporated: The Corporations That Built British Colonialism* (Cambridge, MA: Harvard University Press, 2023).
16. Michael A. McDonnell, *Masters of Empire: Great Lakes Indians and the Making of America* (New York: Hill and Wang, 2017).
17. Jonathan Dull, *The French Navy and the Seven Years' War* (Lincoln: University of Nebraska Press, 2005), ch.1.
18. David L. Preston, *Braddock's Defeat: The Battle of the Monongahela and the Road to Revolution* (New York: Oxford University Press, 2015).
19. Anderson, *Crucible of War;* Baugh, *Global Seven Years War*.
20. Shovlin, *Trading with the Enemy;* Eliga H. Gould, "Peacemaking," in Burnard, Hart, and Houllemare, *Oxford Handbook of the Seven Years' War*, 137–58; Edmond Dziembowski, *La guerre de Sept Ans, 1756–1763* (Paris: Perrin, 2015).
21. Jon Wilson, *India Conquered: Britain's Raj and the Chaos of Empire* (New York: Simon and Schuster, 2017); Philip J. Stern, *The Company-State: Corporate Sovereignty and the Early Modern Foundations of the British Empire in India* (New York: Oxford University Press, 2011); James Vaughn, *The Politics of Empire at the Accession of George III: The East India Company and the Crisis and Transformation of Britain's Imperial State* (New Haven: Yale University Press, 2019); and

H. V. Bowen, *Revenue and Reform: The Indian Problem in British Politics, 1757–1773* (Cambridge: Cambridge University Press, 1991).
22. Bob Harris, "War, Empire, and the 'National Interest' in Mid-Eighteenth-Century Britain," in *Britain and America Go to War: The Impact of War and Warfare in Anglo-America, 1754–1815*, ed. Julie Flavell and Stephen Conway (Gainesville: University Press of Florida, 2004), 13–40.
23. Christopher Clark, *The Sleepwalkers: How Europe Went to War in 1914* (London: Penguin, 2013).
24. Simms, *Three Victories and a Defeat*.
25. Nicholas Rogers, *Mayhem: Post-War Crime and Violence in Britain, 1748–53* (New Haven: Yale University Press, 2012), 4–5.
26. Kathleen Wilson, *The Sense of the People: Politics, Culture and Imperialism in England, 1715–1785* (Cambridge: Cambridge University Press, 1998).
27. Steve Pincus, *The Heart of the Declaration: The Founder's Case for an Activist Government* (New Haven: Yale University Press, 2016); Bob Harris, "'American Idols': Empire, War and the Middling Ranks in Mid-Eighteenth-Century Britain," *Past & Present* 150 (1996): 111–41.
28. Bob Harris, *Politics and the Nation: Britain in the Mid-Eighteenth Century* (Oxford: Oxford University Press, 2002), 64.
29. Linda Colley, "The Apotheosis of George III: Loyalty, Royalty and the British Nation, 1760–1820," *Past & Present* 102 (1984): 94–129.
30. Jeremy Adelman, "Empires, Nations, and Revolutions," *Journal of the History of Ideas* 79 (2018): 73–88.
31. John Brooke, *The Chatham Administration, 1766–1768* (London: Macmillan, 1956), 28.
32. Griffin, *Age of Atlantic Revolution*, 65–81.
33. H. V. Bowen, *The Business of Empire: The East India Company and Imperial Britain, 1756–1833* (Cambridge: Cambridge University Press, 2006), 219–59.
34. Jessica Hanser, "From Cross-Cultural Credit to Colonial Debt: British Expansion in Madras and Canton, 1750–1800," *American Historical Review* 124 (2019): 87–107.
35. P. J. Marshall, *East India Fortunes: The British in Bengal in the Eighteenth Century* (Oxford: Clarendon, 1976).
36. Philip J. Stern, "Company, State and Empire: Governance and Regulatory Frameworks in Asia," in H. V. Bowen, Elizabeth Mancke, and John G. Reid, eds., *Britain's Oceanic Empire: Atlantic and Indian Ocean Worlds, c. 1550–1850* (Cambridge: Cambridge University Press, 2012), 130–31.
37. Brijen K. Gupta, *Sirajuddaullah and the East India Company, 1756–1757: Background to the Foundation of British Power in India* (Leiden: E. J. Brill, 1962), 130.
38. Huw V. Bowen, "A Question of Sovereignty? The Bengal Land Revenue Issue, 1765–67," *Journal of Imperial and Commonwealth History* 16 (1988): 158–59.
39. James M. Vaughn, "John Company Armed: The English East India Company, the Anglo-Mughal War and Absolutist Imperialism, c. 1675–1690," *Britain & the World* 11 (2018): 101–37; Margaret R. Hunt, "The 1689 Mughal Siege of East India Company Bombay: Crisis and Historical Erasure," *History Workshop Journal* 84 (2017): 149–69.

40. Marshall, *Making and Unmaking of Empires*, 156.
41. Marshall, *Making and Unmaking of Empires*, 196.
42. Marshall, *Making and Unmaking of Empires*, 201.
43. Rajat Datta, *Society, Economy and the Market: Commercialization in Rural Bengal, c. 1760–1800* (New Delhi: Manohar, 2000).
44. Elizabeth Mancke, "Another British America: A Canadian Model for the Early Modern British Empire," *Journal of Imperial and Commonwealth History* 25 (1997): 5.
45. Brett Rushforth, *Bonds of Alliance: Indigenous and Atlantic Slaveries in New France* (Chapel Hill: University of North Carolina Press, 2012).
46. C. Grant Head, *Eighteenth Century Newfoundland: A Geographer's Perspective* (Toronto: University of Toronto Press, 1976).
47. Marie Peters, "State, Parliament and Empire in the Mid-Eighteenth Century: Hudson's Bay and the Parliamentary Enquiry of 1749," *Parliamentary History* 29 (2010): 171–91.
48. Lisa Ford, *The King's Peace: Law and Order in the British Empire* (Cambridge, MA: Harvard University Press, 2021).
49. Philip Lawson, *The Imperial Challenge: Quebec and Britain in the Age of the American Revolution* (Kingston and Montreal: McGill-Queen's University Press, 1989).
50. J. M. Bumsted, *Land, Settlement and Politics in Eighteenth-Century Prince Edward Island* (Kingston and Montreal: McGill-Queen's University Press, 1982); Bernard Bailyn, *Voyagers to the West: A Passage in the Peopling of America on the Eve of Revolution* (New York: Knopf, 1986).
51. Mancke, "Another British America," 28–29.
52. Mancke, "Another British America," 28.
53. Nancy Christie, "'In These Times of Democratic Rage and Delusion': Popular Religion and the Challenge to Established Order," in G. A. Rawlyk, ed., *The Canadian Protestant Experience, 1760–1990* (Burlington: Welch, 1990).
54. Trevor Burnard, "Placing British Settlement in the Americas in Comparative Perspective," in H. V. Bowen, Elizabeth Mancke, and John G. Reid, eds., *Britain's Oceanic Empire: Atlantic and Indian Ocean Worlds, 1500–1820* (Cambridge: Cambridge University Press, 2012), 413–14.
55. Marshall, *Making and Unmaking of Empires*, 53, 55, 155, 209.
56. P. D. G. Thomas, *Tea Party to Independence* (Oxford: Clarendon, 1991), 14–15; Benjamin Labaree, *The Boston Tea Party* (New York: Oxford University Press, 1964); Benjamin Carp, *Defiance of the Patriots: The Boston Tea Party and the Making of America* (New Haven: Yale University Press, 2010); Bunker, *An Empire on the Edge*.
57. Pincus, Bains, and Reichardt, "Thinking the Empire Whole," 634.
58. [John Dickinson], "A Letter from the Country to a Gentleman in Philadelphia" (1773), 1.
59. Marshall, *Making and Unmaking of Empires*, 270–71; Jonathan Eacott, *Selling Empire: India in the Making of Britain and America* (Chapel Hill: University of North Carolina Press, 2011), 195–207.
60. Burnard, "Placing British Settlement in the Americas in Comparative Perspective," 415.

61. Hannah Weiss Muller, *Subjects and Sovereign: Bonds of Belonging in the Eighteenth-Century British Empire* (New York: Oxford University Press, 2017).
62. Elizabeth Mancke, "Early Modern Expansion and the Politicization of Oceanic Space," *Geographical Review* 89 (1999): 225-36.
63. C. A. Bayly, "The British and Indigenous Peoples, 1760-1860: Power, Perception, and Identity," in Martin Daunton and Rick Halpern, eds., *Europe and Its Others: British Encounters with Indigenous Peoples, 1600-1850* (Philadelphia: University of Pennsylvania Press, 1999), 19-41.
64. Yirush, *Settlers, Liberty, and Empire*, 108.
65. Owen Stanwood, *The Empire Reformed: English America in the Age of the American Revolution* (Philadelphia: University of Pennsylvania Press, 2011); Peterson, *City-State of Boston*.
66. Richard Middleton, *The Bells of Victory: The Pitt-Newcastle Ministry and the Conduct of the Seven Years' War, 1757-1762* (New York: Cambridge University Press, 1985).
67. Agostini, "'The Provincials will work like Giants,'" 89-90.
68. Fred Anderson, *A People's Army: Massachusetts Soldiers and Society in the Seven Years' War* (New York: W. W. Norton, 1984).
69. Peter Way, "Militarizing the Atlantic World: Army Discipline, Coerced Labour, and Britain's Commercial Empire," *Atlantic Studies* 13 (2016): 346.
70. Matthew Dziennik, *The Fatal Land: War, Empire, and the Highland Soldier in British America* (New Haven: Yale University Press, 2015); Geoffrey Plank, *An Unsettled Conquest: The British Campaign against the Peoples of Acadia* (Philadelphia: University of Pennsylvania Press, 2001).
71. Aaron Graham, *Tropical Leviathan: Slavery, Society and Security in Jamaica, 1770-1840* (Oxford: Oxford University Press, 2024).
72. O'Shaughnessy, *Men Who Lost America*, 58.
73. Vaughn, *Politics of Empire*, 1.
74. Elena Schneider, *The Occupation of Havana: War, Trade, and Slavery in the Atlantic World* (Chapel Hill: University of North Carolina Press, 2018).
75. Lawrence Stone, ed., *An Imperial State at War: Britain from 1689 to 1815* (London: Routledge, 1993), 5-6.
76. Stephen Conway, *War, State and Society in Mid-Eighteenth-Century Britain and Ireland* (Oxford: Oxford University Press, 2006), 50.
77. Marshall, *Edmund Burke and the British Empire in the West Indies*, pt. 1; Richard B. Sheridan, "The British Credit Crisis of 1772 and the American Colonies," *Journal of Economic History* 20 (1960): 1161-86; Bunker, *An Empire on the Edge*, ch.3.
78. Walpole's colonial ministers and officials insisted on adherence by the colonies to imperial sovereignty but believed that arguments between metropole and colony were counterproductive and that accommodation worked better than confrontation. Ian K. Steele, "The Anointed, the Appointed, and the Elected: Governance of the British Empire, 1689-1784," in P. J. Marshall, ed., *The Oxford History of the British Empire: The Eighteenth Century* (Oxford: Oxford University Press, 1998), 114-19; James Henretta, *"Salutary Neglect": Colonial Administration Under the Duke of Newcastle* (Princeton: Princeton University Press, 1972).
79. Andrew Beaumont, *Colonial America and the Earl of Halifax, 1748-1761* (New York: Oxford University Press, 2015).

80. Mancke, "Another British America," 1–36.
81. Trevor Burnard and Aaron Graham, "Security, Taxation and the State in Jamaica, 1721–1782," *Early American Studies* 18 (2020): 461–89.

Chapter 2. British Imperial Policy

1. Holger Hoock, *Empires of the Imagination: Politics, War and the Arts in the British World* (London: Verso, 2010), 23.
2. Simms, *Three Victories and a Defeat*, 492.
3. P. D. G. Thomas, *George III: King and Politicians, 1760–1770* (Manchester: Manchester University Press, 2002).
4. James R. Sofka, "The Eighteenth-Century International System: Parity or Primacy?" *Review of International Studies* 27 (2001): 147–63.
5. Ruggiu, "Empires," 108.
6. Shovlin, *Trading with the Enemy*; François-Joseph Ruggiu, "Des nouvelles France aux colonies—Une approche comparée de l'histoire impériale de la France de l'époque moderne," *Nuevo Mundo Mundos Nuevos,* June 14, 2018, https://doi.org/10.4000/nuevomundo.72123; H. V. Bowen, "British Conceptions of Global Empire, 1756–1783," *Journal of Imperial and Commonwealth History* 26 (1998): 1–27; Edmond Dziembowski, *Un nouveau patriotisme français, 1750–1770: la France face à la puissance anglaise à l'époque de la guerre de Sept Ans* (Oxford: Voltaire Foundation, 1998); Allan J. Kuethe and G. Douglas Inglis, "Absolutism and Enlightened Reform: Charles III, the Establishment of the Alcabala, and Commercial Reorganization in Cuba," *Past & Present* 109 (1985): 118–43.
7. David Armitage, "George III and the Law of Nations," *William and Mary Quarterly* 79 (2022): 3–30.
8. Granville Sharp, *A Representation of the Injustice and Dangerous Tendency of Tolerating Slavery* (London, 1769), 48–49, 78–79, 83.
9. Armitage, "George III and the Law of Nations," 25; O'Shaughnessy, *Men Who Lost America*, 41, 46.
10. Bunker, *An Empire on the Edge*, 368–69.
11. O'Shaughnessy, *Men Who Lost America*, 21–22.
12. Griffin, *The Townshend Moment*, 167–77.
13. Alison Gilbert Olson, *Making the Empire Work: London and American Interest Groups, 1690–1790* (Cambridge: Harvard University Press, 1992), 141.
14. John M. Murrin, "The French and Indian War, the American Revolution, and the Counterfactual Hypothesis: Reflections on Lawrence Henry Gipson and John Shy," in Murrin, *Rethinking America from Empire to Republic* (Oxford: Oxford University Press, 2018), 122, 123, 171–72.
15. Murrin, "The French and Indian War, the America Revolution, and the Counterfactual Hypothesis," 124.
16. Olson, *Making the Empire Work*, 134, 142, 143; Lawson, *The Imperial Challenge*, 31.
17. Miller, *Defining the Common Good*, 239; Thomas P. Slaughter, *Independence: The Tangled Roots of the American Revolution* (New York: Hill and Wang, 2014), 222–23.
18. J. C. D. Clark, *The Language of Liberty, 1660–1832: Political Discourse and Social*

Dynamics in the Anglo-American World (Cambridge: Cambridge University Press, 1994), 306.
19. Olson, *Making the Empire Work*, 134, 142–43.
20. Bowen, "British Conceptions of Global Empire, 1756–83," 10; Marshall, *Making and Unmaking of Empires*, 278, 317.
21. Jack P. Greene, "Britain's Overseas Empire before 1780: Overwhelmingly Successful and Bureaucratically Challenged," in *Creating the British Atlantic: Essays on Transplantation, Adaptation, and Continuity* (Charlottesville: University of Virginia Press, 2013), 126.
22. Greene, "Britain's Overseas Empire before 1780," 134.
23. S. J. Connolly, *Divided Kingdom: Ireland, 1630–1800* (Oxford: Oxford University Press, 2008), 348; Griffin, *The Townshend Moment*, 25.
24. Elliott, *Empires of the Atlantic World*, 298–323; Steve Pincus, "Rethinking Mercantilism: Political Economy, the British Empire, and the Atlantic World in the Seventeenth and Eighteenth Centuries," *William and Mary Quarterly* 69 (2012): 30–31.
25. Stephen Howe, *Ireland and Empire: Colonial Legacies in Irish History and Culture* (Oxford: Oxford University Press, 2000), 14.
26. Jack P. Greene, "Introduction: Empire and Liberty," in Greene, ed., *Exclusionary Empire: English Liberty Overseas, 1600–1900* (Cambridge: Cambridge University Press, 2010), 115.
27. Reid, *In a Defiant Stance*, 12, 14–15; Reid, *The Constitutional History of the American Revolution*, abridged ed. (Madison: University of Wisconsin Press, 1995), 44–45; Neil Longley York, *Neither Kingdom nor Nation: The Irish Quest for Constitutional Rights, 1698–1800* (Washington, DC: The Catholic University of America Press, 1994), 87–88, 90–91.
28. Letter from Governor Francis Bernard to Lord Barrington, November 23, 1765, cited in York, *Neither Kingdom nor Nation*, 15–16 fn. 42; Yirush, *Settlers, Liberty, and Empire*, 57–58.
29. J. C. Beckett, "The Irish Parliament in the Eighteenth Century," *Report and Proceedings of the Belfast National History and Philosophical Society*, 2nd series, vol. 4 (1955): 22–23; Beckett, "Anglo-Irish Constitutional Relations in the Late Eighteenth Century," *Irish Historical Studies*, 14 (1964): 25.
30. Connolly, *Divided Kingdom*, 348; Griffin, *The Townshend Moment*, 25.
31. R. B. McDowell, *Ireland in the Age of Imperialism and Revolution, 1760–1801* (Oxford: Clarendon, 1979), 59, 218.
32. Toby Barnard, *A New Anatomy of Ireland: The Irish Protestants, 1649–1770* (New Haven: Yale University Press, 2004), 178.
33. Thomas Bartlett, "The Augmentation of the Army in Ireland, 1767–1769," *English Historical Review* 96 (1981): 549; Vincent Morley, *Irish Opinion and the American Revolution 1760–1783* (Cambridge: Cambridge University Press, 2002), 24; 85–86.
34. Bartlett, "The Augmentation of the Army in Ireland, 1767–1769," 540.
35. McDowell, *Ireland in the Age of Imperialism and Revolution*, 223–26.
36. McDowell, *Ireland in the Age of Imperialism and Revolution*, 226.
37. Marshall, *Making and Unmaking of Empires*, 53, 55, 155, 209.
38. Lucy Sutherland, *The East India Company in Eighteenth-Century Politics* (Ox-

ford: Oxford University Press, 1952), 150–51; Bowen, *Revenue and Reform*, 32–33, 38, 39, 131.
39. Sutherland, *East India Company in Eighteenth-Century Politics*, 138.
40. Sutherland, *East India Company in Eighteenth-Century Politics*, 149, 177; Bowen, *Revenue and Reform*, 49, 51; Nancy F. Koehn, *The Power of Commerce: Economy and Governance in the First British Empire* (Ithaca and London: Cornell University Press, 1994), 202.
41. Koehn, *The Power of Commerce*, 211.
42. Bowen, *Revenue and Reform*, 98; Sutherland, *East India Company in Eighteenth-Century Politics*, 231; O'Shaughnessy, *Men Who Lost America*, 131.
43. Koehn, *The Power of Commerce*, 215–16.
44. Bowen, *Revenue and Reform*, 153, 163, 187; Marshall, *Making and Unmaking of Empires*, 213; Sutherland, *East India Company in Eighteenth-Century Politics*, 248, 251–52, 263–64.
45. Francis D. Cogliano, *No King, No Popery: Anti-Catholicism in Revolutionary New England* (Westport: Greenwood, 1995); Stanwood, *The Empire Reformed*, 143–76.
46. Marshall, *Making and Unmaking of Empires*, 186. For the Acadian removal, see Plank, *An Unsettled Conquest;* John Grenier, *The Far Reaches of Empire: War in Nova Scotia, 1710–1760* (Norman: Oklahoma University Press, 2008).
47. John Garrigus, *Before Haiti: Race and Citizenship in French Saint-Domingue* (New York: Palgrave Macmillan, 2006).
48. Stephen Conway, "War, Imperial Expansion and Religious Developments in Mid-Eighteenth-Century Britain and Ireland," *War in History* 11 (2004): 125–47.
49. Lawson, *The Imperial Challenge*, 115.
50. Lawson, *The Imperial Challenge*, 91.
51. Jessica L. Harland-Jacobs, "Incorporating the King's New Subjects: Accommodation and Anti-Catholicism in the British Empire, 1763–1815," *Journal of Religious History* 39 (2015): 203–23; Aaron Wallis, "The Standing of New Subjects: Grenada and the Protestant Constitution after the Treaty of Paris," *Journal of Imperial and Commonwealth History* 42 (2014): 1–21.
52. Harland-Jacobs, "Incorporating the King's New Subjects," 210.
53. O'Shaughnessy, *Empire Divided*, 124–26; Marshall, *Making and Unmaking of Empires*, 187–88.
54. O'Shaughnessy, *Empire Divided*, 124–26; Mark R. Anderson, *The Battle for the Fourteenth Colony: America's War of Liberation in Canada, 1774–1776* (Hanover: University Press of New England, 2013), 17–18, 26, 37; Gustave Lanctot, *Canada and the American Revolution, 1774–1783* (Cambridge, MA: Harvard University Press, 1967), 31. For population figures, see Holly A. Mayer, "Canada, Congress, and the Continental Army: Strategic Accommodations, 1774–1776," *Journal of Military History* 78 (2014): 513.
55. Lawson, *The Imperial Challenge*, 47.
56. Lawson, *The Imperial Challenge*, 98, 124.
57. Christie, *Northern Bastille*, 38, 116–18.
58. Anthony Bruce, *Anson: Royal Naval Commander and Statesman, 1697–1762* (London: Helion, 2023).
59. Glyndwr Williams, "The Pacific: Exploration and Exploitation," in P. J. Marshall,

Oxford History of the British Empire: The Eighteenth Century (Oxford: Oxford University Press, 1998), 554.
60. Williams, "The Pacific," 558.
61. Anne Salmond, *Aphrodite's Island: the European Discovery of Tahiti* (Berkeley: University of California Press, 2009); Nicholas Thomas, *Cook: The Extraordinary Voyages of Captain James Cook* (New York: Walker, 2003); Kate Fullagar, *The Warrior, the Voyager, and the Artist: Three Lives in an Age of Empire* (New Haven: Yale University Press, 2023).
62. Kate Fullagar, "America and the Pacific: The View from the Beach," in Gould et al., *Cambridge History of America and the World*, 1:367.
63. Maxine Berg, "Sea Otters and Iron: A Global Microhistory of Value and Exchange at Nootka Sound, 1772–1792," *Past & Present* 242 (2019): 50–82.
64. K. R. Howe, *Where the Waves Fall: A New South Sea Islands History from First Settlement to Colonial Rule* (Sydney: Allen and Unwin, 1984).
65. Matthew Dziennik, "'Till these Experiments be Made': Senegambia and British Imperial Policy in the Eighteenth Century," *English Historical Review* 130 (2015): 1135–36. See also Christopher Leslie Brown, "Empire without America: Africa in the Era of the American Revolution," in D. R. Peterson, ed., *Abolitionism and Imperialism in Britain, Africa and the Atlantic* (Athens: Ohio University Press 2010), 84–100; Paul E. Lovejoy, "Forgotten Colony in Africa: The British Province of Senegambia," in Lovejoy and Suzanne Schwarz, eds., *Slavery, Abolition, and the Transition to Colonialism in Sierra Leone* (Trenton: Africa World Press, 2015), 109–25.
66. Stern, *The Company-State: Corporate Sovereignty and the Early Modern Foundations of the British Empire in India* (Oxford: Oxford University Press, 2011), ch. 2.
67. Dziennik, "'Till these Experiments be Made,'" 1143.
68. Elliott, *Empires of the Atlantic World*, 303.
69. Emma Christopher, *A Merciless Place: The Fate of Britain's Convicts after the American Revolution* (Oxford: Oxford University Press, 2010), 95–96.
70. Dziennik, "'Till these Experiments be Made,'" 1161.
71. O'Shaughnessy, *Empire Divided*, 84–86, 96, 109, 131; Olson, *Making the Empire Work*, 159, 163–68.
72. Perry Gauci, "The Attack of the Creolian Powers: West Indians at the Parliamentary Elections of Mid-Georgian Britain, 1754–74," *Parliamentary History* 33 (2014): 201–22.
73. O'Shaughnessy, *Empire Divided*, 65–67.
74. James R. Fichter, *Consumption, Politics, and Revolution, 1773–1776* (Ithaca: Cornell University Press, 2023), 90, 104–5, 106.
75. J. G. A. Pocock, "1776: The Revolution against Parliament," in *Virtue, Commerce, and History*, 266. Robert Livingston Schuyler argues that, as early as the Tudors, Parliament claimed authority outside the realm of England, as it demonstrated in legislating for Wales; see Schuyler, *Parliament and the British Empire: Some Constitutional Controversies Concerning Legislative Jurisdiction* (New York: Columbia University Press, 1929), 8–9.
76. Julian Hoppit, *Britain's Political Economies: Parliament and Economic Life, 1660–1800* (Cambridge: Cambridge University Press, 2017); Aaron Graham, "Legislatures,

Legislation and Legislating in the British Atlantic, 1692–1800," *Parliamentary History* 37 (2018): 369–88.
77. Barbara Black, "The Constitution of Empire: The Case for the Colonists," *University of Pennsylvania Law Review* 124 (1976): 1157; Reid, *In Defiance of the Law*, 177–78.
78. Hinderaker, *Boston's Massacre*, 187.
79. Clark, *The Language of Liberty, 1660–1832*, 66.
80. Joanna Innes, *Inferior Politics: Social Problems and Social Policies in Eighteenth-Century Britain* (Oxford: Oxford University Press, 2009), 3, 4, 21–22, 42, 74, 83, 88, 171.
81. Alison Gilbert Olson, "Parliament, Empire, and Parliamentary Law, 1776," in J. G. A. Pocock, ed., *Three British Revolutions: 1641, 1688, 1776* (Princeton: Princeton University Press, 1980), 291, 295–96, 301–2.
82. Miller, *Defining the Common Good*, 160, 227; Clark, *The Language of Liberty, 1660–1832*, 88.
83. Eliga H. Gould, "Liberty and Modernity: The American Revolution and the Making of Parliament's Imperial History," in Greene, *Exclusionary Empire*, 115; Miller, *Defining the Common Good*, 222.
84. Clark, *The Language of Liberty, 1660–1832*, 111.
85. H. T. Dickinson, "Britain's Imperial Sovereignty: The Ideological Case against the American Colonies," in Dickinson, ed., *Britain and the American Revolution* (London: Longman, 1989), 81; Yirush, *Settlers, Liberty, and Empire*, 16, 38–50, 79, 112, 216–17, 266.
86. Christopher Tomlins, *Freedom Bound: Law, Labor, and Civil Identity in Colonizing English America, 1580–1865* (Cambridge: Cambridge University Press, 2010), 261, 296.
87. Yirush, *Settlers, Liberty, and Empire*, 75.
88. William Knox, "Considerations on the Great Question, What Is to Be Done with America," ed. Jack P. Greene, *William and Mary Quarterly* 30 (1973): 295, 296, 297, 302, 305.
89. Jack P. Greene, *The Constitutional Origins of the American Revolution* (New York: Cambridge University Press, 2011), 39, 68, 69; Greene, *Negotiated Authorities: Essays in Colonial Political and Constitutional History* (Charlottesville: University of Virginia Press, 1994).
90. H. T. Dickinson, "Britain's Imperial Sovereignty," 64–97.

Chapter 3. Empire of Coercion

1. Lowell J. Ragatz, *The Fall of the Planter Class in the British Caribbean, 1763–1833* (New York: Century, 1928).
2. Marie Peters, "The Myth of William Pitt, Earl of Chatham, Great Imperialist, Part I: Pitt and Imperial Expansion, 1738–1763," *Journal of Imperial and Commonwealth History* 21 (1993): 54–55.
3. Barbara L. Solow, "Slavery and Colonisation," in Solow, ed., *Slavery and the Rise of the Atlantic System* (Cambridge: Cambridge University Press, 1991), 1.
4. David Eltis, Frank L. Lewis, and David Richardson, "Slave Prices, the Atlantic Slave Trade, and Productivity in the Caribbean," *Economic History Review* 58

(2005): 673–74; Burnard, *Planters, Merchants, and Slaves: Plantation Societies in British America, 1650–1820* (Chicago: University of Chicago Press, 2015).

5. B. W. Higman, *Plantation Jamaica, 1750–1850: Capital and Control in a Colonial Economy* (Kingston: University of the West Indies Press, 2005), 293; Mark Overton, *Agricultural Revolution in England: The Transformation of the Agrarian Economy, 1500–1850* (Cambridge: Cambridge University Press, 1996).

6. Keith McClelland, "Redefining the West India Interest: Politics and the Legacies of Slave-Ownership," in Catherine Hall et al., *Legacies of British Slave-Ownership: Colonial Slavery and the Formation of Victorian Britain* (Cambridge: Cambridge University Press, 2014), 127–62.

7. Ahmed Reid, "Sugar, Slavery and Productivity in Jamaica, 1750–1807," *Slavery & Abolition* 37 (2016): 159–82.

8. Higman, *Plantation Jamaica*, 238.

9. Eltis, Lewis, and Richardson, "Slave Prices," 684.

10. J. R. Ward, *British West Indian Slavery, 1750–1834: The Process of Amelioration* (Oxford: Clarendon, 1988); Lorena S. Walsh, *Motives of Honor, Pleasure and Profit: Plantation Management in the Colonial Chesapeake, 1607–1763* (Chapel Hill: University of North Carolina Press, 2010).

11. Abbé Raynal, as cited in Michael Duffy, *Soldiers, Sugar, and Seapower: The British Expeditions to the West Indies and the War with Revolutionary France* (Oxford: Clarendon, 1987), 6.

12. Christopher L. Brown, "Empire without Slaves: British Concepts of Emancipation in the Age of the American Revolution," *William and Mary Quarterly* 61 (1999): 273–306.

13. Steve Pincus, "The Pivot of Empire: Party Politics, Spanish America and the Treaty of Utrecht (1713)," in Jason Peachey, ed., *Making the British Empire, 1660–1800* (Manchester: Manchester University Press, 2020), 17–37. But see J. H. Elliott, "Party Politics and Empire in the Early Eighteenth Century," in Peachey, *Making the British Empire*, 38–55.

14. John Oldmixon, *The British Empire in America*, 2 vols. (London, 1708), 1:xxii, xxvi, xxx.

15. Edward Littleton, *The Groans of the Plantations* (London, 1689), 1.

16. Barbara Arneil, "Trade, Plantations, and Property: John Locke and the Economic Defense of Colonialism," *Journal of the History of Ideas* 55 (1994): 591–609; Lucas G. Pinheiro, "A Factory Afield: Capitalism and Empire in John Locke's Political Economy," *Modern Intellectual History* 19 (2022): 1–28.

17. Sophus Reinert, *Translating Empire: Emulation and the Origins of Political Economy* (Cambridge, MA: Harvard University Press, 2011).

18. John Cary, *An Essay on the State of England in Relation to Its Trade, Its Poor, and Its Taxes* (Bristol, 1695), 74–77, 84.

19. Sir Dalby Thomas, cited in Eric Williams, *Capitalism and Slavery* (Chapel Hill: University of North Carolina Press, 1944), 55.

20. Joshua Gee, "A Letter to a Member of Parliament, Concerning the Naval-Stores Bill" (London, 1720), 18.

21. Malachy Postlethwayt, ed., *Universal Dictionary of Trade and Commerce*, 2 vols., 4th ed. (London, 1764), vol. 1: entry under "Colonies."

22. William Wood, *A Survey of Trade*, 2nd ed. (London, 1719), 132–33, 173–74.

23. Wood, *A Survey of Trade*, 179, 191.
24. Cited in Peter Earle, *The World of Defoe* (London: Weidenfeld and Nicholson, 1976), 162–63.
25. Edward Ward, "A Trip to Jamaica," in H. W. Troyer, ed., *Five Travel Scripts Commonly Attributed to Edward Ward* (New York: Columbia University Press, 1933), 13.
26. Cited in Richard S. Dunn, *Sugar and Slaves: The Rise of the Planter Class in the English West Indies, 1624–1713* (Chapel Hill: University of North Carolina Press, 1972), 239.
27. Hans Sloane, *A Voyage to the Islands of Madera, Barbados, Nieves, S. Christophers and Jamaica . . .* , 2 vols. (London, 1707 and 1725), 1:lvii.
28. [Charles Leslie], *A New and Exact Account of Jamaica* (Edinburgh: R. Fleming, c. 1740), 38, 336–38; Jack P. Greene, ed., *The Natural, Moral, and Political History of Jamaica . . . by J[ames] K[night]* (Charlottesville: University of Virginia Press, 2021), 492–93.
29. Daniel Defoe, *Colonel Jack*, ed. Samuel Holt Monk (1722; New York: Oxford University Press, 1989), 128, 133.
30. Simon Newman, "Freedom-Seeking Slaves in England and Scotland, 1700–1780," *English Historical Review* 134 (2019): 1136–68.
31. David Bindman, "The Black Presence in British Art: Sixteenth and Seventeenth Centuries," in Henry Louis Gates, ed., *The Image of the Black in Western Art: From the Age of Discovery to the Age of Abolition* (Cambridge, MA: Harvard University Press, 2010), 235–70.
32. George Van Cleve, "*Somerset's Case* and Its Antecedents in Imperial Perspective," *Law and History Review*, 24 (2006): 601–45.
33. Newman, "Freedom-Seeking Slaves," 1161–62.
34. Horace Walpole to Sir Henry Mann, February 25, 1750, in Peter Cunningham, ed., *The Letters of Horace Walpole* (London: R. Bentley, 1891), 2:197.
35. Julian Hoppit, *A Land of Liberty? England 1689–1727* (Oxford: Oxford University Press, 2000), 268.
36. Trevor Burnard, *Jamaica in the Age of Revolution* (Philadelphia: University of Pennsylvania Press, 2020), 161–63, 168.
37. Adam Smith, *An Inquiry into the Nature and Causes of the Wealth of Nations* (1776), ed. R. H. Campbell and A. S. Skinner, 2 vols. (Oxford: Oxford University Press, 1976). See also Richard Pares, "Merchants and Planters," *Economic History Review Supplements* 4 (1960); S. D. Smith, "*Merchants and Planters* Revisited," *Economic History Review* 53 (2002): 434–65; Emma Rothschild, "Adam Smith in the British Empire," in Sankar Muthu, ed., *Empire and Modern Political Thought* (Cambridge: Cambridge University Press, 2012), 184–98; and Seymour Drescher, *The Mighty Experiment: Free Labor versus Slavery in British Emancipation* (New York: Oxford University Press, 2002).
38. Adam Smith, *Theory of Moral Sentiments* (London, 1759), 402–3.
39. "UK Economic History: Slavery," *Financial Times*, June 13, 2020.
40. Robert Winder, *Bloody Foreigners: The Story of Immigration to Britain* (London: Abacus, 2013), 129.
41. Pares, "Merchants and Planters," 47–50.
42. Pares, "Merchants and Planters," 37–45.

43. Williams, *Capitalism and Slavery*, 5.
44. Stephen Epstein, "Attitudes toward Blackness," in Craig Perry et al., eds., *The Cambridge World History of Slavery* (Cambridge: Cambridge University Press, 2021), 2:237.
45. Katherine Gerbner, *Christian Slavery: Conversion and Race in the Protestant Atlantic World* (Philadelphia: University of Pennsylvania Press, 2018), 83-90.
46. Gerbner, *Christian Slavery*, 89.
47. Sanghera, *Empireworld*, 151-52.
48. Robert C. Allen, *The British Industrial Revolution in Global Perspective* (Cambridge: Cambridge University Press, 2009); E. A. Wrigley, *Energy and the English Industrial Revolution* (Cambridge: Cambridge University Press, 2015); William J. Ashworth, *The Industrial Revolution: The State, Knowledge and Global Trade* (London: Bloomsbury 2017); Tirthankar Roy and Giorgio Riello, *Global Economic History* (London: Bloomsbury, 2019); and Priya Satia, *Empire of Guns: The Violent Making of the Industrial Revolution* (London: Penguin, 2018).
49. Hall et al., *Legacies of British Slave-Ownership;* Katie Donington, *The Bonds of Family: Slavery, Commerce and Culture in the British Atlantic World* (Manchester: Manchester University Press, 2020).
50. Joseph E. Inikori, *Africans and the Industrial Revolution in England: A Study in International Trade and Economic Development* (Cambridge: Cambridge University Press, 2002); Jan de Vries, *The Industrious Revolution: Consumer Behavior and the Household Economy, 1650 to the Present* (New York: Cambridge University Press, 2008); Robin Blackburn, "The Scope of Accumulation and the Reach of Moral Perception: Slavery, Market Revolution and Atlantic Capitalism," in Catherine Hall et al., eds., *Emancipation and the Remaking of the British Imperial World* (Manchester: Manchester University Press, 2014), 19-35.
51. Patrick K. O'Brien, "The Nature and Historical Evaluation of an Exceptional Fiscal State and Its Possible Significance for the Precocious Commercialization and Industrialization of the British Economy from Cromwell to Nelson," *Economic History Review* 64 (2011): 408-46; C. Knick Harley, "Slavery, the British Atlantic Economy, and the Industrial Revolution," in A. B. Leonard, David Pretel, et al., *The Caribbean and the Atlantic World Economy* (New York: Palgrave Macmillan, 2015), 161-83.
52. Nuala Zahedieh, "Colonies, Copper, and the Market for Inventive Activity in England and Wales, 1680-1730," *Economic History Review* 66 (2013): 805-25; Chris Evans, "'Voyage Iron': An Atlantic Slave Trade Currency, Its European Origins, and West African Impact," *Past & Present* 239 (2018), 41-70; and Nicholas Radburn, "The British Gunpowder Industry and the Transatlantic Slave Trade," *Business History Review* 97 (2023): 363-84.
53. Paul Hudson, "Slavery, the Slave Trade and Economic Growth," in Hall et al., *Emancipation and the Remaking of the British Imperial World*, 36-59.
54. Trevor Burnard, "Plantations and the Great Divergence," in Roy and Riello, eds., *Global Economic History*, 102-17.
55. Richard Pares, "The Economic Factors in the History of the Empire," *Economic History Review* 7 (1937): 119; Thomas Truxes, *The Overseas Trade of British America: A Narrative History* (New Haven: Yale University Press, 2021), 7-9.

56. Ralph A. Austen, "Monsters of Protocolonial Economic Enterprise: East India Companies and Slave Plantations," *Critical Historical Studies* 139 (2017): 139–78.
57. Cited in Patrick Richardson, *Empire and Slavery* (London: Longmans, 1968), 4.
58. Mark Peterson, "Capitalism," in Joseph C. Miller, ed., *The Princeton Companion to Atlantic History* (Princeton: Princeton University Press, 2015), 71.
59. For criticism, see Sean Wilentz, "A Matter of Facts," *Atlantic,* January 22, 2020; William Hogeland, "Against the Consensus Approach to History: How Not to Learn about the American Past," *New Republic,* January 25, 2021; Letters from Noah Feldman and James Oakes, *New York Review of Books,* June 23, 2022, 62. For a particularly acrimonious exchange, see "Communications," *American Historical Review* 125 (2020): 768–74.
60. Daryl Michael Scott, "African American Exceptionalism in the Service of American Exceptionalism," *American Historical Review* (2022), 1816; Nikole Hannah-Jones, Caitlin Roper, Ilena Silverman, and Jake Silverstein, eds., *The 1619 Project: A New Origin Story* (New York, 2021), xxv; Jeannette Eileen Jones, "Exploring 'American' Slavery," *American Historical Review* (2022): 1858; Robert Parkinson, *The Common Cause: Creating Race and Nation in the American Revolution* (Chapel Hill: University of North Carolina Press, 2016); Holton, *Liberty Is Sweet.* Burnard, *Jamaica in the Age of Revolution,* 151–73.
61. Robert Parkinson, *The Common Cause: Creating Race and Nation in the American Revolution* (Chapel Hill: University of North Carolina Press, 2016); Holton, *Liberty Is Sweet.*
62. Burnard, *Jamaica in the Age of Revolution,* 151–73.
63. Holton, *Forced Founders,* 66–69.
64. Burnard, *Planters, Merchants, and Slaves,* 144–45; Bruce A. Ragsdale, *A Planter's Republic: The Search for Economic Independence in Revolutionary Virginia* (Madison: University of Wisconsin Press, 1996), 126–27.
65. David Richardson, *Principles and Agents: The British Slave Trade and Its Abolition* (New Haven: Yale University Press, 2022), 25; Sean Kelley, *American Slavers: Merchants, Mariners, and the Transatlantic Commerce in Captives, 1644–1865* (New Haven: Yale University Press, 2023).
66. Richardson, *Principles and Agents,* 25.
67. SlaveVoyages.org, http://www.slavevoyages.org.
68. Christopher Leslie Brown, *Moral Capital: Foundations of British Abolitionism* (Chapel Hill: University of North Carolina Press, 2006), 100.
69. Trevor Burnard, "Anthony Benezet: *A Short History of Guinea* and Its Impact on Early British Abolitionism," in Burnard, Joy Damousi, and Alan Lester, eds., *Humanitarianism, Empire and Transnationalism in the Anglophone World, 1760–1995* (Manchester: Manchester University Press, 2022), 37–59; Geoffrey Plank, *John Woolman's Path to the Peaceable Kingdom: A Quaker in the British Empire* (Philadelphia: University of Pennsylvania Press, 2012); Marcus Rediker, *The Fearless Benjamin Lay: The Quaker Dwarf Who Became the First Revolutionary Abolitionist* (London: Verso, 2017).
70. Christopher Leslie Brown, "The Problem of Slavery," in Gray and Kamensky, *Oxford Handbook of the American Revolution,* 431.
71. Edelson, *New Map of Empire,* 140–96; Marshall, *Edmund Burke and the British*

Empire in the West Indies; P. J. Marshall, "A Polite and Commercial People in the Caribbean: The British in St. Vincent," in Elaine Chalus and Perry Gauci, eds., *Revisiting the Polite and Commercial People: Essays in Georgian Politics, Society, and Culture in Honour of Professor Paul Langford* (Oxford: Oxford University Press, 2019), 173–90.

72. William Knox, *Three Tracts Respecting the Conversion and Instruction of the Free Indians with the Negro Slaves in the Colonies* (London, 1768), 27.
73. Marshall, *Making and Unmaking of Empires*, 196.
74. Trevor Burnard, "Slavery and the Enlightenment in Jamaica, 1760–1772: The Afterlife of Tacky's Rebellion," in Damien Tricoire, ed., *Enlightened Colonialism: Imperial Agents, Narratives of Progress and Civilizing Policies in the Eighteenth Century* (Basingstoke: Palgrave Macmillan, 2017), 227–46.
75. Marshall, *Making and Unmaking of Empires*, 195.
76. David Arnold, "Hunger in the Garden of Plenty: The Bengal Famine of 1770," in Alessa Johns, ed., *Dreadful Visitations: Confronting National Catastrophe in the Age of Enlightenment* (London: Routledge, 1999), 86.
77. Marshall, *Making and Unmaking of Empires*, 175.

Chapter 4. Settlers and Indigenous Peoples

1. Mark Peterson, "Demography," in Burnard, Hart, and Houllemare, *Oxford Handbook of the Seven Years' War*, 635–54.
2. Greene, "Britain's Overseas Empire before 1780," 116.
3. Peter H. Wood, "From Atlantic History to a Continental Approach," in Jack P. Greene and Philip D. Morgan, eds., *Atlantic History: A Critical Appraisal* (New York: Oxford University Press, 2009), 284–86.
4. John J. McCusker and Russell R. Menard, *The Economy of British America, 1607–1789* (Chapel Hill: University of North Carolina Press, 1985), 103, 112, 136, 153, 172, 203.
5. J. David Hacker, "From '20. and odd' to 10 Million: The Growth of the Slave Population in the United States," *Slavery & Abolition* 41 (2020): 840–55; Philip D. Morgan, "Slavery in the British Caribbean," in David Eltis and Stanley L. Engerman, eds., *The Cambridge World History of Slavery*, vol 3: *AD 1420–1804* (Cambridge: Cambridge University Press, 2011), 383–85; Philip Morgan, J. R. McNeill, Matthew Mulcahy, and Stuart B. Schwartz, *Sea and Land: An Environmental History of the Caribbean* (New York: Oxford University Press, 2022), 162–83.
6. Daniel K. Richter, *The Ordeal of the Longhouse: The People of the Iroquois League in the Era of European Colonialism* (Chapel Hill: University of North Carolina Press, 1992); and Kathleen DuVal, *The Native Ground: Indians and Colonists in the Heart of the Continent* (Philadelphia: University of Pennsylvania Press, 2006).
7. Morgan, McNeill, Mulcahy, and Schwartz, *Sea and Land*, 162–83.
8. S. Max Edelson, "Changing American Geographies," in Gould, Mapp, and Pestana, *Cambridge History of America in the World*, 1:55.
9. Thomas Paine, *Common Sense . . .* (London, 1776).
10. Patrick Griffin, "Mobility and the Movement of Peoples," in Gould et al., *Cambridge History of America in the World*, 1:166.

11. Robert Michael Morrissey, *Empire by Collaboration: Indians, Colonists and Governments in the Illinois Country* (Philadelphia: University of Pennsylvania Press, 2015); Pekka Hämäläinen, *Lakota America: A New History of Indigenous Power* (New Haven: Yale University Press, 2019); Elizabeth A. Fenn, *Encounters at the Heart of the World: A History of the Mandan People* (New York: Hill and Wang, 2004); Michael Witgen, "A Nation of Settlers: The Early Republic and the Colonization of the Northwest Territory," *William and Mary Quarterly* 76 (2019): 391–98; and Bethel Saler, *The Settlers' Empire: Colonialism and State Formation in America's Old Northwest* (Philadelphia: University of Pennsylvania Press, 2019).
12. Benjamin Franklin, *Observations on the Increase of Mankind,* in *The Papers of Benjamin Franklin,* ed. Leonard W. Labaree et al. (New Haven: Yale University Press, 1959–): 4:225–34.
13. James Otis, *The Rights of the British Colonies Asserted and Proved* (Boston, 1764), in Bernard Bailyn, ed., *Pamphlets of the American Revolution, 1750–1776* (Cambridge, MA: Harvard University Press, 1965): 1:435–36, 439–40.
14. Clare A. Lyons, *Sex among the Rabble: An Intimate History of Gender and Power in the Age of Revolution, Philadelphia, 1730–1830* (Chapel Hill: University of North Carolina Press, 2006); Christine Walker, "As Though She 'Was a Virtuous Woman': Colonial Changes to Gender Roles, Marital Practices, and Family Formation in Atlantic America, 1720–1760," *Journal of Colonialism and Colonial History* 21 (Summer 2020), http://doi.org/10.1353/cch.2020.0016; Trevor Burnard, *Mastery, Tyranny and Desire: Thomas Thistlewood and His Slaves in the Anglo-Jamaican World* (Chapel Hill: University of North Carolina Press, 2004), 202–4, 226–27, 261–66.
15. Benjamin Franklin, "The Speech of Miss Polly Baker, *Gentleman's Magazine,* 15 April 1747," in *Papers of Benjamin Franklin,* 3:120–25.
16. Trevor Burnard, "From 'Little Better than Slaves' to 'Cowskin Heroes': Poor White People in Jamaica, 1655–1782," Joseph C. Miller Memorial Lecture Series, ed. Abdelkader Al Ghouz, Jeannine Bischoff, and Sarah Dusend, vol. 4 (Berlin: EB-Verlag Dr. Brandt, 2021).
17. Franklin, *Observations on the Increase of Mankind,* 4:225–34.
18. Benjamin Franklin, "American Discontents," *London Chronicle,* January 5–7, 1768, in *Papers of Benjamin Franklin,* 15:12.
19. Trevor Burnard, "Benezet: *A Short History of Guinea* and Its Impact," 37–59; Rothschild, "Adam Smith in the British Empire," 184–98.
20. Charles Carroll of Carrollton to William Graves, September 7, 1773, *Maryland Historical Magazine* 32 (1937): 219.
21. Peter Lindert and Jeffrey Williamson, "American Colonial Incomes, 1650–1774," *Economic Historical Review* 69 (2016): 54–77; Robert Allen et al., "The Colonial Origins of the Divergence in the Americas: A Labor Market Approach," *Journal of Economic History* 72 (2012): 863–94.
22. Lindert and Williamson, "American Colonial Incomes," 54–77.
23. Vincent Geloso, "Predation, Seigneurial Tenure, and Development in French Colonial America," *Social Science History* 44 (2020): 747–70. For a counterview, see Michael Gauvreau and Nancy Christie, "The Inhabitants 'Appear Are Not Such

Fools as a Menny Thinks': Credit, Debt, and Peasant Litigation in Post-Conquest Quebec," in Nancy Christie, Michael Gauvreau, and Matthew Gerber, eds., *Voices in the Legal Archives in the French Colonial World: "The King is Listening"* (New York: Routledge, 2020), 215–39.

24. Truxes, *Overseas Trade of British America*, 330–37; Elizabeth Boody Schumpeter, *English Overseas Trade Statistics, 1697–1808* (Oxford: Oxford University Press, 1960), 17–18; Bureau of the Census, *Historical Statistics of the United States, Colonial Times to 1970* (Washington, DC: US Government Printing Office, 1973).

25. Thomas M. Truxes, *Irish-American Trade, 1660–1783* (Cambridge: Cambridge University Press, 1988), 49.

26. Jacob M. Price, "New Time Series for Scotland's and Britain's Trade with the Thirteen Colonies and States, 1740 to 1791," *William and Mary Quarterly* 32 (1975): 318–21.

27. Burnard, *Planters, Merchants, and Slaves*, 167.

28. Burnard, *Planters, Merchants, and Slaves*, 9–10.

29. Burnard, *Planters, Merchants, and Slaves*, 18–19, 285n42.

30. McCusker and Menard, *Economy of British America*, 18.

31. Richard Pares, *War and Trade in the West Indies 1739–1763* (Oxford: Clarendon, 1936); and Williams, *Capitalism and Slavery*.

32. Albert B. Southwick, "The Molasses Act—Source of Precedents," *William and Mary Quarterly* 8 (1951): 389–405.

33. Loïc Charles, Guillaume Daudin, Paul Girard, and Guillaume Plique, "Exploring the Transformation of French and European Trade and Economy in the Long Eighteenth Century," *Historical Methods* 54 (2022): 228–58.

34. Ralph Davis, "English Foreign Trade, 1700–1774," *Economic History Review* 25 (1962): 294; Davis, *The Rise of the Atlantic Economies* (Ithaca: Cornell University Press, 1973), 255; C. Knick Harley, "Slavery, the British Atlantic Economy, and the Industrial Revolution," in Leonard, Pretel, et al., *The Caribbean and the Atlantic World Economy*, 168, 174.

35. Harley, "Slavery, the British Atlantic Economy, and the Industrial Revolution," 161, 174–75; Nicholas F. R. Crafts, *British Economic Growth during the Industrial Revolution* (Oxford: Oxford University Press, 1985), 127.

36. Sven Beckert, *Empire of Cotton: A Global History* (New York: Vintage, 2014).

37. Davis, "English Foreign Trade, 1700–1774," 300–303.

38. T. H. Breen, *The Marketplace of Revolution: How Consumer Politics Shaped American Independence* (New York: Oxford University Press, 2004).

39. R. C. Nash, "The Organization of Trade and Finance in the British Atlantic Economy, 1600–1830," in Peter A. Coclanis, ed., *The Atlantic Economy during the Seventeenth and Eighteenth Centuries* (Columbia: University of South Carolina Press, 2005), 131; Manuel Covo, *Entrepot of Revolutions: Saint-Domingue, Commercial Sovereignty, and the French-American Alliance* (Oxford: Oxford University Press, 2022), ch. 1.

40. David Richardson, "Slavery, Trade, and Economic Growth in Eighteenth-Century New England," in Barbara Solow, ed., *Slavery and the Rise of the Atlantic System* (Cambridge: Cambridge University Press, 1991), 244, 253–57.

41. James F. Shepherd and Gary M. Walton, *Shipping, Maritime Trade and the Eco-*

nomic Development of Colonial America (Cambridge: Cambridge University Press, 1972), 115, 128, 134.
42. Peter Pellizzari, "Supplying Slavery: Jamaica, North America, and British Intra-Imperial Trade, 1752–1769," *Slavery & Abolition* 41 (2020): 528–54.
43. Pellizzari, "Supplying Slavery," 528–29.
44. Gregory O'Malley, *Final Passages: Captives in the Intercolonial Slave Trade* (Chapel Hill: University of North Carolina Press, 2014); Cathy Matson, *Merchants and Empire: Trading in Colonial New York* (Baltimore: Johns Hopkins University Press, 1988); Truxes, *Defying Empire*.
45. Burnard, *Planters, Merchants, and Slaves*, 111; Kenneth Morgan, "Robert Dinwiddie's Reports on the British American Colonies," *William and Mary Quarterly* 65 (2008): 305–46, quote at 305.
46. Burnard, *Planters, Merchants, and Slaves*, 110–14; Morgan, "Robert Dinwiddie's Reports," 305–46.
47. Giorgio Riello, "Cotton Textiles and the Industrial Revolution," *Past & Present* 255 (2022): 87–139.
48. R. P. Thomas and Deirdre McCloskey, "Overseas Trade and Empire," in Roderick Floud and McCloskey, eds., *The Economic History of Britain since 1700*, vol. 1: *1700–1860* (Cambridge: Cambridge University Press, 1981), 100–101.
49. S. D. Smith, "British Exports to Colonial North America and the Mercantilist Fallacy," *Business History* 37 (1995): 58.
50. Gert Oostindie, "Modernity and the Demise of the Dutch Atlantic, 1650–1914," in Leonard, Pretel, et al., *The Caribbean and the Atlantic World Economy*, 108.
51. Mark Peterson, "Boston à l'heure française: religion, culture et commerce à l'époque des revolutions atlantique," *Annales historiques de la Révolution française* 363 (2011): 7–31.
52. Pekka Hämäläinen, "How Native Americans Shaped Early America," in Gould et al., *Cambridge History of America in the World*, 1:198.
53. Paul W. Mapp, *The Elusive West and the Contest for Empire, 1713–1763* (Chapel Hill: University of North Carolina Press, 2011).
54. Colin G. Calloway, *The American Revolution in Indian Country: Crisis and Diversity in Native American Communities* (Cambridge: Cambridge University Press, 1995).
55. Jeffrey Ostler, *Surviving Genocide: Native Nations and the United States from the American Revolution to Bleeding Kansas* (New Haven: Yale University Press, 2019), 75–76.
56. Colin G. Calloway, "Life, Land, and Liberty: The Native Americans' Revolution," in Klooster, *Cambridge History of the Age of Atlantic Revolutions*, 1:422.
57. Calloway, "Life, Land, and Liberty," 425–26.
58. James H. Merrell, *The Indians' New World: Catawbas and Their Neighbors from European Contact through the Era of Removal* (Chapel Hill: University of North Carolina Press, 1989); Pekka Hämäläinen, "The Shapes of Power: Indians, Europeans, and North American Worlds from the Seventeenth to the Nineteenth Centuries," in Juliana Barr and Edward Countryman, eds., *Contested Spaces of Early America* (Philadelphia: University of Pennsylvania Press, 2014), 65.
59. Susan Sleeper-Smith, "Women, Kin and Catholicism: New Perspectives on the Fur Trade," *Ethnohistory* 47 (2000): 423–52. For wider contexts, see Richard White,

The Middle Ground: Indians, Empires, and Republics in the Great Lakes Region, 1650–1815 (Cambridge: Cambridge University Press, 1991); and Michael Witgen, *An Infinity of Nations: How the Native New World Shaped Early America* (Philadelphia: University of Pennsylvania Press, 2012).

60. Wayne E. Lee, "The Military Revolution of Native North America: Firearms, Forts and Polities," in Lee, ed., *Empires and Indigenes: Intercultural Alliance, Imperial Expansion, and Warfare in the Early Modern World* (New York: New York University Press, 2011), 49–80.

61. Cited in Daniel Richter, "Native Peoples of North America and the Eighteenth-Century British Empire," in P. J. Marshall, ed., *The Oxford History of the British Empire: The Eighteenth Century* (Oxford: Oxford University Press, 1998), 357.

62. Cited in Michael A. McDonnell, "North American Breakdown," in Burnard, Hart, and Houllemare, *Oxford Handbook of the Seven Years' War*, 425.

63. Jean M. O'Brien, *Firsting and Lasting: Writing Indians Out of Existence in New England* (Minneapolis: University of Minnesota Press, 2010); Christine M. DeLucia, *The Memory Lands: King Phillip's War and the Place of Violence in the Northeast* (New Haven: Yale University Press, 2018).

64. Pekka Hämäläinen, *The Comanche Empire* (New Haven: Yale University Press, 2009).

65. Hämäläinen, *Lakota America*, 1–2.

66. Elizabeth A. Fenn, *Encounters at the Heart of the World* (New York: Hill and Wang, 2014).

67. Anderson, *Crucible of War*, 457–68.

68. Colin Calloway, "Red Power and Homeland Security: Native Nations and the Limits of Empire in the Ohio Country," in Michael A. McDonald and Kate Fullagar, eds., *Facing Empire: Indigenous Experiences in a Revolutionary Age* (Baltimore: Johns Hopkins University Press, 2018), 145.

69. George Washington to William Crawford, September 17, 1767, *The Writings of George Washington, 1745–1799*, ed. John C. Fitzpatrick, 39 vols. (Washington, DC: Government Printing Office, 1931–1944), 2:469; Colin G. Calloway, *The Indian World of George Washington: The First President, the First Americans and the Birth of the Nation* (Oxford: Oxford University Press, 2018).

70. Stuart Banner, *How the Indians Lost Their Land: Law and Power in the Frontier* (Cambridge, MA: Harvard University Press, 2007), 85–95; Colin G. Calloway, *The Scratch of a Pen: 1763 and the Transformation of North America* (New York: Oxford University Press, 2006); Tessa Murphy, *The Creole Archipelago: Race and Borders in the Colonial Caribbean* (Philadelphia: University of Pennsylvania Press, 2021); Allan Greer, *Property and Dispossession: Native, Empires, and Land in Early Modern North America* (Cambridge: Cambridge University Press, 2018); D. H. Murdoch, "Land Policy in the Eighteenth-Century British Empire: The Sale of Crown Lands in the Ceded Islands, 1763–1783," *Historical Journal* 27 (1984): 549–74.

71. Jane T. Merrit, *At the Crossroads: Indians and Empire on a Mid-Atlantic Frontier, 1700–1763* (Chapel Hill: University of North Carolina Press, 2003).

72. François Furstenberg, "The Significance of the Trans-Appalachian Frontier in Atlantic History, c. 1754–1815," *American Historical Review* 19 (2008): 647–77.

73. William B. Hart, "The Unsettled Periphery: The Backcountry on the Eve of the American Revolution," in Gray and Kamensky, *Oxford Handbook of the American Revolution*, 33.
74. Patrick Griffin, *American Leviathan: Empire, Nation, and Revolutionary Frontier* (New York: Hill and Wang, 2007); Matthew C. Ward, *Breaking the Backcountry: The Seven Years' War in Virginia and Pennsylvania* (Pittsburgh: University of Pittsburgh Press, 2003).
75. Eric Hinderaker and Peter C. Mancall, *At the Edge of Empire: The Backcountry in British North America* (Baltimore: Johns Hopkins University Press, 2003).
76. Gregory Evans Dowd, *A Spirited Resistance: The North American Struggle for Unity, 1745–1815* (Baltimore: Johns Hopkins University Press, 1992); Patrick Spero, *The Fight for Independence in the American West, 1765–1776* (New York: W. W. Norton, 2018).
77. Susan Sleeper-Smith, *Indigenous Property and American Conquest: Indian Women of the Ohio River Valley, 1690–1792* (Chapel Hill: University of North Carolina Press, 2018).
78. Elizabeth A. Fenn, *Pox Americana: The Great Smallpox Epidemic of 1775–82* (New York: Hill and Wang, 2001).
79. Nicholas Canny, *Making Ireland British, 1580–1650* (Oxford: Oxford University Press, 2001); Jane Ohlmeyer, *Cambridge History of Ireland*, vol 2: *1550–1730* (Cambridge: Cambridge University Press, 2018); Micheál Ó Siochrú, *God's Executioner: Oliver Cromwell and the Conquest of Ireland* (London: Faber and Faber, 2008).
80. Thomas Devine, *Scotland's Empire 1680–1815* (London: Allen Lane, 2004); Andrew Mackillop, *Human Capital and Empire: Scotland, Ireland, Wales and British Imperialism in Asia, ca. 1690–1820* (Manchester: Manchester University Press, 2021); Dziennik, *Fatal Land;* Stephen Mullen, *The Glasgow Sugar Aristocracy: Scotland and Caribbean Slavery, 1775–1838* (London: University of London Press, 2022).
81. Patrick Griffin, *The People with No Name: Ireland's Ulster Scots, America's Scots Irish, and the Creation of a British Atlantic World, 1689–1764* (Princeton: Princeton University Press, 2001).
82. Bob Harris, "The Anglo-Scottish Treaty of Union, 1707 in 2007: Defending the Revolution, Defeating the Jacobites," *Journal of British Studies* 49 (2010): 28–46.
83. Daniel Szechi, *The Jacobites: Britain and Europe, 1688–1788* (Manchester: Manchester University Press, 2019); Dziennik, *Fatal Land*.
84. Szechi, *Jacobites*.
85. Andrew Thompson, "Empire and the British State," in Sarah Stockwell, ed., *The British Empire: Themes and Perspectives* (Oxford: Oxford University Press, 2011), 38.
86. Sylvie Kleinman, "Tone and the French Expeditions to Ireland, 1796–1798: Total War or Liberation?" in Pierre Serna, Antonino De Francesco, and Judith A. Miller, eds., *Republics at War, 1776–1840: Revolutions, Conflicts and Geopolitics in Europe and the Atlantic World* (New York: Palgrave Macmillan, 2013), 87–89; John E. Cookson, *The British Armed Nation, 1793–1815* (Oxford: Oxford University Press, 1997).
87. James Kelly, "Coping with Crisis: The Response to the Famine of 1740–41," *Eigh-

teenth-Century Ireland 27 (2012): 99–122; David Dickson, *Arctic Ireland: The Extraordinary Story of the Great Frost and Forgotten Famine of 1740–41* (Belfast: White Row, 1997).

88. Jonathan Swift, *A Modest Proposal* ... (Dublin, 1729), 14.
89. Ian McBride, "The Politics of *A Modest Proposal*: Swift and the Irish Crisis of the Late 1720s," *Past & Present* 244 (2019): 89–122.
90. Eliga Gould, "The Path Not Taken: American Independence and the Irish Counterpoint," in Patrick Griffin and Francis D. Cogliano, eds., *Ireland and America: Empire, Revolution, and Sovereignty* (Charlottesville: University of Virginia Press, 2021), 89.
91. Truxes, *Irish-American Trade, 1660–1783*, 34–35, 47.
92. James Horn, "British Diaspora: Emigration from Britain, 1680–1815," in Marshall, *Oxford History of the British Empire: The Eighteenth Century*, 46–49.
93. Dickson, *Arctic Ireland*, 69.
94. Thomas Bartlett, "'A People Made Rather for Copies than Originals': The Anglo-Irish, 1760–1800," *International History Review* 12 (1990): 11–25.
95. Gould, "The Path Not Taken," 91.
96. Matthew Dziennik, *Colonial Soldiers in the Age of Revolution: A Global History* (Oxford: Oxford University Press, 2024).
97. Connolly, *Divided Kingdom*, 341.
98. J. G. Simms, *The Williamite Confiscations in Ireland, 1690–1703* (London: Faber, 1956), ch. 12; L. M. Cullen, "Catholics under the Penal Laws," *Eighteenth-Century Ireland* 1 (1986): 23–36.
99. Thomas Bartlett, *The Fall and Rise of the Irish Nation: The Catholic Question, 1690–1830* (Dublin: Gill and Macmillan, 1992).
100. Peter Rushton and Gwenda Morgan, *Treason and Rebellion in the British Atlantic, 1685–1800: Legal Responses to Threatening the State* (London: Bloomsbury, 2020), 122.
101. Connolly, *Divided Kingdom*, 304; Connolly, *Religion, Law and Power: The Making of Protestant Ireland, 1660–1760* (Oxford: Oxford University Press, 1992), 219–20.
102. Timothy D. Watt, *Popular Protest and Policing in Ascendancy Ireland, 1691–1761* (Woodbridge: Boydell and Brewer, 2018).
103. Greene, "Overwhelmingly Successful."

Part Two. The War and Its Effects

1. E. H. Carr, *What is History?* (London: Penguin, 1961), 87.
2. F. R. Ankersmit, "Historical Representation," *History and Theory* 27 (1988): 205–28.
3. Stephen Conway, *The British Isles and the War for American Independence* (Oxford: Oxford University Press, 2000), ch. 6; Joanna Innes and Mark Philp, eds., *Re-imagining Democracy in the Age of Revolution: America, France, Britain, Ireland, 1750–1850* (Oxford: Oxford University Press, 2013).
4. Christopher Clark, *Revolutionary Spring: Fighting for a New World, 1848–1849* (London: Allen Lane, 2023), 745.

5. Cited in Marshall, "Britain's American Problem," in Gray and Kamensky, *Oxford Handbook of the American Revolution*, 24.
6. Trevor Burnard, "Slavery and the Causes of the American Revolution in Plantation British America," in Andrew Shankman, ed., *The World of the Revolutionary American Republic: Expansion, Conflict, and the Struggle for a Continent* (New York: Routledge, 2014), 81–111.
7. Stephen Conway, "Britain, Ireland, and the American Revolution, c. 1763–1785," in Klooster, *Cambridge History of the Age of Atlantic Revolutions*, 1:297–307.
8. Truxes, *Overseas Trade of British America*, ch. 6.
9. Maya Jasanoff, "The Other Side of Revolution: Loyalists in the British Empire," *William and Mary Quarterly* 65 (2008): 218.
10. For Malaya, see C. A. Bayly and Tim Harper, *Forgotten Wars: The End of Britain's Asia Empire* (London: Allen Lane, 2007).
11. Miranda Spieler, "France and the Atlantic World," in Peter McPhee, ed., *A Companion to the French Revolution* (Oxford: Blackwell, 2013), 57–72; Annie Jourdan, "Tumultuous Contexts and Radical Ideas (1783–89): The 'Pre-revolution' in a Transnational Perspective," in David Andress, ed., *The Oxford Handbook of the French Revolution* (Oxford: Oxford University Press, 2013), 92–108.
12. Paul Ginsborg, *Daniele Manin and the Venetian Revolution* (Cambridge: Cambridge University Press, 1979), 367. For an interesting example of the counterfactual parlor game, see J. C. D. Clark, "British America: What If There Had Been No American Revolution?" in Niall Ferguson, ed., *Virtual History: Alternatives and Counterfactuals* (New York: Basic, 1999).
13. Hamish Scott, "The Seven Years' War and Europe's *Ancien Régime*," *War in History* 18 (2011): 419–55.
14. Peter Onuf, "The Empire of Liberty: Land of the Free and Home of the Slave," in Shankman, *The World of the Revolutionary American Republic*, 195–217; Seymour Drescher, "Revolution in England? Abolitionism," in Klooster, *Cambridge History of the Age of Atlantic Revolutions*, 2:396–420.
15. David Ramsay, *History of the American Revolution*, 2 vols. (Philadelphia: Aitken, 1789), 2:356. For revolution as modernity, see Arendt, *On Revolution*, 12.
16. Peter S. Onuf, "American Exceptionalism and National Identity," *American Political Thought* 1 (2012): 77–100.
17. Abbé Raynal, *The Revolution of America* (London: Lockyer Davis, 1781), 80.
18. Ezra Stiles, *The United States Elevated to Glory and Honor* (New Haven: Thomas and Samuel Green, 1783), 52.
19. Jane Kamensky, *A Revolution in Color: The World of John Singleton Copley* (New York: W. W. Norton, 2016); Leora Auslander, *Cultural Revolution: Everyday Life and Politics in Britain, North America and France* (Berkeley: University of California Press, 2009); Nathan Perl-Rosenthal, *The Age of Revolutions and the Generations Who Made It* (New York: Basic, 2024).
20. Cited in Gray and Kamensky, introduction to *Oxford Handbook of the American Revolution*, 8.
21. Gray and Kamensky, introduction to *Oxford Handbook of the American Revolution*, 3.
22. Bayly, *Imperial Meridian*; J. R. Ward, "The Industrial Revolution and Imperialism, 1750–1850," *Economic History Review* 47 (1994): 44–65.

23. Vincent T. Harlow, *The Founding of the Second British Empire, 1763–93*, 2 vols. (London: Longmans, 1955, 1964); P. J. Marshall, "Britain and the World in the Eighteenth Century: Reshaping the Empire," *Transactions of the Royal Historical Society* 8 (1998): 1–18.
24. Conway, "Britain, Ireland, and the American Revolution," 315–16.
25. Alan Taylor, *The Civil War of 1812: American Subjects, Irish Rebels, and Indian Allies* (New York: Knopf, 2010); P. J. Cain and A. G. Hopkins, "The Theory and Practice of British Imperialism," in Raymond E. Dumett, ed., *Gentlemanly Capitalism and British Imperialism: The New Debate on Empire* (London: Harlow, 1999), 206–10.
26. Lance E. Davis and Robert J. Cull, "International Capital Movements, Domestic Capital Markets, and American Economic Growth, 1820–1914," in Stanley Engerman and Robert Gallman, eds., *The Cambridge Economic History of the United States: The Long Nineteenth Century* (Cambridge: Cambridge University Press, 2000), 733–812.
27. Susan Sleeper-Smith, "Native America after 1763," in Burnard, Hart, and Houllemare, *Oxford Handbook of the Seven Years' War* (New York: Oxford University Press, 2024), 521–38.
28. Gregory Evans Dowd, "Indigenous Peoples without the Republic," *Journal of American History* 104 (2017); 19–41.
29. Rob Harper, *Unsettling the West: Violence and State Building in the Ohio Valley* (Philadelphia: University of Pennsylvania Press, 2018).
30. Wayne Lee, "A Contest of Wills: The Spectrum and Experience of Political Violence in the American Revolution," in Klooster, *Cambridge History of the Age of Atlantic Revolutions*, 1:243.
31. Colin G. Calloway, *The Victory with No Name: The Native American Defeat of the First American Army* (New York: Oxford University Press, 2015).
32. Calloway, "Life, Land, and Liberty," 447.

Chapter 5. The Loyal Colonies

1. Anderson, *Battle for the Fourteenth Colony*, 52–53; Lanctot, *Canada and the American Revolution*, 29.
2. Anderson, *Battle for the Fourteenth Colony*, 14–15.
3. Anderson, *Battle for the Fourteenth Colony*, 14–15.
4. Lanctot, *Canada and the American Revolution*, 207; Holly A. Mayer, "Quebec and Nova Scotia, Congress, and the Continental Army: Strategic Accommodations, 1774–1776," *Journal of Military History* 78 (2014): 504, 532.
5. Greene, *Constitutional Origins of the American Revolution*, 70; Lanctot, *Canada and the American Revolution*, 49.
6. Greene, *Constitutional Origins*; Anderson, *Battle for the Fourteenth Colony*, 69, 169, 339.
7. Lanctot, *Canada and the American Revolution*, 96–97.
8. Anderson, *Battle for the Fourteenth Colony*, 264.
9. Mayer, "Quebec and Nova Scotia, Congress, and the Continental Army," 519–22.
10. Anderson, *Battle for the Fourteenth Colony*, 229; Nancy Christie, "Merchant and

Plebian Commercial Knowledge in Montreal and Quebec, 1760–1820," *Early American Studies* 13 (2015): 856–80.

11. Donald Creighton, *The Empire of the St. Lawrence: A Study in Commerce and Politics* (Toronto: University of Toronto Press, 2002), 3.

12. Christie, *Northern Bastille*, 71–72.

13. Anderson, *Battle for the Fourteenth Colony*, 46, 163, 117–18, 129, 229, 240, 219, 86; Lanctot, *Canada and the American Revolution*, 45, 54, 57, 72, 74, 75, 95.

14. Wilfred Brenton Kerr, *Bermuda and the American Revolution, 1760–1783* (Princeton: Princeton University Press, 1936), 45, 47, 50, 56, 59–60, 70, 82; Henry C. Wilkinson, "They Build Small Ships of Cedar: Bermuda and American Independence," in *The American Revolution and the West Indies*, ed. Charles W. Toth (Port Washington, NY: Kennikat Press, 1975), 152, 154, 157, 159, 160, 162, 163–64; Michael Jarvis, *In the Eye of All Trade: Bermuda, Bermudians, and the Maritime Atlantic World, 1680–1783* (Chapel Hill: University of North Carolina Press, 2010), 376, 386–89, 391, 392, 396, 412, 419, 421, 422.

15. Kerr, *Bermuda and the American Revolution*, 26–28, 89, 90, 91; Wilkinson, "They Build Small Ships of Cedar," 155, 162; Jarvis, *In the Eye of All Trade*, 383–84, 385, 387, 410, 411, 440.

16. Morley, *Irish Opinion and the American Revolution*, 330; Neil Longley York, *Neither Kingdom nor Nation: The Irish Quest for Constitutional Rights, 1698–1800* (Washington, DC: Catholic University of America Press, 1994), 23; Schuyler, *Parliament and the British Empire*, 40–102.

17. York, *Neither Kingdom nor Nation*, 13–22; James Kelly, "'Era of Liberty': The Politics of Civil and Political Rights in Eighteenth-Century Ireland," in Greene, *Exclusionary Empire*, 82, 89.

18. Kelly, "'Era of Liberty,'" 91; York, *Neither Kingdom nor Nation*, 43–49, 59–68; R. Coupland, *The American Revolution and The British Empire* (New York: Longmans, Green and Company, 1930), 92–93.

19. York, *Neither Kingdom nor Nation*, 252.

20. O'Shaughnessy, *Empire Divided*, 82–108.

21. Jack P. Greene, "The Jamaica Privilege Controversy, 1764–66," in Greene, *Negotiated Authorities: Essays in Colonial, Political, and Constitutional History*, 350–94.

22. Morley, *Irish Opinion*, 15. But see J. G. Simms, *Colonial Nationalism, 1698–1776: Molyneux's The Case of Ireland—Stated* (Cork, Ireland: Mercier Press, 1976).

23. Trevor Burnard, "Dominant Minorities: The Irish Protestants and White Jamaicans in the British Empire in the 1780s," in Cogliano and Griffin, *Ireland and America: Empire, Revolution*, 126–54.

24. Andrew J. O'Shaughnessy, "The Stamp Act Crisis in the British Caribbean," *William and Mary Quarterly* 51 (1994): 203–26; O'Shaughnessy, "The Formation of a Commercial Lobby: The West India Interest, British Colonial Policy and the American Revolution," *Historical Journal* 40 (1997): 75–95.

25. York, *Neither Kingdom nor Nation*, 252. See also Harry T. Dickinson, "Why Did the American Revolution Not Spread to Ireland?" *Valahian Journal of Historical Studies* 18–19 (2012): 170.

26. S. H. H. Carrington, "Economic and Political Developments in the British West Indies during the Period of the American Revolution" (PhD diss., London Uni-

versity, 1975), 245–47; Jack P. Greene, *Peripheries and Center: Constitutional Development in the Extended Polities of the British Empire and the United States, 1607–1788* (Athens: University of Georgia Press, 1986), 139. See also Herbert C. Bell, "The West India Trade before the American Revolution," *American Historical Review* 22 (1917): 272–78, 287; and F. R. Augier et al., *The Making of the West Indies*, 5th ed. (London: Longmans, 1964), 108.

27. Gipson, *The British Empire before the American Revolution*, 13:75–76; Selwyn H. H. Carrington, *The British West Indies during the American Revolution* (Dordrecht, Netherlands: Foris, 1988), 129.
28. *JAJ*, December 9 and 22, 1774 (Kingston, Jamaica: Alexander Aikman, 1811–1829); C.O. 150/53, TNA; John Knowles to Samuel and William Vernon, Montego Bay, April 27, [1775], Special Collections, box 656, Newport Historical Society, Newport, Rhode Island.
29. Morley, *Irish Opinion*, 95.
30. Dickinson, "Why Did the American Revolution Not Spread to Ireland?" 164.
31. Maurice R. O'Connell, *Irish Politics and Social Conflict in the Age of the American Revolution* (Philadelphia: University of Pennsylvania Press, 1965), 32; Dickinson, "Why Did the American Revolution Not Spread to Ireland?" 164–65.
32. O'Connell, *Irish Politics*, 27; Morley, *Irish Opinion*, 102; J. C. Beckett, "Anglo-Irish Constitutional Relations in the Later Eighteenth Century," *Irish Historical Studies* 14, no. 53 (1964): 26.
33. Morley, *Irish Opinion*, 82.
34. O'Connell, *Irish Politics*, 28, 124.
35. Morley, *Irish Opinion*, 96, 81.
36. Morley, *Irish Opinion*, 149, 152, 153, 125.
37. O'Shaughnessy, *Empire Divided*, 147–51; *Journal of the Assembly of Grenada*, April 10, 1776, C.O. 104/4, TNA.
38. Angus Calder, *Revolutionary Empire: The Rise of English-Speaking Empires from the Fifteenth Century to the 1780s* (New York: E. Dutton, 1981), 755.
39. O'Connell, *Irish Politics*, 71.
40. O'Connell, *Irish Politics*, 172–73, 190, 73, 85, 171, 84, 194.
41. Herbert Butterfield, *George III, Lord North and the People, 1779–80* (New York: Russell and Russell, 1968), 113, 364, 257.
42. O'Shaughnessy, *Empire Divided*, 58–81.
43. Gearóid Ó Tuathaigh, *Ireland Before the Famine, 1798–1848* (Dublin: Gill Books, 1972), 2.
44. Truxes, *Irish-American Trade, 1660–1783*, 49.
45. L. M. Cullen and T. C. Smout, "Economic Growth in Scotland and Ireland," and Cullen, "Merchant Communities, the Navigation Acts and Irish and Scottish Responses," in *Comparative Aspects of Scottish and Irish Economic and Social History, 1600–1900*, ed. Cullen and Smout (Edinburgh: John Donald, 1977), 3–18; L. M. Cullen, *An Economic History of Ireland since 1660* (London: B. T. Batsford, 1972), 53, 54, 55, 59.
46. Thomas M. Truxes, *Overseas Trade of British America*, 290.
47. Toby Barnard, *A New Anatomy of Ireland: The Irish Protestants, 1649–1770* (New Haven: Yale University Press, 2003), 2.
48. Barnard, *New Anatomy of Ireland*, 256; Toby Barnard, *Making the Grand Figure:*

Lives and Possessions in Ireland, 1641–1770 (New Haven: Yale University Press, 2004), 149–50.
49. McDowell, *Ireland in the Age of Imperialism and Revolution*, 156.
50. Morley, *Irish Opinion*, 61–62.
51. Barnard, *New Anatomy of Ireland*, 20.
52. December 23, 1774, *JAJ*, 6:569–70.
53. Morley, *Irish Opinion*, 21, 17; Sarah E. Yeh, "In an Enemy's Country: British Culture, Identity, and Allegiance in Ireland and the Caribbean, 1688–1763" (PhD diss., Brown University, 2006).
54. Calder, *Revolutionary Empire*, 531.
55. Cullen, *Economic History of Ireland*, 83; Louis Nelson, *Architecture and Empire in Jamaica* (New Haven: Yale University Press, 2016).
56. Barnard, *New Anatomy of Ireland*, 33.
57. Barnard, *New Anatomy of Ireland*, 19, 243.
58. T. H. Breen, *The Marketplace of Revolution: How Consumer Politics Shaped American Independence* (New York: Oxford University Press, 2004).
59. Calder, *Revolutionary Empire*, 676; Dickinson, "Why Did the American Revolution Not Spread to Ireland?" 159–60; J. C. Beckett, "The Irish Parliament in the Eighteenth Century," *Report and Proceedings of the Belfast Natural History and Philosophical Society*, 2nd series, vol. 2 (1955), 21–22.
60. Beckett, "The Irish Parliament in the Eighteenth Century," 20.
61. Schuyler, *Parliament and the British Empire*, 193.
62. Edmund Morgan, "Slavery and Freedom: The American Paradox," *Journal of American History* 59 (1972): 2.
63. Richard S. Dunn, review of *American Slavery, American Freedom: The Ordeal of Colonial Virginia* by Edmund S. Morgan, *William and Mary Quarterly*, 33 (1976): 671.
64. Robert Parkinson, *The Common Cause: Creating Race and Nation in the American Nation* (Chapel Hill: University of North Carolina Press, 2016).
65. Brown, "Problem of Slavery," in Gray and Kamensky, *Oxford Handbook of the American Revolution*, 428.
66. Holton, *Forced Founders: Indians, Debtors, Slaves, and the Making of the American Revolution in Virginia* (Chapel Hill: University of North Carolina Press, 2000).
67. Gary B. Nash, *The Unknown American Revolution: The Unruly Birth of Democracy and the Struggle to Create America* (New York: Penguin, 2005), ch. 4.
68. Holton, *Forced Founders*, 160.
69. Nash, *Unknown American Revolution*, 161.
70. Holton, *Forced Founders*, 154.
71. Robert Olwell, *Masters, Slaves, and Subjects: The Culture of Power in the South Carolina Low Country* (Ithaca: Cornell University Press, 1998); J. William Harris, *The Hanging of Thomas Jeremiah: A Free Black Man's Encounter with Liberty* (New Haven: Yale University Press, 2009).
72. Burnard, *Planters, Merchants, and Slaves*, 238–39.
73. Philip D. Morgan and Andrew O'Shaughnessy, "The Arming of Slaves during the American Revolution," in Morgan and Christopher Leslie Brown, *The Arming of Slaves: Classical Times to the Modern Age* (New Haven: Yale University Press, 2007), 180–208.

74. Claudius Fergus, "'Dread of Insecurity': Abolitionism, Labor and Security in Britain's West India Colonies, 1760–1823," *William and Mary Quarterly* 66 (2009): 757–80.
75. George Metcalf, *Royal Government and Political Conflict in Jamaica, 1729–1783* (London: Longman, 1965), 189. See also Sarah Yeh, "Colonial Identity and Revolutionary Loyalty: The Case of the West Indies," in Stephen Foster, ed., *The Oxford History of the British Empire: British North America in the Seventeenth and Eighteenth Centuries* (Oxford: Oxford University Press, 2013), 195–226; Greene, "Liberty, Slavery, and the Transformation of British Identity in the Eighteenth-Century West Indies," *Slavery & Abolition* 21 (2000): 1–31; Greene, "Liberty and Slavery: The Transfer of British Liberty to the West Indies, 1627–1865," in Greene, *Exclusionary Empire*, 50–76; and Andrew O'Shaughnessy, "The West India Interest and the Crisis of American Independence," in Roderick A. McDonald, ed., *West Indies Accounts; Essays in the History of the British Caribbean and the Atlantic Economy* (Kingston: University of the West Indies Press, 1996), 126–48.
76. Seymour Drescher, "The Shocking Birth of British Abolitionism," *Slavery & Abolition* 33 (2012): 572–89.
77. Brown, "Problems of Slavery," in Gray and Kamensky, *Oxford Handbook of the American Revolution*, 427–46.
78. Burnard and Graham, "Security, Taxation, and the State," 461–89.
79. Burnard, *Planters, Merchants, and Slaves*, 243.
80. Burnard, *Jamaica in the Age of Revolution*, 202.
81. Michel Ducharme, *The Idea of Liberty in Canada during the Age of Atlantic Revolutions, 1776–1838* (Montreal: McGill-Queen's University Press, 2014), 16–27, is especially good in discussion of Canada. Ducharme makes the distinction between different concepts of liberty.
82. Staughton Lynd and David Waldstreicher, "Free Trade, Sovereignty, and Slavery: Toward an Economic Interpretation of American Independence," *William and Mary Quarterly* 68 (2011): 598.
83. Lynd and Waldstreicher, "Free Trade, Sovereignty, and Slavery," 630.
84. Brad A. Jones, *Resisting Independence: Popular Loyalism in the Revolutionary British Atlantic* (Ithaca: Cornell University Press, 2020).
85. Martin Howard, *A Letter from a Gentleman in Halifax, to His Friend in Rhode Island* (Newport, RI: S. Hall, 1765); and Howard, *A Defense of the Letter from a Gentleman at Halifax, to His Friend in Rhode Island* (Newport, RI: S. Hall, 1765).
86. Jerry Bannister and Liam Riordan, eds., *The Loyal Atlantic: Remaking the British Atlantic in the Revolutionary Era* (Toronto: University of Toronto Press, 2012).

Chapter 6. The War of Empires

1. J. R. Seeley, *The Expansion of England* (Boston: Roberts, 1883), 24. For the first Hundred Years' War, see Jonathan Sumption, *The Hundred Years' War*, 5 vols. (London: Faber and Faber, 1990–2023).
2. Hamish Scott, "The Seven Years' War and Europe's *Ancien Régime*," *War in History* 18 (2011): 421.

3. Piers Mackesy, *The War for America, 1775–1783* (1964; reprinted with an introduction by John Shy, Lincoln: University of Nebraska Press, 1993); John Shy, *A People Numerous and Armed: Reflections on the Military Struggle for American Independence,* rev. ed. (Ann Arbor: University of Michigan Press, 2000).
4. Piers Mackesy, *Could the British Have Won the War of Independence?* (Worcester, MA: Clark University Press, 1976).
5. "Piers Gerald Mackesy, 1924–2014," *Biographical Memoirs of Fellows of the British Academy,* 15 (2016): 301–2.
6. Richard Overy, *Blood and Ruins: The Last Imperial War, 1931–1945* (London: Allen Lane, 2021).
7. Shy, *People Numerous and Armed;* Jim Piecuch, *Three Peoples, One King: Loyalists, Indians, and Slaves in the Revolutionary South, 1775–1782* (Columbia: University of South Carolina Press, 2008).
8. David Halberstam, *The Best and the Brightest* (New York: Random House, 1972); Neil Sheehan, *A Bright Shining Lie: John Paul Vann and America in Vietnam* (London: Picador, 1990).
9. Julie Flavell, *The Howe Dynasty: The Untold Story of a Military Family and the Women Behind Britain's Wars for America* (New York: Liveright, 2021).
10. Carter Makasian, *The American War in Afghanistan: A History* (New York: Oxford University Press, 2023).
11. John Newsinger, *British Counterinsurgency* (Basingstoke: Palgrave Macmillan, 2015).
12. Newsinger, *British Counterinsurgency,* 33–66.
13. Timothy Harper, *Underground Asia: Global Revolutionaries and the Assault on Empire* (Cambridge, MA: Harvard University Press, 2021).
14. N. A. M. Rodger, *The Command of the Ocean: A Naval History of Britain, 1649–1815* (New York: W. W. Norton, 2005).
15. Christopher P. Magra, *Poseidon's Curse: British Naval Impressment and Atlantic Origins of the American Revolution* (New York: Cambridge University Press, 2016), and Magra, *The Fisherman's Cause: Atlantic Commerce and the Maritime Dimension of the American Revolution* (New York: Cambridge University Press, 2009).
16. Larrie D. Ferreiro, *Brothers at Arms: American Independence and the Men of France and Spain Who Saved It* (New York: Vintage, 2017), 143; Ferreiro, "Pierre-Augustin Caron De Beaumarchais," in David K. Allison and Ferreiro, eds., *The American Revolution: A World War* (Washington, DC: Smithsonian, 2018), 67.
17. Ferreiro, *Brothers at Arms,* 73.
18. Gabriel Paquette and Gonzalo M. Quintero Saravia, "Spain and the American Revolution," in Paquette and Saravia, eds., *Spain and the American Revolution* (London: Routledge, 2020), 12.
19. Barbara Tuchman, *The First Salute: A View of the American Revolution* (New York: Knopf, 1988).
20. Klooster, *Illicit Riches;* Wim Klooster and Gert Oostindie, *Realm between Empires: The Second Dutch Atlantic, 1680–1815* (Ithaca: Cornell University Press, 2018).
21. Young to Heylinger, May 20, 1776, John Colpoys to Young, November 27, 1776, Adm. 1/309/488, 589; F. C. Van Oosten, "Some Notes Concerning the Dutch Caribbean During the American Revolutionary War," *The American Neptune* 36 (1976): 165; Florence Lewisohn, "St. Eustatius: Depot for Revolution," *Revista/*

Review Interamericana 5 (1975-76): 625; John E. Selby, *The Revolution in Virginia, 1775-1783* (repr., Charlottesville: University of Virginia Press, 2007), 171-72; Richard Sampson, *Escape in America: The British Convention Prisoners, 1777-1783* (Chippenham: Picton, 1995), 19.

22. Ferreiro, *Brothers at Arms*, 335.
23. Paquette and Saravia, "Spain and the American Revolution," 11.
24. Ferreiro, *Brothers at Arms*, 91.
25. Kathleen DuVal and Gonzalo M. Quintero Saravia, "Benardo de Gálvez: Friend of the American Revolution, Friend of Empire," in Andrew J. O'Shaughnessy, John A. Ragosta, and Marie-Jeanne Rossignol, eds., *European Friends of the American Revolution* (Charlottesville: University of Virginia Press, 2023), 156.
26. Paquette and Saravia, "Spain and the American Revolution," 11.
27. Alan Lemmers, "Revolution and the Dutch Republic," in Allison and Ferreiro, *The American Revolution: A World War*, 120.
28. Paquette and Saravia, "Spain and the American Revolution," 11, 13.
29. José M. Guerrero and Larrie D. Ferreiro, "Uniforms, Supplies, and Money from Spain," in Allison and Ferreiro, *The American Revolution: A World War*, 87.
30. Stephen Mihm, "Funding the Revolution: Monetary and Fiscal Policy in Eighteenth-Century America," in Gray and Kamensky, *Oxford Handbook of the American Revolution*, 332.
31. William V. Wenger, *The Key to American Independence: Quantifying Foreign Assistance to the American Revolution* (El Segundo, CA: independently published, 2021), ix, 112, 113.
32. Ryan K. Smith, *Robert Morris's Folly: The Architectural and Financial Failures of an American Founder* (New Haven: Yale University Press, 2014).
33. Simms, *Three Victories and a Defeat*, 677.
34. H. M. Scott, *British Foreign Policy in the Age of the American Revolution* (Oxford: Clarendon, 1991), 3.
35. Timothy D. Walker, "Old Partners and Intersecting Interests: Trade and Diplomacy between Portugal and the United States during the Era of George Washington (c. 1781-1805)," in O'Shaughnessy, Ragosta, and Rossignol, *The European Friends of the American Revolution*, 175-204.
36. Paul Gilje, "Ideology *and* Interest: Free Trade and the League of Armed Neutrality, and the American Revolution," in O'Shaughnessy, Ragosta, and Rossignol, *The European Friends of the American Revolution*, 43-66.
37. Scott, *British Foreign Policy in the Age of the American Revolution*, chs. 3-4.
38. Morgan and O'Shaughnessy, "Arming Slaves in the American Revolution," 196, 198, 199. In 1778, Irish Catholics became officially eligible to enter the army. Patrick Walsh, "Ireland and the Royal Navy in the Eighteenth Century," in John McAleer and Christer Petley, eds., *The Royal Navy and the British Atlantic World, c. 1750-1820* (London: Palgrave Macmillan, 2016), 63.
39. Minute of Cabinet (in King's handwriting). At Lord North's, Saturday, January 17, 1778, Geo. 2760, Royal Archives at Windsor Castle.
40. Robert Parkinson, *Thirteen Clocks: How Race United the Colonies and Made the Declaration of Independence* (Chapel Hill: University of North Carolina Press, 2021).

41. Jonathan R. Dull, *The French Navy and American Independence: A Study of Arms and Independence, 1774–1787* (Princeton: Princeton University Press, 2019).
42. David Syrett, "The Organization of British Trade Convoys during the American War, 1775–1783," *Mariner's Mirror* 62 (1976), 170, 171, 178; *The Annual Register*, 1778; D. H. Murdoch, ed., *Rebellion in America: A Contemporary British Viewpoint, 1769–1783* (Santa Barbara, CA: 1979), 522.
43. Hannah Farber, *Underwriters of the United States: How Insurance Shaped the American Founding* (Chapel Hill: University of North Carolina Press, 2021), 23.
44. O'Shaughnessy, *Men Who Lost America*, 39–40, 74, 167, 338, 344.
45. Andrew Lambert, "The British Grand Strategy," in Allison and Ferreiro, *The American Revolution*, 40, 42–43.
46. William B. Willcox, "Sir Henry Clinton: Paralysis of Command," in George Athan Billias, ed., *George Washington's Generals and Opponents* (New York: Da Capo, 1994), 100, fn. 8; Conway, *The War of American Independence, 1775–1783* (London: E. Arnold, 1995), 158; Dull, *The French Navy and American Independence*, 359–76; R. Arthur Bowler, "Logistics and Operations in the American Revolution," in *Reconsiderations on the Revolutionary War: Selected Essays*, ed. Don Higginbotham (Westport, CT: Greenwood, 1978), 67.
47. O'Shaughnessy, *Men Who Lost America*, 213.
48. O'Shaughnessy, *Men Who Lost America*, 178–86.
49. Lord George Germain to Governor John Dalling of Jamaica, December 7, 1780, C.O. 137/78/335, TNA.
50. Dr. Benjamin Moseley, *A Treatise on Tropical Diseases: On Military Operations; and the Climate of the West-Indies* (London: T. Cadell, 1789), 133; Sir John Fortescue, *The War of Independence: The British Army in North America, 1775–1783*, with an introduction by John Shy (1911; abridged ed., London: Greenhill, 2001), 196–97; "Kemble's Journal 1780," *The Kemble Papers: The Journals of Lieut.-Col. Stephen Kemble, 1773–1789*, 2 vols. (New York: New York Historical Society, 1885), 2:36; John Hunter, *Observations on the Disease of the Army in Jamaica* 3rd ed. (London: T. Payne, 1808), 20, 48.
51. DuVal and Saravia, "Benardo de Gálvez: Friend of the American Revolution, Friend of Empire," 158–59; J. Barton Starr, *Tories, Dons and Rebels: The American Revolution in British West Florida* (Gainesville: University Presses of Florida, 1976), 1, 141, 143, 144–45, 160, 173–74, 190–92, 211.
52. Paquette and Saravia, "Spain and the American Revolution," 15; and Ferreiro, "The Rise and Fall of the Spanish-French Bourbon Armada," 66.
53. Ferreiro, "The Rise and Fall of the Spanish-French Bourbon Armada," 65–66.
54. "Memorandum. Paper Read in the Cabinet by Lord Sandwich, Delivered to the King and Communicated to Lord North—Sept 14, 1779," *The Private Papers of John, Earl of Sandwich*, ed. G. R. Barnes and John Owen, 4 vols. (London: Navy Records Society, 1932–38), 3:170–71.
55. Lambert, "British Grand Strategy," 38.
56. David Syrett, *Shipping and the American War, 1775–83: A Study of British Transport Organization* (London: Bloomsbury, 1970), 89, 161; Norman Baker, *Government and Contractors: The British Treasury and War Supplies, 1775–1783* (London: Athlone, 1971), 91.
57. Paquette and Saravia, "Spain and the American Revolution," 17; Larrie D. Ferreiro,

"The Rise and Fall of the Spanish-French Bourbon Armada," in Paquette and Saravia, *Spain and the American Revolution*, 70.
58. Jeremy Black, *War for America: The Fight for Independence 1775–1783* (New York: St. Martin's, 1994), 204.
59. O'Shaughnessy, *Empire Divided*, 219–25.
60. Nicholas Tracy, *Navies, Deterrence and American Independence: Britain and Seapower in the 1760s and 1770s* (Vancouver: University of British Columbia Press, 1988), 14; George Martelli, *Jemmy Twitcher* (London: Jonathan Cape, 1962), 258.
61. Tuchman, *The First Salute*, 235. See also Germain to Vaughan, April 4, 1781, and July 4, 1781, C.O. 318/8/103, 127, TNA.
62. Sam Willis, *Fighting at Sea in the Eighteenth Century: The Art of Sailing Warfare* (Woodbridge, Suffolk: Boydell, 2008), 59, 71, 101.
63. Rodger, *The Command of the Ocean*, ch. 22.
64. Rodger, *The Command of the Ocean*, ch. 22.
65. N. A. M. Rodger, *The Insatiable Earl: A Life of John Montagu, Fourth Earl of Sandwich* (New York: W. W. Norton, 1993), 292.
66. Roy Adkins and Lesley Adkins, *Gibraltar: The Greatest Siege in British History* (New York: Viking, 2017).
67. Paquette and Saravia, "Spain and the American Revolution," 16.
68. Emma Rothschild, "A (New) Economic History of the American Revolution," *New England Quarterly* 91 (2018): 110–23; Arthur M. Schlesinger, Sr., "The Uprising against the East India Company," *Political Science Quarterly*, 32 (1917): 60–79.
69. C. J. Bryant, "Indigenous Mercenaries in the Service of European Imperialists: The Case of the Sepoys in the Early British Indian Army, 1750–1800," *War in History* 7 (2000): 12.
70. Daniel Baugh, "Why Did Britain Lose Command of the Sea?" in Jeremy Black and Philip Woodfine, eds., *The British Navy and the Use of Naval Power in the Eighteenth Century* (Leicester: Leicester University Press, 1988), 152.
71. Stephen Conway, "'A Joy Unknown for Years Past': The American War, Britishness and the Celebration of Rodney's Victory at the Saints," *History* 86 (2001): 187, 189, 190, 197, 198; Troy Bickham, *Making Headlines: The American Revolution as Seen through the British Press* (De Kalb: Northern Illinois University Press, 2009), 164–67.
72. O'Shaughnessy, *Empire Divided*, 235–36; Joan Coutu, *Persuasion and Propaganda: Monuments of the Eighteenth-Century British Empire* (Montreal: McGill-Queen's University Press, 2006), 240–49.
73. Henry B. Wheatley, ed., *The Historical and Posthumous Memoirs of Sir Nathaniel William Wraxall, 1772–1784*, 5 vols. (London: Bickers & Son, 1884), 2:319, 320, 321.
74. Alan Atkinson, *The Europeans in Australia: A History*, vol. 1 (Melbourne: Oxford University Press, 1998).

Chapter 7. Imperial Futures

1. Bayly, *Imperial Meridian*, 164–92; Jeremy Adelman, "An Age of Imperial Revolutions," *American Historical Review* 113 (2008): 319–40; and Geoffrey Parker, "Crisis and Catastrophe: The Global Crisis of the Seventeenth Century Reconsidered," *American Historical Review* 113 (2008): 1053–79.

2. Gray and Kamensky, "Introduction: American Revolutions," in Gray and Kamensky, *Oxford Handbook of the American Revolution*, 3.
3. Polasky, "Atlantic Revolutions," 510–11. For wider context, see Klooster, *Cambridge History of the Age of Atlantic Revolutions*.
4. Trevor Burnard, "The Other British Colonies," in Klooster, *Cambridge History of the Age of Atlantic Revolutions*, 1:270.
5. Edmund S. Morgan, *The Birth of the Republic, 1763–1789* (Chicago: University of Chicago Press, 1956).
6. Pekka Hämäläinen, *Indigenous Continent: The Epic Conquest for North America* (New York: Liveright, 2022); and Ned Blackhawk, *The Rediscovery of America: Native Peoples and the Unmaking of U.S. History* (New Haven: Yale University Press, 2023).
7. Daniel Richter, *The Ordeal of the Longhouse: The Peoples of the Iroquois League in the Era of European Colonization* (Chapel Hill: University of North Carolina Press, 1992).
8. Hämäläinen, "How Native Americans Shaped Early America," 1:196.
9. Brian DeLay, *War of a Thousand Deserts: Indian Raids and the U.S.-Mexican War* (New Haven: Yale University Press, 2009).
10. Colin Calloway, *The Indian World of George Washington* (New York: Oxford University Press, 2018).
11. Katherine Carté Engel, "Connecting Protestants in Britain's Eighteenth-Century Atlantic Empire," *William and Mary Quarterly* 75 (2018): 37–70; Katherine Carté, *Religion and the American Revolution: An Imperial History* (Chapel Hill: University of North Carolina Press, 2021), 70, 65.
12. Samuel Fisher, "Fit Instruments in a Howling Wilderness: Colonists, Indians, and the Origin of the American Revolution," *William and Mary Quarterly* 73 (2016): 647–80.
13. Alan Taylor, *Divided Ground: Indians, Settlers and the Northern Borderlands of the American Revolution* (New York: Knopf, 2006), 133; Philip Bucknor, "Whatever Happened to the American Empire?" *Journal of the Canadian Historical Association* 4 (1993): 7; and Walter L. Hixson, *American Settler Colonialism: A History* (New York: Palgrave Macmillan, 2013), 7–9.
14. Mackillop, *Human Capital and Empire*; Prasanna Parthasarathi, *Why Europe Grew Rich and Asia Did Not: Global Economic Divergence, 1600–1850* (Cambridge: Cambridge University Press, 2011).
15. Alan Lester and Fae Dussart, *Colonization and the Origins of Humanitarian Governance* (Cambridge: Cambridge University Press, 2014); Nigel Penn, *The Forgotten Frontier: Colonist and Khoisan on the Cape's Northern Frontier in the Eighteenth Century* (Athens: Ohio University Press, 2005); Elizabeth Elbourne, *Empire, Kinship and Violence: Family Histories, Indigenous Rights and the Making of Settler Colonialism, 1770–1842* (Cambridge: Cambridge University Press, 2023), 232–69.
16. Frederick E. Hoxie, "Retrieving the Red Continent: Settler Colonialism and the History of American Indians in the US," *Ethnic and Racial Studies* 31 (2008): 1158–59, 1162.
17. Dowd, "Indigenous Peoples without the Republic," 41.

18. Julie Chun Kim, "The Caribs of St. Vincent and Indigenous Resistance during the Age of Revolutions," *Early American Studies* 11 (2013): 117–32.
19. Julie Chun Kim, "Natural History of Indigenous Resistance: Alexander Anderson and the Caribs of St. Vincent," *The Eighteenth Century: Theory and Interpretation,* 55 (2014): 217–33.
20. Heather Freund, "'Who Should Be Treated with Every Degree of Humanity?': Debating Rights for Planters, Soldiers, and Caribs/Kalingo on St. Vincent, 1763–1773," *Atlantic Studies* 13 (2015): 125–43.
21. Richard B. Sheridan, "The British Credit Crisis of 1772 and the American Colonies," *Journal of Economic History* 20 (1960): 161–86.
22. Marshall, *Making and Unmaking of Empires,* 182. For land acquisition, see D. H. Murdoch, "Land Policy in the Eighteenth-Century British Empire: The Sale of Crown Lands in the Ceded Islands, 1763–1783," *Historical Journal* 27 (1984): 549–74.
23. Marshall, "A Polite and Commercial People in the Caribbean," 173–90; Jack P. Greene, *Evaluating Empire and Confronting Colonialism in Eighteenth-Century Britain* (Cambridge: Cambridge University Press, 2013), 1–19; J. Paul Thomas, "The Caribs of St. Vincent: A Study of Imperial Maladministration, 1763–1773," *Journal of Caribbean History* 18 (1983): 60–72.
24. Trevor Burnard, "Slavery and the Enlightenment in Jamaica, 1760–1772: The Afterlife of Tacky's Rebellion," in Damien Tricoire, ed., *Enlightened Colonialism: Imperial Agents, Narratives of Progress and Civilizing Policies in the Eighteenth Century* (Basingstoke: Palgrave Macmillan, 2017), 227–46.
25. Edward Cox, "Fedon's Rebellion 1795–1796: Causes and Consequences," *Journal of Negro History* 67 (1982), 7–19; David Barry Gaspar and David Patrick Geggus, eds., *A Turbulent Time: The French Revolution and the Greater Caribbean* (Bloomington: Indiana University Press, 1997); Michael Duffy, *Soldiers, Sugar and Seapower: The British Expeditions to the West Indies and the War against Revolutionary France* (New York: Oxford University Press, 1987).
26. Kit Candlin, "The Role of the Enslaved in the 'Fedon Rebellion' of 1795," *Slavery & Abolition* 39 (2018): 685–707.
27. Kim, "The Caribs of St. Vincent and Indigenous Resistance during the Age of Revolutions"; Kit Candlin, *The Last Caribbean Frontier, 1795–1815* (Basingstoke: Palgrave Macmillan, 2012); Murphy, *The Creole Archipelago,* 201–28.
28. Joy Damousi, Trevor Burnard, and Alan Lester, introduction to *Humanitarianism, Empire and Transnationalism,* 6–13; Alan Lester, "Humanitarian Governance and the Circumvention of Revolutionary Human Rights in the British Empire," in Michael Barnett, ed., *Humanitarianism and Human Rights: A World of Difference?* (Cambridge: Cambridge University Press, 2020), 107–26; Amanda B. Moniz, *From Empire to Humanity: The American Revolution and the Origins of Humanitarianism* (New York: Oxford University Press, 2016).
29. P. J. Marshall, ed., *The Speeches of the Right Hon. Edmund Burke,* vol. 5: *India: Madras and Bengal, 1774–1785* (Oxford: Oxford University Press, 1981), 385.
30. Robert Skinner and Alan Lester, "Humanitarianism and Empire: New Research Agendas," *Journal of Imperial and Commonwealth History* 40 (2012): 729–47.
31. Andrew Porter, "Trusteeship, Anti-Slavery and Humanitarianism," in Porter, ed.,

The Oxford History of the British Empire: The Nineteenth Century (Oxford: Oxford University Press, 1999), 198.

32. Max M. Edling, "United States Expansion and Incorporation in the Long Nineteenth Century," *Journal of Imperial and Commonwealth History* 49 (2021): 431, 433, 434; Nicholas Guyatt, *Bind Us Apart: How Enlightened America Invented Racial Segregation* (New York: Basic, 2016).
33. Edling, "Expansion and Incorporation," 445.
34. Trevor Burnard, "Ireland, Jamaica and the Fate of White Protestants in the British Empire in the 1780s," in Angela McCarthy, ed., *Ireland in the World: Comparative, Transnational, and Personal Perspectives* (Routledge: London and New York, 2015), 15–33.
35. Williams, *Capitalism and Slavery*, 122.
36. Soile Ylivoni, "Whiteness, Polite Masculinity, and West-Indian Self-Fashioning," *Cultural and Social History* 18 (2021): 669–89.
37. Kenneth Morgan, "Robert Dinwiddie's Reports on the British American Colonies," *William and Mary Quarterly* 65 (2008): 305.
38. Trevor Burnard, "Powerless Masters: The Curious Decline of Jamaican Sugar Planters in the Foundational Period of British Abolition," *Slavery & Abolition* 32 (2011): 185–98; Burnard, *Jamaica in the Age of Revolution*; Burnard and Richard Follett, "Caribbean Slavery, British Antislavery and the Cultural Politics of Venereal Disease," *Historical Journal* 55, no. 2 (2012), 427–52; Burnard and Deirdre Coleman, "The Savage Slave Mistress: Punishing Women in the British Caribbean, 1750–1834," *Atlantic Studies* 19 (2022): 34–59; and Burnard, "Tropical Hospitality, British Masculinity and Drink in Late Eighteenth-Century Jamaica," *Historical Journal* 65 (2022): 202–33.
39. Bruce A. Ragsdale, *Washington at the Plow: The Founding Farmer and the Question of Slavery* (Cambridge, MA: Harvard University Press).
40. Christopher Leslie Brown, "Antislavery in America, 1760–1820: Comparisons, Contours, Contexts," in Gould et al., *Cambridge History of America and the World*, 1:423–24; Paul Polgar, *Standard Bearers of Equality: America's First Abolition Movement* (Chapel Hill: University of North Carolina Press, 2019).
41. David Brion Davis, *The Problem of Slavery in the Age of Revolution, 1770–1823* (Ithaca: Cornell University Press, 1975), 213–54; Burnard, "Anthony Benezet: *A Short History of Guinea* and Its Impact on Early British Abolitionism"; and Matthew Mason, *Slavery and Politics in the New Nation* (Charlottesville: University of Virginia Press, 2006).
42. J. R. Oldfield, *Transatlantic Abolitionism in the Age of Revolution: An International History of Antislavery* (Cambridge: Cambridge University Press, 2013).
43. Manisha Sinha, *The Slave's Cause: A History of Abolition* (New Haven: Yale University Press, 2016).
44. Richard S. Newman, *The Transformation of American Abolitionism: Fighting Slavery in the Early Republic* (Chapel Hill: University of North Carolina Press, 2002).
45. James Alexander Dun, *Dangerous Neighbors: Making the Haitian Revolution in Early America* (Philadelphia: University of Pennsylvania Press, 2016).
46. Richardson, *Principles and Agents*, 122–31. See also James E. Bradley, *Religion,*

Revolution and English Radicalism: Non-conformity in Eighteenth-Century Politics and Society (Cambridge: Cambridge University Press, 1992). For Wesley, see Brycchan Carey, "John Wesley's *Thoughts upon Slavery* and the Language of the Heart," *Bulletin of the John Rylands University Library of Manchester* 85 (2003): 273-81.
47. Seymour Drescher, "History's Engines: British Mobilization in the Age of Revolution," *William and Mary Quarterly* 66 (2009): 737-56.
48. J. G. A. Pocock, "British History: A Plea for a New Subject: A Reply," *Journal of Modern History* 47 (1975): 627.
49. Marshall, *Remaking the British Atlantic*, ch. 1; Nicholas B. Dirks, *The Scandal of Empire: India and the Creation of Imperial Britain* (Cambridge, MA: Harvard University Press, 2009); Burnard, *Jamaica in the Age of Revolution*, ch. 3.
50. Julian Hoppit, *The Dreadful Monster and its Poor Relations: Taxing, Spending and the United Kingdom, 1707-2021* (London: Allen Lane, 2021).
51. Conway, *The British Isles and the War for American Independence*, 252-59.
52. Bayly, *Imperial Meridian*, 8.
53. P. J. Marshall, "A Nation Defined by Empire, 1755-1776," in Alexander Grant and Keith J. Springer, eds., *Uniting the Kingdom? The Making of British History* (London: Routledge, 1995), 221. See also Eliga H. Gould, "A Virtual Nation: Greater Britain and the Imperial Legacy of the American Revolution," *American Historical Review* 104 (1999): 476-89.
54. Trevor Burnard, *Writing Early America: From Empire to Revolution* (Charlottesville: University of Virginia Press, 2023), 159-63.
55. Glenn Burgess, *George Orwell's Perverse Humanity: Socialism and Free Speech* (London: Bloomsbury, 2023), 55, 82.
56. Ian Christie, *Stress and Stability in Late Eighteenth-Century Britain: Reflections on the British Avoidance of Revolution* (Oxford: Oxford University Press, 1984). For the ubiquity of the long eighteenth century as a theme in British history, see Frank O'Gorman, *The Long Eighteenth Century*, 2nd ed. (London: Bloomsbury, 2016).
57. Joanna Innes and Mark Philp, eds., *Re-Imagining Democracy in the Age of Revolutions: America, France, Britain, Ireland, 1750-1850* (Oxford: Oxford University Press, 2015).
58. O'Shaughnessy, *Men Who Lost America*, 4.
59. O'Shaughnessy, *Men Who Lost America*, 5.
60. Flavell, *Howe Dynasty*; O'Shaughnessy, *Men Who Lost America*; Linda Colley, "The Apotheosis of George III: Loyalty, Royalty and the British Nation, 1760-1820," *Past & Present* 102 (1984): 94-129.
61. O'Shaughnessy, *Men Who Lost America*, 45-46.
62. Vincent T. Harlow, *The Founding of the Second British Empire, 1763-1793*, 2. vols. (London: Longmans, 1952, 1964), 1:62.
63. James Belich, *Replenishing the Earth: The Settler Revolution and the Rise of the Anglo World, 1780-1939* (Oxford: Oxford University Press, 2009).
64. Marshall, *Remaking the British Atlantic*, 123, 191-92. See also O'Shaughnessy, *Empire Divided*, 238-46.
65. Helen Taft Manning, *British Colonial Government after the American Revolution*,

1782–1820 (New Haven: Yale University Press, 1933; repr., Hamden, CT: Archon, 1966), 72, 73, 99, 149, 294, 295, 361–63; Schuyler, *Parliament and the British Empire*, 198.

66. Manning, *British Colonial Government*, 9–10.
67. Cited in Christie, *Northern Bastille*, 123–24.
68. Cited in Taylor, *American Revolutions*, 330.
69. Christie, "Merchant and Plebian Commercial Knowledge in Montreal and Quebec, 1760–1820," 856–80.
70. Simon Schama, *Rough Crossings: Britain, the Slaves and the American Revolution* (London: Vintage, 2009); Maeve Ryan, *Humanitarian Governance and the British Antislavery World System* (New Haven: Yale University Press, 2022).
71. Alan Taylor, "The War of 1812 and the Struggle for a Continent," in Andrew Shankman, ed., *The World of the Revolutionary American Republic: Land, Labor, and the Conflict for a Continent* (New York: Routledge, 2014), 259.
72. Eliga H. Gould, *The Persistence of Empire: British Political Culture in the Age of the American Revolution* (Chapel Hill: University of North Carolina Press, 2000), 182.
73. Alan Atkinson, "The Free-Born Englishman Transported: Convict Rights as a Measure of Eighteenth-Century Empire," *Past & Present* 144 (1994): 88–115.
74. Suzanne Schwarz, "Commerce, Civilisation, and Christianity: The Development of the Sierra Leone Company," in David Richardson, Schwarz, and Anthony J. Tibbles, eds., *Liverpool and Transatlantic Slavery* (Liverpool: Liverpool University Press, 2007), 252–76.
75. Ryan, *Humanitarian Governance*, 16. See also Padriac Scanlan, *Freedom's Debtors: British Antislavery in Sierra Leone in the Age of Revolution* (New Haven: Yale University Press, 2017); Catherine Hall, *Macaulay and Son: Architects of Imperial Britain* (New Haven: Yale University Press, 2012); Lauren Benton and Lisa Ford, *Rage for Order: The British Empire and the Origins of International Law, 1800–1850* (Cambridge, MA: Harvard University Press, 2016).
76. Michel Ducharme, *The Idea of Liberty in Canada during the Age of Atlantic Revolutions, 1776–1838* (Montreal: McGill-Queen's University, 2014).
77. Jane Errington, *The Lion, the Eagle and Upper Canada: A Developing Colonial Ideology*, 2nd ed. (Montreal and Kingston: McGill-Queen's University Press, 2012); Jeffrey L. Nairn, *The Capacity to Judge: Public Opinion and Deliberative Democracy in Upper Canada, 1791–1854* (Toronto: University of Toronto Press, 2000); and Nancy Christie, ed., *Transatlantic Subjects: Ideas, Institutions, and Social Experience in Post-revolutionary British North America* (Montreal: McGill-Queen's University Press, 2008).
78. Brad A. Jones, *Resisting Independence: Popular Loyalism in the Revolutionary British Atlantic* (Ithaca: Cornell University Press, 2021), 210.
79. Conway, "'A Joy Unknown for Years Past.'"
80. Brad A. Jones, "'In Favour of Popery': Patriotism, Protestantism, and the Gordon Riots in the Revolutionary British Atlantic," *Journal of British Studies* 52 (2013): 74–102. See also Jerry Bannister and Liam Riordan, eds., *The Loyal Atlantic: Remaking the British Atlantic in the Revolutionary Era* (Toronto: University of Toronto Press, 2012).

81. Manning, *British Colonial Government after the American Revolution, 1782–1820*, 228–29; Morgan and O'Shaughnessy, "Arming Slaves in the American Revolution," 196, 198, 199.
82. Francis and Mary Wickwire, *Cornwallis: The Imperial Years* (Chapel Hill: University of North Carolina Press, 1980), 8, 88, 92, 98, 175; Dalrymple, *Love and Betrayal in Eighteenth-Century India*, 3.
83. Kariann Yokata, *Unbecoming British: How Revolutionary America Became a Postcolonial Nation* (Cambridge: Cambridge University Press, 2010).
84. A. G. Hopkins, *American Empire: A Global History* (Princeton: Princeton University Press, 2016).
85. Kinsley Brauer, "The United States and British Imperial Expansion, 1815–1860," *Diplomatic History* 12 (1988): 24.
86. Patrick Griffin, "Imperial Confusion: America's Post-colonial and Post-revolutionary Empire," *Journal of Imperial and Commonwealth History* 49 (2021): 420.
87. Griffin, "Imperial Confusion," 414.
88. Gould et al., introduction to *Cambridge History of America and the World*, 1:25.
89. Max M. Edling, "United States Expansion and Incorporation in the Long Nineteenth Century," *Journal of Imperial and Commonwealth History* 49 (2021): 445.
90. Beckert, *Empire of Cotton*, 205.
91. Jay Sexton, "The British Empire after A. G. Hopkins' *American Empire*," *Journal of Imperial and Commonwealth History* 49 (2021): 469.
92. Richard Huzzey, *Freedom Burning: Anti-Slavery and Empire in Victorian Britain* (Ithaca: Cornell University Press, 2012).
93. Sexton, "British Empire," 439.
94. Matthew Birchall, "History, Sovereignty, Capital: Company Colonization in South Australia and New Zealand," *Journal of Global History* 16 (2021): 141–57.

Acknowledgments

THIS PROJECT STARTED MANY YEARS AGO but was an embryonic project until early 2023 when Andrew accepted a fellowship at the Wilberforce Institute at the University of Hull, where Trevor was director, and when both Trevor and Andrew began work in earnest on this project. We are grateful to the University of Hull for providing a conducive environment for authoring this book. Our book is heavily reliant on the scholarship of an exceptionally substantial number of people writing on the American Revolution and the eighteenth-century British Empire. It would be invidious to name all the people who have helped us. But we are grateful to Eric Hinderaker and Patrick Griffin, who gave this manuscript a remarkably close and welcomingly positive reading for Yale University Press. Adina Popescu at Yale University Press has been constantly encouraging. Nancy Christie helped us with the history of Quebec, Nova Scotia, Newfoundland, and Canada, providing guidance to a vigorous historiography on empire in early Canada. Peter Onuf, Marie Houllemare, Emma Hart, and François-Joseph Ruggiu have been enthusiastic about what we have been doing.

We thank the participants in a conference about themes central to this book, held at the Wilberforce Institute in March 2023, especially Stephen Conway, a leading expert in the twin topics of the American Revolution and British imperialism who gave a riveting keynote address. We mourn the loss in April 2023, at a tragically youthful age of thirty-eight, of Aaron Graham, an attendee at this conference and a prolific author in Andrew's and Trevor's historical specialty of Jamaica in the period of slavery. Trevor would also like to note the contribution made to this volume by his close friend, Ed Gray, who sadly died in December 2023, aged just fifty-nine.

We realize that in advancing an account of the American Revolution written from an imperial perspective we stand on the shoulders of giants, from Charles Andrews and Lawrence Henry Gipson in the distant past to more contemporary scholars. Two of our mentors stand out in particular—

Jack Greene and Peter Marshall, each of whom has insisted during his long and extraordinary career that the history of imperialism in the age of the American Revolution is vital for understanding that conflict. Our work is indebted at every turn to their scholarship.

We dedicate this work to our families in Britain, Australia, and New Zealand and to the memories of our fathers, Raymond Burnard (1935-1998) and John O'Shaughnessy (1927-2023). In particular, we'd like to acknowledge our brothers—Nicholas for Andrew and Murray and Russell for Trevor.

Trevor Burnard sadly passed away upon the completion of this book at the age of sixty-three in August 2024. He was diagnosed with cancer when we began the project but managed to write numerous drafts, as well as undertake other projects, including the completion of a book by the late Aaron Graham, and running the Wilberforce Institute at Hull. He was stoical and uncomplaining in the face of his suffering. Trevor stood out for his generosity, his kindness, his support of colleagues, his mentorship of younger scholars, his prolific productivity, and most of all for his integrity. His wife Deborah was by his side throughout and always a wonderful, much loved companion.

Index

Note: Page numbers in italics refer to figures.

abolitionist movement, 116, 117, 119, 153, 179, 181, 224, 226–28, 237, 246
absenteeism, 176
Acadia, 70, 82
Acts of Union, 218
Adam (enslaved man), 8
Adams, John, 90, 154, 193
Afghanistan, 188, 189, 215
Africa: British Empire in, 17, 19, 30, 64, 96, 197; and the Hundred Years' War, 185; Seven Years' War in, 43, 48; trade with, 87, 237; wealth from, 112. *See also* Senegambia; Sierra Leone; South Africa
Age of Empire, 2, 155, 217, 246
Age of Revolution, 21, 26, 27, 155, 216, 217, 230, 246
Allen, Ethan, 161
Alleyne, John Gaye, 167
American Revolution: and the abolitionist movement, 227–28; alternate outcomes, 152–53, 186–87, 245; and Canada, 217–19; causes of, 33–41; as civil war, 21, 183; consequences of, 149–57; cost of, 229; counterinsurgency, 188–89, 215; Ethiopian regiment, 179–80; as global war, 16, 19, 20–21, 28, 152, 197–202, 217; impact of, 216, 228–33; as imperial event, 31, 217–18; as inspiration for other revolutions, 23, 26; and Ireland, 218; and Jamaica, 217–18; parallels to Vietnam, 187–88; and South Asia, 218; synopsis, 10–13, 16
American Slavery, American Freedom (Morgan), 177–78
Amherst, Jeffery, 1st Baron, 139, 196
Andrew Doria, 192
Andrews, Charles McLean, 3, 20
Anglicization, 17, 30, 37
Anglo-Mysore War, 197, 212, 213, 242, 242, 243

Anishinaabes, 44
Anne (Queen), 28, 100
Anson, George, 85
Antigua, 77, 90, 163, 175, 176, 196, 198, 242; Shirley Heights, 242
Antill, Edward, 161
antislavery. *See* abolitionist movement
Apongo (enslaved man), 117
Arab Spring, 19
Arbuthnot, Mariot, 207
Arendt, Hannah, 23–24
Arnold, Benedict, 161
Articles of Confederation, 160
Asia: British Empire in, 17, 64; trade with, 246; wealth from, 112. *See also* South Asia
Australia: Aborigines in, 156, 221; Botany Bay, 235; and the British Commonwealth, 37; and the British Empire, 10, 17, 86, 155, 229, 242, 244; Cook's voyages to, 10, 216; settler societies in, 64
Austria, 19, 39, 194, 195, 229; monarchial reforms, 39; and the Seven Years' War, 45, 153; taxes in, 63, 229
Austrian Netherlands, 191
authoritarianism: in America, 91–92; in the British Empire, 11, 26, 40, 88, 92, 119, 143, 151, 159, 184, 229, 233, 235, 239, 244; in Canada, 55, 234, 238; cosmopolitan, 60; Indigenous peoples, 138; in Ireland, 17; in Massachusetts, 13; in West Africa, 88

Bacon, John, 214
Bahamas: and the Boston Board of Customs, 91; British army in, 196, 198, British control in, 75, 177; capture of by Spain, 197, 202, 215; Loyalists in, 184, 233; New Providence, 202. *See also* Caribbean
Bailyn, Bernard, 33–34

295

Baker, Polly, 124
Ball, John, 191
Bank of America, 197
Bank of England, 45
Barbados: absenteeism in, 176; and the British Empire, 198, 222; plantations in, 98, 99, 108; racism in, 109; slave code, 103; slavery in, 109; sovereignty in, 164; St. Anne's Fort, 242; Stamp Act in, 166, 167; taxes paid by, 89; wealth distribution in, 129; white population of, 174, 177. *See also* Caribbean
Barras, Jacques-Melchior Saint-Laurent, Comte de, 210
Bartlett, Thomas, 144
Basques, 29
Baugh, Daniel, 45
Bay of Honduras, 224
Bayly, C. A., 46
Beachy Head, Battle of, 210
Beaumarchais, Pierre-Augustin Caron de, 190
Beckford, William, 79, 129
Bedford, John Russell, 4th Duke of, 72
Belize, 197
Benezet, Anthony, 116
Bengal: Britain in, 27, 36, 91, 235, 243; British acquisition of, 61, 194; under the East India Company, 28, 51–53, 59, 79–80, 118; fabric from, 119; famine in, 53, 118, 218, 221; government in, 80–81; Indigenous population of, 34, 59, 148; and the slave trade, 119; taxation in, 51–52, 64, 79, 88, 218; threat of rebellion in, 175. *See also* India
Berkeley, William, 178
Bermuda: and the Boston Board of Customs, 91; Britain in, 96, 163; loyalty to the British Empire, 183; support for the American Revolution, 162–64
Bernard, Francis, 76
Bingham, William, 191
Black Carib War, 118, 175. *See also* Carib Wars
Blackstone, William, 94
Bladen, Martin, 61
Blathwayt, William, 61
Board of Customs (Boston), 90

Board of Customs (English), 91
Board of Trade, 55, 74, 75, 93–94, 132
Boston Committee of Correspondence, 160
Boston Massacre, 12, 93
Boston Tea Party, 58, 74, 80, 218
Botetourt, Norborne Berkeley, Baron, 73
Bougainville, Louis-Antoine de, 86
Bourbons, 70, 203, 211, 239
Braddock, Edward, 47
Brathwaite, John, 213
Britain: Bristol, 102; in Central America, 200; conflict with Dutch Republic, 185; conflict with France, 48–49, 171, 185–86, 192; conflict with Germany, 194; conflict with Spain, 185; danger of invasion in, 198; economic development in, 110–11; expeditions to the Pacific, 10, 86, 216; as global power, 67; Gordon Riots, 172, 218, 239; hostile to non-whites, 117–19; impact of the American Revolution in, 228–33; imperial reform in, 50–51, 61; and the Kalingos, 221–24; Liverpool, 102; London, 6, 10, 40, 48, 54, 65, 101, 102, 103, 116, 129, 150, 163, 176, 214, 239; relationship with France, 65–66; and the Seven Years' War, 43, 120; and the slave trade, 115–17; slavery in, 104–5; sources of wealth, 111–13; trade with Jamaica, 131. *See also* British Empire; England
British army: in the American colonies, 62–63; in Canada, 63, 161–62, 189, 198, 199, 215; in the Caribbean, 75, 90–91, 169, 174–75, 177, 195, 198, 242; Catholics in, 145, 212; in Central America, 195; commanders of, 188; conflicts with Indigenous people, 118; defects of, 188, 194, 195, 196, 199; First West India Regiment, 196, 242; in Florida, 198; global reach of, 198; harsh treatment of soldiers by, 62–63; Hessians in, 195, 196; highlanders in, 142; increasing size of, 65; in India, 52, 58, 68, 77–78, 195, 198, 212–13, 240–41, 243–44; Indigenous peoples in, 195; in Ireland, 58, 76–77, 78, 174, 175, 198; Irish recruits, 145; Loyalists in, 195; and the Mutiny Acts, 93; in New York, 198, 199, 207, 208, 215; in North America, 16, 63, 72, 74, 139, 170, 187, 189, 190, 195,

INDEX

198–99, 205, 208, 215; and the Quartering Act, 74; recruiting Blacks, 5, 180–81, 196, 242; in Senegambia, 196; sepoys in, 52, 195, 212; transportation of, 203
British Commonwealth, 37
British Empire: in Africa, 17, 19, 30, 64, 96, 197; in America (map), *165*; in the American colonies, 5, 16–17, 30, 64; in Asia, 17, 64; attempts at reform, 75; in Australia, 155; in Canada, 21, 27, 36, 40, 53–56, 61, 66, 88, 96, 155, 229, 234–35; in the Caribbean, 36, 37, 40, 89, 96, 107, 152, 153, 197, 200, 222, 232–33; colonies loyal to, 18–19, 21, 31, 151, 159–84; expansion of, 3–4, 120, 123, 151, 217, 229, 242, 246; in Florida, 55, 61, 66, 200, 201; and the French Revolution, 26; as global empire, 96, 212; imperial economy, 127–33; in India, 6, 19, 34–36, 40, 51–53, 58–61, 69–70, 88, 155, 197, 232, 245; Indian Department, 88; and Indigenous populations, 156–57; in Ireland, 17, 18, 20, 21, 27–28, 40, 44, 72, 96, 141–43, 153, 235; in the Mediterranean, 197; in Scotland, 17, 21, 30, 34, 65, 141–43; in Senegambia, 36; and the Seven Years' War, 40, 47; and the slave trade, 6, 19; slavery in, 119; in South Asia, 28, 30, 152, 212; trade in, 70; and the United States, 24, 245–46. *See also* Britain; British army; England; Royal Navy
British navy. *See* Royal Navy
Brown, Christopher, 179
Brunias, Agostino, *136*, *137*
Buckinghamshire, John Hobart, 2nd Earl of, 171, 231
Burgoyne, John, 64, 80, 190–91, 192, 199
Burke, Edmund, 2, 26, 224
Bute, John Stuart, 3rd Earl of, 69, *84*
Byrd, William III, 180
Byron, John, 86

Camden, Battle of, 192
Campbell, John, 85–86, 201
Campbell v. Hall, 91
Canada: Acadia, 70; and the American Revolution, 217–19; British acquisition of, 127, 133, 194; British army in, 161–62, 198, 199, 215; British colonies in, 21, 27, 36, 40, 53–56, 61, 66, 88, 96, 155, 229, 234–35, 244; and the British Commonwealth, 37; British immigrants to, 238; Catholics in, 17, 81–85, 139, 238; conquest of, 53–54, 122, 218; defense of, 218; fishing in, 54, 56; France in, 46; French vs. English legal systems in, 91; fur trade in, 54; governors of, 243; Hudson's Bay, 54; imperial policies in, 18, 81–85; Indigenous peoples in, 56, 195, 221; Loyalists in, 233, 234–35, *236*, 238; loyalty to the Empire, 17; Maritime provinces, 54, 56, 82; Montreal, 20, 47, 54, 161–62, 196, 198; Newfoundland, 54, 55, 56; Old vs. New Subjects, 161; population of, 125; Prince Rupert's Land, 54; settler societies in, 64; and the Seven Years' War, 30. *See also* Nova Scotia; Quebec
Canada Constitutional Act (1791), 218, 234, 243
Cape Colony, 221, 229, 244
capitalism: agricultural, 99; in the Atlantic world, 114; and colonialism, 3; hyper-, 113; merchant, 113
Carib Wars, 199; First (Black), 118, *136*, 175; Second, 221–22, 223
Caribbean: absenteeism in, 176; and the American Revolution, 213, 217; Bermuda, 163; Black population of, 121, 122, 177; British army in, 242; British colonies in, 36, 37, 40, 89, 96, 107, 152, 153, 197, 200, 222, 232–33; British convoys in, 196–97; British navy in, 199; British view of, 102, 228; Catholics in, 17, 22, 139, 223; contentious reputation of, 89; differences with North America, 172–76; Dutch Republic in, 47, 174, 206; exports to, 127; extractive societies in, 64; fortification of, 242; funding for, 107–8; governors of, 73; and the Hundred Years' War, 185; imperial policies in, 89–91; imperialism in, 34; importance of, 111–13; Indigenous peoples in, 17, 96, 98, 118, 156, 221–24; and the Irish triangle, 173–74; loyalty to the British Empire, 159, 170–72, 178, 183; map, *14–15*; Montserrat, 198; opposing the American Revolution, 170–72; plantations in, 22, 98–99, 98–100,

Caribbean (*continued*)
107–8, 116, 132, 147; population of, 121, 124, 125; Protestants in, 30; resistance in, 230; Royal Navy in, 210; Saint-Domingue Rebellion, 176; Scotland and, 141; and the Seven Years' War, 30, 43, 48, 62, 64, 222; slave trade in, 98, 108, 115–16, 120, 131, 182, 224, 229, 232; slavery in, 87, 98–108, 109, 110, 111, 115–16, 117, 147–48; sovereignty in, 105; Spain in, 198; and the Sugar (Revenue) Act, 74, 167; supporting the American Revolution, 164–69; taxation in, 94; tension in, 29; Tortola, 163; trade with, 91, 100–102, 119, 130–31, 235; Virgin Islands, 163; wealth distribution in, 128–30. *See also* Antigua; Bahamas; Barbados; Cuba; Dominica; French Caribbean; Grenada; Haiti; Jamaica; Nevis; St. Kitts; St. Lucia; St. Vincent; Tobago; Trinidad

Caribs (Kalingos), 96, 118, 156, 221–24

Carleton, Guy, 83, 161, 215

Carlisle Peace Commission, 171

Carolina Pioneer Corps, 196

Carolinas, 151. *See also* North Carolina; South Carolina

Carr, E. H., 149

Carroll, Charles, 125–26

Cartagena, 132

Carteret, Philip, 86

Cary, John, 101

Catawbas, 135

Catherine II (Russia), 194–95

Catholic Relief Act (1778), 84, 172

Catholics: in Acadia, 82; assimilation of, 82, 83; in Britain, 84, 239; in Canada, 17, 81–85, 139, 238; in the Caribbean, 17, 22, 139, 223; emancipation of, 61; in England, 81, 140; French, 17, 55, 81–83, 85, 122, 139, 140, 175, 223; in Ireland, 22, 69, 81, 84–85, 142–47, 148, 151, 170, 174, 177, 212; in Nova Scotia, 175; in Quebec, 22, 34, 81–85, 122, 175; rights of, 118

Ceded Islands, 221–22. *See also* Dominica; Grenada; St. Vincent

Central America, 195, 197–98, 200, 201

centralization, 17, 26, 29, 39, 41, 61, 92, 151, 229

Channel Islands, 28, 197, 198

Charles I, 232

Charles II, 38

Chatham ministry, 79. *See also* Pitt, William (the Elder)

Cherokee War, 139

Cherokees, 135, 139

Chesapeake Bay, 207

Chesapeake Capes, Battle of, 205–10, 212

Chesterfield, Phillip Dormer Stanhope, 4th Earl of, 145

Chickasaws, 135, 141

Choctaws, 135, 141

Choiseul, Étienne François, Duc de, 40, 195, 203

Christianity: and the abolitionist movement, 228; and slavery, 109–10

Christie, Ian, 230

Church of England, 85. *See also* Protestantism

Churchill, Winston, 186–87

citizenship: access to, 224, 245; in the British Empire, 61

Civil War, 119

Clark, George Rogers, 191

Clarke, Alured, 243

Clarke, Simon, 7

Clarkson, John, 23, 237

Clarkson, Thomas, 226, 237

Clay, Henry, 244

Clinton, Henry, 181, 199, 200, 203, 207, 209, 210

Clive, Robert, 48, 52, 60, 64, 79–80

Coercive Acts (1774), 5, 12, 13, 74, 161, 218

coffee, 101, 130

Colden, Cadwallader, 73

Collinson, Peter, 57

Colonel Jack (Defoe), 103–4

colonialism: and the British Empire, 3–4; and capitalism, 3; in the Carolinas, 135; eighteenth-century, 143, 164; growth of, 2; increased pace of, 24. *See also* settler colonialism

colonization: of Canada, 54; French, 55; of Ireland, 143; in the Pacific, 87, 91; in the Pacific Ocean, 29; in Scotland, 141; in Senegambia, 91

Comanches, 137–38, 219

INDEX

Commissioners of Customs, 74
common law, 92, 94
Concord, Battle of, 92
Connecticut, 62, 63, 85. *See also* New England
Continental Army: in Canada, 161–62; European support for, 190–91, 196; foreign assistance for, 191–93; payments for, 194; as protection against slave rebellion, 179–80; under Washington, 13, 16, 193
Continental Congress, 13, 160, 161, 162, 168, 181, 191, 194
Continental Navy, 192
Cook, James, 10, 86, 216
Coote, Eyre, 212
Copley, John Singleton, 211
Cornwallis, Charles, 205, 208, 212, *242*, 243
Coromantee risings, 8, 175
Coromantee Sam (enslaved man), 8
corruption, 52–53, 78, 80, 229, 239
cotton: from America, 106, 130, 233, 245, 246; from Britain, 111, 132, 245; from India, 111, 119, 221
counterrevolution, 21, 26, 115, 238
Court of Proprietors, 78, 80, 81
credit crisis (1772), 178
Creeks, 135, 137, 141
Creoles, 8, 200
Croghan, George, 134
Cuba, 47, 132, 165, 233. *See also* Caribbean; Havana
Currency Act (1751), 92
Curzon, Samuel, 191
Customs Board, 74

Dalling, John, 200
Dalrymple, Alexander, 86
Dampier, William, 85
D'Arcy, Patrick, 164
Dartmouth, William Legge, Earl of, 74
Davy, Sergeant, 105
Day, Thomas, 9
Deane, Silas, 150, 163, 190, 192
Death of Major Peirson, The (Copley), 211
Declaration of Independence, 1, 5, 8–9, 10, 21, 36, 71, 95, 114, 192, 196, 218, 220
Declaration of Rights, 168

Declaratory Act (1720), 75, 93, 172, 218
Defeat of the Floating Batteries at Gibraltar, The (Copley), 211
Defoe, Daniel, 102, 103
Delaware (state), 163
Delawares (tribe), 134, 141, 219
democracy: in Canada, 56, 238; danger to, 27; liberal, 56
Denmark, 195
Devonshire, William Cavendish, Duke of, 72, 104
Dickinson, John, 59, 160, 166
Digby, Robert, 208
Dinwiddie, Robert, 132
Discovery, HMS, 10
disease: in the Caribbean, 176, 201; in Central America, 200; in Cuba, 62; and Indigenous peoples, 138, 141; malaria, 200; in Senegambia, 88, 89; smallpox, 141; venereal, 10, 87, 124, 226
diwani, 51, 60, 64, 88, 218
Dobbs, Arthur, 55
Dogger Bank, 211
Dominica: British army in, 242; and the British Empire, 221; fortification of, 242; free ports in, 90, 173; French occupation of, 198; Indigenous people in, 98; market scene, *137*; threat from Black Caribs, 185. *See also* Caribbean; Saintes, Battle of the
Domville, William, 164
Dorset, Lionel Cranfield Sackville, 1st Duke of, 72
Dunmore, James Murray, 4th Earl of, 5, 73, 115, 134, 164, 179–81, 182, 184
Dunn, Richard S., 178
Duportail, Louis Lebègue, 192
Dutch Republic: and the American Revolution, 193; at the Cape of Good Hope, 213; in the Caribbean, 21, 47, 174, 190, 197, 202, 206; conflict with England, 28, 171, 185, 197, 206; in the East Indies, 206; financial market expansion, 39; League of Armed Neutrality, 185, 195; navy of, 211; at Negapatam, 213; St. Eustatius, 174, 191–92. *See also* Europe; Holland; Netherlands
DuVal, Kathleen, 4
d'Yve, Thérèse Philippine, 23

East Florida. *See* Florida

East India Act (1783), 78, 224

East India Company: conflicts with Indian powers, 46, 69–70; *diwani* rights, 51, 60, 64, 88, 218; escorts for ships, 197; governing India, 58–61, 77–78; government bailout of, 80–81; inquiry into, 78–79; problems of, 43, 44, 221; reforms to, 78–80; and the Seven Years' War, 46; sovereignty of, 51–53, 78–79, 155; state support of, 28, 118, 229; troops recruited by, 196

East Indies, 206

Egmont, John Perceval, Earl of, 56

empire: in America, 16–17, 24, 232, 238; current interest in, 35; European, 38, 46–47, 49, 66, 70, 233; French, 26, 28–29, 38–39, 40, 46, 48, 51, 70, 123; global, 18, 30, 64, 68, 69, 244; historic significance of, 2–5, 245; Holy Roman, 49; in India, 51–53, *240–41*; mercantile, 5–6; military, 239, 242–44; resistance to, 12; in South Asia, 46; Spanish, 26, 28–29, 38, 40, 47, 51, 55, 64, 69, 70, 88, 198, 219, 233. *See also* British Empire

empire-building, 6, 25

England: agriculture in, 99; American exports to, 127; and the British Empire, 17, 30, 34; conflict with Dutch Republic, 171, 197, *202*, 206; conflict with France, 197, 200, *202*, 210, 212, 239; conflict with Spain, 171, 197, *202*, 239; personal wealth in, 112, 128; politicians in, 72; support for the Patriots in, 35; trade with America, 127–28. *See also* Britain; Great Britain

English Civil War, *33*, 35

English Reformation, 35, 93

Enlightenment, 2, 5, 23, 61, 103, 106, 111; Scottish, 228

Epstein, Stephen, 109

Estaing, Charles Henri Hector, Comte d', 210

Europe: Britain's lack of allies in, 232; Britain's loss of prestige in, 231; British Empire in, 152; great power politics, 70; and the Hundred Years' War, 185; League of Armed Neutrality, 185, 195; military alliances, 194–95; Seven Years' War in, 43, 48; support for Americans, 216; trade with, 132. *See also* Dutch Republic; France; Germany; Holland; Spain

expansion: American, 13, 24, 25, 36, 91, 122, 123, 140, 221; in the Anglophone world, 224; in the British Empire, 29, 30, 36, 48, 49, 53, 56, 86, 120, 123, 141, 151, 214, 222, 234, 242, 244, 246; economic, 39, 89; in the French Empire, 29, 65, 123; global, 234; Native American, 137–38; of settler colonization, 232; of slave trade and plantation system, 39, 182; of trade, 46, 89, 173; in the West Indies, 129; westward, 13, 25, 140, 219, 222

Falkland Islands, 198

Fauquier, Francis, 115

federalism, 94, 225, 246

Federalist Party, 27

Fédon, Julien, 223

Ferreiro, Larrie D., 193, 205

First Carib War, *136*

First Maroon War, 66, 175, 218

fishing, 54, 56

Flood, Henry, 167, 176

Florida: and the Boston Board of Customs, 91; boundaries of, 29; British acquisition of, 55, 61, 66; British army in, 198; British loss of, 200; East, 61, 198, 200, 202; Pensacola, 198, 201, 202, 205; settlement of, 55; Spanish, 29, 55, 197–98; speculation in, 66; St. Augustine, 189, 198, 199, 215; West, 61, 198, 200, 201, 202, 205

Fort Detroit, 198

Fort Duquesne, 47

Fort Moultrie, 163

Fort Niagara, 198

Fort Orange, 192

Fort Pitt, 193

Fox, Charles James, 78, *209*, 214

France: alliance with Spain, 198; and the American Revolution, 13, 16, 20–21, 31, 65, 152, 171, 189–93, 193–94, 197, 229; attack on Gibraltar, 211–12; attempted invasion of Jersey, 211; bankruptcy of the monarchy, 39; Britain's mistrust of, 132; in the Caribbean, 21, 82, 90, 107, 198; conflict with Britain, 35, 48–49, 192; conflict with England, 120, 171, 185–86,

INDEX 301

197, 200, 202, 210, 212, 239; empire of, 26, 28–29, 38–39, 40, 46, 51, 70, 123; in India, 197; and Jamaica, 218; in North America, 136; Pacific expedition, 86; relationship with Britain, 65–66; and the Seven Years' War, 19, 43, 47, 133, 138, 153, 195, 219; as threat, 176, 181. *See also* Europe; French Caribbean; French navy; French Revolution

Franklin, Benjamin, 10, 34, 57–58, 61, 160, 163, 192; on population, 123–26

Franklin, William, 73

Frederick II, "the Great" (Prussia), 69, 192, 195

free market, 113, 130

free trade, 99, 106, 172, 173

Free Trade Acts (1778 and 1779), 172

Freeman's Farm, Battle of, 192

French Caribbean, 21, 90, 92, 107, 130, 133, 171, 172–73, 182, 190, 195, 197, 198, 202, 203, 207, 222, 233; Guadeloupe, 22, 47, 214; Martinique, 47, 191, 199, 206, 212, 214

French navy, 201–2, 206, 208–10, 212–13

French Revolution, 23, 24, 65, 142, 152, 154, 190, 229, 231, 234, 244; responses to, 26–27

fur trade, 54, 135

Gage, Thomas, 134

Gainsborough, Thomas, 214

Gallagher, John, 3

Gálvez, Bernardo de, 193, 201–2, 205

Gálvez, Matías, 201

Gaspee, HMS, 163

Gee, Joshua, 101

Geneva, 23

genocide, 137, 141, 221, 224

George I, 98

George II, 47, 49, 67, 68, 98

George III: accession to the throne, 68–69; British Empire at the death of, 216; and the Caribbean, 169, 200; charged with tyranny, 1, 95, 170, 184; coronation of, 68; and Europe, 194; and the Indigenous peoples, 220–21; loyalty to, 169; as monarch, 50, 70–72, 73, 79, 99; Pitt and, 63, 97; political cartoons, 205, 209; popu-larity of, 232; portrait, 201; and the Quebec Act, 84–85; response to loss of the colonies, 150, 231; and the Royal Navy, 203; statue of, 161

Georgia: and the American Revolution, 151, 181; boundary with Florida, 29; British army in, 198, 215; British colony in, 120; Savannah, 210, 215

Germain, George, 171, 187, 200, 203, 231

Germany: Hanover, 49, 50, 68–69, 142, 170; under the Nazis, 194; war in Europe, 45, 195. *See also* Europe; Prussia

Gibbon, Edward, 2

Gibraltar, 28, 196, 197, 198, 210; assault on, 211–12

Gibraltar, HMS, 207

Gillray, James, 209, 214

Gipson, Lawrence Henry, 20, 153

global wars: American Revolution as, 16, 19, 20–21, 28, 152, 197–202, 217; European, 232; threat of, 6. *See also* Seven Years' War

globalization, 4, 132

Glorious Revolution, 22, 71, 111, 230

Goodrich family, 163

Gordon Riots, 172, 199, 218, 239

Graaff, Johannes de, 192

Gradis, Abraham, 40

Grasse, François-Joseph-Paul, Comte de, 193, 201, 206–7, 210, 212–13, 214

Grattan, Henry, 167, 176

Graves, Thomas, 207–8

Great Britain, 1, 20, 28, 58, 69, 84, 104, 132, 161, 175, 177, 180, 181, 214, 216. *See also* Britain; England; Scotland; Wales

Grenada: and the British Empire, 30, 81, 82, 83, 221; fortification of, 242; French capture of, 171, 198; French Catholics in, 81, 82, 83, 140; loyalty to the British Empire, 170; plantations in, 17; slave revolt in, 8, 223; speculation in, 66, 222; wealth distribution in, 129. *See also* Caribbean

Grenville, George, 51, 93, 94, 142, 234

Grizell, John, 7

Grotius, Hugo, 70

Guadeloupe, 22, 47, 214. *See also* Caribbean; French Caribbean

Guatemala, 201

Guernsey, 196, 198

Guichen, Luc Urbain de Bouëxic, Comte de, 211

Haiti: as Black republic, 165, 227–28; slave revolt in, 8, 227. *See also* Caribbean; Saint-Domingue
Haitian Revolution, 9, 23, 108, 223
Halifax, George Montagu-Dunk, 2nd Earl of, 72, 74, 82, 218
Hanoverians, 50, 59, 71, 142
Hardwick, Philip Yorke, Earl of, 142
Harlow, Vincent, 232
Hartley, David, 58
Hartnole, John, 182
Hastings, Warren, 218, 239, 243
Hat Act (1732), 94
Haudenosaunee (Iroquois), 135, 137, 219
Haudenosaunee confederation, 135
Havana, 192, 193; conquest of, 47, 62, 64, 132. *See also* Cuba
Hawaii, 10
Hazen, Moses, 162
Hearts of Steel, 175
Henry VIII, 29, 140, 230
Hessians, 195, 196
Highland Scots, 141, 142, 146
Hinchinbrook, HMS, 200
Hobbes, Thomas, 70
Hodgson, Marshall, 46
Holland. *See* Dutch Republic; Europe; Netherlands
Holton, Woody, 179–80
Holy Roman Empire, 49
Home, Robert, *242*
Honduras, 118, 197, 200, 215; Bay of, 224
Hood, Samuel, 207, 208–9
Howard, Martin, 183
Howe, Richard, 187
Howe, William, 187, 199
Hudson's Bay Company, 54, 55, 56
Hughes, Edward, 213
humanitarianism, 117, 118, 223, 224–25, 228, 233, 234, 237, 239
Hume, David, 2, 5–6, 9
Hundred Years' War, 185
Hutcheson, Francis, 228
Hutchinson, Thomas, 73
Hyder Ali, 212, 213

illegitimacy, 124
Illinois, 191, 198
immigrants: British, 238; to Canada, 55–56; from Ireland, 170
imperialism: after the American Revolution, 155; authoritarian, 233; British, 17, 19, 47, 56, 57–58, 59; in Canada, 56; in the Caribbean, 34; in India, 59; in the Pacific, 85–87; slave-based, 100–102; in the United States, 2, 16, 19–20, 24–25, 31, 155–57, 244–45. *See also* British Empire
India: and the American Revolution, 20; Andhra Pradesh, 212; Annagudi, 213; Bednore, 213; Bombay, 28, 198; Britain in, 6, 19, 34, 35, 40, 51–53, 58–61, 69–70, 88, 155, 197, 232, 245; British army in, 52, 58, 68, 77–78, 195, 198, 212–13, *240–41*, 243–44; under Cornwallis, 243–44; corruption in, 52–53, 78, 80, 229, 239; Cuddalore, 213; deindustrialization of, 221; fabrics from, 112; France in, 197; governance of, 91; governors of, 243; and the Hundred Years' War, 185; imperial policies in, 77–81; independence of, 37; Indigenous peoples of, 96; Kingdom of Mysore, 197, 212, 213, 242, *242*, 243; Madras, 20, 28, 53, 213; Mangalore, 213; as model for West Africa, 87–88; Scotland and, 141; and the Seven Years' War, 30, 36, 46–47, 48; speculation in, 66; Tamil Nadu, 212; taxation in, 51–52; textiles from, 111, 119, 132, 221; trade with, 87, 112; and the War of the Austrian Succession, 49; wealth of, 61. *See also* Bengal; East India Company; South Asia
India Act (1784), 218
Indian Department, 88
Indian Ocean, 197, 204, 206, 213
Indigenous peoples: Aborigines, 156, 221; in the American colonies, 36; and the American Revolution, 134, 156; and the British Empire, 151, 156, 195–96; of California, 120; in Canada, 56, 195, 221; in the Caribbean, 17, 96, 98, 118, 156, 221–24; decline in population, 121; enslaved, 54; and European settlers, 117–18, 120–21, 123, 133–41, 220–21; and the federal govern-

ment, 25; of the Great Plains, 120; in India, 96; land taken from, 11, 25, 30, 34, 122, 123, 148, 156–57, 219, 220, 245; Miskito Indians, 195, 200; in New York, 63; in North America, 88, 96, 98, 122; in the Pacific, 86–87; of the Pacific Northwest, 87, 120–21; population of, 121–22; rebellion of, 69; rights of, 118; San people, 156, 221; in Senegambia, 87; and the Seven Years' War, 47, 134; sovereignty of, 6, 123; in the sub-arctic, 121; subjugation of, 118; treatment of, 61, 96; and the United States, 156, 219–20; violence against, 12; and westward expansion, 156–57. *See also* Native Americans

Industrial Revolution, 35, 110–11, 114, 130, 133, 155, 229

industrialization, 65–66, 245

Iredell, James, 183

Iredell, Thomas, 183

Ireland: absenteeism in, 176; agriculture in, 99; and the American Revolution, 35, 164–70, 218; Belfast, 169, 170; and the British Empire, 17, 18, 20, 21, 27–28, 40, 44, 72, 96, 141–43, 153, 235; and the British military, 58, 76–77, 78, 91, *168*, 169–70, 174, 175, 198, 198–99; Catholics in, 22, 69, 84, 151; connection to slavery, 119; as conquered country, 75; Cork, 173; counterinsurgency, 189; differences with North America, 172–76; Dublin, 20, 77, 143, 145, 164, *168*, 169, 170; famine in, 143, 144; Galway, 174; Glasgow, 173; government in, 75–76; Great Rebellion, 175; imperial policies in, 75–77, 140; included in Articles of Confederation, 160; independence of, 37; loyalty to the British Empire, 159, 170–72, 178, 183; opposing the American Revolution, 170–72; personal wealth in, 112; Protestants in, 30; resistance in, 57, 144–47, 175, 176, 198, 230; sectarian problems in, 82; settler societies in, 64, 143; sovereignty in, 93, 94; taxation in, 167; trade with, 128, 129

Irish Privy Council, 75

Irish Union Act (1801), 234

Irish Volunteer movement, 171, 172, 199

Iron Act (1749), 94

Iroquois Confederation, 135

Islas Malvinas, 198

Jacobites, 48, 50, 73, 82, 104, 142, 146

Jacobitism, 65, 73

Jamaica: and the American Revolution, 20, 217–18; annual duty to Britain, 89–90; Battle of the Saintes, 152, 198, *208*, 210–11, 214, 215, 218, 228, 238–39; British army in, 90, 169; British views of, 103; constitutional dispute, 69; Coromantee risings, 175; free ports in, 90, 173; governor of, 73, 243; Hanover plot, 7–9, 175; imperial policies in, 89; importance of, 97, 132, 213; invasion of, 214, 215; investment in, 46; Kingston, 20; loyalty to the British Empire, 182; Maroon Wars, 66, 175, 218, 223; Maroons, 7, 117, *136*, 195; payment of army subsidies, 90, 91; petition repudiating parliamentary sovereignty, 168–69; plantations in, 98, 102; and Poynings' Law, 75, 76; and the Seven Years' War, 62; shipping to, 197; slave labor in, 101; slave revolt in, 6–9, 18, 68, 117–18, 124, 147, 175, 199, 218, 223; Spanish bullion trade, 89; standard of living in, 127; and the Sugar (Revenue) Act, 167; Tacky's Revolt, 63, 90, 175; threat of invasion by Spain and France, 197, 218; trade with Britain, 131; wealth distribution in, 127, 128, 129. *See also* Caribbean

James II and VII, 38, 61, 142, 232

Jefferson, Thomas, 1, 2, 5, 6, 27, 71, 115, 157, 220, 245; as governor of Virginia, 164, 178

Jefferys, Thomas, 14–15

Jeremiah (enslaved man), 180

Jersey, 196, 198, 211

Johnson, Lyndon, 187

Johnson, Rashauna, 25

Johnson, William, 139

Johnstone, George, 211

Jones, John Paul, 190

Jumonville, Joseph Coulon de Villiers du, 44

Jumonville Glen, Battle of, 44

Kalb, Johann de, 192

Kalingos (Caribs), 156, 221–24

Kaskaskia, 198

Kempenfelt, Richard, 211
Kennedy, John F., 187
Khoikhoi (San) people, 156, 221
Knight, James, 103
Knowles, Charles, 89
Knox, William, 46, 74, 82, 95, 117
Kościuszko, Tadeusz, 192
Kumar, Krishan, 4–5

Lafayette, Marquis de, 23, 192, 216
Lajeunesse, Prudent, 162
Lake Nicaragua, 200
Lakotas, 138, 219
land speculation, 117
Lansdowne, William Petty-Fitzmaurice, Marquess of, 9
Lascelles family, 108
Latin America, 246. *See also* Central America
Law of Nations, 70
Lay, Benjamin, 116
League of Armed Neutrality, 185, 195
Lee, Arthur, 52–53, 243
Leeward Islands, 89, 98, 167, 176, 191. *See also* Antigua; Caribbean; Guadeloupe; Montserrat; Nevis; St. Eustatius; St. Kitts; Virgin Islands
Legacies of British Slave-Ownership project, 111
Les Îles des Saintes, 214. *See also* Saintes, Battle of the
Leslie, Charles, 103
Lesser Antilles, 90. *See also* Caribbean
Lexington, Battle of, 92
Little Bighorn, Battle of, 219
Littleton, Edward, 100
Locke, John, 100–101
Lord Dunmore's War, 134
Lords of Trade, 76
Louis XIV, 105
Louis XVI, 27
Louisbourg, 47
Louisiana: Baton Rouge, 201; and the British Empire, 139; and France, 29, 133; Lake Pontchartrain, 201; Manchac, 198, 201; Maurepas, 201; Natchez, 201; New Orleans, 191, 201; Spanish, 193
Loyalism, 151, 179–84

Loyalists: in the American colonies, 183–84, 195; after the American Revolution, 151, 183–84, 233–39; in Bermuda, 163; Black, 23; in Canada, 184, 233, 234–35, 236, 238; in the Caribbean, 233; in Ireland, 189. *See also* Tories
Lucas, Charles, 164
Lyttelton, William Henry, 139, 166, 180–81

Macartney, George, 213
Macaulay, Catharine, 2
Macaulay, Zachary, 237
Mackesy, Joseph (Pat), 186–87
Mackesy, Piers, 186, 188, 189
Mackinaw City, 198
Mahicans, 134
Maine, 66
Makram Empire, 46
Malaya (Malaysia), 152, 189, 229
Malayan War, 189
Manchac, 198, 201
Manchester, William Montagu, 5th Duke of, 243
Manigault, Peter, 129
Mansfield, Willliam Murray, 1st Earl of, 13, 84, 239
Marathas, 242
Marches of the British Armies, The (Rennell), 240–41
Maroon Wars: First, 66, 175, 218; Second, 66, 223
Maroons, 7, 117, 195
marriage, 123–24
Martinique, 47, 191, 199, 206, 212, 214. *See also* Caribbean; French Caribbean
Marx, Karl, 106
Maryland: agent for, 191; and the American Revolution, 151; colonization of, 56; and the Northwest Territories, 85; population of, 125–26; and the Seven Years' War, 45; shipments to Bermuda, 163
Massachusetts: Boston, 12–13, 20, 37, 58, 72, 74, 90, 131, 151, 161, 182, 199, 210; Boston Committee of Correspondence, 160; and the British army, 62, 63; governors of, 73, 76; Indigenous peoples, 137; Protestantism in, 83; Provincial Congress, 160. *See also* New England

INDEX

305

McNamara, Robert, 187
Memeiskas, 44
mercantilism, 5, 99, 114, 133
Methodists, 228
Mexican-American War, 219
Mexico, 29, 114, 219
Miamis, 44, 219
Middle Passage, 116, 121
Millar, John, 228
Minden, Battle of, 187, 231
Minnesota, 138
Minorca, 28, 47, 196, 197, 198, 205
Miskito Indians, 195, 200
Mobile, Alabama, 198, 201
Modest Proposal, A (Swift), 143
Mohawks, 140
Molasses Act (1733), 90
Molyneux, William, 164, 170
Monongahela, Battle of, 47
Montesquieu, Charles de, 71
Montgomery, Robert, 161
Montserrat, 198
Moore, Henry, 73
Morgan, Edmund, 177–78
Morris, Robert, 194, 197
Morristown, 194
Mosnier, Jean-Laurent, 214
Mosquito Shore, 29, 200
Mughal Empire, 46, 51, 60
Munsees, 134
Murray, Augusta, 73
Murrin, John, 153
Mutiny Act (1765), 11–12, 93
Mysore (India), 197, 212, 213, 242, 242, 243
Mysore Wars: Second, 212; Third, 243

Naples, 195
Napoleonic Wars, 65, 142, 190, 244
Nash, Gary, 179
national debt, 5, 45, 49, 61, 63–64, 229
nationalism, 25; colonial, 144; economic, 155; Protestant, 144
Native Americans: Anishinaabes, 44; Catawbas, 135; Cherokees, 135, 139; Chickasaws, 135, 141; Choctaws, 135, 141; Comanches, 137–38, 219; Creeks, 135, 137, 141; Delawares, 134, 141, 219; in the Great Lakes region, 136; Haudenosaunee (Iroquois), 135, 137, 219; Lakotas, 138, 219; Mahicans, 134; Memeiskas, 44; Miamis, 44, 219; Mohawks, 140; Munsees, 134; Očéthi Šakówin (Seven Council of Fires), 138; Odawas, 139; Osages, 219; Shawnees, 141; Sioux, 138; Wampanoags, 137. *See also* Indigenous peoples
Navigation Acts, 94, 173
Negapatam (Nagapattinam), 213
Nelson, Horatio, 200, 209, 214, 215
Netherlands: and the American Revolution, 21; Austrian, 191; revolution in, 23. *See also* Dutch Republic
Nevis, 108, 111, 129, 166, 167, 198. *See also* Caribbean
New England: as anti-Catholic, 22; and Britain, 12–13, 36, 61, 95; and the British army, 45; vs. the Caribbean, 90; Federalists in, 27; Indigenous peoples, 137; Jamaica's hostility to, 182; and the Quebec Act, 83; resentment of Britain by, 62; and the Seven Years' War, 62; as source of military-age men, 132; value to the empire, 132; wealth distribution in, 127, 129; and West Indian trade, 131. *See also* Thirteen Colonies
New France, 46, 139
New Granada, 38
New Jersey, 73. *See also* New England
New Mexico, 137
New Orleans, 191, 201
New South Wales, 229, 235
New York: and the American Revolution, 189; British army in, 198, 199, 207, 208, 215; governors of, 73; Hudson Valley, 140; naval battles, 210; and the Northwest Territories, 85; refusal to pay army subsidies, 91; and the Seven Years' War, 45; shipping to, 197. *See also* New England
New Zealand: and the British Commonwealth, 37; and the British Empire, 244; Cook's expeditions to, 10, 216
Newcastle, Thomas Pelham-Holles, 1st Duke of, 67, 72, 132
Newenham, Edward, 164
Newfoundland, 29, 54, 91
Newman, Simon, 104
Nicaragua, 198, 215

North, Frederick, 2nd Earl of Guilford: and the Caribbean, 213; and colonial policies, 74, 77, 218; and India, 79–80, 81; and North America, 93, 95, 142, 231–32; political cartoons, *84, 204*; and the Quebec Act, 84; resignation of, 78, 150, 215, 231–32

North America: Black population of, 121–22; Britain in, 96; British army in, 16, 63, 72, 74, 96, 139, 170, 187, 189, 190, 195, 205, 208, 215; British military victories in, 68; Chesapeake region, 103, 122, 137, 164; expansion of British colonies in, 120–21; French, 127; Great Lakes region, 12, 44, 135, 136, 138, 139; Hudson Valley, 140; Illinois country, 191; and the Irish triangle, 173–74; Mississippi Valley, 122, 138, 198, 201, 219; Missouri Valley, 138, 219; Northwest Territories, 91; Ohio River Valley, 12, 34, 44, 49, 70, 122, 123, 134, 139, 140, 222; population increase in, 121–26; Seven Years' War in, 12, 34, 43, 47, 48, 62, 63; slavery in, 147–48; South, 219; standard of living in, 126–27; trade in, 111–13; trade with, 127–28, 132; Upper Midwest, 198; West and Southwest, 219. *See also* Canada; Thirteen Colonies; United States

North Carolina, 135, 151, 163
North Sea, 48, 197, 206, 211
Northwest Passage, 10, 55
Northwest Territories, 85, 91
Nova Scotia: British army in, 63, 198; and the British Empire, 54, 55, 120; constitutional reform in, 184; defense of, 203; governors of, 56, 229; Halifax, 196, 198, 200, 218, 238; loyalty to the British Empire, 159, 178, 183; Protestants in, 161; support for Americans, 160–62

Oakboys, 176
Observations on the Increase of Mankind (Franklin), 123–26
Očéthi Šakówin (Seven Council of Fires), 138
Odawas, 139
O'Hara, Charles, 177
Oldmixon, John, 100
Omai (Tahitian), 10, 86

Orwell, George, 230
Osages, 219
Oswald, Richard, 40
Otis, James, 124
Ottoman Empire, 46

Pacific islands, 85–87, 91
Paine, Thomas, 2, 122
Panama, 142
Panther, HMS, 207
Pares, Richard, 107, 108, 111, 113
Parker, Hyde, 211
Parker, Peter, 163
Parkinson, Robert, 179
Patriots: and Canada, 160, 161–62, 184; ideology of, 92; objections of, 38, 43–44, 52, 54; as rebels, 154, 188–89; slaveholding, 115; support for, 35, 65
Paxton Boys, 12, 140
Peace of Paris, 19, 22, 40, 152, 156–57, 215, 218
Peachey, James, *236*
Pelham, Henry, 132
Penal Laws, 174
Pennsylvania: and the Northwest Territories, 85; Paxton Boys, 140; population of, 123, 125; Quakers in, 116, 119; wealth distribution in, 129
Perth, James Drummond, Duke of, 104
Peru, 114
Philadelphia Abolition Society, 227
Philippines, 43, 48
Phillip, Arthur, 235
Pinney family, 108
Pitt, William (the Elder): colonial policy of, 72; India Act, 218; opponents of, 64; and the Seven Years' War, 6, 19, 50, 62, 63, 67; on sugar planters, 97, 114; on the war in Europe, 44, 47, 195; on the wealth of the colonies, 61
Pitt, William (the Younger), 26, 85, 97, 229
Plantations Committee of the Privy Council, 74
Plassey, Battle of, 52
Pocock, Nicholas, *208*
Pollock, Oliver, 191
Pombal, Sebastião José de Carvalho e Melo, Marquis de, 195
Pompey (enslaved man), 104–5

INDEX

Pontiac's War, 12, 69, 118, 134, 138
Popple, Henry, *165*
Porto Novo, Battle of, 212
Portugal, 195, 197. *See also* Europe
Postlethwayt, Malachy, 101-2
Poynings' Law, 75, 76
Presbyterians, 141, 170, 171, 172
Price, Charles, 167
Price, Richard, 150
Prince William, HMS, 207
privateers, 9, 163-64, 190, 196-97
Proclamation of 1763, 139-40
Protestant internationalism, 81, 220
Protestantism: in the American colonies, 5, 13, 30, 81-82, 83; in Britain, 85, 225, 239; and the British Empire, 220-22; and British identity, 96; in Canada, 55; in the Caribbean, 30, 159, 164, 225; in Ireland, 17, 30, 143, 144-45, 147, 151, 159, 164, 166, 169, 174, 175, 225; in Quebec and Nova Scotia, 11, 12, 13, 83, 161, 238; sectarian, 238; and slavery, 110
Prussia, 39, 69, 153, 194, 195. *See also* Europe; Germany
Pufendorf, Samuel, 70
Purea (Tahitian chieftainess), 86
Purrier, John, 9

Quakers, 116, 119, 181, 227
Quartering Act (1764), 74
Quebec: Battle of, 53-54; British acquisition of, 64, 127; British army in, 189, 198; as British colony, 30, 54, 55, 56; conquest of, 47; constitutional reform in, 184; defense of, 203; French Catholics in, 55, 83-85, 122, 140; as French society, 55; included in Articles of Confederation, 160; loyalty to the British Empire, 159, 178, 183; Montreal, 196, 198; Protestants in, 161; support for Americans, 160-62. *See also* Canada
Quebec Act (1774), 17, 54, 74, 81-85, 82, *84*, 140, 218, 234; opposition to, 5, 12, 83, 85, 161
Quito (New Granada), 38

racism, 25, 108-10, 124, 235; British, 117-19; in Canada, 235; in Franklin's population analysis, 124-25

Ramsay, David, 154
Rao, Gautham, 25
Raynal, Abbé, 100, 154
Regulating Act (1778), 80, 218
Rennell, James, *240-41*
Renunciation Act, 172
representation, 74, 85, 94, 95, 149-50, 153, 179, 232, 238
republicanism, 2, 33-34, 154, 164, 225, 230, 233, 235
resistance: to British rule, 117; in the Caribbean, 222, 230; to empire, 12; in Grenada, 223; in Haiti, 223, 227; in Ireland, 57, 144-47, 175, 176, 198, 230; in Jamaica, 6-9, 18, 68, 117-18, 124, 147, 175, 199, 218, 233; in Scotland, 48, 50, 73, 82, 142, 146, 147; to slavery, 117-18; in St. Vincent, 199
Resolution, HMS, 10
Revenue Act (1764), 74
revolution: agricultural, 130; causes of, 18, 35-37, 46, 119; colonial, 195; and empire, 2, 31; fear of, 198, 231; historical view of, 35, 154; modern, 19; scientific, 111; support for, 177, 181; sympathetic, 23, 216. *See also* Age of Revolution; American Revolution; counterrevolution; French Revolution; Glorious Revolution; Haitian Revolution; Industrial Revolution
Revolutionary Settlement (1688-89), 25, 93, 95
Revolutionary War. *See* American Revolution
Reynolds, Joshua, 86, 214
Rhode Island: British army in, 198; naval battles, 210; shipping to, 197; and the slave trade, 116. *See also* New England
Rhodesia, 37
Richmond, Charles Lennox, Duke of, 242
Roatán island, 224
Robinson, Isaiah, 192
Robinson, Ronald, 3
Robinson Crusoe (Defoe), 103
Rochambeau, Jean-Baptiste Donatien de Vimeur, Comte de, 193, 207
Rockingham, Thomas Watson-Wentworth, 1st Marquess of, 82
Rodney, George, 198, 206, 207, 210, 211, 213, 214, 238-39; artistic tributes to, 214
Roman Empire, 3

Roosevelt, Franklin, 192
Royal African Company, 28, 101
Royal Navy: Battle of Chesapeake Capes, 205–10, 212; Battle of the Saintes, 152, 198, *208*, 210–11, 214, 215, 218, 228, 238–39; in the Caribbean, 199–200, 210, 213, 214; in Central America, 200; Channel Fleet, 198, 203, 206, 212; vs. the Dutch fleet, 211; in the Falkland Islands, 198; First Fleet, 235; global demands on, 197–98, 203–5; in India, 210; in the Indian Ocean, 197, 204, 206, 213; in Jamaica, 205; Leeward Island Squadron, 206, 208–9; in the Mediterranean, 198, 205, 206, 210; North American Squadron, 207, 208–9; providing convoys for shipping vessels, 196–97, 203; strength of, 190; successes against France and Spain, 210–15; weakness against France and Spain, 202–5
Royal Proclamation (1763), 11, 18
Ruggiu, François-Joseph, 40
Russia, 39, 194, 195
Rutledge, Edward, 180

Safavid Empire, 46
Saint Tropez, Pierre André de, 213
Saint-Domingue, 23, 38–39, 40, 130, 131, 133. *See also* Haiti
Saint-Domingue Rebellion, 176
Saintes, Battle of the, 152, 198, *208*, 210–11, 214, 215, 218, 228, 238–39
Saint-Simon, Claude-Anne de Rouvroy, Marquis de, 207
Saldanha Bay, 211
San Juan River, 200
San people, 156, 221
Sandwich, John Montagu, Earl of, 190, 203–4, 206, 210, 213
Sandwich, HMS, 207
Saratoga, Battle of, 16, 80, 190–91, 200
Saxony, 194
Schlesinger, Arthur Jr., 187
Schuyler, Philip, 162
scientific revolution, 111
Scotland: agriculture in, 99; and the British Empire, 17, 21, 30, 34, 65, 141–43; colonization of, 141; famine in, 142; Glasgow, 238; and Great Britain, 28; Highlanders, 141, 142, 146; personal wealth in, 112; rebellion in, 57; resistance in, 147; and slavery in, 105, 119; support for the Patriots, 35, 238; trade with the American colonies, 128. *See also* Great Britain
Scott, Daryl Michael, 114–15
Scottish Rebellion, 73
Second Carib War, 221–22, 223
Second Maroon War, 66, 223
Second Mysore War, 212
Seeley, John, 185
Senegal, 61
Senegambia: British army in, 196; in the British Empire, 28, 36, 159; colonization in, 91; imperial policies in, 87–89; and the slave trade, 87, 119. *See also* West Africa
Sepoy Rebellion, 117
sepoys, 52, 117, 195, 212, 213
settler colonialism: in North America, 57, 86, 123, 135, 141; ideology of, 25; in Ireland, 143, 146. *See also* colonialism
settler political theory, 95
Seven Years' War: in Africa, 48; and the American Revolution, 11, 36, 43–44; Battle of Wandiwash, 52, 212; British acquisitions, 62–63; and the British Pacific expeditions, 86; British victories, 19, 65–66, 194; in the Caribbean, 30, 43, 48, 62, 64, 222; cost of, 39–40, 45–46; counterinsurgency, 188; effect on power relations between Indigenous peoples and settlers, 138–39; in Europe, 43, 48; France in, 219; as global war, 43–44, 47; imperial consequences of, 28, 29, 61–64, 66–67; influence on subsequent revolutions, 21–22; narrative of, 30, 44–47; in North America, 12, 34, 43, 47, 48, 62, 63; in the Philippines, 48; Pitt's strategies, 6, 19, 50, 62, 63, 67; in South Asia, 30, 43, 46–47, 48; understanding, 47–51
Sharp, Granville, 105, 116
Shawnee War, 134
Shawnees, 141
Shelburne, William Petty-Fitzmaurice, Earl of, 9, 74, 82
Shy, John, 186–88

INDEX

Sierra Leone, 23, 233, 235, 237–38; Freetown, 235
Sierra Leone Company, 235
Simcoe, John Graves, 243
Sioux, 138
1619 Project, 114, 118
slave codes, 103
slave trade: abolition of, 233, 237; Atlantic/transatlantic, 40, 46, 47, 101, 111, 115–16, 119, 120, 121, 131, 182, 218, 224; in Britain, 102; Britain's role in, 6, 115–17; in the Caribbean, 98, 108, 115–16, 120, 131, 182, 224, 229, 232; European, 39; growth of, 39; and humanitarianism, 225; opposition to, 115; as source of British wealth, 113; in West Africa, 29, 87, 98, 115
slavery: abolition of, 233; in America, 23; in the American colonies, 5, 101, 151, 153; and the American Revolution, 113–17, 180–82; and antislavery, 225–28; in Barbados, 109, 166; battle over, 245; and Blackness, 109; in the British Empire, 19, 22, 97, 119; and British wealth, 111–13; in Canada, 54; in the Caribbean, 87, 98–108, 109, 110, 111, 115–16, 117, 119, 147–48, 225–26; and Christianity, 109–10; and the Civil War, 119; defense of, 148; in France, 105; Franklin's opposition to, 125; in Great Britain, 104–5; harshness of, 102–7; and imperial policy, 100–102; importance of, 106–7; in Ireland, 104; in Jamaica, 181; and Loyalism, 179–84; in North America, 147–48; opposition to, 105, 106, 116; politics of, 180; in Saint-Domingue, 40; Smith's view of, 105–6; in the United States, 244; in Virginia, 13, 103–4, 114, 115, 177–78, 182. *See also* resistance
Sloane, Hans, 103
Smith, Adam, 2, 3, 5–6, 125, 228; on slavery, 105–6
smuggling, 29, 30, 41, 133, 174
Society Islands, 10
Solano y Bute, José, 207
Somerset, James, 105
Somerset case, 13, 105, 218
South Africa: Cape Colony, 221, 229, 244; independence of, 37; settler societies in, 64. *See also* San people

South America, 198
South Asia: and the American Revolution, 218; British Empire in, 28, 30, 152, 212; Seven Years' War in, 30, 43, 46–47, 48; trade with, 132. *See also* India
South Carolina: and the American Revolution, 181, 187; British army in, 198; Charleston, 163, 189, 198, 200, 205, 215; Cherokee War, 139; fears of slave rebellion in, 180; Savannah, 210, 215; slavery in, 100; wealth distribution in, 129
South Dakota, 138
South Pacific, 96
South Sea Bubble, 66, 85
sovereignty: in the American colonies, 94–95; in Barbados, 164; British, 6, 28, 58, 82, 86, 94, 222–23, 246; in the Caribbean, 222–23; of the East India Company, 51–53, 78–79; in Grenada, 82; imperial, 3, 4, 94; in India, 52, 58, 88; Indigenous, 6, 123; in Ireland, 93, 94; in Jamaica, 168; parliamentary, 38, 88, 93, 95, 163, 164, 167, 168, 184; popular, 235; settler, 220, 246; of the United States, 154, 192
Spain: alliance with France, 198; American colonies, 29, 137; and the American Revolution, 20, 21, 31, 152, 171, 190–91, 193–94, 195, 197; attack on Gibraltar, 211–12; in the Bahamas, 215; in the Caribbean, 29, 198; in Central America, 200, 201; and the Comanches, 219; conflict with England, 120, 171, 185, 197, 202, 239; and Cuba, 233; empire of, 26, 28–29, 38, 40, 47, 51, 55, 64, 70, 88, 198, 219, 233; in Florida, 29, 55, 197–98; former colonies of, 197; and Jamaica, 89, 218; in Louisiana, 193; in North America, 219; in the Pacific, 85; in South America, 198; Spanish navy, 201–2, 204–5, 207; as threat, 176, 181. *See also* Europe
Spanish Armada, 198
speculation, 66
St. Clair, Arthur, 219
St. Eustatius, 174, 191–92, 213
St. Kitts: absentee ownership in, 176; Brimstone Hill, 242; British army in, 242; elections in, 177; French occupation of, 198; shipping to, 197; Stamp Act riots,

St. Kitts (*continued*)
166, 167; wealth in, 129. *See also* Caribbean
St. Lawrence River, *236*
St. Lucia, 196, 198, 199, 215. *See also* Caribbean
St. Thomas, 174
St. Vincent: and the British Empire, 98, 221; Carib Wars, 96, 118, *136*, 175, 199; fortification of, 242; French occupation of, 171, 198; Kalingos in, 222–24; naval battle, 204. *See also* Caribbean
Stamp Act (1765), 12, 18, 38, 39, 83, 89, 218; in Bermuda, 163; exemptions from, 90–91; opposition to, 94, 183; repeal of, 93; in the West Indies, 166
Stark, Caleb, 191
Steelboys, 176
Steuben, Frederick Wilhelm von, 192–93
Stiles, Ezra, 154
Stone, Lawrence, 33, 35, *36*
Stormont, Lord, 231
Stuarts, 13, 35, 48, 69, 142
Suffolk Resolves, 161
Suffren, Pierre André de, 206, 213
Sugar (Revenue) Acts (1764 and 1766), 11, 74, 90, 167, 173
sugar plantations, 98–100, 101, 114, 129–30, 172–73, 176
Sullivan, Lawrence, 81
Sussex, Augustus Frederick, 1st Duke of, 73
Swift, Jonathan, 143, 164
Sydney, Lord, 235

Tacky's Revolt, 63, 90, 175
Tahiti, 10, 86
Talbot, Charles, 104
Taliban, 189
Tarleton, Banastre, 187
Tasmania, 221
taxation: in the American colonies, 12, 18, 25, 38, 39, 58–59, 63, 90–91, 92, 93, 94, 95, 112, 138, 153, 171, 179; in Austria, 63, 229; in Bengal (*diwani*), 51–52, 60, *60*, 64, 88, 218; in Britain, 45, 63–64, 79, 229; in the British Empire, 39, 91; in Canada, 83, 235; in the Caribbean, 66, 71, 89, 90, 91, 94, 167; by the Continental Congress, 194; in French colonies, 39, 127; in Ireland, 76, 77, 164, 167; in Jamaica, 66, 89; land tax, 79; opposition to, 92; in the Spanish colonies, 38; of tea, 58–59
Taxation of the Colonies Act (1778), 91
Taylor, Alan, 24
Taylor, Simon, 7–8
Tea Act (1773), 74, 80, 93
Test Act (1704), 172
Texas, 137
Theory of Moral Sentiments (Smith), 106
Third Mysore War, 243
Thirteen Colonies: autonomy of, 75; British military in, 62–63; economic growth in, 127; equality/inequality in, 126; failure of reform in, 40, 41, 54; governors of, 72–73, 81; growth of, 37; imperial policies in, 73–75; lack of support from other colonies, 35, 160, 172; Loyalists in, 183–84, 195; political divisions in, 62; rebellion of, 9, 18, 21, 30, 35, 38, 133, 148, 150–51, 217, 246; relationship with Britain, 61, 72, 168; and the Seven Years' War, 44, 51; slave trade in, 115, 119, 182; taxation of, 90; trade with England, 127–28; trade with Scotland and Ireland, 128; wealth distribution in, 127, 128–29. *See also* New England; North America; United States; *and individual colonies by name*
Thistlewood, Thomas, 182
Thomas, Dalby, 101
Thornton, Henry, 237
Thurlow, Lord, 231
Tipu Sultan, 212, 213, 242, 243
tobacco, 99–100, 114, 129
Tobago: British acquisition of, 61; French occupation of, 198, 207, 215; loyalty to Britain, 170. *See also* Caribbean
Torbay, HMS, 207
Tories, 50, 162, 183. *See also* Loyalists
Tortola, 163
Townshend, Charles, 76, 87
Townshend, George, 4th Viscount, 72, 76, 77, 143, 218
Townshend Duties, 58, 76, 90, 93, 163
trade: with Africa, 87, 237; between America and England, 127–28, 130–31; with the American colonies, 129; Americanization

of, 130, 132; with Asia, 246; with Britain, 129; in the Caribbean, 91, 100–102, 119, 130–31, 235; with Europe, 132; free trade, 99, 106, 172, 173; fur trade, 54, 135; globalization of, 132; with India, 87, 112; inter-imperial, 129–33; with Ireland, 129; Irish triangle, 173–74; with Latin America, 246; in North America, 91, 111, 132; in overseas territories, 70; in the Pacific, 86; with plantations, 112; regulation of, 93–94, 159; in Senegambia, 89; with South Asia, 132; at St. Eustatius, 191; in sugar, 97, 98, 99, 101, 105; in tobacco, 99; transatlantic, 144; with West Africa, 132, 147. *See also* slave trade
Trafalgar, Battle of, 209, 211, 213, 214, 215
Treaty of Aix-la-Chappelle, 44
Treaty of Aranjuez, 198
Treaty of Mangalore, 213
Treaty of Paris (1763), 43, 47
Treaty of Paris (1783), 16
Treaty of Utrecht, 54
Trelawney, William, 73
Trinidad, 166, 222, 234. *See also* Caribbean
Triumph, HMS, 207
Trumbull, John, 211
Truxes, Thomas, 113
Tuchman, Barbara, 18
Tucker, Henry, 162
Tucker family, 162, 163
Tudors, 35
Tupaia (Tahitian), 86
tyranny, 1, 13, 52–53, 57, 92, 93, 95, 170, 184, 230, 238

Union of 1707, 142
United States: and the British Empire, 24, 245–46; as empire, 24, 31, 218–20, 238, 244–45; sovereignty of, 154, 192, war in Afghanistan, 188. *See also* North America; Thirteen Colonies; *and individual states by name*
US Constitution, 218

Valley Forge, 194
van Bibber, Abraham, 191
Vaughn, James, 64
Vergennes, Charles Gravier, Comte de, 190
Vietnam, 152
Vietnam War, 186, 187–88, 189, 232
Ville de Paris, HMS (formerly French), 214
Virgin Islands, 120, 163, 170. *See also* Leeward Islands
Virginia: agent for, 191; and the American Revolution, 151, 179–80; as British colony, 13, 45, 62, 95; Chesapeake Bay, 207, 208–10, 212; fears of slave rebellion in, 179–80; governor of, 73; and the Northwest Territories, 85; and Poynings' Law, 75, 76; slavery in, 13, 103–4, 114, 115, 177–78, 182; supplies to Bermuda from, 163
Virginia Company, 52

Wabash, Battle of, 219
Wadden Sea, 206
Wager (enslaved man), 117
Wakefield, Edward Gibbon, 246
Wales, 17, 28, 30, 34, 35, 72; personal wealth in, 112, 128. *See also* Great Britain
Walker, George, 131, 133
Walker, Thomas, 161
Wallis, Samuel, 86
Walpole, Horace, 105
Walpole, Robert, 45, 102
Wampanoags, 137
Wandiwash, Battle of, 52, 212
War of 1812, 155, 235
War of American Independence. *See* American Revolution
War of the Austrian Succession, 44, 45, 48–49
War of the Bavarian Succession, 194
Ward, Edward, 103
Wars of the Three Kingdoms, 230
Washington, George: aide to, 191; in Barbados, 177; and Canada, 160; leading the Continental Army, 13, 16, 193; and Native Americans, 141; Newenham's dedication to, 169; in the Seven Years' War, 44, 141; and slavery, 227
Washington, Martha, 227
Wealth of Nations, The (Smith), 5, 6, 105–6
Wenger, William V., 193–94
Wesley, John, 228
West, Benjamin, *60*, 151, *201*, 237

West Africa: Britain in, 21, 28, 29, 229; Gorée, 198; India as model for, 87–88; and the slave trade, 29, 87, 98, 115; trade with, 132, 147. *See also* Senegambia
West Florida. *See* Florida
West Frisia, 206
West Indies. *See* Caribbean
Western Proclamation (1763), 93
Whatley, Thomas, 94
Wheatley, Francis, *168*
Whigs, 50, 155, 232, 238; Country, 78
Whipple, Abraham, 163
white supremacy, 108–9, 110, 117, 124, 224, 235
Whiteboys, 17, 69, 146–47, 175, 176
Wilberforce, William, 237
Wilkes, John, 70
William III, 230
Williams, Eric, 107, 108–9, 110, 111
Wilmot, John Eardley, 151, 237
Winder, Robert, 107
Windward Islands: British acquisition of, 61, 96; duties paid to Britain, 89, 91; slavery in, 224; speculation in, 66. *See also* Grenada; Martinique; St. Lucia; St. Vincent
Wolfe, James, 48, 64
Wood, William, 102
Woolman, John, 116
Wooster, David, 162
world war. *See* global wars
World War II, 186–87, 194
Wraxall, Nathaniel, 214, 215
Wraxall, Peter, 136
Wyvill Association Movement, 172

Yale, Elihu, 104
Yorke, Philip, 104
Yorktown, battle of: American victory at, 16; British defeat at, 152, 177, 205, 208, 212, 231; Washington at, 193

Zabin, Serena, 25
Zong (slave ship), 227